LEWIS CARROLL

A BIOGRAPHY

Lewis Carroll

A Biography

Anne Clark

J. M. Dent & Sons Ltd

London   Toronto   Melbourne

First published 1979
© Anne Clark 1979

Printed in Great Britain
by Biddles Ltd, Guildford, Surrey
for J. M. Dent & Sons Ltd
Aldine House, Albemarle Street, London

This book is set in 11 on 12pt VIP Baskerville

British Library Cataloguing in Publication Data

Clark, Anne
    Lewis Carroll.
    1. Carroll, Lewis – Biography   2. Authors,
    English – 19th century – Biography
    I. Title
    828'.8'09   PR4612

ISBN 0-460-04302-1

Contents

Plates

Acknowledgments

The author wishes to acknowledge the help and encouragement she has received from the following: Mr Wm S. Akin, Miss G. Beck, Rev. Stanley Beckett, Mr N. V. Clark, Professor Morton N. Cohen, Mr Denis Crutch, Canon Ivor Ll. Davies, Mr John N. S. Davis, Mrs Edna De Prez, The Dodgson Family Estate, Father J. B. Gaffney, Dr S. H. Goodacre, Professor E. Guiliano, Mrs I. H. M. Jaques, Mr Philip Jaques, Miss Pamela Keen, Canon Littleton, Mr Christopher MacDonald, Dr J. N. A. Mason, The Lewis Carroll Society, The Lewis Carroll Society Daresbury Branch, The Lewis Carroll Society of North America, Mr Graham Ovenden, Mrs V. E. Ryan, Mrs M. J. St Clair, Mr Hugh St Clair, David and Maxine Schaefer, Mr R. B. Shaberman, Mr Colin Sims, Mr Jeffrey Stern, Mr A. Gordon Thomas, Dr Warren Weaver, Mr Trevor Winkfield, Mr John Wing.

Plates by kind permission of the National Portrait Gallery, the Dodgson Family Collection in Guildford Muniment Room, Mrs I. H. M. Jaques, the Lewis Carroll Society of North America, Mr Graham Ovenden, Mrs M. J. St Clair, Mr David Schaefer.

Note about Abbreviations

The following frequently quoted books are abbreviated in the references as follows:

Collingwood, *The Life and Letters of Lewis Carroll*, by Stuart Dodgson Collingwood, 1898.
Green, *The Diaries of Lewis Carroll*, edited by Roger Lancelyn Green, 1953.
Hatch, *A Selection from the Letters of Lewis Carroll to His Child-Friends*, by Evelyn M. Hatch, 1933.
Hudson, *Lewis Carroll*, by Derek Hudson, 1954. Revised edition 1977.
Handbook, *The Lewis Carroll Handbook*, by S. H. Williams, F. Madan and R. L. Green, 1962.

1   Mid Seas of Corn

If the Rev. Charles Dodgson had not chosen to devote himself to religion and the care of his pastoral flock and family, he might easily have become a literary giant, for he possessed in abundance the raw material of genius. As a scholar he was a perfectionist, attaining at Oxford the rare distinction of a double first in Mathematics and Classics. His skill in translation was matched by an elegant prose style, and his finely developed sense of humour was complemented by a riotous imagination capable of producing the most delightful nonsense. Had his firm Christian faith been matched by a belief in his own talents, he might have left the world so much more than the few neglected volumes of sermons, letters and translation which comprise his entire literary offering to posterity. He was, however, convinced that true genius was confined to a privileged few, and was too modest to claim such distinction for himself. 'The deference universally paid to splendid talents,' he wrote, 'and the eminence to which they often so rapidly attain, is a proof of their comparative rarity, and a proof, therefore, that the great mass of good must be produced by the aggregate force of those whose single efforts may seem to be of little value and efficacy.'[1] And so it was that he preferred to identify with those who fell short of genius, and on whom the onus of working for the general good of mankind pressed heavily. The spiritual welfare of his people, the relief of the local poor, the ordered running of his parish and the clarification of religious doctrine occupied almost all his time. That which remained was devoted to his family, his friends – mostly clerical – and the pursuit of culture.

To his eldest son, Charles Lutwidge Dodgson, he fortunately passed on all his talents. His earnest desire was that this child, so like himself, should, by assiduous application to his work, achieve academic distinction, become a parson, marry and raise a family: in short, that his son's life should be a carbon copy of his own. The boy responded as well as he was able. He honoured his father above all men, emulated him and sought earnestly to please him. But though he imitated his father's career to the point of becoming a mathematical lecturer at his own old college, and became a deacon of the Church, he never took Priest's Orders, nor did he marry and have children. For the young Charles was possessed with an irrepressible genius. The seeds of literary ambition germinated within him in his infancy, and he was compelled to let them grow and flourish. And although, paradoxically (for it was his own gift), it is doubtful whether his father ever fully understood the boy's genius, he gave him every facility to develop it.

The name of Charles Lutwidge Dodgson nevertheless remained obscure. Perhaps the more modest view of his talents which his father encouraged him to adopt from birth was partly responsible for his decision to publish his more fanciful works under a pseudonym. The tall, thin don, who smiled but rarely laughed, strode poker-straight about the streets of Oxford for nearly half a century. Although his outline was familiar to many, few realized his fame. Latinize his Christian names, however, and reverse their order, and he appears as the world knows him best: Lewis Carroll, amateur conjurer, inventor of games and puzzles, photographer par excellence, nonsense poet, friend of little girls and author of *Alice*.

Charles Dodgson Senior was born at Hamilton, Lanark, in the year 1800. For generations the various branches of the Dodgson family tree had borne an abundant crop of clergyman, most distinguished of whom was his grandfather the Bishop of Elphin, a wild and beautiful diocese in the west of Ireland. His father, Captain Charles Dodgson of the Fourth Royal Irish Dragoon Guards, paid for his deviation from the family tradition of entering the ministry by dying on active service at Philipstown in Ireland in December 1803. Only two weeks after the Captain's death, his young widow Lucy gave birth to their second child, Hassard. Nine years later she provided Charles and Hassard with a stepfather in the person of the Rev. George Marwood, of Busby Hall, Stokesley, Yorkshire. He became Canon Residentiary of Chichester Cathedral, and the couple had one daughter. Though Charles was mostly absent from home, first at Westminster School, and later at Oxford, his domestic background was a religious one which naturally turned his thoughts in the direction of the Church.

After taking his Master's Degree at Christ Church, Oxford, in 1825, Mr Dodgson accepted a Studentship – the equivalent of a Fellowship in other colleges – and became a public tutor and mathematical lecturer. His colleagues respected him not only for his scholarship, but also for his spirited delivery of spontaneous anecdotes. Nevertheless, his career at the College was short, for although by a curious anomaly the Dean and Canons were allowed to marry, the Students were bound by a rigidly enforced rule of celibacy which was not dispensed with until the latter half of the nineteenth century. When at Christ Church, Hull, on 5 April 1827 he married his cousin, Frances Jane Lutwidge, Mr Dodgson forfeited his right to a Studentship.

Fanny Lutwidge, who like himself was a grandchild of the Bishop of Elphin, was in every way the ideal wife for Mr Dodgson. Socially she was well connected, an important consideration in the nineteenth century. Her father, Major Charles Lutwidge of the First Royal Lancashire Militia, had inherited the very substantial estate of Holmrook, near Whitehaven, but he had sold it to his uncle, Admiral Skeffington Lutwidge, preferring to live in Hull, where he was a collector of customs. Even more important, Fanny Lutwidge possessed personal qualities which enabled her to shoulder many heavy responsibilities and to be a constant help to her husband in the difficult life which lay ahead of them. A contemporary described her as 'one of the sweetest and gentlest women that ever lived, whom to know was to love. The earnestness of her simple faith and love shone forth in all she did and said: she seemed to live always in the conscious presence of God.'[2]

Loss of Studentship was not a serious problem for Mr Dodgson, for he was appointed instead to the living of All Saints' Church, Daresbury, a living in the gift of the Dean and Chapter of Christ Church, Oxford. In those days Daresbury was not even large enough to rate as an independent parish, being nothing more than a small chapelry embracing a group of six neighbouring villages, which altogether contained only 1500 inhabitants, though these were scattered over some 9000 acres. Though Daresbury was only seven miles south of Warrington, to where the railway already extended, a more secluded spot could scarcely be imagined. The village was connected with the outside world by tollroads, but its diminutive population of less than 200 people attracted very little traffic, so that even the passing of a market-bound farmer in a broad, horse-drawn shandray was an event significant enough to bring the children running from their houses. It was not very far from major industrial centres like Liverpool and Manchester, but the impact of the industrial era had not touched it. Even today, despite the addition of a nuclear power station and a motorway just over the hill, it has somehow managed to retain its essentially rural character.

The parsonage in Morphany Lane that went with the Daresbury living was built in 1819 by a local builder, Thomas Haddock, at a cost of £1275.[3] It was a detached, double fronted, two-storey building with a typically Georgian semi-circular fanlight above the door and a tiny ornamental porch to relieve the otherwise plain exterior. The house was gutted by fire in 1884 during a temporary vacant period, and only the well now remains. In surviving photographs it appears much smaller than it really was. Constructed on medieval courtyard lines around the well, it was designed to allow a much greater degree of self-sufficiency than is necessary nowadays.[4] The house itself was L-shaped, and the various outhouses, which included a shippon for four cows, stables and gig-house with laundry above, almost totally enclosed the courtyard. There were seven bedrooms, two sitting rooms, two kitchens and a study: but the best room in the house was the schoolroom, vitally necessary for a curate whose income was so small that he was compelled to supplement it by taking in paying pupils. Surrounded by enough pasturage to sustain its own livestock, and with agricultural land stretching away as far as the eye could see, it was indeed 'An island-farm, mid seas of corn/Swayed by the wandering breath of morn.'[5]

No sooner had they settled in at the parsonage than the curate and his wife began raising children. Most healthy young couples of their era went in for large families, and the Dodgsons were no exception. Over the next seventeen years they produced eleven children, all of whom thrived – a minor miracle in Victorian England – and all but the last of whom were born at Daresbury Parsonage. The first two were girls, Fanny and Elizabeth, born in 1828 and 1830 respectively, but on 27 January 1832 the eldest son was born. This was Charles Lutwidge Dodgson, alias Lewis Carroll. On 11 July 1832 he was baptized at his father's church by the Rev. George Heron in the old stone font which still gathers moss in Daresbury churchyard, where it was deposited when the church was rebuilt in 1872.

The community into which the Dodgson children were born was primarily agricultural. The Cheshire landscape was not rugged or grand like that of Yorkshire or Lancashire, nor dramatically beautiful like Wales or Cumberland. Its loveliness consisted rather of gentle fruitful meadows, a patchwork of greens, browns and yellows encircled by the hedgerows with their tangle of wild flowers, in some ways more akin to the south of England than the north. Though communicatons are better now, it is still recognizably the same landscape that was familiar to Charles Dodgson in his formative years. Grain was the chief local product, although potato growing was becoming increasingly important. Most local farmers had some livestock, and all but the very poorest families kept a pig or two in a sty at the bottom of the garden. Farm labourers took a 'baggin' of home-made bread and cheese and buttermilk to work, and even Mr Dodgson walked about the parish with his lunch tied up in a red and white spotted handkerchief. Life was hard, with men, women and children alike starting work early and continuing until late at night; these hours were only curtailed in the winter months. Such considerations applied not only to the parishioners but also to the entire Dodgson household, and the habit of rising early and working late remained with Charles throughout his life.

From the windows of the parsonage Charles could look out and see Morphany Hall, a long, low, black and white house occupied by the Dodgsons' nearest neighbours, James Darbyshire and his wife, 'Aunt

Dar' to the Dodgson children. The Darbyshire boys were among his earliest playmates, and with them he could follow his favourite pursuits of tree-climbing and scrambling in and out of the grass-grown marl-pits, those relics of the old Cheshire custom of marling, or excavating large quantities of loam and spreading it on farmland as a kind of topdressing. The moat around Morphany Hall provided an abundance of rushes, which as an infant Charles once diligently gathered and peeled, in the quaint belief that the pith could be used for the relief of the poor.

Household tasks were difficult and time consuming, even in a home like the Dodgsons' where there were servants. Looking after her large family and supervising the domestic staff was a full-time occupation for Mrs Dodgson, who had to help her husband with his work among the poor of the parish and cope with her own state of chronic pregnancy into the bargain. The older children had to help in the care of the younger ones, and Charles, as the eldest son, quickly established himself as a natural leader who liked nothing better than to amuse his brothers and sisters – and chiefly the latter, since sisters outnumbered brothers by seven to three. His ability to entertain little girls, developed in those Daresbury days, had an overwhelming impact on the course of his future, and he spent his entire life trying to recreate the warm, familiar pattern of his home circle, casting himself in the leading role of protector and entertainer rolled into one. The animated responses of his lively brothers and sisters were the tinder that fired his own brilliant inventiveness, and his lightning drawing ability and surprising manual dexterity were the twin accessories that gave impetus to his flights of fancy. It is easy to overlook this intellectually precocious boy's skill with his hands; yet at eight years of age he was already ordering elementary carpentry equipment and at fourteen made for his sister Elizabeth a miniature tool kit measuring only two inches by one-and-a-half, but perfect in every detail. And the same boy who faced life with a persistent nervous stammer enjoyed nothing more than to dress up as a conjurer in a long white robe and brown wig, mystifying his family with his sleight of hand.

As the son of a dedicated parson, Charles was disciplined from infancy into regular church attendance. Twice every Sunday his entire family, including the servants, made the mile-and-a-half journey along winding country lanes and cobbled streets to join the local congregation, which rapidly expanded under Mr Dodgson's ministry. The quaint admonition to bellringers on the ancient square tower, an acrostic on the word Daresbury, gave Charles an early taste for this ingenious form of metrical composition, of which he produced more than forty examples to entertain his child friends:

Dare not to come into this Sacred Place
All you good Ringers, but in awfull Grace.
Ring not with Hatt, nor Spurs nor Insolence.
Each one that does, for every such offence
Shall forfeit Hatt or Spurs or Twelve Pence.
But who disturbs a Peal, the same Offender
Unto the Box his sixpence shall down Tender.
Rules such no doubt in every Church are used
You and your Bells that may not be abused.

The splendid Jacobean carved oak pulpit from which Charles' father preached is still in use today, but the Dodgson pew did not survive the rebuilding of the church in 1872. This pew had been the subject of a minor dispute in 1839, shortly after Daresbury Hall changed hands, for in those days it was the custom among the wealthier classes to purchase land within the parish church and to erect on it a private pew. The dispute began when Mr Dodgson discovered that a plate bearing the name of Mr Samuel Chadwick, the new owner of Daresbury Hall, had been fixed on the door of his own pew, and after unsuccessfully trying to arrange a meeting with him, he wrote:

> What I wished to explain about the Pew was, that as it stands *partly* in the *Old* chancel of the church the proprietor of Daresbury cannot claim it as his property, though he has a perfect right if he wishes to demand that the part of the seat which stands on his own ground shall be removed. The fact is that when I first came here, there was no seat for the clergyman and as seats were not saleable, the only thing to be done was to build one in the chancel, but the chancel being inconveniently small for the purpose Mr Heron who thought with me that the clergyman ought to have a pew of his own, was kind enough to say that I was at liberty to carry the back of his seat into *his* part of the church in order to make it sufficiently wide. On this permission the pew was built as it now stands, and of course entirely at my expense.
>
> General Heron advised that I should pay Mr Heron [the former owner] some *nominal* sum and that he should give me a written acknowledgement that he gave up his property in the ground and Mr Heron promised to do so, but this was never done, and as the property has now come to your hands it rests entirely with you to say whether you will allow the pew to stand as it does. If you do not object to this, I propose that a plate with the words *Ministers Pew* should be set upon the door, and I do not think any future owner of Daresbury would be inclined to alter the arrangement.[6]

Matters were thus amicably settled in that painstaking manner and with that punctilious attention to correct form that characterized the code of conduct passed on by Mr Dodgson to his eldest son.

Sundays in the Dodgson household were strictly kept, yet no more so than in countless homes throughout the length and breadth of Britain. Careful preparations were made to ensure that work was restricted to the absolute minimum, so that Mary Cliffe, the children's nursemaid, and the other servants could keep the Sabbath. Cold meals replaced the hot lunches which the children would often have preferred. Such pastimes as painting and playing with toys were absolutely forbidden, though between services and Sunday School – instituted at Daresbury by Charles' father – religious reading was approved, and indeed actively encouraged. 'Man is recommended and encouraged to read the word of God'[7] proclaims a card in a tiny linen bag of handwritten texts and pious sentiments which belonged to Charles,[8] and his personal prayer book prescribes for Sunday use 'Oh Lord! help us to keep holy this Thy day – grant that we may lay aside all worldly thoughts and employments, and attend seriously to the good of our immortal souls . . . and give us grace that we may remember and profit by the instruction we may this day receive . . .'[9]

The same little home-made prayer book underlines the value set on private morning and evening prayers in the family. If consciousness of their own sinful nature was overemphasized by today's standards, it was all simply part and parcel of the Victorian attitude to religion, with God the Father exhibiting the ever watchful, absolutely dominant attitude expected from the ideal Victorian father. 'I acknowledge and bewail my unworthiness of the least of the many blessings I enjoy – my constant wanderings into sin, and forgetfulness of Thee – but oh! gracious Father, deal not with me according to my sins, but according to Thine infinite love and mercy . . .'[10] Small wonder that the child daily disciplined in this way spent in adult life many wakeful hours of religious torment. 'There are sceptical thoughts, which seem for the moment to uproot the firmest faith: there are blasphemous thoughts, which dart unbidden into the most reverent souls: there are unholy thoughts, which torture, with their hateful presence, the fancy that would fain be pure.'[11]

Throughout their Daresbury days the Dodgson children were educated at home by their parents. Their mother kept a careful log of Charles' progress in a little book[12] divided into three sections and headed 'Religious Reading: Private', 'Religious Reading with Mama' and 'Daily Reading: Useful – Private'. Charles was less precocious than his own satirical hero of 'The Ligniad', which he wrote at Oxford, who 'even from his tender toothless years/Boldly essayed to swallow and digest/Whole tomes of massive learning, ostrich-like',[13] yet he nevertheless took an immense pleasure in the acquisition of learning. At seven years of age he plodded dutifully through *Pilgrim's Progress*, and various other books based on the scriptures. At his mother's knee on Sundays he studied Baker's *Scripture Characters* and *The Juvenile Sunday Library*.

Hannah More, Mary Butt Sherwood and Maria Edgeworth were warmly approved by the Dodgsons as suitable authors for their children to study. All three had certain basic aims in common: namely, to foster such virtues as honesty, hard work, obedience and contentment with small means. Examples in their books were drawn direct from real-life situations, vice was punished and virtue inevitably rewarded, usually by the fortuitous appearance on the scene of a benefactor of superior social status.

The Shepherd of Salisbury Plain, written by Hannah More for *Cheap Repository Tracts*, diligently studied by little Charles Dodgson and parodied by him in later life, was typical of many. The philosophical shepherd, his crippled wife and five children live happily in a miserable hovel with a leaking thatch. A kindly gentleman, impressed by the shepherd's faith, hard work, thrift and cheerfulness in the face of all adversity, gives him a crown, which he uses to repay a debt to the doctor instead of buying meat for his family. When the parish clerk dies the shepherd is rewarded with his job and his house whereupon, with the assistance of the kindly gentleman, he sets up a Sunday school in the kitchen.

The Cheapside Apprentice, another of the *Tracts* read by Charles, illustrates the extreme disrepute of the public theatre in the early part of the nineteenth century. 'To lounging about the purlieus of a play-house I owe my ruin', laments Mr Francis H. 'I was generally allowed to be a handsome, well-made young man; this unfortunately drew me upon the notice of a set of those wretched women, who nightly crowd the theatres, and the avenues to them . . .' Consorting freely with loose women, he begets a child and squanders his money. Finally he commits robbery and is condemned to hang. On the eve of his execution he repents and writes a hymn:

> . . . Condemned to die by human laws,
>   I own my sentence just,
>   With mercy mild judge thou my cause,
>   Who art my only trust.

This basic distrust of the theatre was deeply ingrained in the earlier Victorians, including Charles' father, and attendance at public theatres, even in the mid nineteenth century, was considered by many churchmen positively to preclude men from taking Holy Orders, as Charles was later to discover.

One of the most severe criticisms of the stories of Hannah More and her contemporaries is that they unconsciously fostered a rigid class system, with acceptance of a life of the severest hardship as the natural lot ordained by God for the poor. Heavy manual labour was not necessarily considered harmful to children. In *The Lancashire Collier Girl*, a brother and sister aged seven and nine years work all day dragging baskets of coal from the coalface to the mouth of the pit.

It must be owned that they may sometimes have exerted themselves even beyond their strength, which is now and then the case with children, through the fault of those who exact work from them: but since in their case the father had an eye on them during the hours of labour, while they had a prudent and tender mother also to look after them at home, there is no particular reason to suppose, that at the time of which we are speaking, they were very much over-worked.

No remedy is offered in the story for the plight of the children exploited in this way. The young Charles Dodgson, who read these stories with all the avid interest of his eager imagination, felt a natural desire to help the poor. But his interest was never stirred beyond a vague desire to do good on an individual basis, and in adult life he accepted the status quo in such matters because he felt that anything he might do would be ineffectual. Seventeen years later he read Charles Kingsley's first novel, *Alton Locke*, and in his diary wrote:

It tells the tale well of the privations and miseries of the poor, but I wish he would propose some definite remedy, and especially that he would tell us what he wishes to substitute for the iniquitous 'sweating' system in tailoring and other trades.

If the book were but a little more definite, it might stir up many fellow-workers in the same good field of social improvement. Oh that God, in His good providence, may make me hereafter such a worker! But, alas, what are the means? Each has his own nostrum to propound, and in the Babel of voices nothing is done. I would thankfully spend and be spent so long as I were sure of really effecting something by the sacrifice, and not merely lying down under the wheels of some irresistible Juggernaut.[14]

Edgeworth's Early Lessons, conceived jointly by Maria Edgeworth and her father, and completed and published by Maria after her father's death, features prominently in Charles' reading list for 1839. So, too, does *The Parents' Cabinet of Amusement and Instruction*, which contains elementary geography, history, poems and moral tales; and to feed Charles' insatiable curiosity for gadgetry, an excellent explanation of such items as an eight-day clock, a pendulum and Davy's Safety Lamp. One particularly significant item is a poem entitled 'Apparent Course of the Sun', of which the following lines are a fair sample:

At Midnight, while we in forgetfulness lie,
And the pale twinkling stars are bespangling the sky.
In China the clocks are already at seven,
In frigid Kamtschatka 'tis almost eleven;
'Tis noon in New Zealand, – the savage reclining
Beneath the thick shade, on his fern root is dining.

This poem surely sparked his interest in the difficulty of determining 'Where does the day begin', which he maintained over a period of many years, including it in one of his earliest family magazines, *The Rectory Umbrella*, and writing a letter to *The Times* about it on 18 April 1857. The following is an extract:

> Suppose yourself to start from London at midday on Tuesday, and to travel with the sun, thus reaching London again at midday on Wednesday. If at the end of every hour you ask the English residents in the place you have reached the name of the day, you must at last reach some place where the answer changes to Wednesday. But at that moment it is still Tuesday (1 p.m.) at the place you left an hour before. Thus you find two places within an hour in time of each other using different names for the same day, and that not at midnight when it would be natural to do so, but when one place is at midday and the other at 1 p.m. Whether two such places exist, and whether, if they do exist, any communication can take place between them without utter confusion being the result, I shall not pretend to say: but I shall be glad to see any rational solution suggested for the difficulty as I have put it.[15]

The Parents' Cabinet also includes the tale of a child called Charles, whose friend George shows him his pet rabbits: 'There was the mother with six young ones; all such pretty clean animals. Three of them had skins entirely white; two had black spots on their backs; and one of them had a pair of beautiful brown ears with all the rest of its body as white as snow.' It would be futile to pretend that here was the origin of the famous White Rabbit, or indeed to look for sources for any of the domestic, farmyard or wild animals found in the writings of Lewis Carroll. The sole exception is the Cheshire Cat, whose geographical connection with Charles' birthplace encourages us to seek him in those Daresbury days. Most convincing of the explanations of the origin of the Cheshire Cat is that he was originally John Catheral of Chester, whose coat of arms, dated 1304, included a cat. When angry, Catheral always bared his teeth in a grin, and died grinning while defending the town of Chester. In his honour, Cheshire cheeses were thereafter made in the shape of a cat, complete with grin.

Charles' father was more than a living example of upright character and personal intellectual attainment on whom the boy unconsciously modelled himself, for from the beginning he took an active, indeed vital, part in his son's early education. From infancy Charles was fascinated by mathematics, his father's favourite subject. In later years his family recalled this vividly: 'One day when Charles was a very small boy, he came up to his father and showed him a book of logarithms, with the request "Please explain". Mr Dodgson told him that he was much too young to understand anything about so difficult a subject. The child listened to what his father said, and appeared to think it irrelevant, for he still insisted, "*But*, please explain!" '[16] And a letter from his mother, written from the bedside of her sick father in Hull, proves that in his Daresbury days he had already begun Latin: 'It delights me, my darling Charlie, to hear that you are getting on so well with your Latin, and that you make so few mistakes in your Exercises.'[17]

It is commonly supposed that Charles left Daresbury only once during his father's incumbency there, when the family went on a holiday to Beaumaris on the Isle of Anglesey. The three-day journey by horse-drawn carriage involved crossing the famous Menai suspension bridge. But his first surviving letter, written in baby-talk in a guided hand, comes from a place called 'Marke', so far unidentified. His father was often absent from home on church business, especially from 1836 onwards, when he was appointed Examining Chaplain to the Bishop in the newly created diocese of Ripon, and he may occasionally have taken his eldest son with him. Family ties were strong on both sides, and the abundant documents of later years record innumerable visits to various relatives, mostly in the north of England. Charles was well acquainted with his paternal grandfather, whose home was in Hull, and whose declining health prevented him from undertaking the long journey to Daresbury. He was almost certainly staying in Hull in 1836, the year of his grandmother's death, when Ruth Middleditch, the Lutwidge family's housemaid, presented him with a small oil painting of a dog.[18] A book of skeleton maps owned by Charles,[19] probably dating from 1843, shows various routes between Daresbury, Anglesey, Oxford, London, Hull and so on. These may be his father's journeys, but if so there are some notable omissions, and they could be Charles' own travels.

Nor was life at Daresbury totally devoid of social contacts. Charles' lifelong friend, Thomas Vere Bayne, three years older than himself, came over every Sunday with his father, the Headmaster of Warrington Grammar School, who sometimes assisted at services. During Mr. Dodgson's incumbency at Daresbury the living at Middleton in Lancashire was held by Richard Durnford, first President of the Oxford Union, who ultimately became Bishop of Chichester and was a regular visitor at the parsonage. Another close acquaintance was John Wilson Patten, Member of Parliament for North Lancashire for over forty years. Wilson Patten was a staunch campaigner for the welfare of the industrial population, and only left the House of Commons when he was created a baron. Bachelor George Heron, the family friend who baptized Charles Lutwidge Dodgson, was heir to Moore Hall and Daresbury Hall, and became Canon of Chester. In his honour the Dodgsons' youngest son was named Edwin Heron Dodgson. A substantial landowner in the district, Lord Francis Egerton, also knew Mr Dodgson well, and held him in particularly high esteem. To him Mr Dodgson confided his deep concern for the spiritual welfare of the large floating population of bargees on the Bridgewater Canal, which ran through the outskirts of the chapelry. The barge people would never have entered an ordinary parish church, where they would have felt out of their own environment, but Mr Dodgson was convinced that if a floating church could be provided for them at Preston Brook, where the barge horses were unharnessed and stabled en route to Manchester, they could be persuaded to take part in services. Lord Egerton consequently purchased a barge and equipped it for the purpose, and here Mr Dodgson held services every Sunday, even baptizing in the little stone font babies brought to him by gypsy-like, clog-shod women.

Lord Egerton was one of thirty-one private individuals, including Lord Derby, Edward Lear's patron, who in 1840 sponsored the Warrington Exhibition. Over 11,000 people attended the exhibition and its associated elegant soirées, including the Dodgsons and Charles. The remarkably wide range of exhibits included 323 'curiosities and antiquities', 250 Natural History specimens and 42 pieces of 'philosophical apparatus', an array guaranteed to feed the mind of a child as imaginative as Charles.

At the exhibition silhouettes were cut of Charles and his parents, these being the earliest likeness of the boy and the only surviving one of his mother (Plate 1). A look at the parents' profiles emphasizes their consanguinity, for they shared the same high forehead and finely chiselled mouth, the noses being broadly similar, though in Mrs Dodgson marginally too prominent for ideal feminine beauty. Their double descent from the Bishop of Elphin was probably responsible for the close facial resemblances between all the Dodgson children, perhaps best seen in large family groups (Plate 2), and in a comparison of the pictures of Edwin and the earliest surviving photograph of Charles.

The seeds of nonsense-writing can also be traced to that marvellous old character, the Bishop of Elphin, whose rumbustious jokes are a reminder that he was born in the age of Fielding, Smollett and Sterne. Lewis Carroll's nephew-biographer, Stuart Dodgson Collingwood, quotes substantial extracts from the Bishop's letters to the Percy family. These he describes as 'interesting and giving some idea of the life of a rural clergyman' apparently without noticing their ripe humour and bawdy double-entendre:

> I am obliged to you for promising to write to me, but don't give yourself the trouble of writing to this place, for 'tis almost impossible to receive 'em, without sending a messenger 16 miles to fetch 'em.
>
> 'Tis impossible to describe the oddity of my situation at present, which, however, is not void of some pleasant circumstances.
>
> A clogmaker combs out my wig upon my curate's head, by way of a block, and his wife powders it with a dredging-box.
>
> The vestibule of the castle (used as a temporary parsonage) is a low stable; above it the kitchen, in which are two little beds joining to each other. The curate and his wife lay in one, and Margery the maid in the other. I lay in the parlour between two beds to keep me from being frozen to death, for as we keep open house the winds enter from every quarter, and are apt to sweep into bed to me.

Elsdon was once a market town as some say, and a city according to others, but as the annals of the parish were lost several centuries ago, it is impossible to determine what age it was either the one or the other.

There are not the least traces of the former grandeur to be found, whence some antiquaries are apt to believe that it lost both its trade and charter at the Deluge.

. . . There is a very good understanding between the parties [i.e., churchmen and Presbyterians of the parish] for they not only intermarry with one another, but frequently do penance together in a white sheet, with a white wand, barefoot, and in the coldest season of the year. I have not finished the description for fear of bringing on a fit of the ague. Indeed, the ideas of sensation are sufficient to starve a man to death, without having recourse to those of reflection.

If I was not assured by the best authority on earth that the world is to be destroyed by fire, I should conclude that the day of destruction is at hand, but brought on by means of an agent very opposite to that of heat.

I have lost the use of everything but my reason, though my head is entranced in three night-caps, and my throat, which is very bad, is fortified by a pair of stockings twisted in the form of a cravat.

As washing is very cheap, I wear *two* shirts at a time, and, for want of a wardrobe, I hang my great coat upon my own back, and generally keep on my boots in imitation of my namesake in Sweden. Indeed, since the snow became two feet deep (as I wanted a 'chaappin of Yale' from the public-house), I made an offer of them to Margery the maid, but her legs are too thick to make use of them, and I am told that the greater part of my parishioners are not less substantial, and notwithstanding this they are remarkable for agility.[20]

Essentially a man of his era, Mr Dodgson was not morally free to dwell on the shape of his parishioners' legs or their goings on in the sheets, but his sense of humour was no less keen. Collingwood writes that 'In moments of relaxation his wit and humour were the delight of his clerical friends, for he had the rare power of telling anecdotes effectively. His reverence for sacred things was so great that he was never known to relate a story which included a jest upon words from the Bible.'[21]

A letter written by Mr Dodgson to Charles from Leeds in 1840 amply demonstrated his own adroitness at nonsense prose. He had undertaken to make some trifling purchases for his son and launches into an account of setting the whole town in an uproar to get them:

Then what a bawling & a tearing of hair there will be! Pigs & babies, camels & Butterflies, rolling in the gutter together – old women rushing up the chimneys & cows after them – ducks hiding themselves in coffee cups, & fat geese trying to squeeze themselves into pencil cases – at last the Mayor of Leeds will be found in a soup plate covered up with custard & stuck full of almonds to make him look like a sponge cake that he may escape the dreadful destruction of the town.[22]

It was a highly infectious form of nonsense, densely packed with the germs of the *Alice* books: the close association of pigs and babies, the futile attempts to fit large creatures in small receptacles, the use of the chimney in a crisis, and the continual preoccupation with food. Ducks in coffee cups are not far removed from dormice in teapots or from 'Put cats in the coffee and mice in the tea/And welcome Queen Alice with thirty times three!',[23] and the White Queen diving into a tureen full of soup is a natural descendant of the Mayor of Leeds lurking in the custard.

This was a powerful spur to nonsense writing. Yet superficially at least the same incentives applied equally to all the Dodgson children – all intelligent, nourished at the same breast, rocked in the same cradle, instructed by the same parents. Every one of the children shared some common characteristics with their famous brother, yet some vital element was missing. The girls were of course hobbled by the trappings of conventional Victorian society, condemned to a life of mere accomplishment and charitable works. Fanny delighted in music and botany, and Elizabeth loved literary criticism and creative writing. Mary aspired to translations, paintings and the arts in general, Louisa was as gifted as her father at mathematics. Nevertheless, the girls were decidedly *hors de combat* in the literary field. Skeffington, the second son, was without literary ambition and most closely resembled his father in terms of career and family life, for he became a parson with a wife and large, thriving family, while Edwin, the youngest child, having a true evangelistic vocation, became a missionary in Zanzibar and Tristan da Cunha. Curiously, the best raconteur, his famous brother excepted, was Wilfred, the most physically active of the boys, a fisherman and hunter, good at rowing and fighting, and the only one of the Dodgson boys who took up a career in commerce.

Though in later life all his brothers and sisters looked on Charles with a kind of awe, they made virtually no comment on the nature of his genius, for the fact is they did not really comprehend it. In retrospect it seems strange that Dr Pusey, a Canon of Christ Church, referred to Charles' 'solid qualities', and even more so that his father regarded him as a 'steady, likely-to-do-good man, who in the long run wins the race against those who now and then give a brilliant flash and, as Shakespeare says, "straight are cold again" '.[24]

Even in those early Daresbury days Mr Dodgson had notionally mapped out a career for Charles. 'Looking at the constitution of the Chapter of Christ Church,' he wrote to his brother Hassard, 'it is certainly not impossible that I might be able some day to get for Charles a Studentship from some individual member.'[25] It does not seem to have occurred to him that Charles had the talent to earn a Studentship on the strength of his own merit. His hope was that his son would ultimately graduate, obtain a Studentship, and finally marry and accept a church living. But he forgot that Charles had witnessed too much of his own struggle to bring up a large family in a remote rural area on a limited and uncertain income to wish to repeat that process. 'I am going on as well as a man can be supposed to do, without prospects, living upon a precarious income and subject to constant drawback on his domestic comforts,' he wrote to Dr Bull at Christ Church in 1832. 'I already begin to experience the anxieties incidental to my situation, having at the moment two vacancies for Pupils unfilled.'[26] His income in that year from the Daresbury living was only £191 10s 11d, from which he had to meet rates, taxes and repair bills. Max Müller, the eminent nineteenth-century German philologist who became Taylorian Professor of Modern Languages and first Professor of Comparative Philology at Oxford, wrote, 'A man who at that time could take a Double First was indeed a strong man, well fitted for any work in after life. He would not necessarily turn out an original thinker, a scholar, or a discoverer in physical science, but he would know what it is to know anything thoroughly.'[27] It seems incredible that a man of Mr Dodgson's academic distinction and practical application to his pastoral duties should moulder for sixteen years in such circumstances. Small wonder that Mr Dodgson embraced the cause of poor clergymen. In one of his earliest works, *The Providence of God Manifested in the Temporal Condition of the poorer Clergy* (1839), he wrote:

> The proceeds of all the Benefices in England and Wales, if equally divided among the Incumbents, would furnish an income to each of barely £300 a year. But the actual distribution of these revenues is still more worthy of remark. The total number of Benefices is something more than 10,700. Of these, while the Income of only 1451 exceed £500, those of nearly 5000 are below £200 and those of nearly 200 below £100 a year. The number of Curates exceeds 5000, the average amount of whose stipends is about £80, the great majority of them being less than £100. These numbers are of course reducible by the subtraction of those cases in which the Benefices are united with each other, or with Cathedral Preferment: but such cases are accidental and comparatively rare exceptions, and by recent legal enactments will be rendered still rarer; not mainly interfering with the fact, that about 10,000 Clerical Incomes are below £200 and that a sum less than £100 a year for each is the whole remuneration actually provided for the labours of, at the very least, 6000, Parochial Pastors.
>
> Nor is this all. Poverty and affluence are in fact relative terms. The views, which one man takes of the comforts and necessities of life, do not fairly measure those of another. The circumstances of birth and education, the position in society, which the individual occupies, all these must be taken into account, before we can rightly estimate the proportion which his means bear to his wants, in other words the degree of his wealth or poverty. In cases of ordinary poverty, these circumstances serve in general as so many indications of its hardships. In the case of the poor Clergyman they are so many aggravations. To say nothing of the great expenditure attending the peculiar Education required, and most properly required, as an indispensable qualification for Ministerial

office, – an expense which, as in all other cases, might be taken into
account in the estimate of the pecuniary value of his after labours – all the
circumstances attendant and consequent on that Education, the mental
refinement, the habits and connexions necessarily formed, all bringing
him into immediate contact with the higher walks of life, tend only to
enhance the privations of narrow worldly means, and to unfit him for the
rough encounter of those coarser hardships of Poverty . . .[28]

Such privations had little appeal for the young Charles Dodgson,
whose father had inevitably handed down to him from his infancy the
education and mental refinement to which he referred. Charles alone of
all the Dodgson sons was old enough in those Daresbury days to
appreciate just what those privations could mean. But if Mr Dodgson
suffered, and his family with him, he had friends who not only valued
him for his exceptional educational attainments and devotion to the
Church, but also actively encouraged and enhanced his career by
drawing on his talents. One of these friends was Dr Pusey, Canon of
Christ Church.

Edward Bouverie Pusey was an exact contemporary of Mr Dodgson,
having been born of a wealthy family in 1800, and educated at Eton and
Christ Church, Oxford. When on 30 June 1824 he read out his prize-
winning Latin essay in the Sheldonian Theatre at Oxford, he presented
the manuscript to Mr Dodgson. Its concluding paragraph summarizes
the religious convictions both of author and recipient:

> Silent are the arts of Greece, shattered the empire of Rome, but the Faith
> of Christ, as on surest testimony we are fully certified, will in the eternal
> courses of the ages gather strength, and last until the day when, all that is
> evil or inhuman being extinguished, it shall embrace in one bond of love
> the uttermost parts of the earth.[29]

In 1828 Pusey was appointed Regius Professor of Hebrew at Oxford,
a post which carried with it a Canonry at Christ Church. When, some
five years later, Pusey joined the Oxford Movement, founded by Keble
and Newman, and shortly afterwards made his first contribution to
Tracts for the Times with a tract on fasting, Newman commented, 'He at
once gave us a position and a name'. During the summer vacation of
1836 Pusey conceived the idea of producing a *Library of the Fathers*
containing translations of the works of the early Christian Fathers. In
his view it was of the utmost importance at this time, when the Tractarians were quoting extensively from the Fathers, to enable Englishmen to read in their own language the teachings of an undivided
Christendom propounded by the Fathers. In the words of his prospec-
tus, he wished to emphasize that 'the Anglican branch of the Church
Catholic is founded upon Holy Scripture and the agreement of the
universal Church', and that what mattered in the final analysis was not

the opinions of individual bishops, which could, and did, vary, but the teaching held by all people, in all times and all Churches.

After discussing his schemes in detail with Newman, he wrote to him concerning the great importance of accuracy so as 'not to give people room to say we have put in anything; and even a degree of roughness may well be admitted, if one can obtain energy'. The task of choosing suitable translations was formidable in view of Pusey's rigorous standards. One of the first men whom he approached for help in his series was Mr Dodgson, who somehow, in the busy, crowded parsonage at Daresbury, surrounded by the cares of his family, his parish duties, and his schoolmastering, found time to translate Tertullian, in an enormous volume of 499 pages, with an introduction and notes by Dr Pusey. The choice of subject may have been indicative of the character of the editor, or the author, or both, for Tertullian (*c.* 160–240) was noted as a man whose views of doctrine and morality were both rigid and narrow. The first volume in *The Library of the Fathers*, *Saint Augustine's Confessions*, appeared in 1838, and Mr Dodgson's in 1842. The forty-eighth and last of the series was brought out in 1885, three years after Pusey's death. Rivingtons', the publishers, insisted on a subscription list for the series, and it is an indication of its popularity that while there were only 800 subscribers for the first volume, numbers had risen to 3700 by 1853.

Robert Bickersteth, the famous evangelical who in 1856 was appointed Bishop of the diocese in which Mr Dodgson served, was one of the many who wrote warmly to Pusey in support of the series. 'Few things could be more seasonable or more beneficial to the Church of England, to which, I feel more and more, it is a real privilege in these days of disunion to be united; it is my hearty prayer that the great Head of the Church may very greatly prosper the design for extended good,' he wrote. That Mr Dodgson managed to complete this enormous work of translation was an indication not only of his personal scholasticism but also of his perseverance under adversity. During the next decade or so he was to establish himself by his theological writings as one of the acknowledged leaders of the moderate High Church party. Following his lead in this as in all other matters in his formative years was the young Charles. Though in the latter part of his life he modified his views to some extent, it is clear that the opinions of his father in religious matters predominated throughout a great part of his life. It is perhaps significant that although Charles Lutwidge Dodgson was remarkable in adult life for his ingenuity, originality and wide-ranging sphere of interests, he remained untypically conservative and inflexible in matters of religion and mathematics. These are the two subjects in which his debt to his father was greatest.

During Charles' early childhood Mr Dodgson's personal fortunes were constantly in the mind of an old friend whose patronage had far-reaching consequences for the entire Dodgson household. This was Charles Thomas Longley, who enjoyed a remarkable career in the Church and who during the last eight years of his life was Archbishop of Canterbury. In his early contacts with the eldest son of his old friend, Longley could not have guessed that he would in years to come be Charles' most photographed male adult sitter, and that though he would rise to the position of Primate of all England, his name would be forgotten by all but a few Church historians, while the pen-name of that small boy would become immortal.

Longley was six years older than Mr Dodgson. He was educated at Cheam, Westminster and Christ Church, Oxford, where he obtained a first class B.A. degree in Classics, ultimately attaining his M.A., B.D. and D.D. He was Greek reader at Christ Church until 1822, and was tutor and censor from 1825–8. In 1825 and 1826 he was examiner in the Classical schools and was proctor in 1827. His terms of office therefore directly coincided with Mr Dodgson's period at the College, and they shared a common interest in religion and Classics.

When Mr Dodgson moved to Daresbury in 1827 they followed widely different paths. From 1829 until 1836 Longley was headmaster of Harrow School where he greatly increased the numbers of pupils, but was known as a weak disciplinarian. On 15 October 1836 Melbourne, who was Prime Minister at this period, appointed him Bishop of the newly created Diocese of Ripon. Longley's declared policy was of 'bringing about him one or two tried friends of equal standing and experience with himself, who might cordially co-operate with him in carrying out measures for the Benefit of his Diocese'.[30] In accordance with this he immediately appointed Mr Dodgson his first Examining Chaplain. It was a mark of the unusually high esteem in which the Bishop held him that at his first ordination in Ripon Minister, Mr Dodgson, not Bishop Longley, preached the sermon. Published in 1837, the sermon develops its theme from the parable of the talents (Matthew XXV, 24, 25), and in it Mr Dodgson sets forth his belief in the ultimate authority of the Bible:

> The Bible is the poor man's library, the most indigent strive to possess it; the most careless retain at least some feeling of reverence for it. In all their doubts and difficulties, an appeal to it is unanswerable; its authority is decisive, and a single text of Scripture will often prove more convincing, than volumes of the most subtle arguments of human wisdom.[31]

The young Charles' enthusiasm for the Bible as a constant source of reference in any doubt or difficulty lasted a lifetime, and owed its basis to his father's early teaching and his personal conviction that in imparting to him a thorough knowledge of the Testaments he was equipping him in the best possible way to face the life that lay ahead of him. Just how detailed was the knowledge that Charles was expected to acquire is indicated in *Confirmation. An Appendix to a plain catechism, intended chiefly for the Instruction of young persons before Confirmation, containing the texts*, which his father published in 1839: an incredibly dull book by today's standards, but one which provided the candidate with all the knowledge thought necessary in those days, and more besides. From 1837 on, Mr Dodgson brought out one book every year until his days at Daresbury came to an end. By the end of his life he had published no less than twenty-four books, all of them on religious subjects, and was an avid researcher and exhaustive critic of the enormous quantity of religious books published in Victorian England. From his infancy Charles had before him the example of a father who worked tirelessly to publish books, an activity which gave immense satisfaction to the family at Daresbury Parsonage.

From the time of his appointment as Longley's Examining Chaplain in 1836, Dodgson's new duties, which included responsibility for the Diocesan Training School, made more and more inroads into his time. Being compelled by financial necessity to persevere in taking private pupils, he was, moreover, hampered by being unavailable for duties remote from home during the academic term. What worried Bishop Longley was 'the painful position in which the Diocesan is placed, by being compelled year after year to call on his Chaplain to discharge the laborious and responsible Duties of that office, without any prospect of being able to reward him'.[32]

In the spring of 1840 Longley wrote to Lord Melbourne asking him to appoint Mr Dodgson to the valuable Crown living of Catterick in the North Riding of Yorkshire. According to Lord Ashley (later the Earl of Shaftesbury) who also wrote to Melbourne in favour of the appointment, 'Melbourne acknowledged both the fitness of the Candidate, and the claim of the Bishop, but gave away the benefice to gratify Lord Zetland!'[33] Longley had to be satisfied with an assurance that Mr Dodgson would be suitably rewarded when the opportunity arose.

Melbourne's position at that time was a curious one. In 1839 he had been defeated in the House on the Jamaica Question, and Sir Robert Peel had been called on to form a Tory Government. An immediate clash arose, however, between Peel and Queen Victoria on the so-called Bedchamber Affair, in which the Queen refused to dismiss from her household certain Ladies of the Bedchamber whose husbands had served as ministers in Melbourne's defeated administration. Totally without constitutional precedent Melbourne stepped in and formed a government, ostensibly to spare the Queen embarrassment in a difficult situation. A vote of no confidence again led to Melbourne's defeat in 1841, and he and his government resigned on 30 August 1841.

Less than three weeks later Longley wrote to Peel in a further effort to

gain preferment for Mr Dodgson. Somewhat tactlessly he drew Peel's
attention to Melbourne's assurances, given at a time when Peel had
every justification for regarding himself as the real Prime Minister, and
asking Peel to honour the assurances given by the usurper, Melbourne.
Longley's reasons for seeking Mr Dodgson's preferment were undeni-
ably just and reasonable:

> The Patronage which it has been in the power of the Ecclesiastical
> Commrs. to the newly appointed See of Ripon is chiefly prospective –
> vested interests being respected: and . . . viewing the present Lives, there
> is no probability of any Patronage of value falling to the first Bishop of
> the See, within any Period that can be calculated upon, the only Living
> in his gift which has already fallen vacant in the course of five years,
> being one of about £100 a yr without a House. The first Bishop of Ripon
> therefore finds himself destitute of the means . . . of rewarding merit.[34]

Casting his eye over the Crown livings in his diocese, with a critical
eye to their value and to the likely life-expectancy of the incumbents, he
lighted on Croft (Catterick having only recently been filled). Croft was
a rich and sought-after living whose rector was elderly and ailing. He
accordingly asked Peel to promise the living of Croft to Mr Dodgson on
the death of the existing tenant. If Peel was irritated by Longley's want
of tact, he betrayed no hint of it in his reply, but he was nevertheless
firm in his refusal to give any promises:

> I must observe that I have resolved with respect to every appointment,
> Civil or Ecclesiastical, with which I have any concern, not to enter into
> any engagement nor to give any assurances calculated to raise expecta-
> tions until the appointment be actually vacant – and in compliance with
> that Rule to which I always have adhered, I must reserve to myself the
> unfettered discretion of dealing as I may think fit with the livings you
> mention should a vacancy occur in either of them during my Tenure of
> official power.[35]

It was more than fifteen months before the Rev. James Dalton, M.A.,
Rector of Croft, obliged his Bishop by transferring to a Higher Sphere,
but immediately the news of his death reached Longley, he wrote the
following letter to Peel:

> Palace Ripon
> Jany 6 184[3]
>
> My dear Sir,
>   I take the liberty of informing you that the living of Croft in my
> Diocese concerning which I ventured to address a memorial to you some
> time since, has just become vacant by the death of the Rev'd Mr Dalton
> and I should be most unwilling to trespass longer on your valuable time
> than to say that should your choice of his successor fall on the Rev'd
> Charles Dodgson, the Church, and more especially the Diocese of Ripon
> which he so efficiently served as my Examining Chaplain, would have
> reason to thank you for having selected for Preferment a Clergyman of

high Professional Character, of first rate ability, and of much Theological attainment – one indeed who would adorn the very first Stations in the Church.

Mr Dodgson, who was in both the first classes of Oxford, and served the offices of Public Tutor & Mathematical Lecturer at Christ Church with distinguished Reputation, has been taking Private Pupils for the last sixteen years at a small Perpetual Curacy in a remote village in Cheshire – and with a family of nine Children he is naturally earnestly desirous of some advance in his Profession. It is not only in my own opinion only, but that also persons who feel no personal interest in Mr Dodgson's Preferment, that it would be a benefit to the Church if such Talents as his could be left to their unfettered exercise in the Service.

I need scarcely add, that should your decision in this case happily be in Mr Dodgson's favour, I should feel truly grateful for the relief it would afford me in the discharge of this newly created Diocese.

I have the honour to remain

My dear Sir

Yr faithful & obed. Servt.

C. T. Ripon.[36]

Sir Robt. Peel.

Longley also approached as many influential friends as he could think of and urged them to add their pleas to his own. They needed little persuasion. Peel, who had had only one previous church living to dispose of in eighteen months of office, received numerous applications from deserving clergymen up and down the country; but the most vociferous appeals came from the supporters of Mr Dodgson, who bombarded Peel with letters. Among these supporters were James Archibald Stuart-Wortley-MacKenzie, First Baron Wharncliffe, and Frederick John Robinson, First Earl of Ripon. Lord Francis Egerton described 'the care which he has extended to a very generally neglected but not ungrateful class, that of canal navigators',[37] and the local Member of Parliament, John Wilson Patten, wrote, 'I may confidently say that as regards his character as a clergyman he would receive the unanimous recommendation of a very extensive district in which that character is known and highly appreciated'.[38]

A nineteenth-century Prime Minister had far less political business than his modern counterpart, but as Sir Robert waded through his pile of letters nominating Mr Dodgson for the post, replying personally to each in his small, neat handwriting, his patience understandably wore thin. His reply to the Bishop reveals his irritation:

Whitehall Jany 13 1843

My dear Lord,

I have determined, purely on the grounds of his very high character and attainments, and professional Services within the Diocese of Ripon, to prefer the Rev'd Charles Dodgson to the numberless Competitors with him for the Living of Croft in the North Riding of Yorkshire.

Excuse me for saying that I wish I had been left at liberty to make my selection of Mr Dodgson (which I was perfectly prepared to do) on the single ground of his merits and claims – without the intervention of various Colleagues of mine and Members of Parliament who have been urged to address me in favour of Mr Dodgson, necessarily involving me in a very extensive correspondence and not influencing my decision.

I have written to Mr Dodgson apprizing him of my intentions in his favour.

I have etc.

Robert Peel.[39]

But no hint of this irritation appears in Sir Robert's letter to Mr Dodgson himself, to whom he wrote, 'There is no part of my public Duty which is more gratifying to me, than the appropriation of such Church Patronage as may be at my disposal, to the Reward and Encouragement of active professional Exertions by men of unblemished private Character and great intellectual attainment. In conformity with this principle, and exclusively upon the ground of your professional services and claims, I have resolved to appoint you to the Living of Croft in the North Riding of Yorkshire.'[40] Sir Robert added a proviso that the appointment was made on the strict understanding that Mr Dodgson would live at Croft and carry out the parish duties in person. In his acceptance, he wrote, 'I beg to assure you that I shall be anxious to commence my residence at Croft with as little delay as circumstances will admit of.'[41] The pleasant, open fields of Daresbury had become a poverty trap and an intellectual prison from which the family at the parsonage could hardly wait to escape.

REFERENCES

1   Charles Dodgson, *A Sermon preached in the Minster at Ripon on Sunday January 15th 1837.*
2   Collingwood, p. 8.
3   Edna de Prez, 'Where the sun came peeping in at Morn', *Cheshire Life*, April 1974.
4   Cheshire Archives E.E.P. 1137.
5   'Faces in the Fire', 1860.
6   Daresbury Parish Magazine, August 1906.
7   Paraphrase of St John, 5, 39.
8   D.F.C. 5/4.
9   D.F.C. 5/2.
10 Ibid.
11 *Pillow Problems.*

12 D.F.C. 5/3.
13 E. Guiliano (ed.), *Lewis Carroll Observed*, New York 1974, p. 84.
14 Green, p. 71.
15 Green, p. 105.
16 Collingwood, pp. 12–13.
17 Collingwood, p. 14.
18 D.F.C. 5/1.
19 D.F.C. 5/5.
20 Collingwood, pp. 4–5.
21 Collingwood, p. 8.
22 Hudson, p. 24.
23 *Through the Looking-Glass*, p. 203.
24 Green, p. 8.
25 Green, p. 8.
26 Christ Church Treasury Papers.
27 Max Müller, *My Autobiography*, 1901.
28 *A Sermon preached in the Collegiate Church of Manchester, on Thursday July 18th, 1839, at the meeting of the Society for the Relief of the Widows and Orphans of the Clergy of the Archdeaconry of Chester.*
29 Maria Trench, *The Story of Dr Pusey's Life*, 1900, p. 22.
30 Memorial from Bishop Longley to Sir Robert Peel, 18 September 1841, B.L. Ms. 40489, f. 187.
31 *A Sermon Preached in the Minster at Ripon on Sunday January 15th, 1837.*
32 Memorial from Bishop Longley to Sir Robert Peel, 18 September 1841, B.L. Ms. 40489, f. 187.
33 Letter from Lord Ashley to Sir Robert Peel, 21 September 1841, B.L. Ms. 40489, f. 191.
34 Memorial from Bishop Longley to Sir Robert Peel, 18 September 1841, B.L. Ms. 40489, f. 187.
35 Letter from Sir Robert Peel to Bishop Longley, 22 September 1841, B.L. Ms. 40489, f. 193.
36 B.L. Ms. 40522.
37 B.L. Ms. 40522, f. 205.
38 B.L. Ms. 40522.
39 B.L. Ms. 40522.
40 B.L. Ms. 40522, f. 371.
41 B.L. Ms. 40522, f. 373.

2   Unwillingly to School

Despite the family's eagerness to move, there were practical reasons preventing an immediate transfer to their new home. The late incumbent had had to cope with illness and old age in his final years, and had to some extent neglected both the parish and the rectory. His sons now needed time to clear their father's furniture and effects, while Mr Dodgson for his part wished to arrange a number of repairs and alterations before his family took up occupation of the premises. He described the house as 'a good old-fashioned Rectory, with no *beauty* outside or inside',[1] and criticized the proportions of some of the rooms. Among the alterations which he carried out was the raising of the ceiling of the first floor bedroom, which he and his wife proposed to occupy. This entailed the raising and relaying of the floor of the nursery, a large room of identical area immediately above. More than a century later the floorboards were raised again when the house was converted to three flats, more suitable in size for twentieth-century living. Underneath was found a mysterious cache of miscellaneous odds and ends. These included pieces of clay pipe, the lid of a dolls' teapot, a little shoe and a penknife. A tiny white glove, without which no self-respecting Victorian child would venture outside the garden gate, a silver thimble, as indispensable as fingers to the little Victorian needlewoman, and small scraps of paper and parchment belonging to Mr and Mrs Dodgson formed part of this treasure trove. Most important, however, was a small piece of wood on which Charles had written

> And we'll wander through
> the wide world
> and chase the buffalo.

Accompanying the hoard was another piece of wood bearing the inscription: 'This floor was laid by Mr Martin and Mr Sutton June 19th 1843.' Perhaps these evocative treasures were assembled beneath a loose board over a period of years; but more probably they were deliberately collected to represent each and every member of the Dodgson household, triumphantly transported to Croft on a pre-visit, and ceremonially hidden under the floor boards by Charles or one of his siblings before the workmen nailed the last board in place.

Although Mr Dodgson preached his last sermon at Daresbury in April 1843, the family did not actually move to Croft until the autumn. This was not only on account of the repair work and the settling of parish affairs in Daresbury, but also because Mrs Dodgson was pregnant again. Her tenth child, Henrietta, was born at Daresbury Parsonage on 2 June 1843, and was baptized by the Rev. T. L. Claughton in Daresbury Parish Church on 23 July 1843. There were now no further obstacles to the family's removal.

The township of Croft straddles the Tees where the road from Northallerton to Darlington crosses the swiftly-flowing river. Its ancient bridge 'of sixe myghtye pillars, and of seven arches of stone work' was described in 1531 as 'the moste directe and sure way and passage for the Kinge or Sovraigne Lordes armye and ordynance to resort and passe over into the North parties and marches of this realme'.[2] In the past this strategic position had given it a relative importance as a watering place which had tended to decline with the opening in 1825 of the railway from Stockton to Darlington, only four miles from Croft. Nevertheless, it was still a popular resort in the hunting season, when gentlemen packed its excellent hotel, and sometimes even overflowed into its boarding houses. Besides the regular population of seven hundred people of Croft, the parish included the inhabitants of the neighbouring townships of Dalton and part of Stapleton, plus the hamlets of Halnaby, Jolby and Walmire. With this thriving community Croft offered a range of social contacts for the whole family such as would never have been possible in Daresbury.

The transfer to Croft represented a tremendous improvement in the family fortunes. Mr Dodgson could now count on a secure income for life from the living and letting of the glebe of well over a thousand pounds a year, plus a substantial house with a well-stocked garden and three-and-a-half acres of land as an emolument. He could keep enough livestock to provide all the dairy produce, eggs and bacon that the family needed, and the kitchen garden with its abundance of fruit trees would not only supply their own daily needs of fruit and vegetables, but would also enable them to give some away to the poor and needy. He would have to increase his domestic staff by a further maidservant, and would need an outdoor man to look after the garden, plus occasional casual labour. But he was fortunate in being able to engage the former incumbent's gardener, who knew the work and was known for his industry and skill. At least one of the permanent staff at Daresbury, Mrs Vines, moved with the Dodgsons to Croft.

Had the family wished, they could now have enjoyed a life of high style. The Rectory was enormous, with ample servants' quarters as well as generous family accomodation. There were two huge living rooms, two kitchens, two libraries, a schoolroom and innumerable bedrooms.

Additional domestic offices included a servants' hall, housekeeper's room, pastry room, dairy room, bacon room, needlework room, butler's pantry and wine cellar. Although the size of the house made it unecessary, most of the children preferred to share a room, and two of the girls even shared one with a maidservant. But Charles had a large room of his own on the second floor, not only in recognition of his status as the eldest son, but also because he needed privacy for study. His room was approached by a passageway lit by a dormer window, invisible from the ground, and inscribed by workmen on the outside:

> T Young Painted July 23 1836
> Plumer an Glazer an Tiner 9th August 1830
> Edward Johnson Plumber Darlington 1834

These names read mirror-fashion day by day may have given Charles an early preoccupation with mirror-writing, which he ultimately introduced into *Through the Looking-Glass* with the first verse of the nonsense poem 'Jabberwocky'.

Outside there was a coach house, stabling for seven horses, a tithebarn, henhouse and piggery. The Rev. James Dalton, the last incumbent, had been a notable botanist, and while at Croft botanized extensively in the seasonally flooded woodlands of Upper Teesdale. (His splendid herbarium of over two thousand sheets plus sixty-seven pencil and water colour vignettes of Bryophytes are still in the Yorkshire Museum.)[3] In the thirty-eight years that he had held the living, Mr Dalton had extended this interest by building up in the garden a wonderful collection of plants, many of them rare and exotic, which attracted numerous visitors. The garden was Mrs Dodgson's particular delight. Its abundant produce enabled her to indulge her natural instinct of generosity, and she loved to share her good fortune with others. Always an affectionate daughter, she often sent flowers to her father in Hull, and plant cuttings to her sisters, keeping careful record of the latter, in order to avoid duplication. The ancient 'umbrella tree', a yew, stands in the rectory garden to this very day, and a shoot from the old robinia on the front lawn has grown into a respectable sized tree.

Although the Dodgsons were conscious of a certain superior status in the community and preserved an air of gentility, they preferred a comparatively simple way of life, with the accent on education, culture, and, above all, on self-discipline and Christian charity. Before long the extent of that charity was demonstrated in an act of generosity that was to prove of lasting benefit to the children of the district. On his very first visit to Croft Mr Dodgson had been disturbed to find that only thirty-five children of the parish were in receipt of any form of religious education. Indeed there was no school of any description in Croft. He accordingly conceived the plan of giving up a portion of his glebe amounting to some 15,000 square yards for the provision of a school, whose aims were to be:

> 1st – To train up the Children in Christian Knowledge, according to the doctrines and principles of the Established Church of England, and under the direction and superintendence of the Clergyman of the Parish. 2nd – To provide instruction for them in other useful things, such as Reading, Writing, Arithmetic, and, for the Girls, Needlework.[4]

By October 1844 he had demolished a former cow house to make way for the new building, engaged an architect from Durham, completed the legal formalities and prepared the site. On the 23rd of the same month the first stone was laid by Bishop Longley, and the school was completed early in 1845. It consisted of two large rooms, one for boys and one for girls, capable of holding about sixty pupils. Total costs for building and equipping the school were £422.7.4½d, of which £175 was met by various grants. A collection taken in the parish church provided £15, and the remaining £232.7.4½d was supplied by private subscription. Of this the staggering sum of £121.17.4½d was donated by Mr Dodgson himself, and his own and his wife's families contributed a further £52.10s. Nor did their generosity end there. Annual running costs, which included £60 for the schoolmaster and £27 for the school-mistress, were expected to be in the region of £100, while the income from the pupils was approximately £20 a year. In the first year Mr Dodgson not only contributed £30 and obtained a further £7 from his wife and sister-in-law, but acted as permanent guarantor for the running costs. Though he was freed from the irksome financial necessity of taking paying children by his removal from Daresbury, he had now voluntarily undertaken a permanent charitable liability, and a superintendence which he dutifully carried out for the rest of his life, giving up much of his own time to teaching the children. His wife and, as they advanced in years, his children also helped in the school, and it was here, over a decade later, that Charles Lutwidge Dodgson, during his vacation, enjoyed his first experience of teaching.

Another major preoccupation at that time was the condition of St Peter's Church, situated next to the Rectory, though almost completely screened from view by the tall trees in the garden. Of Norman origin, it was rebuilt and elongated in the early fourteenth century, but on Mr Dodgson's arrival in the parish he found that the roof was unsound and in 1845 he replaced the original with a very good oak copy, which is still there. His obligations in respect of the upkeep of his church living had always been taken very seriously, and his advice to the clergy clearly states his views on the subject:

> I cannot but earnestly impress upon every Incumbent that the annual income of his benefice is charged with the repairs of his Parsonage, of his

Glebe Buildings and Fences, and, in many cases, of the chancel of his
Parish Church: and that by neglecting to make the necessary outlay, as
the need arises, he is constantly accumulating a burden, which may fall
unexpectedly, and press hardly and heavily, on a widow, or a fatherless
family, or both; or will become nothing less than a robbery of his
successor, should he leave no estate sufficient to meet the liability.[5]

While the entire Dodgson household occupied themselves with
charitable works in the parish however, the parents did not neglect
their own children. One major advantage of his improved financial
status was that Mr Dodgson could now invest money in his children's
future. For his daughters he considered that insurances provided the
best securities, but for his sons he felt that an investment in their
education would reap the greatest dividends in later life. He was
determined to obtain the very best education possible for his eldest son.
So it was that Charles Dodgson, at the age of twelve, left home on
1 August 1844, equipped by his devoted family with a superfluity of
clothes and comforts, and became a boarder at Richmond School, some
ten miles away.

Though it had existed from the fourteenth century, Richmond
School did not acquire a significant reputation as an educational
establishment until the appointment as headmaster in 1796 of James
Tate I, an outstanding personality who not only extended the size of the
school but achieved a remarkable academic record. Described as 'a
man dripping with Greek', he wrote a number of books on classical
subjects; but his success as a headmaster lay not so much in his
personal erudition as in his ability to fire his pupils with the love of
learning. A former pupil wrote: 'His nice appreciation of character told
him where he was to begin and how far he could go with each of his
pupils, and his enthusiastic love for what he taught, together with his
child-like simplicity of manner and unaffected kindness, won the hearts
of his scholars, whilst he raised and quickened their intellect.'[6] When in
1833 he resigned his headmastership to become a Canon of St Paul's
Cathedral, he was succeeded by his son, James Tate II, to whom he had
passes on both his love of learning and his ability to assess character
and potential. Perhaps because he was dogged by ill-health, James
Tate II lacked his father's energy and decision in managing the school,
and was consequently less successful as a headmaster. A mild man with
a gentle voice he was quite unable to offer stern reproofs or severe
punishments. 'Scrupulously neat in his own person, and always fault-
lessly dressed,' wrote one former scholar, 'I have known him break off
suddenly when reproving a boy, and notice with commendation the
cleanness of his hands.'[7] A more suitable headmaster to bring out the
best in a boy as sensitive and shy as the young Charles Dodgson could
not be imagined, and whatever James Tate's deficiencies as a head-

master, the influence of his father was still so strong that the reputation of the school was unequalled when Charles arrived there.

Chief emphasis at the school was laid on the teaching not simply of religion but more specifically of Christianity as understood in the Church of England. The moral example of the headmaster was of paramount importance, and under the school's constitution he was liable to expulsion if he became 'a Notorious Drunkard or Gamester, or a constant frequenter of Gaming or Tippling Houses, or became guilty of Fornication, Adultery, or Incest'. Neither James Tate nor his brother Thomas, who was usher, or second master, at the school, showed an inclination to any of these vices, though Thomas, a strapping, robust man differed greatly from his brother, and was widely disliked by the boys for his wilfulness and inflexibility of purpose.

About 120 boys attended the school when Charles Dodgson was there. Free places, usually totalling about twenty, were available, but these were reserved for 'Children Natives in the Burrough and the children of the Burgesses and other persons inhabitating in the said burrough and exercising any Trade, Mystery, or Manual Occupation therein . . .'. Charles, as a boarder, had to pay. He was placed in the headmaster's own house, Swale House, or the 'Cloaca Maxima' (Main Sewer), as the children called it, because it was situated in the Grand Channel at the foot of Frenchgate. The headmaster's personal boarders had to pay more than other boys for the privilege of residing with him, his wife Anne and their family of six children: the fees were over one hundred guineas a year, a charge comparable with that of the foremost public schools of the day. Swale House was enormous, capable of accommodating sixteen boarders as well as the headmaster's own household without any overcrowding. At the end of its pleasant garden was a row of three studies, each of which was shared by two or three of the most senior boys.

The old schoolhouse was replaced in 1850 and ultimately demolished, but Richmond School as Charles knew it was a one-storey building erected in 1677 and situated in a corner of the churchyard. Originally it had consisted of a single room forty-five feet long and twenty feet wide, but in 1815 a second had been added. Heating was by a large open fire. The headmaster had a rostrum at one end, and the boys sat on benches round the walls in enclosures that looked like pews. Charles, like all the other pupils, had a sloping book-board with a shelf beneath where he could keep text books, writing materials and so forth.

Despite his shyness, Charles settled down quickly at the school. As a newcomer he was expected to undergo various initiation ceremonies in the churchyard where the children used to play, and these he described to his eldest sisters Fanny and Memy in a letter written only five days after the start of term:

The boys have played two tricks upon me which were these – they first
proposed to play at 'King of the Cobblers' and asked if I would be king,
to which I agreed. Then they made me sit down and sat (on the ground)
in a circle round me, and they told me to say 'Go to work' which I said,
and they immediately began kicking me and knocking me on all sides.
The next game they proposed was 'Peter, the red lion', and they made a
mark on a tombstone (for we were playing in the churchyard) and one of
the boys walked with his eyes shut, holding out his finger to touch, trying
to touch the mark; then a little boy came forward to lead the rest and led
a good many very near the mark; at last it was my turn; they told me to
shut my eyes well, and the next minute I had my finger in the mouth of
one of the boys, who had stood (I believe) before the tombstone with his
mouth open.[8]

Once he had proved his mettle, the teasing stopped. He acquired a
room-mate called Ned Swire, whose brother was also a boarder, and
liked several of his companions. His parents, who drove over from Croft
on 10 August 1844 to find out at first hand how he was getting on at the
school, were well satisfied with the way in which he adapted himself to
his first experience of life outside the family circle.

Archery, football and fives, wrestling, leapfrog and fighting were all
popular at the school in those days, and on half holidays the boys used
to play cricket on the racecourse, or drag a brass cannon on a wooden
carriage to Willance's Leap, where they fired it aimlessly. In winter
when the snow was deep enough, they used to drag wooden benches
from the schoolhouse to the top of the churchyard walk, jumping
aboard and careering down the path into a piled-up buffer of snow at
the bottom. On Wednesday and Saturday afternoons, when the boys
had time off, they were allowed the free run of the Castle, the ruins of St
Agatha's Abbey at Easby and the Green Walks, their favourite haunt in
the summer months. Here some of the boys indulged in a quiet smoke,
strictly against the rules, and one old boy of the school described how
'in many a crevice and cleft in the rocks, caves, and branches of trees
were the pipes hid after an indulgence in the narcotic delight'.[9] But
Charles was never a breaker of rules. Throughout his life he remained
strictly a non-smoker.

The school year was divided into terms of twenty weeks, each followed by six weeks' holiday, for although Richmond was a market town
with flourishing lead and wool industries, it was not readily accessible,
even in 1844. Standard tuition covered only religious instruction plus
Latin and Greek grammar and literature; nothing else was taught
except French, mathematics and accounts, for which extra payment
had to be made. Most free boys needed the two latter subjects because
they were expected to follow their fathers' trades, but the paying pupils
needed classics for university entrance. Teaching was done by the
headmaster, aided by a single usher and a visiting French master.

Though Charles learned French as a schoolboy, he profited very little from it, and did not take much real interest in the language until the possibility of having *Alice* translated into French encouraged him to take it up again.

Charles quickly proved his scholatic ability, achieving an outstanding rating in mathematics. At the end of the first term the headmaster wrote of him, 'He has past [sic] an excellent examination just now in mathematics, exhibiting at times an illustration of that love of precise argument, which seems to him natural. He is not however *classed* because the subjects in which he and two others were tried, do not allow of a strict comparison with the other Mathematical Pupils.'[10] Classical studies came less easily to him, but he showed considerable promise despite grammatical errors and difficulties with Latin metrical form, for schoolboys of his era had not only to achieve proficiency in prose composition, but to write Latin verse, modelling themselves on the great classical poets, and observing scrupulously the complicated rules of syllabic quantity. He was, in the words of his headmaster, 'marvellously ingenious in replacing the ordinary inflexions of nouns and verbs, as detailed in our grammars, by more exact analogies, or convenient forms of his own devising',[11] and when he read aloud from Virgil or Ovid, failed to observe the correct scansion.

James Tate II showed an almost uncanny ability to analyse Charles Dodgson's true potential. After only a single term he wrote to Mr and Mrs Dodgson:

> I do not hesitate to express my opinion that he possesses, along with other and natural endowments, a very uncommon share of genius. Gentle and cheerful in his intercourse with others, playful and ready in conversation, he is capable of acquirements and knowledge far beyond his years, while his reason is so clear and so jealous of error, that he will not rest satisfied without a most exact solution of whatever appears to him obscure. . . . You must not entrust your son with a full knowledge of his superiority over other boys. Let him discover this as he proceeds. The love of excellence is far beyond the love of excelling; and if he should once be bewitched into a mere ambition to surpass others I need not urge that the very quality of his knowledge would be materially injured, and that his character would receive a stain of a more serious description still.[12]

On 26 November 1845, the last day of term, in the company of his fellow scholars, Charles Dodgson boarded the Mail Coach to Darlington for the last time. He had availed himself of all that Richmond School had to offer a boy of his age, and was now ready to proceed with the next stage of his education.

Westminster, his father's own old school, would have seemed an obvious choice for Charles to progress to, for Christ Church drew a high percentage of its men from this source. It had fallen into a sharp decline in the first half of the nineteenth century, however, and on careful consideration Mr Dodgson decided that this was not the place for Charles. Perhaps this was fortunate, for shortly afterwards Westminster School was plagued with major outbreaks of infectious illness, for which inadequate sewers were blamed. The number of pupils declined alarmingly, and in view of the fatalities it was not surprising that anxious parents withdrew their boys. Rugby, on the other hand, under the headmastership of the famous Dr Thomas Arnold, and encouraged by the new London to Birmingham Railway, which made it more readily accessible, had risen to the foremost ranks of public schools. When Arnold had accepted the headmastership in 1828, most public schools found their numbers dwindling because parents were increasingly reluctant to submit their sons to the brutality of school life. Yet his methods had met with widespread approbation, and despite fees which stood at more than fifty guineas a term, Mr Dodgson resolved to send his eldest son there. Charles Dodgson's name was accordingly entered in the school register on 27 January 1846. He was exactly fourteen years old.

Arnold had been dead for nearly four years when Charles arrived at Rugby, and his place had been taken by Dr Archibald Campbell Tait, who became Archbishop of Canterbury in 1868. The news of his appointment as headmaster had had a mixed reception, but on the whole the choice had been a popular one. 'The election of Tait is a matter of great thankfulness to us and shows that the Trustees have rightly estimated his testimonials' wrote the Rev. Charles Mayor, Arnold's Assistant Master and young Dodgson's favourite mathematics teacher. But the alleged dullness of his sermons and a certain weakness in Classics gave concern in some quarters, and Arnold's great friend Arthur Penryn Stanley was openly horrified. On 29 July 1842 he wrote to Tait: 'The awful intelligence of your election has just reached me . . . I conjure you . . . to lay aside every thought for the present except that of repairing your deficiencies. . . . Read Arnold's sermons. At whatever expense of orthodoxy (so called) for the time, throw yourself thoroughly into his spirit. Alter nothing at first. See all that is good and nothing that is bad in the masters and the Rugby character.'[13] Stanley's fears seem to have been unfounded. 'His tenure of headmastership was a very remarkable instance of goodness and good sense (and, I need hardly add, very good abilities), enabling a man to fill a post for which he was not specially designed,'[14] wrote Dean Bradley.

Tait was not a public schoolboy, though he had been a scholar and later a tutor at Balliol College, Oxford. In 1841 with three other tutors, he had published a protest against *Tract XC*, the most famous of the statements of the Tractarians. Mr Dodgson held fairly liberal views for his era, and to some extent supported Newman and his followers, yet found some of the tenets of *Tract XC* wholly unacceptable. In the years which followed, nothing was more feared among the Anglican clergy than the conversion of their fellows to Roman Catholicism. Anyone in whom the Tractarian movement inspired such fears would have been glad to send his children to Rugby with Tait as headmaster, and by the time Charles arrived there, numbers had risen from 330 in Arnold's day to nearly 500.

As at Richmond, Charles was placed in the headmaster's own house, School House, which contained about eighty boys, compared with only sixteen in Swale House, Richmond. His opinion of Dr Tait is not recorded, but on the whole the head was well liked by his pupils. He was described as

> a most dignified and courteous gentleman, with a grave manner, an impressive voice, and an occasional sparkle of deep feeling or quiet humour, which we felt lying in the background, ready either to flash out upon our faults or make allowances for our shortcomings. . . . He knew exactly where to overlook and where to interfere, and when he did punish or rebuke, it was done in the best manner, with a force and dignity, and judgement which left nothing to be desired.[15]

Yet although he had a reputation for taking a warm interest in individual boys, it is clear that comparatively few boys could expect much personal attention from a headmaster in a school of this size.

From every point of view life at Rugby was a personal disaster for young Dodgson. He could not accept the transition from the intimate family atmosphere of Richmond School, where work had been a pleasure and the kind old schoolmaster a well-loved friend, to the vast impersonality of Rugby. 'There is, or ought to be, something very ennobling in being connected with an establishment at once ancient and magnificent . . .' wrote Dr Arnold. Yet Charles was far from ennobled by the atmosphere of the school. He did not object to the work, though this was rigorous: the boys worked from 7 a.m. until 10 p.m. six days a week, and only marginally less on Sundays, when normal studies were replaced by Biblical ones. But the endless imposition of lines for trifling offences took all the pleasure out of learning and wasted hours which could have been better spent. Even worse was the bullying to which younger pupils were subjected. Though Tait modified the powers of the Praeposters, or sixth formers, who had dominated the school even in Arnold's day, and severely curbed their right to inflict punishments, he could not eliminate bullying altogether. As a scholarly boy who was poor at games, Charles was an obvious target for abuse. Worse still, his distressing stammer caused him acute embarrassment. Yet he could have borne all the humiliation and misery had he been safe from interference at night. Though the practice of sleeping four or five to a bed, which had so shocked Dr Arnold, had been abolished, there were no separate sleeping quarters. Like all the younger boys in the dormitories, Charles was often stripped of his bedclothes, and spent many cold, wretched nights longing for the warm family atmosphere at Croft Rectory and counting the days till the school holidays.

Nevertheless in his contacts with his family young Dodgson always preserved his cheerfulness, giving no hint of these deep-seated unhappinesses. At least he benefited from the separate studies that the boys enjoyed. The addition of a row of these tiny gaslit rooms was one of Tait's best innovations at the school. Charles H. Newmark's excellent description conveys the new boy's pride in his study:

> But he is not quite right until his study is properly furnished, the smell of paint gone off, and the stiffness taken out of the chintz sofa cover. The fitting up is done by the Rugby upholsterers with great expedition, and the study is made *habitable* in the course of a couple of days; but for the first week or two there is an unpleasant smell of newness which pervades the curtains, table cloth and bookshelves . . .
>
> But when the *minutiae* are at length arranged to the satisfaction of the occupant, how supremely comfortable is a Rugby study! What a mistaken idea it is to have large rooms for other than state purposes, such as the reception of company, or the display of ornaments; but for coziness our recollections of school life will tell us that six feet square is quite enough. What could be more perfect happiness than sitting before the fire in our study, with one foot on either hob, superintending the boiling of our 'night-cap', or the frying of some sausages on a Saturday night.[16]

Remarkable though it now seems, it was the practice in Charles Dodgson's day for boys to cook food freely in their studies. A more dangerous habit than to allow five hundred boys to cook separately over open fires in such confined quarters can scarcely be imagined. During his nine years as headmaster Tait practically bankrupted the local pastry cooks, or 'guttle shops' as the boys called them, by introducing communal breakfasts, but the pupils continued to cook snacks at will, particularly in the evenings.

Dodgson could never have been described as a sportsman, although his nephew, Collingwood, tells us that he was always ready to defend weaker boys from bullying with his own fists. He always enjoyed walking, and one of his letters from Rugby describes two visits on foot to Brinklow, some six miles from the school, where he sketched the remains of a Roman encampment. He also describes the Rugby playground, containing an ancient burial mound and filled with trees which the boys used for gymnastics and swinging. Though he claimed never to have played cricket, he was clearly interested in the sport, if only as a spectator, and already while at Rugby had two framed cricketing prints. Of the famous Rugby sport of 'big-side' football, he makes no reference, but the boys themselves made sure that none of their fellows escaped their traditional matches. An excellent contemporary account gives us a picture of what the game was like in Charles Dodgson's day:

> The first indications of a match at football are the prevalence of white trowsers at calling-over, even in the winter time. Further convincing proofs are soon given in the indistinctly-heard repetition of a monosyllable, which, upon a nearer approach, is found to be the word Match, issuing from a line of Praeposters who are stationed at the door to prevent escape of any who might otherwise feel inclined to 'cut'.
>
> The whole school, whether Fags, Praeposters or Fifth Form, being thus assembled in the close, the match is announced . . .
>
> The next preliminary proceeding is the divesture of jackets, braces, and other impediments to a free use of the limbs, and also of hats, which would probably
> > Go in a *hat*, that out a *hat*,
> > Never would come again![17]

Standard dress for the game was the velvet cap and jersey, contrasting pleasingly with the white trousers. In Charles Dodgson's time the two teams consisted simply of School House versus all the rest, with the best twenty players on each side circulating freely about the pitch, and the rest divided into two halves, one to defend goal and the other to attack the opposing goal.

Predictably, Dodgson's academic record was outstanding, and he rarely returned home for the holidays without prizes. His proud mother, meticulous as ever, kept a record of the books he won. It was against the rules for any scholar to win more than one prize per term, and though in his form of more than fifty boys he was often placed first in more than one subject, his prizes averaged out at one per half year from December 1846 onwards. Usually the choice of books, which rested with the scholar himself, was biographical, historical and religious. Even at the age of fourteen he was consciously building up for himself a library which would be of lasting value, and in choosing books either as prizes or from his own money he relied heavily on his father's opinion. Of his total of eleven prize books from Rugby, at least three were for Classics, including Latin composition, which effectively dispels any suggestion that he was weak in these subjects. It would be fairer to say that he was better at Mathematics than Classics, and that as his life progressed, his greater inclination to the former led him to devote himself to Mathematics at the expense of his work in Latin and Greek. As time went on, Divinity also emerged as a subject in which he excelled, and in his last term at the school, the headmaster wrote to his father, 'his examination for the Divinity prize was one of the most creditable exhibitions I have ever seen'.[18]

Sadly very little remains of the correspondence which passed between Croft and Rugby during Charles' four years at the school.

Collingwood reproduces an amusing sketch with which Charles illustrated an incident described by one of his sisters. It is captioned: 'The only sister who *would* write to her brother, though the table had got folded down!' The other sisters are depicted 'sternly resolved to set off to Halnaby and the Castle, tho' it is yet "early early morning".'[19] There was certainly no shortage of news from the Rectory to satisfy Charles' avid interest in family matters.

In his first year at the school the Dodgsons' youngest child, Edwin, was born, and in the following year (1847) Mr Dodgson was made first Rural Dean of the newly formed Eastern Division of the Deanery of Richmond. The constant coming and going to relatives and the daily preoccupations of his brothers and sisters were all of interest to this boy who would clearly have preferred to exchange life in a large public school for the intimate atmosphere of home. In May 1849, responding to his sister Elizabeth's complaint that his letters were too short, he wrote her a mammoth reply running into some 1400 words. The final paragraph gives an excellent picture of daily life at Croft Rectory:

> Will you answer my question about the clocks, when you next write? How do you get on with the poetry book with Willy and Long? Shall I send you or bring you any more numbers of it? And have you seen the *Vast Army*? There is a 3rd part of *Laneton Parsonage* come out, have you seen it? How do you like the *Diversions of Hollycott*? Will my room be ready for me when I come home? And has it got any more 'visitors'? Have you been many walks with Aunt and Cousin Smedley? And how long are they going to stay with you? Are my two pictures of cricketing framed yet? When is Papa going to the Ordination? And when to the Durham examination? Has Fanny yet finished Alison's *Europe*? Have you finished your *Hutchinson*? Are the mats finished? Is Skeffington's ship finished? Have you left off fires yet? Have you begun the evening walks in the garden? does Skeffington ride Henderson's donkey much now? has Fanny found any new flowers yet? have you got any babies to nurse? Mary any new pictures to paint? Has Mr Stamper given up the ballroom yet? Will you tell me whose and when the birthdays in next month are? Will you condense all these questions into one or answer each separately? Lastly, do you believe that I subscribe myself your afette Brther sincerely or not? Is this letter long enough?[20]

Another paragraph in the same letter gives an interesting insight into young Dodgson's notions of the value of genuine truthfulness:

> I have not yet been able to get the 2nd vol: Macaulay's *England* to read: I have seen it however & one passage struck me when 7 bishops signed the invitation to the pretender, & King James sent for Bishop Compton (who was one of the 7) and asked him 'whether he or any of his ecclesiastical bretheren had had anything to do with it?' He replied after a moment's thought, 'I am fully persuaded, your majesty, that there is not one of my bretheren who is not as innocent as myself.' This was certainly no actual lie, but certainly as Macaulay says, it was very little different from one. On the next day the King called a meeting of all the

bishops, when Compton was present, but the other 6 absented themselves. He then for form's sake put the question to each of them 'whether they had had anything to do with it?' Here was a new difficulty which Compton got over by saying, when it came to his turn, 'I gave your lordship *my* answer yesterday.' It certainly showed talent, though exerted in the wrong direction.'[21]

Though exhilarated by his examination successes, young Dodgson always looked forward to the end of term, which at Rugby School was always preceded by a night of revelry and feasting, with the traditional veal pies, oysters and other delicacies, after which the tiny gas-lit studies were nailed up as a precaution against pilferers.

His homecoming was eagerly awaited by his sisters and brothers, who counted on him to tell them stories and lead their games. For he was a born entertainer who always brought a magic sparkle to Croft Rectory. Paradoxically, despite his innate shyness, he had inbred instincts for showmanship, and when he dressed in a long white robe and brown wig to perform conjuring tricks for the other children, or invented puppet shows for their amusement, all his shyness vanished and his stammer with it.

In the summer vacation of 1847, when some of the younger Dodgson children went down with whooping cough, Charles was invaluable, nursing them with infinite patience and playing with them continually. At sixteen years of age there seemed little prospect of his contracting the disease. Yet ironically, though he escaped the family epidemic, he contracted whooping cough at Rugby in March 1848. The attack was a severe one and it was not until July that he was able to attend matins again. The persistent cough he developed at this time suggests secondary bronchiectasis, which was to trouble him intermittently throughout his life. In October of the same year he was confined to the quarantine block at Rugby with mumps. When the glandular swelling receded he complained that he was more deaf than usual. His father wrote to the headmaster with an account of his earlier attack of 'infantile fever' – probably a feverish cold with accompanying otitis media – which had resulted in residual deafness in the right ear. Nerve deafness resulting from mumps is rare but incurable,[22] and led Dodgson in 1856 to consult Dr Joseph Toynbee, an aural surgeon, although this was to no avail. When in later years he was out walking with friends, he always walked on the right, and in public places selected the extreme right of the auditorium.

Encouraged by his eldest son's progress at Rugby, Mr Dodgson wrote in January 1849 to his old friend Dr Pusey, tactfully enquiring whether he might feel able to nominate Charles for a Studentship at Christ Church. Pusey was well known for the strict impartiality of his selections, uncorrupted for almost twenty years of office, during which time he had had the painful duty of refusing the sons of friends. 'I can only say that I shall have *very great* pleasure, if circumstances permit me to recommend your son. Only, I could not pass over a young man of decidedly superior attainments (if the man should be decidedly superior to your son) without violating a principle upon which I have so long acted, and committed myself again and again.'[23]

Charles left Rugby in December 1849. Scholastically he had achieved all that his parents could have expected of him, but the atmosphere of the school had not encouraged his natural development as a scholar and as an individual. What he had attained had been in spite of, rather than because of, the system at Rugby. What he regarded as the ideal in education was the system which he later found in operation at Twyford School, Hampshire, where his Oxford friend Kitchin was headmaster. This was the school eventually chosen for his brothers, and for his little cousin, Jimmy Dodgson. Though he wholeheartedly approved Kitchin's teaching methods, however, he felt that these depended too heavily on his individual personality. 'I like very much the system of freedom and intimacy which prevails here between master and boys', he wrote of a visit to Twyford School in December 1857, 'though there must often be a risk of the boys passing over the bounds of respect due to their masters. It is quite the system of ruling by love, and with a master like Kitchin seems to answer well, but I should doubt if there are many in whose hands it would succeed.'[24] As for his own experiences at Rugby, he wrote, 'I cannot say that I look back upon my life at a Public School with any sensation of pleasure, or that any earthly considerations would induce me to go through my three years again'.

REFERENCES

1 Green, p. 8.
2 *A History of Yorkshire North Riding*, 1914, Vol. 1, p. 163.
3 See 'Note on the Herbaria of John and James Dalton', Colin Sims, *Journal of the Society of Bibliography of Natural History*, Vol. 5, No. 2, 1969.
4 Charles Dodgson, *A Short Account of the First Establishment of the Croft National School*, 1845.
5 Charles Dodgson, *Charge delivered to the Clergy and Churchwardens of the Archdeaconry of Richmond*, 1855.
6 L. P. Wenham, *The History of Richmond School, Yorkshire*, 1958, p. 70.
7 Ibid, p. 168.
8 Collingwood, p. 22.

9   L. P. Wenham, *The History of Richmond School, Yorkshire*, 1958, pp. 82–3.
10   D.F.C. 6/1.
11   Collingwood, p. 25.
12   Ibid.
13   P. T. Davidson and W. Benham, *Life of Archibald Campbell Tait*, pp. 113–14.
14   Ibid, p. 119.
15   Charles H. Newmark, *Recollections of Rugby, by an Old Rugbean*, 1848, p. 132.
16   Ibid, p. 147.
17   Ibid, p. 132.
18   Collingwood, p. 29.
19   Ibid, p. 32.
20   Green, pp. 17–18.
21   Green, p. 17.
22   Dr Selwyn H. Goodacre, 'The Illnesses of Lewis Carroll', *The Practitioner*, August 1972.
23   D.F.C. 7/1a.
24   Green, p. 132.

3 The Rectory Magazines

Charles Dodgson's earliest preserved work of literary composition was not in English, but in Latin. It was composed at Richmond School, and copied into his diary on 25 November 1844. Latin verse composition was one of Mr Tate's chief pleasures, and he had himself written a treatise on Ovidian distich. 'Every Wednesday afternoon (a nominal half-holiday)', wrote a former Richmond pupil, 'our home lesson was the production of ten or twelve lines of "longs and shorts" on some well-worn adage highly interesting to the youthful mind, such as Vita brevis, ars longa, or on some event in the Roman History.'[1] While not precisely conforming to this definition, Charles' effort was probably the result of similarly spontaneous inspiration. 'Evening' was the subject he chose, and the poem read as follows:

> Phœbus aqua splendet descendens, æquora tingens
> Splendore aurato. Pervenit umbra solo.
> Mortales lectos quaerunt, et membra relaxant.
> Fessa labore dies; cuncta per orbe silet.
> Imperium placidum nunc sumit Phœbe corusca.
> Antris procedunt sanguine ore ferae.[2]

Less than a month later Mr Tate wrote of him that 'whether in reading aloud or metrical composition [he] frequently sets at naught the notions of Virgil or Ovid as to syllabic quantity'.[3] Apart from making obvious grammatical errors Charles exhibits that common schoolboy fault, an inability to use the dictionary correctly. When his descending sun-god shines through the water, ghosts (he means 'shades') tumble on the sod in a manner altogether too physical for the confines of the Latin language, and when his mortals seek relaxation with books the day is too literally exhausted. His management of the syllabic quantities in these hexameter lines shows that he had already developed an ear for quantitative verse, but his inexpert handling of the caesura, correct in only three of the lines, would seem to indicate that he was as yet too heavily steeped in the traditions of English poetry, with its tendency to shorter lines and freedom from the obligatory caesura, to master quickly the intricacies of the formal Latin model.

In 1845, according to Collingwood, Charles entered the field of creative English literature with a contribution to the Richmond School Magazine which he entitled 'The Unknown One'. Even in 1898, when he wrote his uncle's biography, Collingwood tells us that it had not been preserved: indeed, there is no record that Richmond School had a magazine at that period. Despite Collingwood's speculation that the story was probably a sensational one, calculated to appeal to the schoolboy imagination, this should not be taken for granted. Even at the age of thirteen Charles already exhibited strong tendencies to humour, and parody in particular.

Also in the year 1845 he produced his first family magazine, entitled *Useful and Instructive Poetry*, for Wilfred and Louisa, his brother and sister. As the first surviving indication of the future literary potential of Lewis Carroll this is of immense interest, consisting of a small collection of humorous verse, including some in limerick form. In style and presentation it is very similar to Edward Lear's *Book of Nonsense*. Though this was not published until 1846, it was composed between 1832 and 1836 to entertain the small children of the Earl of Derby, who employed Lear to illustrate his zoological specimens at Knowsley, only a few miles from Daresbury. It is possible that Lear's verse circulated in manuscript or orally in the district. However, Charles Dodgson never once referred to Lear and the limerick can be traced back at least a hundred and fifty years before these two masters of nonsense verse employed them. Like Lear, Charles Dodgson ransacked the globe for rhymable towns, dwelling on personal eccentricities and wildly improbable incidents. But the final line in Lear's limericks was usually a repetition of the first, while the thirteen-year-old Charles Dodgson's final line was a distinct development in the theme, as in the tale of a relative of the young man of Oporto:

> His sister named Lucy O'Finner,
> Grew constantly thinner and thinner,
> The reason was plain,
> She slept out in the rain,
> And was never allowed any dinner.

Though Charles Dodgson could never hope to match Lear's accomplishment as an artist, his illustrations for *Useful and Instructive Poetry* are spirited and entertaining, complementing the humour of the verse and in their basic approach not unlike those of Lear. There were five monthly issues of this little magazine, which so delighted the Dodgson family that three years later it was bound up into a manuscript volume which still exists. Several of its items indicate thought patterns that constantly recur in Dodgson's adult life. 'A Quotation from Shakespeare with slight improvements' is a reminder of his adaptions of speeches from *Much Ado About Nothing* and of his lifelong desire to produce an expurgated Shakespeare for girls, 'The Trial of a Traitor' of his preoccupation with courtroom procedures, and 'A Tale of a Tail' ('It was a tail of desperate length / A tail of grisly fur') of his ultimate typographical masterpiece with numerous variants, 'The Mouse's Tail'. The obvious prototype of Humpty Dumpty is 'The Headstrong Man', as stubborn as the title suggests, who tumbles from a wall, but whose resulting injuries, unlike Humpty Dumpty's, do not prevent his climbing to an equally insecure perch in a tree.

What also emerges in this juvenile *jeu d'espirit* is a remarkably direct dramatic style drawing heavily on the traditional ballad model. The pathos of the original is parodied with wit and brevity, and the humour depends for its effect chiefly on violent reprisal so extreme as to be absurd. 'Brother and Sister' is worth quoting in its entirety:

> 'Sister, sister, go to bed!
> Go and rest your weary head.'
> Thus the prudent brother said.
>
> 'Do you want a battered hide,
> Or scratches to your face applied?'
> Thus his sister calm replied.
>
> 'Sister, do not raise my wrath.
> I'd make you into mutton broth
> As easily as kill a moth!'
>
> The sister raised her beaming eye
> And looked on him indignantly
> And sternly answered, 'Only try!'
>
> Off to the cook he quickly ran
> 'Dear Cook, please lend a frying-pan
> To me quickly as you can.'
>
> 'And wherefore should I lend it you?'
> 'The reason, Cook, is plain to view.
> I wish to make an Irish stew.'
>
> 'What meat is in that stew to go?'
> 'My sister'll be the contents!'
>   'Oh!'
> 'You'll lend the pan to me, Cook?'
>   'No!'
>
> MORAL: Never stew your sister.

Charles' lifelong preoccupation with time and the nature of the physical forces of the universe is also demonstrated in a short poem:

> Were I to take an iron gun,
> And fire it off towards the sun;
> I grant 'twould reach its mark at last,
> But not till many years had passed.

But should that bullet change its force,
And to the planets take its course;
'Twould *never* reach the *nearest* star,
Because it is so very far.

His interest in all things scientific is apparent from the number of scientific books on his shelves. A favourite author of his was Richard Anthony Proctor (1837–88), a distinguished astronomer and prolific writer, who founded the London scientific weekly *Knowledge* and clashed with the Astronomer Royal, Sir George Airy, over his papers on the *Transit of Venus*. Among several of Proctor's books owned by Charles Dodgson were *The Sun* (1871), *The Moon* (1873) and *Other Worlds than Ours* (1870). Among Dodgson's mathematical papers is the question (unanswered), 'What is the highest point on the moon visible to an observer on the earth?'; but there is no indication of how he proposed to measure lunar height and depth in the absence of a sea level to act as a standard. On 8 April 1856 he wrote to *The Times* in answer to a letter from a Mr Jelinger Symons, who did not believe in the rotation of the moon. Dodgson's letter, which unfortunately was not published, took the form of an explanation of the reason why rotation was a positive necessity. 'In considering the subject,' he wrote, 'I noticed for the first time the fact that though it only goes 13 times round the earth in the course of the year, it makes 14 revolutions round its own axis, the extra one being due to its rotation round the sun.'[4] As his life progressed, his use of scientific fact as a spur to creative literature increased to the point where reality gave way to fantasy, and he crossed the frontiers of Wonderland, Looking Glass Land and Outland.

Useful and Instructive Poetry was not very highly regarded by its youthful author, who wrote, 'It lasted about half a year, and was then very clumsily bound up in a sort of volume: the binding, however, was in every respect worthy of the contents.'[5] Exactly when its successor, *The Rectory Magazine*, was started is debatable; but the endpapers are remnants of his Rugby days and are covered with a conglomeration of miscellaneous entries. The name Dodgson, in fine copperplate, and the date April 1846 are followed by the words in another hand 'excused calling over' and signed 'C. Mayor' (Charles' mathematical teacher). There are several drawings, mostly of horses, and various attempts at Charles' signature, apparently written by friends. One page contains typical schoolboy notes scribbled to him by a classmate in the silence of the form room: 'He said what are you talking for are you Mr Price's pupil I said No Mr Cotton's sir He said very well and wrote down Price.' There are various elementary mathematical calculations, a few lines of Latin and an endorsement 'C. L. Dodgson Sick Room Row'. This probably relates to his isolation, either with his attack of whooping cough or of mumps in 1849, when he would have been confined to the separate sanatorium block which Dr Tait ordered at Rugby School in June 1847.

Only limited reliance can be placed on the endpapers for dating purposes. In *Mischmasch* Charles states that they were bound up in about 1848. The manuscript copy of *The Rectory Magazine* which is in the Humanities Research Centre of the University of Texas is inscribed 'Fifth Edition, carefully revised, and improved, 1850', and on the whole the indications are that Charles in that year merely gathered together copies of all the numbers, added a new title and endpapers, and bound it up, using whatever materials came readily to hand. But the real clue to the year of initiation may lie in Charles' use of pseudonymous initials VX for his serial 'Sidney Hamilton'. Reversal of initials was a frequent device of his, and if the magazine dated from 1847, his age expressed in Latin would have been XV. The state of maturity of the contents is consistent with this dating.

Unlike *Useful and Instructive Poetry*, *The Rectory Magazine* was intended for general contribution under Charles' editorship. 'At first the contributions poured in in one continuous stream, while the issuing of each number was attended by the most violent excitement throughout the entire house,'[6] he wrote. He looked forward to the time when 'teeming with voluntary productions of the most gifted and talented authors and authoresses of this country, *The Rectory Magazine* shall draw from admiring thousands their unanimous and uncalled for plaudits'.[7] But already by the fourth issue we find Charles writing sadly, 'We opened our Editor's box this morning, expecting of course to find it overflowing with contributions and found it – our pen shudders and our ink blushes as we write – empty!'[8]

Eight of the Dodgsons contributed to the magazine, including Aunt Lucy Lutwidge, and there is one additional article whose author is not identified. Nine twelve-page issues were produced, each with an editorial, a serial story entitled 'Sidney Hamilton', 'Answers to Correspondents', and, from the second issue onwards, a ballad and a second serial, 'Crundle Castle'. All of these were by Charles. As submissions from the rest of the family descreased, he made up the deficiencies himself, and the fifth issue is his work alone, while the sixth is his except for a single page offered by Aunt Lucy. All items are entered under assumed initials, but a key is given at the front of the volume. As the number of his articles per issue increased, Charles disguised the shortage of writers by an ever increasing number of assumed initials, and he is represented as Ed. (naturally), VX, BB, FLW, JV, FX and QG. The unidentified author is represented by the initials RY, and this was almost certainly Charles also, for if RZ equalled Lucy Lutwidge reversed, RY might equal Charles Lutwidge reversed, with R standing for Lutwidge.

Charles Dodgson continued to use assumed initials in adult life, with examples like 'K', 'X' and RWG, the latter being the fourth letters of his names. The enigmatic initials 'BB', which were carried over from *The Rectory Magazine* to his earliest traceable printed works, have never ceased to intrigue Carrollian scholars. Possibly the key to their significance lies in the nature of his contributions entered in *The Rectory Magazine* under these initials. His sister Elizabeth, whose initial entries begin with a supposed quotation from Shakespeare, appears as WS, and later, characteristically, as SW. If Elizabeth is Shakespeare, who, then, is Charles? The entries under BB are all mournful ballads, possibly intended as a parody of Burns' more melancholy poems. If so, the mysterious initials might stand for 'Bobby Burns', a theory which tends to be strengthened by Charles' consistent interest in Scottish ballads. An alternative possibility[9] suggests itself in *Poverty Bay: A Nondescript Novel* (1905) by Harry Furniss, the illustrator chosen by Dodgson for *Sylvie and Bruno*. He writes: 'The day I arrived I strolled into the paddocks to find "B.B." (He was known at Eton as "B.B.", short for Beau Brummell, the exquisite, whom he was supposed, by the boys at school, to emulate.)' Harry Furniss always pretended a kind of casual disrespect for Dodgson, whom he caricatured as a complete eccentric. Yet behind the façade was a deep regard and respect for Dodgson's opinions, and nothing is more possible than that Dodgson revealed to him this boyhood nickname at some stage in their many years' collaboration, and that Furniss remembered and ultimately used it. Certainly we know that he was always very particular in his dress, that he arrived at Richmond School with far more clothes than he could possibly need, and that his purchases at Rugby School included gloves and a hat.

Despite its general immaturity, *The Rectory Magazine* is interesting not only because it enables us to compare Charles' work with that of his brothers and sisters in this lively and gifted household, but also because it gives us a number of pointers to the direction which his general literary career would ultimately take. Many of the characteristics of Lewis Carroll's own brand of humour can already be detected in *The Rectory Magazine*, despite its lack of refinement and general clumsiness of execution, and in some cases they are seen to be an integral part of the Dodgson family sense of fun. Thus, while Charles in his editorial 'Rust' puns on ox-eyed (oxide) in a crude illustration, Elizabeth includes a 'cupboard' in her lists of birds in 'Batiania', and prefaces 'Mrs Stoggle's Dinner Party' with 'Eta, beta, Pi'. Nor is the gift of parody his alone: his parodies of the prose serial so popular in the Victorian era are equalled by Elizabeth's, and even Skeffington, nine years old in 1847, makes a gallant effort with 'Farmer Grubbins', which peters out after the second episode. Wilfred, even younger than

Skeffington, parodies the Scottish traditional ballad style with relative success in 'A Tale of the Wars'. Whether his use of bathos was unintentional is open to question:

> The queen fell into a swoon,
>   The porter in a fit:
> The messenger looked round the room,
>   And then went out of it.

The lengthiest of Charles' entries is 'Sidney Hamilton', a nine-part melodrama in which Sidney, estranged from his father, meets with robbery and violence, while his father, falsely accused of attempted theft, is in turn robbed by Sidney's best friend. The story is brought abruptly to a farcical conclusion in which Mr Hamilton's only complaint is of toast wasted at the breakfast table. 'Crundle Castle' is more rewarding to the reader, for it includes not only the first of those 'portmanteau' words which were Lewis Carroll's forté, 'fluff', which he explains as 'probably a combination of flurry and huff, a confusion of words being one of Mrs Cogsby's characteristics', but also the boy Guggy, prototype of Uggug in *Sylvie and Bruno*. Guggy is described as 'a rather overgrown boy of about 6 years old, the delight of his mother, and the detestation of all the neighbourhood'.[10] His unsociable characteristics included kicking his mother's guests, treading on their toes, emptying cake into their laps and even setting fire to them. At the same time Mrs Cogsby, with her social pretensions and devotion to her monstrously spoiled brat, is a simplified version of Uggug's mother, the sub-warden's wife.

Of particular interest and charm is the sole adult contribution, Aunt Lucy's advertisement:

> *Wanted immediately,*
> A maid of all work, in a large but quiet family, where cows, pigs and poultry are kept. She must be able to churn, cure hams and bacon, and occasionally make a cheese. Five only of the children are entirely under her care, but she is expected to do the needlework for seven. She must be able to take twins from a month old, and to bring them up by hand, also carry both out of doors together, as no other servant is kept. She will be required to have Breakfast on the table at 9, luncheon at 12, Dinner at 3 (when she will wait at table), Tea at 6, and Supper at 9. Baking done at home as also the washing, and in winter brewing. No perquisites allowed or going out without leave. All leisure time to be spent in gardening. A cheerfulness of disposition and a willingness to oblige indispensable. Wages £3.3s.0d. a year, with or without tea and sugar accordingly as she gives satisfaction.
>   Apply to R.Z. Happy Grove
>   *Mount Pleasant.*
> by letter, post paid.[11]

The gentle whimsy in this little article gives a unique glimpse of the bustle of activity at Croft Rectory – clearly the 'Happy Grove, Mount

Pleasant' from which it is addressed – where self-sufficiency is the keynote, the daily timetable reads like an endless succession of meal-times for humans and livestock, and gardening is a compulsory hobby. Though only five children require full-time supervision at this stage, Charles and Skeffington are included among those for whom needle-work has to be done, the four eldest girls being by now deemed old enough to do their own.

The Rectory Magazine was Charles' 'unceasing occupation for a period of full six months',[12] though he adds that it was not *full* six months, since he was at school for five of them. In his final editorial he laments its passing and declares 'it would somewhat console us at this moment to see a fit sucessor fill our place'.

That successor was *The Comet*, which 'for the sake of variety, opened at the end instead of the side', and which he anticipated would have a 'tail of boundless length'. Since it was presumably the editor, not the magazine, which was in need of consolation, it would appear that he originally envisaged that another member of the family would emerge as editor. Probably the only other person sufficiently enthusiastic and capable at that time (1848) to act as editor would have been Elizabeth. But in the event, he edited it himself:

> When the Comet next I started,
> They grew lazy as a drone:
> Gradually all departed,
> Leaving me to write alone.[13]

Of its demise he wrote, 'little interest attended this publication, and its contents were so poor, that after 6 months were out, we destroyed all but the last, and published no more'.[14]

Clearly the family's interest in the magazines had waned. Without Charles' unflagging leadership, *The Rosebud*, which followed, taking its name from the cover 'tastefully ornamented with a painted rosebud', probably Mary's handiwork, survived only two issues. *The Star* and *The Will-O-the-Wisp* showed a progressive decline in standard, the latter being remarkable only for its triangular shape.

Two literary items survive to emphasize Charles' early interest in the railway. Today, when jet flights to the ends of the earth are common-place and the launching of yet another astronaut into outer space raises no more than a flicker of interest, it is difficult to imagine the intense impact of the coming of the railway on the human imagination. The sudden ready accessibility to all towns throughout the length and breadth of Britain was the revolution of the age, and though there were some who shook their heads and declared that no good would come of an invention which enabled the lower classes to move more easily from place to place, the enthusiasm of the masses was unreserved.

As an infant in Cheshire, Charles must often have taken the bridle path past the blacksmith's where the local horses were shod, to Daresbury Firs, where he could look down between the trees on the great iron steeds drawing their carriages along the London and North Western Railway and the Lancashire and Cheshire Junction Railway that passed through the township of Keckwick in his father's parish. And after the transfer to Croft, he became a regular user of Darlington Railway Station, from which he travelled to Rugby, and later, to Oxford.

The first of Charles' railway items is a literary trifle in two separate parts, which are preserved in Harvard University Library. Both are instructions for the railway game which Charles invented to amuse his brothers and sisters in Croft Rectory garden. The first, entitled 'Railway Rules', sets out the prices of first, second and third class tickets, and defines the station master's duties, which include sending unruly passengers to prison. The driver acts also as ticket collector, imposing fines on anyone who boards the train without paying, though he is ordered to carry free to the surgeon any passenger who is injured. But when the fare money is divided up equally among everyone, the driver is excluded. The second, called 'Love's Railway Guide', is briefer, more mature and satirical in style. It consists of a timetable and three rules, which read as follows:

> Rule I. All passengers when upset are requested to lie still until picked up – as it is requisite that at least three trains should go over them, to entitle them to the attention of the doctor and assistants.
> II. If a passenger comes to a station after the train has passed the next (i.e. when it is about 100 m. off) he may not run after it but must wait for the next.
> III. When a passenger has no money and still wants to go by the train, he must stop at whatever station he happened to be at, and earn money, by making tea for the station master (who drinks it at all hours of the day and night) and grinding sand for the company (what use they make of it they are *not* bound to explain).[15]

The second literary item is a burlesque ballad opera in three acts specially devised for his own marionette theatre and linking his love of the railway with his lifelong interest in the theatre. Frequent references to Birmingham railway station suggest that it was written during, or immediately after, his schooldays at Rugby, and the epilogue, supposedly spoken by Mr Flexmore, the famous nineteenth-century pantomime clown, indicates that it was performed when his cousins, the Wilcoxes, were staying at Croft:

> Both strangers and relations, we thank you one and all,
> We asked you for your plaudits and you answered to our call,
> Pit, gallery (if such there be) and stalls, and private boxes,
> Spectators all of many names, especially Wilcoxes!

The best account of it is given by Denis Crutch:

> The title '*La Guida di Bragia*' is operatic Italian, and is intended to sound like a translation of 'Bradshaw's Guide'. That notable book was first published by George Bradshaw in 1839, but was called *Bradshaw's Railway Timetable*, and it was not until 1 December 1841, that it appeared under its now familiar title. It was not the first railway guide, nor was it the first publication of that kind from Bradshaw, but it soon became familiar enough to be the object of burlesque in the style of 'The Comic History of England', 'The Comic Blackstone', and others.
>
> With the great interest in the railways it is not surprising that in 1848 there should have appeared *Comic Bradshaw: or, Bubbles from the Boiler*, by Angus B. Reach, an amusing trifle with numerous attractive cuts; strangely it commences with a verse travesty of the Witches in *Macbeth*. Again, in *Punch* in 1856 there is a verse drama called 'Bradshaw: A Mystery' (thought good enough to reprint in 1961) whose hero Orlando is the namesake of a character in 'La Guida di Bragia'.
>
> Neither of these two pieces owes anything to Lewis Carroll, nor he to them; but they were good years for Bradshaw . . .'[16]

Though unsophisticated in style, *La Guida di Bragia* is a competent piece of family entertainment. It opens with a prologue, supposedly spoken by the well-known actor, Ben Webster, who offers an apologia for the marionette theatre:

> Why can't we have, in theatres ideal,
> The good, without the evil, or the real?
> Why may not marionettes be just as good
> As larger actors made of flesh and blood?

Perhaps the most interesting characters in *La Guida di Bragia* are the two station 'horficers', Mooney and Spooney, who change their names with their occupations and who could be regarded as the forerunners of that famous pair, Tweedledum and Tweedledee. Mooney and Spooney have been engaged on the specific understanding that they sing their work, and as they have failed to do so, Bradshaw punishes them by producing a colossal muddle in the timetable. Already Dodgson's gift for parodying Victorian songs is clearly in evidence in this light-hearted little drawing room farce. One of the songs 'Wandering through the wide world, seeking my fortune' is strangely reminiscent of the little piece of wood under the nursery floor: 'And we'll wander through the wide world and chase the buffalo'. Among the many songs parodied are some still familiar today, 'Long long ago', and 'Auld Lang Syne' which begins

> Should all my luggage be forgot,
> And never come to hand,
> I'll never quit this fatal spot
> But perish where I stand.[17]

But perhaps most noteworthy are his various types of communication failure exploited for comic effect. There is the type of failure which occurs from deafness or sheer stupidity:

> *Mooney*: My Spooney, there are moments –
> *Spooney*: Yes, yes, Mooney! it's quite true! there are bolsters.
> *Mooney*: Nonsense, Spooney, how can you talk so? I said 'moments' – let me proceed: there are moments, my dear friend, when I find it *impossible* to express my *'orrid feelings*!
> *Spooney*: Yes, I feel it so, too! It's the same with me! There are moments when I find it *impossible* to press on my *orange peelings*!

Then there is the type of misunderstanding that results from total misuse of words, as portrayed by Mrs Muddle, a kind of lower class Mrs Malaprop, who refuses all her mistress' offers of a travelling companion, because she knows all about collections and steam Indians:

> *Mrs Muddle*: I can manage it all, and when I gets to the station I wants to get out at, says I, why, I'll just nudge the conductor with the pint of my rumbereller!
> *Mooney*: My good woman, you are under some mistake. A railway train is not a bus!
> *Mrs Muddle*: Oh, it ain't, ain't it sir? Then what does it go and conduct itself as a bus for, I'd like to know?
> *Mooney*: I don't understand you, ma'am –
> *Mrs Muddle*: Why, one of them steam Indians went and bust only last week, at least so my neege Eliza told me.
> *Mooney*: Bust? Madam, what in the world do you mean?
> *Mrs Muddle*: Well it *did* bust; don't you go for to denige it, himperence! And now, sir, are you going to ensnare my life for me, or not?

Finally there is the communication failure which results from a dialogue between people who speak different languages, as Mooney and Spooney, under their new names of Moggs and Spicer, discover:

> Enter Kaffir
> *Mooney*: Who are you, sir?
> *Spooney*: Yes, sir, who are you, sir? It is Mr Moggs that speaks to you, sir, and Mr Moggs is a very talented man; you must answer him directly, sir. Is that more like singing, Mooney?
> *Mooney*: Moggs, Moggs, idiot!
> *Spooney*: Oh Moggs, well I never shall remember —
> *Mooney*: But the man hasn't answered yet.
> *Spooney*: No, more he has! Are you going to answer, sir?
> *Kaffir*: —
> *Mooney*: What's that, Spicer? I don't understand French.
> *Spooney*: But it ain't French, it's German.
> *Mooney*: No, that I'll declare it isn't; it must be Dutch.
> *Spooney*: I don't think it's that either: let's ask him. I say, old fellow, what language is that?
> *Mooney*: What a donkey you are, Spicer, he can't understand that, you must talk to him in his own language.

Spooney: How in the world am I to do that, Moggs, when I don't even know what it is?
Mooney: Do as I tell you, sir, and don't be impertinent!
Spooney: Well here goes then: —
Kaffir: —
Mooney: Well, what did he say?
Spooney: Oh, he understood *me* well enough: the difficulty is, I can't understand *him*!

According to his nephew Collingwood, Charles Dodgson's first marionette theatre was made during his childhood at Croft, when 'with the assistance of various members of the family and the village carpenter, [he] made a troupe of marionettes and a small theatre for them to act in. He wrote all the plays himself, the most popular being "The Tragedy of King John" – and he was very clever at manipulating the innumerable strings by which the movements of his puppets were regulated.' But a puppet theatre widely believed in the family to have been that with which Charles used to delight them at Croft cannot have been produced earlier than 1880. For it was made from a set of engraved sheets published by Adolf Engel of Berlin in that year. Though Dodgson's little theatre shows signs of much use, it lacks one or two small details, and has small modifications, such as the addition of three candle holders instead of Mr Engel's footlights, its origin is beyond dispute. The flat, wood-backed figures stood on wooden mounts, and were moved by means of wires up through the flies. This type of figure was far simpler than the type described by Collingwood, and it is most unlikely that Charles employed the type of sophisticated marionettes in popular use today. Dodgson, who maintained a lifelong interest in marionette theatres as a family entertainment, believed strongly that adult professional plays were unsuitable for puppet performances. In April 1855 he conceived the idea of producing a Christmas book for children which he believed would have excellent sales potential, and which he proposed to call 'Practical hints for constructing Marionettes and a theatre'. This was to include several marionette plays. 'All existing plays for such objects seem to me to have one of two faults', he wrote in his diary: '– either (1) They are meant for real theatres, and are therefore not fitted for children, or (2) They are overpoweringly dull – no idea of fun in them. The three already written for our theatre have at least the advantage of being tested by experience and found to be popular.'[18]

Of *The Rectory Umbrella*, which took a year to write and was concluded in 1850, Charles wrote:

Far dost thou eclipse the Maga-
   zines which came before thy day,
And thy coming made them stagger,
   Like the stars at morning ray.[19]

It was a solo effort which demonstrates how remarkably his talents had matured and developed in the five years which had elapsed since he produced *Useful and Instructive Poetry*. The precocious schoolboy had receded, and in his place stood a young man of some eighteen years with an overwhelming interest in the arts, a wealth of literary background with which to feed his gift of parody, and time on his hands to indulge his creative instincts. The result was a mix of poetry and prose, all basically humorous in intention.

The two best poems in *The Rectory Umbrella* are entitled 'Lays of Sorrow', in two parts, both apparently based on actual happenings at Croft Rectory. In the first, the word 'lay' is to be taken literally, for it describes repairs to the old henhouse, the hatching of the eggs, and the hen's ultimate destruction of her own chicks. The first verse illustrates Charles' use of odd and unexpected rhymes for comic effect and acceleration of the rhythm to simulate the rapid blows of hammer and axe.

> The day was wet, the rain fell souse
>   Like jars of strawberry jam, a
> Sound was heard in the old henhouse,
>   A beating of a hammer.
> Of stalwart form, and visage warm,
>   Two youths were seen within it,
> Splitting up an old tree into perches for their poultry
>   At a hundred strokes a minute.

The second 'Lay', an even better poem which parodies Horatius, describes an incident in which his brother Skeffington mounts a donkey but cannot get him to go in the right direction. 'Ulfrid Longbow' (his brother Wilfred Longley) aided by 'fair Flureza' (his sister Louisa Fletcher) comes to the rescue and receives a hero's reward:

> They gave him bread and butter,
>   That was of public right,
> As much as four strong rabbits
>   Could munch from morn till night,
> For he'd done a deed of daring,
>   And faced that savage steed,
> And therefore cups of coffee sweet,
> And everything that was a treat,
>   Were but his right and meed.

Prose items include a series of 'Zoological Papers', most amusing of which is entitled 'Fishs'. Here (with pseudo-scientific seriousness) he treats as actual zoological specimens those toy floating metal fish which can be made to 'swim' with the use of a magnet. Communications failure, that favourite Carrollian device for humour, figures prominently, the author of the 'Scientific paper' describing the 'fishs' being an imaginary German with translation problems. 'Our author tells us that they have "ordinarely angles at them", by which they "can be fanged and heaved out of the water." . . . What the "fanging" consists of we cannot exactly say: if it is anything like a dog "fanging" a bone, it is certainly a strange mode of capture, but perhaps the writer refers to others.'

Another paper reads:

> I have two clocks: one doesn't go at all, and the other loses a minute a day: which would you prefer? 'The losing one,' you answer, 'without a doubt.' Now observe: the one which loses a minute a day has to lose twelve hours, or seven hundred and twenty minutes before it is right again, consequently it is right once in two years, whereas the other is evidently right as often as the time it points to comes round, which happens twice a day. So you've contradicted yourself once: 'Ah, but,' you say, 'what's the use of it being right twice a day, if I can't tell when the time comes?' Why, suppose the clock points to eight o'clock, don't you see that the clock is right *at* eight o'clock? Consequently when eight o'clock comes your clock is right. 'Yes, I see *that*,' you reply. Very good, then you've contradicted yourself *twice*: now get out of the difficulty as you can, and don't contradict yourself if you can help it.'[20]

Sometimes Dodgson's illustrations for *The Rectory Umbrella*, as in 'Ye Fatalle Cheyse' are lively representations of animals and people who have broken loose from the formal picture frame and scamper unrestrained in the margin, much as they do in medieval manuscript books. Like the whale/crocodile with its gaping jaws, popular with the limners of the Middle Ages because it represented the hellmouth, is the monster with its wide mouth at the foot of the page. Also included is a series of parodies of real paintings in the Vernon Gallery in London which he had seen reproduced in Parts 10–15 (1849–50) of *The Vernon Gallery of British Art*, a periodical which must have been available to him at Croft, and which may well have been taken regularly by the Dodgson household. Taken as a whole, Charles Dodgson's family magazines give a unique glimpse of a childhood in which love, wit, humour and learning abounded. From the fertile soil of the collective Dodgson imagination Charles transported the seeds of Wonderland to Oxford, where they lay dormant until they were watered by the tears and warmed by the smiles of a unique little girl: Alice.

REFERENCES

1 L. P. Wenham, *The History of Richmond School, Yorkshire*, 1958, p. 169.
2 Collingwood, p. 23.

 3 Ibid, p. 25.
 4 Ms. Diaries.
 5 *Mischmasch.*
 6 *Ibid.*
 7 *The Rectory Magazine*, f. 1.
 8 Ibid, f. 38.
 9 Drawn to my attention by Mr Denis Crutch.
10 *The Rectory Magazine*, f. 22.
11 Ibid, f. 71.
12 Ibid, f. 97.
13 *The Rectory Umbrella.*
14 *Mischmasch.*
15 Trevor Winkfield (ed.), *The Lewis Carroll Circular*, No. 1, May 1973.
16 'Lewis Carroll and the Marionette Theatre', *Jabberwocky*, Vol. 2, No. 1, Spring 1973.
17 *La Guida di Bragia.*
18 Green, p. 46.
19 Green.
20 Green, p. 26.

4 In Full Academicals

In May 1850 Charles visited Oxford to matriculate at Christ Church. He left no record of his feelings on that occasion, but many famous personalities have described Oxford in the spring, including Mark Pattison, whose father, like Charles Dodgson's, had been an Oxford man, and who came up to matriculate:

> It was May, and Oxford, not then overbuilt and slummy, looked – as Oxford can still look in May – charming. I was intoxicated with delight and my father was as pleased as a child. His constant recurrence to his reminiscences of the place had so rivetted it in my mind that I had, by the aid of an old guide book I found at Hauxdale, mastered the topography by anticipation and was proud, as we walked about the streets, to show that I knew where to find the colleges. My father, of course, took us 'on the water' – his own favourite amusement. We were sculled down to Iffley and he enjoyed paying the over charge, 'eighteenpence each gentleman as we went in the boat, and two shillings the man'; being overcharged made him feel that he was in Oxford . . .

In *Loss and Gain* John Henry Newman conveys his feelings about springtime in Oxford in a passage of tender and affectionate lyricism: 'The planes are so touching just now, with their small multitudinous green hands half-opened; and there are two or three such fine dark willows stretching over the Cherwell; I think some dryad inhabits them: and, as you walk along, just over your right shoulder is the Long Walk, with the Oxford buildings seen between the elms.'[1] Less lyrical is Southey's description of Christ Church: 'The greater part of Christ Church college is antient; nothing can be finer than the great gateway, the great square, and the open ascent to the refectory, though the great square is debased by a little miserable fountain of green and stinking water in the centre, so pitiful, that the famous *Manneké* of Brussels might well be placed in the midst of it, as the appropriate god of the puddle.'[2]

Charles' matriculation formalities began with examination by a tutor, who confirmed his fitness to become an undergraduate, after which he had to be fitted out with the compulsory academic dress. Southey describes the attire of an undergraduate as 'not unlike that of a secular priest. The cap is square, worn diagonally, covered with black cloth, and has a silk tassel in the middle: noblemen have a tassel of gold'.[3] As a commoner, Charles was only entitled to a plain silk tassel. Having satisfied the tutor as to his academic standard, Charles proceeded on 23 May 1850 to the formal matriculation ceremony before the Vice-Chancellor of the University in the ante-room of the Convocation House. On his knees he swore to observe the Statutes, signed his name to the Thirty-Nine Articles, and entered his name in the University Books. Finally, with the words 'Scitote vos in Matriculam Universitatis hodie relatos esse, sub hac conditione, nempe ut omnia Statuta hoc libro comprehensa pro virili observetis', the Vice-Chancellor concluded the ceremony by handing Charles a copy of the University Statutes which he had sworn to obey.

On the whole Charles Dodgson was more fortunate than undergraduates in times past, for the Statutes were in Latin, and it was not until 1845 that an English translation was published. But the Statutes which he had sworn to abide by were an incredible conglomeration of rules, mostly trivial or outmoded. They included 'not to encourage the growth of curls', 'to abstain from that absurd and assuming practice of walking publicly in boots', not to 'introduce new and unusual fashions in dress', to refrain from football, fighting and meeting to debate the Church or government of the University. Punishments set out in the Statutes included fines, forfeiture of weapons, hanging of the undergraduates' dogs, incarceration and banishment. Even more astonishing than the power of the Univeristy authorities over the colleges was their authority over the people of the town. Tailors, for instance, were 'forbidden to depart even a nail's breadth from the received form of fashion of the dress suitable to each degree, under a penalty to be inflicted at the discretion of the Vice-Chancellor',[4] and tavern-keepers were to keep their walls in repair to prevent miscreants out of college after hours from making away, and 'to stop those mazy winding walks, whether in their back areas or gardens, through the labyrinths of which the night-rakes so often steal away . . .'[5]

The many absurdities in the *Oxford University Statutes* were not lost on a humorist of Charles Dodgson's calibre. If any proof were needed, it would be found in his inclusion of the Bellman in the strangely assorted crew of his famous epic, *The Hunting of the Snark*. This University officer is described in the Statutes as the 'ringer, commonly called Le Bellman, or the tintinabulary'. His duty was 'at the death of doctors, masters, scholars and other privileged persons, to put on the clothes of the deceased and give notice of their burial by ringing the bell which he carries in his hand . . .'[6] The Bellman's participation on a journey likely to prove fatal is clearly significant, and perhaps should be regarded as an omen that the Snark would turn out to be a Boojum.

Having matriculated, there was no obstacle to Charles' beginning his career at Christ Church, the college which had been the focal point

1, 2 Charles, aged eight, and his
parents from silhouettes cut at the
Warrington Exhibition in 1840

3 The garden at Croft Rectory: a drawing by Louisa Dodgson, 1868

4   The Dodgson sisters.
Photograph by Lewis Carroll

5   Lewis Carroll's photograph of
his youngest brother Edwin
(right) and friend

6   Agnes Grace Weld, Tennyson's niece. Her photograph gave Lewis Carroll
the entrée to the Tennyson home

7 Farringford, Tennyson's house in the Isle of Wight. Photograph
by Lewis Carroll

8 Hallam Tennyson.   9 Lionel Tennyson.
Photograph by Lewis Carroll   Photograph by Mrs Cameron

10 From Alice's photograph album. Left to right: Lorina, Alice and Edith. Photographed and probably mounted by Lewis Carroll

11 Mrs Foster, née Prickett, Alice's governess. Rumours of her romance with Dodgson were untrue

13 Greville MacDonald, son of the novelist. He wished there were 60,000 volumes of *Alice*

12 Robinson Duckworth. He helped row when *Alice's Adventures* was first told

14 Alice, Lorina, Harry and Edith Liddell in about 1859. Photograph by Lewis Carroll

15 Alice Pleasance Liddell, about 1859. Photograph by Lewis Carroll

of his father's ambitions for him, provided he could get into residence. Shortage of accommodation in the 'House' was a serious and chronic problem, and one which many before him had had to face, including Henry George Liddell, who was soon to cross paths with Dodgson with startling and dramatic effect. For the time being, Dodgson had no alternative but to go home to Croft, where he studied privately, and whiled away the time with his literary pursuits and the entertainment of the family. The sands of 1850 slowly trickled out, without a solution being found. Finally the problem was solved when an old friend of his father's, the Rev. Jacob Ley, offered him the use of a couple of rooms in his own suite. The arrangement, though relatively brief, worked well, and even had certain advantages. Young Dodgson benefited from close contact with an experienced classical scholar who knew the ropes and was able to offer him advice, while at the same time the young man was free to invite his friends to tea, and had no problems more significant than what to do about a name plate.

On 24 January 1851 Dodgson moved in. Two days later personal tragedy took him back to Croft. His mother, only forty-seven years old, had died suddenly. Just a short time previously she had spoken of 'the responsibility incurred by a lot of so much happiness'[7] and had said that at times it really was 'alarming to look round her and feel that she had not a wish unfulfilled'.[8] The cause of death, as shown on her death certificate, was 'inflammation of the brain', a diagnosis so generalized that it is impossible, in the absence of better particulars, to define the exact nature of her final illness; but in her last hours she would have suffered from fever and delirium. The death, so sudden and unexpected, of this gentlest of mothers, who had never been known to utter a harsh word, brought intense personal grief to the bereaved husband and family. They could comfort each other only with the strength of their religious belief, and with the knowledge that 'few surely have ever passed into glory knowing so little of earthly stain or sorrow'.[9] Her death also precipitated a serious domestic crisis. Fanny and Elizabeth were too young to have the responsibility of running such a large establishment thrust upon them overnight, and there was nobody else in the immediate family circle who could be expected to cope with the situation.

There were others only too willing to help, however. First on the scene was Mrs Dodgson's cousin, the well-known Victorian poetess Menella Bute Smedley, who stayed to help the family through the first few weeks of bereavement. Charles' contacts with Menella, brief on this occasion but always affectionate and full of sympathy, were important to him, for the time came when, through her cousin, the novelist Frank Smedley, she was able to help Charles to get work published. Hard on her heels was Mrs Dodgson's younger sister, Lucy Lutwidge, unmarried, a frequent visitor to Croft Rectory, and deeply attached to her nephews and nieces. A gap had been left in Aunt Lucy's life by the death in 1848 of her father, whom she had nursed devotedly through years of ill health. Now she stepped nobly into the void created by her sister's death, moved in permanently with the family, and devoted the rest of her long and happy life to them. Goodness and generosity radiated from her, and the family at the Rectory responded with gratitude to the warmth and expansiveness of her personality. She was one of a multitude of maiden ladies with a finely developed maternal instinct who had been marooned by the curious social structure of Victorian life. Raised in a large family where she was expected to share in the upbringing of her younger brothers and sisters, and trained in domestic economy and the running of a household, she had every qualification for a life of married happiness except a husband. Moreover, since the class system of the day seriously restricted the number of suitors considered eligible for her, she had already reached that point in her life when it appeared that her domestic and maternal instincts must remain unfulfilled. Given that some substitute for the children's mother had to be found, Aunt Lucy was the ideal replacement.

It was not Charles Dodgson's custom to commit his deepest feelings to paper in times of acute personal sorrow. His instincts were to lock his unhappiness in his own heart, preserving a cheerful external demeanour which hid his true thoughts. Yet those who knew him best noted an air of melancholy which hung over him for many months, and there is no doubt that he was profoundly affected by his mother's death. When he returned to Oxford, his eagerness for academic distinction was strengthened by an earnest desire to be self-supporting. Hard work brought relief from sorrow and furthered his quest for financial independence, all the more necessary to his self-respect because there were others at home for whom an equal educational opportunity had to be provided.

For a young man like Dodgson, shy and sensitive, and handicapped in moments of self-conciousness by his distressing stammer, those early days at Christ Church must have been a considerable ordeal. The pattern of his life was now strictly regulated by college routine. Every day he rose promptly at 6.15 a.m. Breakfast, normally a substantial cooked meal of chops, sausages, etc., was prepared for him by Brooks, his personal 'scout', as the college servants were called. He was then ready to attend compulsory chapel service at the summons of the bell, and afterwards to present himself for lectures, dressed in the obligatory academic cap and gown. Dinner was taken at five o'clock in the ancient, oak-panelled hall, where undergraduates and academic staff dined together. A special table was reserved at the top, not for the staff, as one might expect, but for the 'tufts', or noblemen, whose gold-tasselled caps distinguished them from the commoners. Gowned 'servitors' of gentlemanly appearance waited at table, enjoying free education in return for performing certain menial tasks.

One anonymous satirist said of overawed freshmen at the college that 'In Hall they devour their commons with great speed and perturbation, and look as if they thought their messmates were watching their motions, and counting how many mouthfuls they dispatched.'[10] At the time of Dodgson's establishment as an undergraduate there were general complaints of debased standards of meal-taking in Hall, where men were in such haste to begin that they often started before the ancient Latin grace had been said. Silver cutlery, gifts from past scholars, clattered noisily on the pewter plates. Joints of meat were passed around the table, each one carving for himself, and men left the table without waiting for their fellows to finish. Curiously enough it was participation in this somewhat slovenly meal-taking ritual rather than attendance at lectures which established a man's claim to be 'in residence'. These meals, charged individually to the undergraduates, were costly, for the college servants were not paid a proper wage, and subsisted only by grossly overcharging the residents for their provisions.

At that time the Hall was divided into 'messes' of about six people. Among Charles' mess were Philip Pusey, the talented young son of Dr Pusey, who despite his bodily infirmities became an invaluable assistant in his father's religious research; C. J. Cowley-Brown, afterwards Vicar of St John's, Edinburgh, and George Giddlestone Woodhouse, eldest son of the Vicar of Albrighton. Dodgson was particularly close to George Woodhouse in his years as an undergraduate, staying with his family at Albrighton, where Mr Woodhouse Senior was vicar, and after George had left the college, accommodating his younger brother in his own suite until he obtained rooms of his own. In August 1897, after her husband's death, Dodgson wrote to George Woodhouse's widow: 'Of all the friends I made at Christ Church, your husband was the very *first* who spoke to me – across the dinner-table in Hall. That is forty-six years ago, but I remember, as if it were only yesterday, the kindly smile with which he spoke.'[11]

Freshmen at Oxford were often a target for the wit of their seniors. 'They have a startled and uneasy look,' wrote the author of *Hints for Oxford*, 'and seem as if aware of the awkward figure they make in their new caps and gowns. Round all the principal lions they may be seen staring by dozens; or bent on more distant discoveries, they may occasionally be descried wandering about the streets of Bagley, or posting along the Bath road in their full academicals.'[12] Dodgson, however, managed his initiation without any gauche or eccentric behaviour. Apart from missing chapel through oversleeping some six weeks after he went up to Oxford, he settled in very quickly. When Charles went up to Oxford he had already matured to his full height of some 5ft 9in., but he looked taller than he really was on account of his erect posture, coupled with his slim build. Even when he was a child his mother had worried about his being underweight, and in later life his 'painful thinness' was referred to. His essential leanness was the result of plenty of physical exercise, combined with very moderate eating habits. While others took luncheon he was content to nibble a biscuit with a glass of sherry, often pacing restlessly around the room as he did so. His hair was thick, brown and curly, and he tended to wear it slightly longer than most of his contemporaries. His eyes were blue and very mild, and one of them was fractionally higher than the other, giving him a slightly quizzical, asymmetrical look. Though he seldom laughed out loud, a smile was never far from his lips.

Before long Dodgson had made friends with a fellow undergraduate called Richard Colley, who used to have tea with him in Mr Ley's rooms, and with whom he enjoyed long, companionable walks. On a bitterly cold March day in 1851 the two young men took it into their heads to walk over to the court of justice to hear the trials conducted. To their intense annoyance they found their journey had been wasted, for the assizes had already concluded and the judges had left Oxford. This trivial incident was a pointer to Dodgson's lifelong interest in the conduct of the courts. Courtroom procedures made an immense appeal to his sense of the dramatic, and when he portrayed the trial scene in *Alice's Adventures in Wonderland*, he was drawing on direct experience. The friendship with Colley lasted until, having graduated on 10 May 1855 and taken his MA degree in 1859, Colley left Oxford.

Now that he was safely embarked on a career in Mathematics, it is relevant to examine the appropriateness of Christ Church for Charles Dodgson. Arguably the most prestigious of all the Oxford Colleges, immensely wealthy in terms of lands and revenues, and with some ninety church livings at its disposal, Christ Church enjoyed unparalleled academic distinction in the first quarter of the nineteenth century. But whereas between 1821 and 1830, Balliol had gained eleven First Class Honours degrees and Christ Church fifty-one, the next decade produced twenty-two at Balliol and only thirteen at Christ Church, although the latter had twice as many undergraduates as the former. Mark Pattison in his *Memoirs* argues convincingly that the number of Second Class degrees is a more reliable test of the teaching strength of any college, since the First Class men had the innate ability to excel in any event, but the general decline in the standard at Christ Church in the second quarter of the century is undeniable. Nineteenth-century Oxford was, moreover, unlikely to generate true mathematical genius.

Though England was by now beginning to compete in terms of mathematical talent with the advanced and adventurous skills of continental scholars, her finest mathematical talent was concentrated at Cambridge, where the Cambridge Analytical Society had been formed to promote Leibnitzian methods of calculus. Here, too, Arthur Cayley produced his prolific writings on algebraic geometry, and Sir William Rowan Hamilton, concentrating on the development of analysis through mathematical physics and astronomy, clarified the common role of external principles for the laws of optics and dynamics. The Rev. Bartholomew Price, with whom Dodgson read mathematics at Oxford, was author among other things of monumental treatises on Differential Calculus and Infinitesimal Calculus, but he could not match the brilliance of men like Cayley and Hamilton.

Whether Dodgson, as a budding mathematician, was aware of Oxford's deficiencies in his chosen subject from the outset is unclear; but on 12 May 1857 he records in his diary having received a letter from a friend, Mrs Hart, seeking advice about the placing of a promising young mathematician. Dodgson's immediate reaction was that if the boy's powers were really high in Mathematics he would do better at Cambridge. But a few days later he spoke to Bartholomew Price on the subject: 'He strongly advises Oxford,' he wrote, 'as he says he would be *sure* to succeed here, and might very possibly be outstripped at Cambridge. A higher consideration is the more liberal education which Oxford gives.'[13]

Charles Dodgson had embarked on a career in which he would emerge as an exceptionally capable and dedicated scholar who nevertheless lacked fundamental creative mathematical genius. Had he only mapped out for himself a career in logic, an almost uncharted sphere, which he could have entered without preconceived and limiting ideas, and where his natural aptitudes would have guided him without any external assistance, his ultimate scholastic achievement might have been considerably greater. Given such an eventuality the world might never have been introduced to Alice, for his creativity might all have been channelled in the direction of formal text book work. Fortunately his genius found its own natural outlet in his literary works. In the meantime his arrival at Oxford saw him safely launched on the career which his parents had encouraged him to pursue, and he was well satisfied.

A letter to his sister Mary, written a few weeks after he went up to Oxford, gives a foretaste of his fondness for fanciful etymology, and exhibits it as a game in which the family joined. He wrote:

> As Cousin Menella cannot tell the meaning of the word 'kakography', I
> must do my best: the word *now* means 'bad or incorrect writing', but its

original meaning was 'vulgarity', and it is thus derived: 'kay or kai,' a Syriac verb, signifying 'to wear': 'kog or kogh' in Chaldre means 'paper,' and 'graph or graf', is a Hebrew word meaning 'flowers'. Hence 'kakography' meant 'the wearing of paper flowers', and from this came to mean 'vulgarity', as the wearing of such flowers has always been considered among civilized nations as the height of vulgarity. In the same way 'kakographist' meant originally 'she that wears paper flowers', and was a term of great reproach: its meaning is now altogether changed.[14]

One major effect of his removal to Christ Church was that he now enjoyed a freedom which he had never had before, and could enter fully into the social and cultural life of his era. This meant not merely haunting the bookshops, libraries and museums of Oxford, but being able to transfer in the vacations to an even greater sphere of cultural activity: London.

The year 1851 was distinguished by the opening of the Great Exhibition, a notable landmark in Victorian history. The Queen herself regarded it as the outstanding achievement of her Consort, who had played a major role in organizing the exhibition. Albert had had many critics, but these were eventually silenced by the great stimulus to trade and industry, and by the ultimate profit of more than £186,000, which finally formed the nucleus of a fund for the establishment of permanent museums in South Kensington. Overseas buyers were not the only ones who were attracted to the exhibition. People from all walks of life flocked in their thousands to a capital which was eager to accommodate them and cater for their needs. Many workers were given a holiday especially to view this miracle of the age. One Sheffield implement-maker hired two boats, complete with sleeping and cooking facilities, sailed to London and moored them at Westminster while his workers, with a foreman to ensure good behaviour, visited the exhibition.

Young Dodgson was as eager as the rest to see the wonders on display and travelled to London as soon as term ended. In a letter home he gives an account of what he saw:

> I think the first impression produced on you wnen you get inside is one of bewilderment. It looks like a sort of fairyland. As far as you can look in any direction, you see nothing but pillars hung about with shawls, carpets etc., with long avenues of statues, fountains, canopies, etc., etc., etc. The first thing to be seen on entering is the Crystal Fountain, a most elegant one about thirty feet high at a rough guess, comprised entirely of glass and pouring down jets of water from basin to basin; this is in the middle of the centre nave, and from it you can look down to either end, and up both transepts. The centre of the nave mostly consists of a long line of colossal statues, some most magnificent. The one considered the finest, I believe, is the Amazon and Tiger. She is sitting on horseback, and a tiger has fastened on the neck of the horse in front. You have to go to one side to see her face, and the other to see the horse's. The horse's face is really wonderful, expressing terror and pain so exactly, that you

almost expect to hear it scream. . . . There are some very ingenious pieces of mechanism. A tree (in the French Compartment) with birds chirping and hopping from branch to branch exactly like life. The bird jumps across, turns round on the other branch, so as to face back again, settles its head and neck, and then in a few moments jumps back again. A bird standing at the foot of the tree trying to eat a beetle is rather a failure; it never succeeds in getting its head more than a quarter of an inch down, and that in uncomfortable little jerks, as if it was choking.[15]

On 1 November 1851 Dodgson took his first real step towards independence when he won a Boulter Scholarship, worth £20 a year. It was probably at about this time that his father wrote again to Dr Pusey, reporting Charles' academic progress, and at the same time informing him of the death of Mrs Dodgson. On the latter subject Pusey was predictably sympathetic. He had met his own wife when he was eighteen years old, and had loved her passionately through a separation of seven years during which, as a younger son, he had entertained no hope of acceptance as a suitor. A reversal in his romantic fortunes was brought about when his elder brother made a brilliant match, making the connection by marriage now socially desirable. He married her when he was twenty-eight years old, and never recovered from the tragedy of her death eleven years later. In his reply Pusey wrote:

> I have often thought, since I had to think of this, how, in all adversity, what God takes away He may give us back with increase. One cannot think that any holy earthly love will cease, when we shall 'be like the Angels of God in Heaven'. Love here must shadow our love there, deeper because more spiritual, without any alloy from our sinful nature, and in the fulness of the love of God. So, then, if by our very sufferings we are purified, and our hearts enlarged, we shall, in that endless bliss, love more those whom we loved here, than if we had never had that sorrow, never been parted. God does all things in love which He does for those who love him; and so while he chastens we may hope the more from His love, in which he chastens us.[16]

Of Charles' prospects of a Studentship, he commented:

> There was another of more elegant scholarship, I believe. But I had no doubt from the report of the Censors that in the solid qualities which one has to consider in making a person a member of a foundation, your son was far the superior; while he appears to have a good intellect, and after your example to have cultivated it more extensively than the other. The account which I heard from those about his own age, of your son's uniform steady quiet conduct, is all you or any parent could wish.[17]

An interesting literary fragment which Charles wrote in 1851 on the mourning paper which he had adopted following his mother's death gives a humorous account of a Christ Church undergraduate presenting himself for his 'Little Go' examination. Entitled 'The Christ Church Commoner', it purports to be a fragment of an unpublished

novel by the prolific Victorian author of melodramatic stories, George
Payne Rainsford James. The text is as follows:

The Christ-Church Commoner
A Tale
Chap: I
'Respond! Respond! oh Muse!'
Goldsmith.

It was a glowing summer morning: the Orient sun had long risen, and
gilded with his dazzling beam the topmost fane of Tom, the great Tower
of Christ Church. Out of the Eastern gate, known by the name of
Canterbury, is walking a young man, solitary, downcast. His years are
scarcely enough for a clergyman, and yet he wears a white neck-cloth
and bands. Who can he be, and where is he going? Let us follow him: he
approaches a vast range of buildings, ugly and un-architectural: they are
called 'the schools'. As he passes along, men in the street, lounging
against doorposts, look up for a moment, roused by the passing footfall,
gaze on his retreating form, remark to a companion, 'On'y one o' them
'varsity coves in for a little go;' and resume their listless attitude. They
notice nothing of that calm expansive brow, those eyes glistening with
the fire of genius, those chiselled features: they know not *who* has passed
and how should they? Let us follow him in. A long table, covered with
books, and surrounded with chairs; two gloomy-browed examiners, and
twelve pale-faced youths complete the picture. Seats, like those in a
circus, slant up at the end of the room; these are crowded with spectators.

Chap: II
'Veni, vidi, vici'
Caesar.

The youth is sitting at the table: before him lies a small edition of
Sophocles. Sternly does the examiner remark, 'Go on at the four hundred
and fiftieth line'. Slightly shading back with one hand an auburn curl
from his ivory forehead, and resting his head peacefully on the other, in a
low, musical tone, he commences. Some mistakes he makes, small and
few: he is given two pages to translate. . . . They are done: they are
handed in: they are looked over. What is the examiner saying – 'you may
go'. All is over.

. . . .

fragment of an unpublished novel by G. P. R. James.[18]

Charles had already returned to Oxford after the Christmas vacation
when, on Candlemas Day at the consecration of the Church of St
Thomas, in Leeds, his father preached the most famous of all his
sermons. But he received the text in full when his father, in the furore
which followed, published the sermon and associated correspondence.
Charles' personal copy is still preserved in Harvard University Library. The sermon *Ritual Worship*, takes for its text Genesis IV, 4, 5, and
is 'an apologia for the faith and order of the Church of England,
beginning with remarks on the Old Testament patriarchs ("the aged
men" as Dodgson calls them) and ending with the controversies of the

1850s. It is hard to imagine that anything so cautious and circumspect could ever have occasioned a charge of heresy. Yet Dr Goode, the Low Church Dean of Ripon, accused Dodgson of Romanizing tendencies and denounced him to the Bishop'.[19] Dr Goode's accusations led Mr Dodgson to follow up *Ritual Worship* with *A Letter to the Lord Bishop of Ripon* in the same year. In this book, a copy of which Charles also received, he defends his controversial sermon and publishes the Bishop's verdict that 'he is no more a Romanizer than were the Founders of our English Reformation'. Mr Dodgson had known Longley's views on ritual matters for many years. Ten years previously he had written to him regarding Bishop McIlvaine's treatise denouncing the Tractarians, and in particular Dr Pusey's averral that circumcision was 'no means nor channel of spiritual grace'.[20] But the book, though addressed to Bishop Longley, is an appeal from Mr Dodgson, as a leader of those who took a High Church view of the sacraments, to a much wider audience. 'The core of his argument is to do with the real presence of Christ in the eucharistic elements,' writes Canon Ivor Davies: 'I . . . hold most strongly that the language of the Scripture and of the Church is to be regarded as purely *mysterious*, not as metaphorical . . .' Dodgson is contending for the numinous element in religion and is protesting against any attempt to define what is essentially mysterious.'[21] In any event, the dispute appears to have furthered Mr Dodgson's career. In 1852 he was made Canon of Ripon Cathedral, and on 7 June 1854, following the death of the Rev. James Headlam, he was installed Archdeacon of Richmond.

The length of the letters which passed between Charles and his sister Elizabeth had for some years been a standing joke in the family. Even in 1849, when he was at Rugby, Dodgson had ended an enormous epistle to her with the question, 'Is this letter long enough?'[22] Soon after he arrived at Oxford he wrote to Mary, 'Give Elizabeth my best thanks for her letter. I am tired of saying "nice long", so let it always be understood in future.'[23] In June 1852 he wrote another marathon letter to Elizabeth describing the Encaemia at the Sheldonian Theatre in Oxford, a magnificent occasion in which the brilliant colours of the ladies' dresses contrasted in a striking fashion with the subfusc hues of the undergraduates' gowns. On this occasion Edwin Arnold of University College, who later became a brilliant journalist and published his poems in eight volumes in 1888, recited his prize-winning poem, 'The Feast of Balshazza'. This was greeted with enthusiastic applause, and Dodgson liked it very much.

Dodgson began the long vacation of 1852 with a visit to London, where he called at the home of his mother's brother, Skeffington Lutwidge. A barrister and a bachelor, he was in many respects a kindred spirit, and his lively interest in novelties kindled a similar curiosity in young Dodgson. On this occasion Uncle Skeffington showed him many new acquisitions, including a lathe, a refrigerator, and a telescope stand which they used to observe the planets at night. But best of all was a large microscope, through which they examined tiny organisms. 'This is a most interesting sight,' he wrote, 'as the creatures are most conveniently transparent, and you see all kinds of organs jumping about like a complicated piece of machinery, and even the circulation of the blood. Everything goes on at railway speed, so I suppose they must be some of those insects who live a day or two and try to make the most of it.'

He himself was also determined to make the most of it, despite his longer expectation of life. He had discussed with Osborne Gordon, the Classical Moderator, and Robert Faussett, the Mathematical Lecturer, his proposed work schedule for the Long Vacation, and came to the conclusion that '25 hours' *hard* work a day *may* get me through all I have to do, but I am not certain'.[24] The dividends of his extended effort were a Second Class in Classical Moderations and a First Class in Mathematics in December 1852. 'I am getting quite tired of being congratulated on various subjects', he wrote to Elizabeth; 'there seems to be no end of it. If I had shot the Dean I could hardly have had more said about it.'[25]

Pusey now wrote to Mr Dodgson, 'I have great pleasure in telling you that I have been enabled to recommend your son for a Studentship this Christmas. . . . One of the Censors brought me today five names; but in their minds it was plain that they thought your son on the whole the most eligible for the College.'[26] The news of his success brought an immediate letter to Charles from his father, who wrote, 'Your affectionate heart will derive no small addition of joy from thinking of the joy which you have occasioned to me, and to all the circle of your home.'[27]

Studentships at Christ Church were conferred for life, and brought a modest income of £25 a year and the right to remain in residence. There was no positive obligation to work, nor was there any need to prove one's continuing fitness for Studentship, provided that one proceeded to Holy Orders and preserved the vow of celibacy. Marriage meant immediate loss of Studentship. Only the Dean and Chapter were allowed the luxury of wives. A closed community composed almost entirely of celibate men had about it an artificiality which could scarcely be regarded as entirely healthy. Its defects were obvious, and a few years after Dodgson obtained his Studentship the rule of compulsory bachelorhood was withdrawn, though not before Dodgson had already become set in his bachelor ways.

As a Student, Dodgson now had a number of new duties. One of these was to act as Prickbill, a mysterious sounding office reserved for the eight most junior students. It was the Prickbill's job to walk up and down the aisles during morning chapel, identifying those present, and 'pricking' or marking off their names on the weekly 'prick-list'. Identification was not easy, for overcrowding at the obligatory service was notorious, with both undergraduates and Students overflowing into the aisles, sprawling on their knees and looking very much alike in their compulsory academic gowns. And though junior Students were not boys, but mature men, corporal punishment had only recently been abolished, and childish punishments were imposed for minor infringements. Once, when Dodgson failed to prick, he was given two hundred lines to write, and all the other Prickbills with him.

The conduct of services in the Cathedral at that time left much to be desired. The present building incorporates the shrine of the eighth century St Frideswide, who allegedly preserved her virginity from a lascivious royal suitor by hiding in a pigsty. It was built on a scale much smaller than had originally been planned, and until alterations were carried out in 1856, the college congregation crowded most indecorously into the small space between the choir stalls. Old Keys, the verger, not only lived in the South Transept but actually kept a beer store under the pews. Often he stood at the Cathedral door with a great whip in his hand, driving back the dogs who had followed their masters to Chapel. Services were in Latin, read from ancient books with their long Ss, which were a pitfall for the unwary. One chaplain always read out 'fumas' for 'sumas' in the Litany, to the amusement of the undergraduates. Yet in spite of its deficiencies, the choir of Christ Church was 'the navel and seat of life', according to Ruskin. 'In this choir, written so closely and consecutively with indisputable British History, met every morning a congregation representing the best of what Britain had become – orderly as the crew of a man-of-war, in the goodly ship of their temple,' he wrote. 'Every man in his place, according to his age, rank, and learning; every man of sense or heart there recognizing that he was either fulfilling, or being prepared to fulfill, the gravest duties required of Englishmen.'[28]

During his early years as an undergraduate, Dodgson began keeping a diary, and continued to do so for the rest of his life. When he died, Collingwood had access to all thirteen volumes and used them in compiling his uncle's biography. But after the book was written, the family, unaware of their interest to posterity, put them away and forgot all about them. When a centenary exhibition to mark Charles Dodgson's birth was mooted, his surviving nieces began hunting through the family home for items relating to him. On the floor of the cellar they found an old cardboard box containing a bundle of insignificant-looking old grey notebooks. These were the diaries of Charles Dodgson. Sadly four of the volumes were missing, including the first, which covered at least fifteen months. Collingwood unfortunately gives no more than a single sentence from it, dated October 1853. Other documentation for this period of Dodgson's life is comparatively limited, but we know that in May 1853 his cousin, Francis Hume (Frank) Dodgson, two years his junior, son of Mr Dodgson's younger brother Hassard, Matriculated and joined him at Oxford. Frank was a frequent companion in those early Oxford years, and together they enjoyed boating, theatre visits and other social activities until Frank left the University and ultimately emigrated to Australia.

Some trifling event on the cricket field in May 1853 prompted Dodgson to compose a mock epic to his friend Woodhouse entitled 'The Ligniad', in two books. The title, reminiscent of *The Iliad*, is a pun on Woodhouse's name, taken from the Latin 'lignum', meaning 'wood.' Book one deals with his precocity in the classics as an infant, his resolve to read no Greek till he found the lost plays of Euripides, and his stoicism in adversity. The only Greek quotation, taken from Aeschylus' Agamemnon, line 1343,[29] means 'Ah me, I am smitten'. Book two moves on to the cricket match which inspired the epic:

> But now my muse, approaching higher themes,
> Shrinks from the task in trembling, for the field,
> Green and smooth-shaven, spreads before her sight;
> The wickets pitched, the players ranged around;
> And he, the hero, in his glory there;
> A sight to dream of, not to write about!
> Then fare thee well, greatest of little men,
> In Greek, in Latin, in the cricket field:
> Great as a bowler, greater as a bat,
> But as a 'short slip' greater yet than that![30]

During the early months of 1854 Dodgson was preoccupied with the imminent 'Greats' examination in the Classical School. His work schedule involved reading thirteen hours a day for the last three weeks preceding the examination. Part of the examination consisted of a viva voce, and Dodgson's determination to pass was such that he spent the entire night before the viva voce in private study. Philosophy and history were subjects in which his interest developed later in life, and it was scarcely surprising that when the results were published, he was only placed in the Third Class. But this was enough to allow him to proceed to his ultimate aim, the Final Mathematical School.

During the course of that summer he contributed two poems anonymously to Hall's *Oxonian Advertiser*, neither of which he considered worthy of preservation. This is disappointing, since they were his first publications. Though they cannot be positively identified, the small range of poems published at that period were uniformly poor in calibre, and his own estimate of them must have been accurate.

Perhaps that third class was the spur that encouraged Dodgson to spend two months of the summer vacation with a mathematical reading party at Whitby. In charge of the party was Professor Bartholomew Price, whose *A Treatise on Infinitesimal Calculus*, which he published in four volumes between 1852 and 1860, was in preparation. Under his tuition Dodgson found that he was getting on very well in Integral Calculus. Meanwhile, as his friend Thomas Fowler, a member of that same reading party later recalled, he established for himself something of a reputation as a raconteur, sitting by the sea surrounded by children, enthralled by the oral antecedents of Wonderland. At the same time he had his first two identifiable works published. These were a humorous poem 'The Lady of the Ladle', and a Tale, 'Wilhelm von Schmitz', which appeared in *The Whitby Gazette*. Not wishing to give his name he signed them 'BB', the enigmatic initials which he had used in childhood in *The Rectory Magazine*.

In late October 1854, Dodgson gained First Class Honours in the Final Mathematical School. All the members of the Whitby mathematical reading party did well, but Dodgson headed the list, with 279 marks finishing eighteen marks clear of Bosanquet, his nearest rival. 'I feel at present very much like a child with a new toy, but I dare say that I shall be tired of it soon, and wish to be Pope of Rome next,'[31] he commented.

Bartholomew Price had never had such a good set of men in the Final Mathematical School. Dodgson was now well placed for a senior scholarship, and stood next in line for a Lectureship. As he returned to Croft for Christmas, his future looked promising indeed.

He began 1855, the year of the first surviving diary, at Ripon, where his father, as Canon of Ripon Cathedral, was always 'in residence' for the first three months of each year. The Canonry carried with it as an emolument a Victorian residence which survived until 1972, when it was demolished to make way for a commercial development. By modern standards the Residence was large, but the Dodgson family with its essential entourage of household staff was enormous and accustomed to the vastness of Croft Rectory, so that often Charles had to seek a bed elsewhere. On this occasion he stayed at the lodging house of a Mrs Barker, whose husband was an artist. One day she lent him her husband's water-colour sketches to browse through, and he was so impressed with the spirited illustration, executed entirely in blue, of the Mother and Child from Shelley's 'Vision of Ocean', that he later looked up the text and copied the relevant verse into his diary:

> . . . at the helm sits a woman more fair
> Than heaven, when, unbinding its star-braided hair,
> It sinks with the sun on the earth and the sea,
> She clasps a bright child on her up-gathered knee,

It laughs at the lightning, it mocks the mixed thunder
Of the air and the sea . . .

The wild romanticism of the words and the idealized, spirited portrait of mother and child all made an intense appeal to Dodgson's artistic sensibilities.

Much of his leisure was now taken up with cultural pursuits, sometimes alone and sometimes with his family and friends. Concert visits, parties, excursion to local beauty spots and reading occupied much of his time. He was still busy with family literary and artistic projects, producing a sketch of St Cecilia for the title page of his sister Mary's book of sacred poems, and a sketch for the *Art Repository*, another family enterprise. To this he also contributed 'The Carpet-Knight', a slight humorous poem in three stanzas built on a series of puns.

Even in this vacation period, however, Dodgson's preoccupation with mathematical affairs is apparent. Among the many notes on mathematical problems is a diary entry in which he records spotting an oversight in Professor Bartholomew Price's *Treatise on Differential Calculus and its application to geometry*, published in 1848. More significant is his first diary reference to photography, which he suggests might be put to practical use in mathematics by first modelling the complicated figures used in solid geometry and then photographing them. To the day of his death he kept a collection of geometrical models as teaching aids.

On 23 January 1855, just four days before his twenty-third birthday, Dodgson took on his first pupil, a young freshman called Burton, who was working for his 'Little-Go', and who proved an apt pupil. The absurdity of having only a single pupil was not lost on him, as he demonstrated in a letter to his sister and brother, Henrietta and Edwin in which he thanked them for a birthday present, unspecified but 'much better than a cane would have been'. The letter demonstrates his exploitation of communication failure for the purposes of humour:

> My one pupil has begun his work with me, and I will give you a description how the lecture is conducted. It is the most important point, you know, that the tutor should be *dignified* and at a distance from the pupil, and that the pupil should be as much as possible *degraded*.
> Otherwise, you know, they are not humble enough.
> So I sit at the further end of the room; outside the door (*which is shut*) sits the scout: outside the outer door (*also shut*) sits the sub-scout: half-way downstairs sits the sub-sub-scout; and down in the yard sits the *pupil*.
> The questions are shouted from one to the other, and the answers come back in the same way – it is rather confusing till you are well used to it. The lecture goes on something like this: —
> *Tutor*. What is twice three?
> *Scout*. What's a rice-tree?

Sub-scout. When is ice free?
Sub-sub-Scout. What's a nice fee?
Pupil (timidly). Half a guinea!
Sub-sub-Scout. Can't forge any!
Sub-Scout. Ho for Jinny!
Scout. Don't be a ninny!
Tutor. (looks offended . . .)[32]

A week later he began coaching his friend Sandford's younger brother on an informal basis, and received by way of thanks a volume of Hood's poems. Two more regular pupils were soon added, so that by 5 March he was devoting fifteen hours a week to teaching. Meanwhile Dodgson himself was being coached by Bartholomew Price in preparation for the Mathematical Scholarship. But he was disappointed with his performance in the first day's papers for the Senior Mathematical Scholarship and on the second day, having managed only two questions in the morning paper, decided not to present himself in the afternoon. Only two candidates took the last paper, and the Scholarship went to Bosanquet, whom he had beaten so easily in the Final Mathematical School at the end of the preceding term. 'It is tantalizing to think how easily (?) I might have got it, if I had only worked properly.'[33] Four days later Bosanquet won the Johnson scholarship also. '*Eheu fugaces! Video meliora proboque, deteriora sequor* – I do not think the work of this term worth recording,'[34] Dodgson wrote sadly. The plain fact was that he had simply not worked hard enough. He had been seduced, like so many others before him, by the pleasures of literature, by social intercourse with his fellows, by art exhibitions and playreadings: even by skating, which he tried, and which resulted in a bad fall and a cut head. An attack of influenza in early February may have impeded his studies, but would not have had a significant effect on his results.

Dodgson had that term suffered a further disappointment. Robert Fausett, the Mathematical Lecturer at Christ Church, had obtained a commission in the Commissariat and left Oxford in February 1855, expecting to go to the Crimea. As Dodgson stood next in line he clearly had high hopes of succeeding to the Mathematical Lectureship, until he heard rumours that the Dean did not intend to appoint a successor. This, he conjectured, was because of his objection to appointing a BA. In the event matters were postponed when Fausett returned and announced his intention of completing the term.

In one matter, however, Dodgson had achieved success. On 14 February he had been made Sub-Librarian in place of his old friend Bayne, of Daresbury days, who had become ineligible for the post by taking his MA degree. This brought with it an income of £35 a year. In making appointments to the Sub-Librarianship, the Dean always

advised familiarization with the contents of the library, and referred to
the motto 'Nosse bonos libros non minima pars est bonae eruditionis.'
Dodgson immediately began to apply himself to the Dean's advice, and
at the same time formulated a practical scheme for general reading,
subdividing his list into Classics, Divinity, History, Languages (modern), Poetry, Mathematics, Novels, miscellaneous studies, Divinity
reading for ordination (to which he decided to give preference, and on
which he consulted his father) and other subjects. By the end of term he
had completed his reviews of a major section of the books on the
library shelves, and had added twenty-four notable books to his reading list.

During the Easter vacation he entertained the family at Croft with
his Marionette Theatre, selecting for the occasion *The Tragedy of King
John*, which he had written himself. Its success gave him the idea of a
Christmas book for children, giving practical hints for constructing the
theatre and marionettes, plus a series of plays suitable for marionettes
or children. He felt that such a book would be commercially viable, but
the idea was never pursued. This is however the first hint in the diaries
that he had ever considered the possibility of publishing children's
books.

A few days later he went into Darlington and bought a copy of
Chambers' Euclid for Louisa, who at fifteen years already demonstrated a
wide range of talents, and who in later years was her brother's equal in
mathematics. Dodgson was highly critical of the book, and made many
deletions and insertions, asserting quite rightly that an author was duty
bound to distinguish any interpolations of his own from the text of the
original writer. It was a theme which he took up again and exploited in
Euclid and his Modern Rivals, published in 1879 and the most readable of
all his mathematical works.

When he returned to Christ Church, it was not to the rooms in
Peckwater Quad which he had occupied as an undergraduate, but to a
suite of rooms in Chaplain's Quad commensurate with his status as a
fully fledged Student. The block was demolished over a century ago,
but his new quarters were large enough to enable him to coach his
pupils, and to give a 'large wine' to all his friends from time to time, as
custom demanded. His friend George Kitchin, Mathematical
Examiner at Christ Church, now arranged to send fourteen of his men
to Dodgson for tuition. These Dodgson interviewed and assessed,
dividing them into sets and allocating thirteen hours a week to teaching
them. This would equate to roughly two pupils per term, and would
bring him in approximately £50. With £35 from his Sub-Librarianship,
£25 a year from his studentship and £20 from a Bostock Scholarship,
which he gained in May 1855, his income was now raised to the level of
near independence. And although he had no official lecturing position,

his private arrangement with Kitchin greatly enhanced his prospects of getting the coveted Mathematical Lectureship.

Although most of his time was now taken up in lecturing and preparation, in sorting the enormous number of mathematical examination papers passed on to him by Kitchin, and in library work, Dodgson nevertheless managed to make some progress on *The Fifth Book of Euclid proved Algebraically* by a College Tutor which he finally published anonymously in 1858. Some doubt has been expressed about his authorship of this book, which has been attributed to his friend Thomas Fowler of Lincoln College, particularly since Dodgson could not strictly be called a tutor. Nevertheless, his diary entry about the composition of this book is unequivocal, and it must properly be regarded as his first published mathematical work.

On 2 June 1855 Thomas Gaisford, the old Dean of Christ Church, died after a very short illness. Despite his seventy-six years, he had been active virtually till the end, and only one week before his death had been with Dodgson and Osborne Gordon in the Library, putting away newly acquired books and apparently in perfect health. The news of his death following a series of hourly bulletins cast gloom over the entire college. Known affectionately as the 'Old Bear', he had held his office since 1831, when he exchanged the Prebendal Stall at Durham for the Deanery. Though his rule had been authoritarian, he had inspired love and respect in many. Pusey, who maintained that changes in the old order at the University had broken Gaisford, wrote of his death to Gladstone, 'This will, at the best, make a very sad change. He was a representative of the best of the past, which has been passing away, and respect for him was a check to revolution in many institutions.'[35]

But Gaisford had not been without enemies. His dislike of change in the University was such that he had deliberately hindered the work of the Oxford University Commission set up in 1850, which he declared 'can be productive of no good, and may eventually breed discord and disunion'.[36] His policy towards the commissioners was to show his contempt by ignoring all their correspondence. Writing to Gladstone in May 1854, Jelf attributed the decline in the academic standards at Christ Church directly to Gaisford. 'I believe that what we want is Dean Jackson redivivus. If in the event of a vacancy a thoroughly good man were selected for that place, the ancient glories of "the House" would revive.'[37] In his view the Dean of Christ Church required a remarkable range of qualities. 'The man we want must be, not only a wise scholar, and apt to teach, but a thorough gentleman, a man skilful and experienced in *governing* young men of the upper classes, a man of sound judgement, courteous manner, business habits, incomparable integrity.'[38]

Pusey had terrible forebodings about the identity of Gaisford's successor. 'Now nothing but what is evil is threatened as his successor. They imagine Liddell,'[39] he confided to Gladstone. Some eighteen months earlier Liddell had preached a controversial sermon at Oxford which had led to complaints to the Vice-Chancellor of the University. 'We must bear the struggle with rationalism: but it is miserable to hear it coming down upon the young men from those who ought to teach them the truth,'[40] Pusey wrote of Liddell's sermon.

Five days after Gaisford's death *The Times* announced his successor: Henry George Liddell, Headmaster of Westminster School and personal Chaplain to the Prince Consort. Pusey's worst fears were realized, but the news of his appointment was greeted with cheers in the House of Commons. As for Dodgson, like many of the younger members of the University, he had no personal knowledge of him, and accordingly reserved his judgment; yet he noted in his diary the lack of enthusiasm at Christ Church for Liddell's appointment. The majority of Liddell's critics were concerned not so much by his religious views as by his reputation, gained while serving on the Royal Commission, as a vigorous and forceful university reformer. William Richmond, the artist, said that Liddell was 'as handsome a specimen of aristocratic manhood as could be seen in a lifetime'. His father was the brother of a baron, his mother the niece of an earl. A Charterhouse schoolboy, he had matriculated at Christ Church in 1829, in due course obtaining a double first and remaining a Student and tutor there until he was appointed headmaster of Westminster School in 1846.

The work for which Liddell is chiefly remembered is his *Greek Lexicon*, still the most authoritative work in this field, which he produced jointly with his friend Robert Scott, Master of Balliol. Though it was first published in 1843, he continued to revise it until his death more than fifty years later, normally devoting several hours a day to it. Its purpose was to 'foster and keep alive the accurate study of the Greek tongue; that tongue which has been held one of the best instruments for training the young mind; that tongue which, as the organ of Poetry and Oratory, is full of living force and fire, abounding in grace and sweetness, rich to overflowing'.

Liddell was a man of diverse abilities, not all of them academic. He had great artistic talent, possessing an excellent eye, highly developed critical faculties and considerable ability as a draughtsman. In the opinion of William Richmond, he could have become a successful artist, and many of his elaborate doodles which he produced on his blotter at Chapter meetings are preserved to prove his skill. Ruskin, who became a lifelong friend and owed much to Liddell's encouragement, wrote of him:

> He was, and is, one of the rarest types of nobly presenced Englishmen,
> but I fancy it was his adverse star that made him an Englishman at all –

the prosaic and practical element in him having prevailed over the sensitive one. He was the only man in Oxford among the masters of my day who knew anything of art; and his keen saying of Turner that 'he had got hold of a false ideal' would have been infinitely helpful to me at that time, had he explained and enforced it. But I suppose he did not see enough in me to make him take trouble with me, – and, what was much more serious, he saw not enough in himself to take trouble, in that field, with himself.[41]

Although a contemporary of Keble and Newman, Liddell had been virtually untouched by the Tractarian movement. Though not opposed in principle to reform at Oxford, he proved something of a disappointment to those who expected him to bring about in his new capacity as Dean those recommendations which he had strongly, even belligerently, advocated prior to his appointment. Truth to tell, he disliked controversy, and had no intention of stirring up the type of hostility he had encountered at Westminster School. It was clear from the outset that he was unlikely to rouse support for reform from the existing Chapter at Christ Church, who were conservative in the extreme, and still influenced by the policies of Gaisford. At the time of his appointment, Liddell was only forty-four years old. The Chapter over which he now presided included not only Dr Pusey, who had been Canon of Christ Church since 1828, but also the aged Dr Barnes, who had been a Canon for fifty-five years.

The new Dean was a family man. His wife, the former Miss Lorina Reeve, was considered a beauty, with dark hair, Spanish-type features and an imperious bearing. One son, Arthur, aged only three years, had died during an outbreak of scarlet fever at Westminster School, but at the time of Liddell's appointment as Dean of Christ Church there were four surviving children: Harry, the eldest, Lorina Charlotte, named after her mother, Edith, little more than a baby – and Alice, at three years old already utterly delightful. But several months were to elapse before the young Liddells were able to move into the Deanery with their parents.

REFERENCES

1 Maisie Wood, *Young Mr Newman*, 1948, p. 35.
2 *Letters from England*, p. 173.
3 Ibid.
4 G. R. M. Ward (translator), *Oxford University Statutes*, 1845, p. 160.

 5 Ibid, p. 154.
 6 Ibid, p. 204.
 7 Green, p. 29.
 8 Ibid.
 9 Ibid.
10 *Hints for Oxford*, 1823, p. 10.
11 Article, Roger Lancelyn Green, 'Carroll's "The Ligniad" ', *Lewis Carroll Observed*, Edward Guiliano (ed.), New York, 1976, p. 82.
12 *Hints for Oxford*, 1823, p. 10.
13 Ms. Diaries.
14 D.F.C. 18/5/4.
15 Collingwood, pp. 51–2.
16 *The Story of Dr Pusey's Life*, by Maria Trench, 1900, p. 150.
17 D.F.C. 7/2b.
18 Trevor Winkfield (ed.), *The Lewis Carroll Circular*, No. 1.
19 Ivor Ll. Davies, 'Archdeacon Dodgson', *Jabberwocky*, Vol. 5, No. 2, Spring 1976.
20 Lambeth Palace Library Ms. Longley I, f. 224.
21 Ivor Ll. Davies, 'Archdeacon Dodgson', *Jabberwocky*, Vol. 5, No. 2, Spring 1976.
22 See p. 44.
23 Green, p. 35.
24 Ibid.
25 Collingwood, p. 57.
26 Collingwood, p. 55.
27 Green, p. 33.
28 *Praeterita*.
29 Identified by Roger Lancelyn Green.
30 Roger Lancelyn Green, 'Carroll's 'The Ligniad'', An Early Mock Epic in Facsimile', *Lewis Carroll Observed*, E. Guiliano (ed.), New York, 1976, p. 90.
31 Green, p. 37.
32 Hatch, p. 18.
33 Green, p. 45.
34 Ibid.
35 B.L. Ms. 44281, f. 181.
36 H. L. Thompson, *Memoir of Henry George Liddell, DD*, London 1899.
37 B.L. Ms. 44381, ff. 31–2.
38 Ibid.
39 B.L. Ms. 44281, f. 181.
40 Ibid.
41 John Ruskin, *Praeterita*.

5 Dodgson Photographing

Dodgson, oblivious to the existence of his future heroine, was busy lecturing his private pupils, pursuing his personal schedule of studies, and following his multifarious interests. Immediately term ended he transferred to an even larger sphere of cultural activity: London.

Here he booked in at one of his favourite hotels, the Old Hummums at the corner of Great Russell Street. Established in the seventeenth century as a Turkish bath, it had once, like most bagnios, been the scene of debauchery and revels. George Augustus Sala, in *The Old Hummums Made New Again*, said that the baths had been revived 'with so many luxurious accessories and with such complete success that it is unnecessary to specify all the manifold arrangements for steaming, stewing, lathering, spraying, coating, pummelling, punching and pitching the bathers'. In view of its doubtful reputation it seems on the face of it surprising that Dodgson should have stayed there, but by his day it had shed its doubtful associations and had become the most respectable of the group of bagnios in the Covent Garden Piazza. It was a favourite haunt of artists and writers, a class with whom Dodgson now aspired to associate, and is described by Dickens in *Great Expectations*:

> In those times a bed was always to be had at any hour of the day, and the Chamberlain, letting me in at his ready wicket, lighted the candle next in order on the shelf, and showed me straight up to the bedroom next in order on his list. It was a sort of vault on the ground floor at the back, with a despotic monster of a four-poster bedstead in it, straddling over the whole place, putting one of its arbitrary legs in the fireplace, and another in the doorway, and squeezing the wretched little washing-stand in a quite Divinely righteous manner.

Having temporarily discarded his academic gown, Dodgson stepped easily into the role of man-about-town, and sometimes accompanied by his friends Bayne and Ranken, threw himself into a whirl of social activity with all the inexhaustible energy of a young man of twenty-three. Yet although he and Ranken had made plans for lionizing in London, it was not the glittering social life of the elegant society drawing-room which attracted him, but the art-exhibitions, the botanical gardens and Lord's cricket ground, and above all the theatre and opera house.

Bellini's 'Norma' was all the rage at this time, and Dodgson saw Madame Arga in the title role at the People's Opera in Drury Lane. He praised the prima donna's personal rendering, and described the music as 'delicious'; but he was disappointed in the supporting cast, and found the costumes and scenery poor. On the following evening he stood in the pit at Covent Garden, having given up his seat to a lady, to hear Giulietta Grisi in the same role. 'She was magnificent in voice and acting, but in appearance is red-faced and coarse, though wonderfully young-looking at fifty,'[1] he wrote. While in London Dodgson saw his first ballet at Drury Lane, and was sharply critical of the performance: 'The studied ugliness of the attitudes struck one a great deal more than anything else. Talk of the poetry of motion! The instinctive grace of cottage children dancing is something far more beautiful. I never want to see another ballet,'[2] he wrote.

For Dodgson, no visit to London was complete without a visit to the Princess's Theatre, on the north side of Oxford Street, which under the management of Charles Kean was in the greatest decade of its history. In the summer of 1855 he saw a performance of *Henry VIII*. Apart from hearing Mrs Fanny Kemble reading Henry V, without costumes or scenery, at Oxford Town Hall, this was Dodgson's first experience of Shakespeare on the stage. Now he saw Kean himself as Cardinal Wolsey, and Kean's wife, Ellen Tree, as Queen Catherine. Unlike Mrs Kemble, they had every advantage that scenery and costumes could give. It had been a feature of Kean's management, since he took over the Princess's in 1851, to offer spectacular scenic effects in all his productions, and to incorporate the newest stage techniques in presenting Shakespeare. None but the best scene painters were employed on his sets. On this occasion the triumph of the performance was Queen Catherine's dream. A transparent gauze behind the sleeping queen imparted a vision-like quality and enabled the audience to see angel figures descending to her. 'Never shall I forget that wonderful evening, that exquisite vision,' wrote Dodgson afterwards. 'Sunbeams broke in through the roof and gradually revealed two angel forms, floating in front of the carved work on the ceiling: the column of sunbeams shone down upon the sleeping queen, and gradually down it floated a troop of angelic forms, transparent, and carrying palm branches in their hands. . . . So could I fancy (if the thought be not profane) would real angels seem to our mortal vision . . .'[3]

Back at Croft, a few days later, Dodgson returned to literary pursuits. His cousin, the poetess Menella Smedley, whom he had met again recently at the Putney house of his uncle, Hassard Dodgson, had been impressed by Dodgson's 'The Three Voices', a parody of Tennyson's 'The Two Voices'. She in turn had shown it to her cousin Frank Smedley, author of the novel *Frank Fairleigh*, which Cruikshank had illustrated. Smedley liked the poem, and expressed an interest in helping to get Dodgson's work published. 'I do not think I have written anything worthy of real publication (in which I do not include *The Whitby Gazette* or *The Oxonian Advertiser*), but I do not despair of doing so some day' he commented. Smedley was as good as his word. By the end of July, he had sent some sample verses by Dodgson to Edmund Yates, editor of *The Comic Times*, who promptly printed 'Poetry for the Million', comprising a brief prose introduction plus 'The Dear Gazelle', a parody based on a verse from Lalla Rookh. Each of the four lines of Moore's stanza in succession forms the first line of a stanza of Dodgson's.

The Comic Times, a weekly magazine which Yates began on 11 August 1855, was regrettably short lived, surviving for only sixteen issues, despite contributions by men of the calibre of Robert Brough, George Augustus Sala, Charles Henry Bennett and Francis Smedley. But before the venture collapsed, Yates published three further contributions by Dodgson. These were a poem, 'She's all my fancy painted Him', and two prose pieces, 'Hints for Etiquette: or Dining Out Made Easy,' and 'Photography Extraordinary'.

Dr Selwyn Goodacre argues most convincingly that 'Hints for Etiquette' is a parody on a chapter, 'Dinners' from *Hints on Etiquette and the Usages of Society: With a Glance at bad habits*, by ΑΓΩΓΟΣ, which by 1849 had run into its twenty-sixth edition. The examples quoted by Dr Goodacre include the following:

> *Hints on Etiquette*: 'If you pass to dine merely from one room to another, offer your left arm to the lady.'
> *Lewis Carroll*: 'In proceeding to the dining room, the gentleman gives one arm to the lady he escorts – it is unusual to offer both.'
> *Hints on Etiquette*: 'Do not ask any lady to take wine, until you see she has *finished* her fish or soup. This exceedingly absurd and troublesome custom is very properly giving way at the best tables to the more reasonable one of the gentleman helping the lady to wine next to whom he may be seated, or a servant will hand it round.'
> *Lewis Carroll*: 'The practice of taking soup with the next gentleman but one is now wisely discontinued; but the custom of asking your host his opinion of the weather immediately on the removal of the first course still prevails.'
> *Hints on Etiquette*: 'Never use your knife to convey your food to your mouth, under any circumstances; it is unnecessary, and glaringly vulgar. Feed yourself with a fork or spoon, nothing else, – a knife is only to be used for cutting.'
> *Lewis Carroll*: 'To use a fork with your soup, intimating at the same time to your hostess that you are reserving your spoon for the beefsteaks, is a practice wholly exploded.'
> *Hints on Etiquette*: '. . . If you should have to carve and help a joint, do not

load a person's plate – it is vulgar; also in serving soup, one ladleful to each is sufficient.'
Lewis Carroll: 'On meat being placed before you, there is no possible objection to your eating it, if so disposed; still in all cases, be guided entirely by the conduct of those around you.'
Hints on Etiquette: 'At every respectable table you will find silver forks; being broader, they are in all respects more convenient than steel for fish or vegetables. Steel forks except for carving, are now never placed on a table.'
Lewis Carroll: 'The method of helping roast turkey with two carving-forks is practicable, but deficient in grace.'
Hints on Etiquette: 'Do not pick your teeth much at table, as, however satisfactory a practice to yourself, to witness it is not at all pleasant.'
Lewis Carroll: 'As a general rule, do not kick the shins of the opposite gentleman under the table, if personally unacquainted with him: your pleasantry is liable to be misunderstood – a circumstance at all times unpleasant.'[4]

'Photography Extraordinary', the second piece by Dodgson to be published in *The Comic Times*, sets out the pseudoscientific theory that photography can be used to 'develope' ideas to the required degree of intensity, and gives an example of a short prose passage and accompanying poem belonging 'apparently to the Milk-and-Water School of Novels' strengthened through two further 'schools'. Experiments on a passage of Wordsworth converted it to 'strong, sterling poetry', and the same experiment on a passage of Byron scorched and blistered the paper. '*Could* this art be applied (we put the question in the strictest confidence) – *could* it, we ask, be applied to the speeches in Parliament!' Dodgson concludes. 'It may be but a delusion of our heated imagination, but we will still cling fondly to the idea, and hope against hope.'

Now that Dodgson was getting more work published, he began in July 1855 to compile a kind of scrap-book into which he pasted or copied his best work to date, published or unpublished, as well as a few items by others from the family magazines. He called this *Mischmasch*, and dated its preface 13 August 1855. It still exists at Harvard, and was published for the first time as a complete anthology together with *The Rectory Umbrella* in 1932. One of the stanzas which he included was the 'Stanza of Anglo-Saxon Poetry' which he contributed to a verse-making game, possibly in the long vacation of 1855, when on a visit to his cousins, the Wilcoxes, who lived at Whitburn, near Sunderland. This ultimately became the first verse of his famous nonsense poem 'Jabberwocky', ultimately expanded into a complete poem and featured in *Through the Looking-Glass*. It is fascinating to find that this most famous of all nonsense poems was not the studied composition of an established author in his fortieth year, but the spontaneous jeu d'esprit of a young man of twenty-three.

During the same vacation he tried teaching for the first time at Croft

National School. First he spent a day sitting in while his father taught the boys, and on the following day began with scripture lessons himself. He enjoyed the experience, and frequently made himself useful in the school, taking the girls' class when not needed by the boys. On the whole he seems to have preferred the girls, whom he was soon teaching regularly four mornings a week, preparing skeleton maps of the Holy Land, Jerusalem and the Temple for their benefit. Initially they were shy with him, but answered well nevertheless.

While visiting Whitburn Dodgson met a little girl who might be regarded as his first child friend. This was the niece of the new Dean of Christ Church, Frederika Liddell, whom he met quite by chance, and described as 'one of the nicest children I have ever seen, as well as the prettiest; dear, sweet, pretty little Frederika!' Dodgson did not admire lifeless, doll-like beauty in children, but sought a kind of animation, combined with gentleness and innocence. Like others in his circle of acquaintances, he looked at children with an artist's eye, and before two days had elapsed he had sketched Frederika sitting on a stile. At a home theatrical evening a week later, he acted with her and others in a charade, and wrote in his diary afterwards: 'Mark this day, oh Annalist, with a white stone' (his usual expression for what we might call a red letter day).

On 18 August 1855, whilst still at Whitburn, Dodgson was informed of the Dean's intention to make him Mathematical Lecturer at the beginning of the next term. This meant that he no longer needed to enter for the scholarship examination again. His father, delighted with the news, immediately wrote urging him to insure his life, invest £100 a year, and lay out additional money in building up his personal library, in order to provide a nest egg against the time when he should decide to accept a living to settle down in. (He did not mention marriage, but this possibility was clearly in his father's mind.)

A month later Dodgson's elation turned to disappointment when his friend Barclay wrote to him from Dieppe with the news that Lloyd, not Dodgson, was to be the new mathematical lecturer at Christ Church. As this was on Kitchin's authority, it was no idle rumour. In fact when he returned to Christ Church Lloyd gave all the 'public' mathematical lectures required during the Michaelmas term leaving Dodgson to his private pupils, who took up nearly eighteen hours' teaching time a week.

Dodgson could not be made Master of Arts of the University until he had completed the requisite number of terms and been formally admitted by the Vice-Chancellor. He took his Master's degree in 1857. But in honour of Liddell's appointment as Dean, Dodgson was made Master of the House on 15 October 1855 and as such was entitled to the privileges of a Master of Arts within Christ Church. The only objection to the allocation of a Lectureship to a Bachelor of Arts was now overcome. As he saw out the old year quietly at Croft in December 1855, he wrote in his diary:

> I am sitting alone in my bedroom this last night of the old year, waiting for midnight. It has been the most eventful year of my life: I began it a poor bachelor student, with no definite plans or expectations: I end it a Master and tutor in Christ Church, with an income of more than £300 a year, and the course of mathematical tuition marked out by God's providence for at least some years to come. Great mercies, great failings, time lost, talents misapplied – such has been the past year.[5]

Return to Oxford brought immediate problems with the Mathematical Lectureship, for of sixty men sent for, only twenty-three turned up to discuss the proposed work schedule. Dodgson's second summons brought no response from the absentees, so that he had to have recourse to the Dean, who helped him to draw up a plan of campaign. Their new proposals included allowing men to work privately without Dodgson's lectures if they so wished, subject to periodic examinations during term, and abolishing compulsory arithmetic lessons for those capable of managing without them.

Dodgson's early difficulties invite the supposition that he might have been the 'Tutor who did not understand how to deal with undergraduates' and who accordingly 'made discipline for a time an arduous task'[6] during Liddell's early months in office. But Dodgson was never an official College Tutor, nor were difficulties with the undergraduates exclusive to him. When he examined four of the men on the work allocated by Lloyd during the previous term, he found they knew none of it. This was part of a general apathy amongst the men which, as a dedicated scholar, Dodgson found difficult to understand.

Small wonder that his enthusiasm quickly waned. 'I am weary of lecturing, and discouraged,' he wrote in November 1856. 'It is thankless, uphill work, goading unwilling men to learning they have no taste for, to the inevitable neglect of others who really want to get on.'[7]

Side by side with his official lecturing work, Dodgson now began teaching at St Aldate's School, where his friend Maurice Swabey was headmaster. His timetable included religious instruction on Sunday mornings and arithmetic on Tuesday and Fridays. He was struck by the difference between these bold, town-bred boys and the quieter country children at Croft National School. But after an initial experiment in teaching a mixed class, he reported that the sexes would need to be segregated, as the girls could not keep up with the boys. Before long he had difficulty in maintaining discipline, and by the end of February he had to abandon it altogether.

Meanwhile Dodgson was still pursuing his personal literary activities. Regrettably *The Comic Times* had collapsed in November

1855, and deserted by their publisher, the regular staff had formed a company to produce *The Train*, a predominantly humorous monthly magazine. Though the company lacked the money to pay for articles or illustrations, the list of contributors was impressive – Yates, Sala, Brough and Smedley in the first number alone. By January 1856 Dodgson was already composing work specifically for *The Train*, producing 'Novelty and Romancement', a prose piece which appeared in October of that year. His first contribution actually to appear in *The Train* was 'Solitude', in March 1856. In the same issue was 'Ye Carpette Knyghte', the poem he wrote at Ripon in January 1855, revised with pseudo-medieval spelling. Though medieval English made a strong appeal to his imagination, he never made any real effort to come to grips with it, and remained permanently ignorant of its basic structure. Yet this did not prevent his continued experimentation with it, and even a piece as slight as 'Ye Carpette Knyghte' was revised on no less than three occasions. A few days after he composed it he records studying early English alphabets in *The Rise and Progress of Writing*, and adds that he had tried, and failed, with its help to decipher manuscript at the end of a great Bible of the age of Henry VIII in Christ Church Library.

Altogether Dodgson made eight contributions to *The Train*. In addition he corrected two items by his old friend Mounsey of Richmond School, a poem about a little Highland girl and a prose piece with the promising title, 'On the singularity of animals having only one tail', which he recommended to Yates. Dodgson initially submitted his work under the old boyhood pseudonymous initials 'BB', but Yates now asked him to substitute a suitable pen-name, rejecting 'Dares', Dodgson's first suggestion, taken from his birthplace, Daresbury. Four more pseudonyms now occurred to him, all based on his own Christian names: 'Edgar Cuthwellis', 'Edgar U. C. Westhill', 'Louis Carroll', and 'Lewis Carroll.' The fateful choice was left to Yates. On 1 March 1856 Dodgson recorded in his diary that '*Lewis Carroll*' was chosen; the famous nom-de-plume was first used for 'Solitude'.

Dean Liddell had meanwhile been staying temporarily with Archdeacon Clerke, the Sub-Dean, until the Deanery could be got ready. A man noted for his good taste and judgment in architectural matters, he had decided on many alterations and improvements to the house. These included magnificent oak panelling in the drawing room and hall, and the construction of a majestic 'Lexicon' staircase, so called because it was paid for out of the profits of that famous book, which by 1855 had run into four editions totalling twenty-three thousand copies. Most important of all, he had opened out on the first floor a gallery measuring forty-four feet long and approached by an arch at the head of the stairs, which was excellent for acoustics and could be used as an additional reception room. This was now a house in which glittering social gatherings of a kind unknown in modest old Gaisford's day could be held. There were many building delays, including a fire at the factory in Lambeth where all the oak panelling was destroyed on the very point of completion, but finally on 12 February 1856 Liddell wrote to his mother:

> Painters and paperers still linger, but we are now very nearly done, and hope to throw open our doors for an evening musical party next week. They are intending to get up the 'Mackbeth' music, choruses, some glees, and other music by the help of some of the young men and ladies, if they are not too prudish to join.[8]

About two weeks later he wrote again:

> So, about 8 o'clock on Thursday evening, think of Madam making her first curtsey at the head of her own stairs in Oxford. This is a strange place for rumours. It has been reported that Mrs Liddell is getting up private theatricals, and that Dr Clerke permits his daughter to personate one of the witches, while the Dean is expected to represent Mackbeth![9]

Mrs Liddell already had high social ambitions, and, anxious to play her own part in assisting her husband's work, was seeking a reputation as a hostess. Her guest list was so long that the soirée had to be repeated in order to accommodate everybody. Dodgson missed that first curtsey, but along with about half the college he was invited to the repeat performance, which took place on Saturday 8 March. Dodgson loved social gatherings as a young man, though not for the dancing. 'I never dance,' he once wrote to a child friend, 'unless I am allowed to do it *in my own peculiar way*. There is no use trying to describe it: it has to be seen to be believed. . . . Did you ever see the Rhinoceros, and the Hippopotamus, at the Zoological Gardens, trying to dance together? It is a touching sight.'[10] To him the only reason for adults to meet together was to enjoy conversation and music.

Of the latter there was no shortage at the Deanery party. Besides the Macbeth music there were songs sung by Ernest de Bunsen, son of a prominent German diplomat, and choruses taken by three popular Oxford men, Twiss, Irvine and Pember. But for Dodgson the chief significance of the evening was the opportunity it afforded him of making friends with little six-year-old Lorina Liddell, the Dean's eldest daughter. Only a few days before he had met Harry, her elder brother, down at the boats and they had instantly struck up a friendship. Harry was a remarkably handsome boy, like all his family, and intelligent and well mannered into the bargain. There was a certain degree of hero-worship in his relationship to the young Don, and he now became his constant companion, eagerly seeking him out at every opportunity, joining in boating expeditions and other treats, and even dropping into

Dodgson's rooms for breakfast. And, *mirabile dictu*, he sometimes brought Lorina with him.

A restless, creative intellect like Dodgson's continually seeks new outlets, and he now felt the need for some other pastime besides reading and writing. Photography intrigued him, not only because the scientific process appealed to his methodical nature, but because it formed a link between his two major interests: art, and people. All his life he had enjoyed drawing, and had an eye for composition, with highly developed critical faculties. But although his sketches were fine little works of art, he was deficient in elementary draughtsmanship, being unable to fulfil his creative instincts to his own satisfaction with paintbrush or pencil. This was especially true of portraiture, in which his chief preoccupation lay. Now, as a photographer, he could compensate for his inferior draughtsmanship by his skill and patience in mastering the technical difficulties, and having once achieved mastery of this new 'black art', could compete with painters on equal terms. It was the heyday of Victorian photography, the era of Mrs Julia Margaret Cameron, a gifted amateur who took up photography in a garden shed at the age of forty-eight, and with whom Dodgson later made friends, and of Rejlander, a painter who originally saw photography as a means of helping artists to paint. The final stimulus to take up this hobby came from Reginald Southey, Dodgson's friend at Christ Church, and from Uncle Skeffington, both of whom already had cameras. Ever intrigued by novelties, Uncle Skeffington was among the very earliest amateur photographers to take up the art after the removal of patents, and in the long vacation of 1855 Charles had accompanied him on photographic expeditions around Croft, where he had photographed the bridge and church, though not very successfully.

The collodion wet-plate process which Dodgson used had been preceded by the Daguerreotype, so called after its French inventor, Daguerre, and by the calotype of Henry Fox Talbot. Both these methods were patented in England. Frederick Scott Archer invented the collodion wet-plate just in time for the Great Exhibition of 1851, but initially Fox Talbot claimed that this was merely a modification of his patented process, and it was not until a professional photographer named Sylvester Laroche successfully challenged the claim in a court of law that Fox Talbot was induced to give up in February 1855 his claim for a fourteen-year extension of his patent. Amateurs were now at last free to take up this amazing new art form.

The method which Dodgson and his contemporaries used was incredibly complicated, and involved immediate access, both before and after the picture was taken, to a photographic darkroom. Collodion had to be poured evenly over a carefully polished plate which was then dipped in silver nitrate solution. Speed was essential, for the plate had to remain wet while the photographer went back to his camera and took the photograph. Finally, back in the darkroom the plate had to be evenly heated over a fire before being varnished, drained and dried. Only then could a print be made.

In March 1856 Dodgson took a train to London and called at Ottiwell's, in Charlotte Street, where he ordered a camera. This was a costly item, £15 without other indispensable accessories, but he did not begrudge the expense. 'It is my one recreation, and I think should be done well,' he wrote. The plate size of this first camera was eight inches by ten inches. During his lifetime he bought at least two other cameras, but worked in five plate sizes altogether, probably using a masking technique to obtain the smaller variants.

In his earliest days of photographic experiment Dodgson usually joined Southey, drawing on his greater experience. On 25 April 1856 the two men went to the Deanery to photograph the Cathedral, using Southey's camera, as Dodgson's had not yet arrived. The Dean's three little daughters were playing in the garden, and Dodgson quickly made friends with them. Southey, like Uncle Skeffington, took special pleasure in landscape photography. This had certain advantages over portraiture, which required an obedient subject prepared to sit stock still for forty-five seconds or more to achieve a satisfactory result. But for Dodgson, no picture could be complete without human interest. He accordingly tried to group the children in the foreground of Southey's picture; but they fidgeted, and the photographs failed.

This was Dodgson's first recorded meeting with Alice Liddell. Photographic 'victims', as he called them, were now vital to Dodgson, and the four Liddell children were on hand. Although they were not patient sitters, they could be cajoled into remaining still with stories, often illustrated with pen and ink drawings. Dodgson began to haunt the Deanery, at first with Mrs Liddell's approval, for photography was still a novelty, and photographs of her beautiful children were not unwelcome. But as time went on, and the pictures failed more often than not, and the mass of paraphernalia became an encumbrance, her patience wore thin.

Like most of his contemporaries, Dodgson had taken an intense interest in the progress of the Crimean war. The public conscience had been awakened by accounts of the wretched plight of the troops, and especially of the wounded, by stories of the work of Florence Nightingale, and above all by a brilliant and moving series of photographs taken by Roger Fenton in the Crimea which were widely exhibited. Dodgson had been to lectures and art displays, and finally to an exhibition of Fenton's photographs. On the day when the signing of the peace treaty was announced, he was staying in Ripon, where the cathedral bells rang out all day. A few days later he submitted a poem about Florence Nightingale, called 'The Path of Roses', to Edmund Yates for *The Train*. Dodgson invariably took a keen interest in the pictures which accompanied his writings, and he now offered a detailed description of an illustration he thought suitable. Both poem and picture appeared a week later. Dodgson's choice of subject was ambivalent, for in May 1855 he had condemned a picture of Florence Nightingale for 'making a sort of romance out of real human suffering'.[11]

The long vacation gave Dodgson the opportunity to return to London. *A Winter's Tale* was in production at the Princess's Theatre, and though less spectacular than *Henry VIII*, it was a pleasing production. Making her debut was a young lady of nine years,[12] destined to become the idol of the London stage: Ellen Terry. Dodgson remarked on the remarkable ease and spirit with which she interpreted the part of Mamilius, which she played for a hundred and three performances, at a wage of fifteen shillings a week. Dressed in a red and silver costume and pushing a tiny toy cart copied from a Greek vase, she eclipsed her accomplished twelve-year-old sister Kate, who appeared as servant to the Old Shepherd, and her father, Ben Terry, who was the Officer of the Court. In the early days of Kate's acting career the Terry family had been split up, Mrs Terry remaining in London with Kate while Ellen toured the provinces with her father. This close bond between Ellen and her father left its mark on her acting career. Ben Terry was proud of his beautiful enunciation, and it was to his early insistence on clear articulation that she owed the wonderful diction for which she became famous.

Dodgson saw the Terry sisters again in the following January in *A Midsummer Night's Dream* at the same theatre. He liked Kate's performance as Titania and Ellen's as Puck, but Ellen herself was not pleased with the part, and claimed that she grew gawky in this role, while the mischief of the character had an adverse effect on her behaviour. She was only mollified by her costume as the Fairy Goldenstar, in a maudlin pantomime which formed part of the double bill.

Photography was very much to the fore when, in August 1856, Dodgson set off with his brothers Skeffington and Wilfred, both now at Oxford, and his friend Collyns, for the Lake District before returning to Croft. Uncharacteristically he took a number of landscapes, though he confessed that he was disappointed in the scenery, which was less impressive than he had been led to expect. But there were lots of portraits, too, mostly of the family, of the Longleys, and of the Bainbridges, his meeting with whom in the summer of 1854 had been the highlight of his visit to Whitby.

Soon after his return to Oxford Dodgson, who found that he had no free evenings at all for reading and relaxation, confessed to finding the autumn series of lectures too demanding. Fearing that he might break down altogether, he managed to rearrange his schedule to leave at least three evenings a week free. Meanwhile he began taking his camera over to the Deanery, in the hope of photographing not only the Liddells, but other selected sitters, like the family of Sir Henry Acland, Regius Professor of Medicine and personal physician to the Prince of Wales. Perhaps it was just a coincidence that when he called with his camera on his only free morning of term, he was just in time to see the entire family drive off from the Deanery; but when he went back at Harry's request a few days later he was told that Mrs Liddell wanted no more photographs until the whole family could be photographed in a group. 'This may be a hint that I have intruded on the premises long enough,'[13] wrote Dodgson, and resolved not to go again unless specifically invited to do so, except to pack up and remove his apparatus. Probably Mrs Liddell was a little offended at his arranging photographic sessions through Miss Prickett, the governess, instead of directly with herself, and at his inviting other people, even close friends of the Dean like the Aclands, to be photographed in her garden.

Other minor signs of strain began to show in his relationship with Mrs Liddell at around this time. In December 1856 Dodgson began teaching Harry mathematics. Mrs Liddell objected on the grounds that Dodgson would be too busy, but he did not take the hint. She was, however, still preoccupied with the Dean's health, and before the end of the year the couple had departed to Madeira for the winter, leaving the children in the care of Miss Prickett. 'Pricks', as the children called her, came from a highly respected local family, but her personal fortune was inadequate to support her, and she took the only situation considered suitable for a lady without means, that of governess. She was no beauty, having somewhat heavy features, but eventually married well. Meanwhile, her connection with the Liddells lent her a certain distinction, and she was capable of offering the children the rudiments of an education with the help of visiting tutors in French, music and drawing, and able to instruct them in the social graces. When she married, she became reasonably prosperous as the proprietress of the Mitre Hotel in Oxford and continued to regard Dodgson with cordiality, lending him clothes in which he could dress up his child models and taking an interest in his books.

With Mrs Liddell out of the way, Dodgson now had free access to the children, and Miss Prickett was glad of his support in her care of the children. He made constant calls at the Deanery, partly to see the children and partly in the hope of hearing news of the health of the Dean, on whose account he was genuinely concerned. His advice was continually sought, and he gave it conscientiously until the inevitable occurred: his interest in the children was misconstrued as an interest in their governess! Dodgson was frankly horrified, and resolved to take no further interest in the children in public. It was a resolution he could not keep, even for a few days, for they were eager for his companionship, and he had not the heart to refuse them.

Meanwhile, Mrs Reeves, the children's maternal grandmother, maintained a close interest in their welfare, and soon after the Dean's departure she wrote to Miss Prickett saying that she feared that Dodgson's maths lessons were overtaxing Harry's brain. Harry had by now become inattentive, and the lessons were consequently abandoned. When, soon afterwards, Harry was accepted at Twyford School, where Dodgson's brothers had been educated, the intimacy between the man and the boy was confined to the school holidays. At the beginning of the Christmas vacation Dodgson travelled to London and chose a magic lantern and slides for Croft National School. He also bought toys which were distributed from a bran pie at the school feast for a hundred and fifty children. The slides were shown in two sessions, each attended by over eighty children, servants and friends. These were the largest audiences Dodgson had ever had. There were forty-seven slides, thirteen songs and a commentary by Dodgson himself, who amended his performance on the second day with imitations, 'to make the comedy more palpable'.[14] He made no note of the subject matter, but when Elizabeth had asked him for suggestions, he had written, 'If I could get proper slides for it, a very good plot might be made up out of incidents in a schoolboy's life, on the model of "The Enraged Musician" (acted by Mrs German Reed).'[15]

On 1 July 1856, when he was at Croft, a significant entry appeared in his diary: 'Walked over with Skeffington to Dinsdale and called on the Smiths. I took some of my photographs to show them and arranged that a party of them are to come on Friday to sit.'[16] Showing photographs, which nearly always resulted in a sitting, was to become a regular part of Dodgson's social life for the next twenty-five years. His photography that summer involved him in a vast amount of work, trimming, arranging and mounting his pictures in albums for display, and for a quarter of a century he never went anywhere without a selection of his portraits. His hobby was to a large extent seasonal, especially in the early period when he had no 'glasshouse', or photographic studio, of his own. But in the winter when the light was too poor for portraiture he busied himself with the arrangement and documentation of his prints. Essentially a methodical man, he later began a photographic register in which he numbered his plates. After his death the register was lost, but the numbering runs into nearly 2700. But even this is not a true guide to his output, for from time to time he erased some of this enormous stock and used the numbers over again, so that the overall total was even higher.

Photography was an expensive hobby, however, and he soon began to attempt to defray some of the expenses by marketing his work commercially. In June 1857 he was invited to a 'Harmonic' evening by Quintin Twiss, a talented undergraduate whose flair for acting and singing made him extremely popular at Oxford. Dodgson seized this opportunity of photographing him in a sailor suit, and again in ordinary clothes with a pipe in his mouth at a jaunty angle. Later he photographed him as the 'Artful Dodger', and with a group of friends. His extrovert nature made him a natural subject, and Dodgson obtained twenty-five orders for copies. Thus encouraged, he took the portraits plus six anatomical photographs to Ryman's, the stationers. Between 1860 and 1861 he actually circulated a printed list of photographs, presumably in order to obtain some financial return as well as to oblige his friends. His photographs of skeletons seemed to have marketable possibilities in Oxford. One of these was of a tunny fish caught by Acland, the Regius Professor of Medicine, when he went to Madeira with the Dean. Dodgson's photograph of the mounted tunny skeleton was circulated with a serious Latin descriptive leaflet, and a line by line travesty. The latter was 'believed to have been rough-hewn by Lewis Carroll, handed round the Common Room, retouched by Gordon, Bode and the rest'.[17] Both leaflets and the photograph are still at Christ Church in a scrapbook kept by Thomas Vere Bayne.

By some curious contradiction Dodgson, who wrote his lighter works under a pseudonym, talked openly and on every possible occasion about his photography. Yet his pictures were almost as personal as his writings, revealing much not only of the sitter but also of the photographer and his relationship with the sitter, however fleeting. The admiraton of an appreciative audience not only satisfied his innate love of showmanship, but also met his deep-seated need for approval.

Having mastered the technical processes, Dodgson was free to concentrate on the composition of his photographs, which became his major forte. His work is notable for absolute simplicity of arrangement, with no complicated backgrounds to distract the eye. Simple accessories, a book, a toy, perhaps a parasol or chess set, often serve to assist the sitter to achieve a natural pose, to draw together the elements of composition and to impart a message to the viewer. His greatest gift was that of relating two or more figures to each other: indeed in 1858 he had described 'grouping' as his 'favourite branch of the subject'.[18] He also had the invaluable knack of arranging the hands of the sitter in a way which appeared entirely natural:

> In single portraits the chief difficulty to be overcome is the natural placing of the hands. Within the narrow limits allowed by the focussing power of the lens there are not many attitudes into which they naturally fall, while if the artist attempts the arrangement himself, he generally

produces the effect of the proverbial bashful young man in society who finds for the first time that his hands are an encumbrance, and cannot remember what he is in the habit of doing with them in private life.[19]

As a photographer Dodgson was an indefatigable lionizer, and often his portraits acted as passports into the homes of the great. In August 1857 Tennyson's wife's sister, Mrs Charles Weld, brought her little daughter Agnes Grace to Croft Rectory, and Dodgson took two photographs of her. Though Francis Palgrave had dedicated a sonnet to her, she was no great beauty; but she had an interesting face and his photograph of her as 'Little Red Riding Hood' made a strong appeal to Victorian taste. In the following year Dodgson exhibited it along with three others at the Photographic Society, and even invited Palgrave to compose a few lines on it, an offer which he declined.

During the long vacation of 1857 Dodgson toured Scotland with his brothers Skeffington and Wilfred, who had joined him at Oxford, and in whose company he was now often to be found. He had sent copies of the photographs via Mrs Weld to Tennyson, who had much admired them, and on his return from his Scottish tour he resolved at least to go and look at Tent Lodge, where the Tennysons were staying. Finally he plucked up enough courage to call, and sent in his card, with the pencilled inscription 'Artist of "Agnes Grace" ', whereupon he was cordially received by Mrs Tennyson. Encouraged by her response he returned again four days later. To his delight Tennyson himself appeared: black-haired, bearded and unkempt, carelessly dressed, but kind and friendly and with 'a dry lurking humour in his style of talking'.[20] The family was due to leave Tent Lodge next day, but Tennyson thought it possible that Dodgson might take photographs at the Ambleside home of his friend James Marshall, MP for Leeds, when the Tennysons arrived there in a few days' time. Accordingly he took Dodgson over to the Marshalls', where they obtained consent. That night Dodgson dined at Tent Lodge, where he showed his photographs to Tennyson, who enjoyed them so much that Dodgson had high hopes of obtaining a sitting.

> Some of the photographs called out a good deal of fun on Mr Tennyson's part. The picture of Skeffington in fishing costume, he said, had the expression (stroking down his beard as he spoke) 'Well! I've come down here to catch a trout, and if I don't catch a trout this season, the great business of my life will be gone'; and his half-length portrait 'By Jupiter! all my labour gone for nothing, and not one single trout!' The anatomical photographs intrigued him, and especially a group of a human skeleton and monkey.

He was struck by the similarity between the skull of the young monkey and that of the human, and likened its gradual alteration to the way in which the human skull at first resembles the statues of the gods, gradually degenerating into human form.

When the subject turned to Ruskin, of whom they talked a good deal, Dodgson wrote that he 'seemed to have a profound contempt for him as a critic, though he allowed him to be a most eloquent writer. He said that Ruskin had written to him, asking to make his aquaintance, that he had answered it in a friendly spirit, and that Ruskin had then sent him an impertinent letter, of which he had taken no notice, nor of any letter received from him since.'[21] The first letter from Ruskin, written from his home in Denmark Hill, reads as follows:

Dear Mr Tennyson,
    I venture to write to you, because as I was talking about you with Mr Woolner yesterday, he gave me more pleasure than I can express by telling me that you wished to see my 'Turners'.
    By several untoward chances I have been too long hindered from telling you face to face how much I owe you. So you see at last I seize the wheel of fortune by its nearest spoke, begging you with the heartiest entreaty I can, to tell me when you are likely to be in London and to fix a day if possible that I may keep it wholly for you, and prepare my 'Turners' to look their rosiest and best. Capricious they are as enchanted opals, but they must surely shine for you.
    Any day will do for me if you give me notice two or three days before, but please come soon, for I have much to say to you and am eager to say it, above all to tell you how for a thousand things I am gratefully and respectfully yours,
                                J. Ruskin.[22]

But the mixed reception of his monodramatic lyric 'Maud', whose form was widely misunderstood, made Tennyson hypersensitive to criticism, and when he received the second letter from Ruskin which, though intended to be complimentary, was not without reservations, he was unduly irritated:

My Dear Sir,
    . I hear of so many stupid and feelingless misunderstandings of 'Maud' that I think it may give you some pleasure to know my sincere admiration of it throughout.
    I do not like its versification so well as much of your other work, not because I do not think it good of its kind, but because I do not think that wild kind quite so good, and I am sorry to have another cloud put into the sky of one's thoughts by the sad story, but as to the general bearing and delicate finish of the thing in its way, I think no admiration can be extravagant.
    It is a compliment to myself, not to you, if I say that I think with you in *all* things about the war.
    I am very sorry you put the 'Some one had blundered' out of the 'Light Brigade'.[23]

It was precisely the most tragical line in the poem. It is as true to its history as essential to its tragedy.

Believe me sincerely yours,

J. Ruskin.[24]

Ruskin was always difficult to satisfy. Only a few weeks before Dodgson's arrival he had written yet again. 'It is a long time since I have heard from you and I do not like the mildew to grow over what little memory you may have of me. It is however no excuse for writing to say that I wanted to congratulate you on the last edition of your poems. Indeed it might be and I hope will be some day better managed, still many of the plates are very noble things, though not, it seems to me, illustrations of your poems.'[25] And later, when Ruskin read the *Idylls of the King* he wrote, 'I shall always wish it had been nobleness independent of a romantic condition of externals in general', and described 'Maud' as one of his own 'pet rhymes'.[26]

A few days later Dodgson's wish to take the Laureate's portrait was realized when he spent a whole day at the Marshalls' and took several photographs of them and of the Tennysons. The photographs of the children were almost bound to succeed better than those of the poet, for Dodgson, who venerated him almost to the point of adulation, was never entirely at ease with him. But it was the portrait of the great man himself that had commercial possibilities, and one of these was published by Joseph Cundall of Bond Street in 1861.

The story of Dodgson's association with little Agnes Grace Weld, without whose photographs Dodgson would probably never have met his favourite literary 'Lion', had a rather sad ending. Agnes, who never married, in later life took a harmless delight in introducing him as 'Lewis Carroll' to her lionizing friends, a habit which he deplored and which caused him much embarrassment. On 4 May 1896 he wrote in his diary:

> I met Miss Agnes Weld, with some foreign lady, to whom she introduced me – a thing I have again and again begged her not to do, and have already explained to her how much I dislike being thus made a 'lion'. Requests being evidently useless, I have at last taken the thing into my own hands, and have written to tell her that in future when I meet her with strangers I shall not recognize her.[27]

Poor Little Red Riding Hood! It was harsh treatment from one lion hunter to another.

REFERENCES

1   Green, p. 53.
2   Ibid, p. 52.

3   Ibid, p. 54.
4   Dr Selwyn Goodacre, 'An Unrecognized Lewis Carroll Parody', *Jabberwocky*, Vol. 5, No. 2.
5   Collingwood, p. 65.
6   H. L. Thompson, *Henry George Liddell: A Memoir*, 1899, p. 167.
7   Green, p. 96.
8   H. L. Thompson, *Henry George Liddell: A Memoir*, 1899, p. 148.
9   Ibid, p. 149.
10 Hatch, pp. 90–1.
11 Ms. Diaries.
12 Ellen Terry always believed herself to be a year younger than she really was. Her birth on 27 February 1847 was registered at Coventry in March of that year.
13 Green, p. 95.
14 Ms. Diaries.
15 Ibid.
16 Ibid.
17 W. Tuckwell, *Reminiscences of Oxford*, 1900, p. 160.
18 Green, p. 142.
19 *The Illustrated Times*, 28 January 1860.
20 Green, p. 125.
21 Ibid, p. 126.
22 Hallam Lord Tennyson, *Alfred Lord Tennyson: A Memoir*, 1899.
23 Ibid, p. 323.
24 Ibid, p. 346.
25 Ibid, p. 381.
26 The line was later reinstated.
27 Ms. Diaries.

6 Difficulties

The diaries for the four years covering 17 April 1858 to 1 May 1862 are unfortunately missing, and little remains to show how Dodgson spent the later part of 1858. In literary terms it appears to have been entirely unproductive, for nothing was published and almost nothing preserved. But in April 1859 he visited the Tennysons again, this time at their own home, Farringford, at Freshwater on the Isle of Wight. The Tennysons had bought Farringford in 1856 with the profits from 'Maud'. On 30 April 1856 Emily Tennyson described its idyllic setting:

> We have agreed to buy, so I suppose this ivied home among the pine-trees is ours. Went to our withy holt: such beautiful blue hyacinths, orchises, primroses, daisies, marsh-marigolds and cuckoo-flowers. Wild cherry trees too with their single snowy blossom, and the hawthorns white with their 'pearls of May.' The park has for many days been rich with cowslips and furze in bloom. The elms are a golden wreath at the foot of the down; to the north of the house the mespilus and horse-chestnut are in flower and the apple-trees are covered with rosy buds. Alfred dug the bed ready for the rhododendrons. A thrush was singing among the nightingales and other birds, as he said 'mad with joy.' At sunset, the golden green of the trees, the burning splendour of Blackgang Chine and St Catherines, and the red bank of the primeval river, contrasted with the turkis-blue of the sea (that is our view from the drawing-room), make altogether a miracle of beauty.[1]

This was the season and the setting when Dodgson, who was staying at Freshwater with his friend Collyns, visited Farringford for the first time. In a letter to his cousin William Wilcox he describes the event:

> There was a man painting the garden railings when I walked up to the house, of whom I asked if Mr Tennyson were at home, fully expecting the answer 'No', so that it was an agreeable surprise when he said, 'He's there, sir,' and pointed him out, and behold! he was not many yards off, mowing his lawn in a wide awake and spectacles. I had to introduce myself, as he is too short-sighted to recognize people, and when he had finished the bit of mowing he was at, he took me into the house to see Mrs Tennyson who, I was very sorry to find, had been very ill. . . . He took me over the house to see the pictures, etc. (among which my photographs of the family were hung 'on the line', framed in those enamel – what do you call them, cartons?). The view from the garret windows he considers

one of the finest in the island, and showed me a picture which his friend
Richard Doyle had painted of it for him; also his little smoking room at
the top of the house, where of course he offered me a pipe; also the
nursery, where we found the beautiful little Hallam, his son, who
remembered me more readily than his father had done.[2]

In the evening he called again for tea by invitation, and adjourned
with Tennyson and a clergyman friend to the smoking room for a
couple of hours. The proofs of the *Idylls of the King* were lying around,
but Tennyson would not let him read them. He was curious to see the
kind of books the poet had most readily to hand at his writing table, and
found that they were all Greek or Latin. The letter continues:

> It was a fine moonlight night and he walked through the garden with me
> when I left, and pointed out an effect of the moon shining through thin,
> white cloud, which I had never noticed before – a sort of golden ring, not
> close round the edge like a halo, but at some distance off. I believe sailors
> consider it a sign of bad weather. He said he had often noticed it and had
> alluded to it in one of his early poems. You will find it in 'Margaret'.[3]

On the following day he dined at Farringford, and met Sir John
Simeon, an old Christ Church man. Tennyson confessed to dreaming
passages of poetry which he always forgot when he woke up, except one
which he dreamed at the age of ten:

> May a cock sparrow
> Write to a barrow?
> I hope you'll excuse
> My infantine muse.[4]

In the smoking room they swapped horror stories, in which Tennyson
revelled. Dodgson described it as one of the most delightful evenings he
had spent for many a long day.

Oxford was in a state of great excitement on his return, for it was
about to receive a singular mark of royal favour. On 17 October 1859
the Prince of Wales came into residence at Christ Church. The entire
college turned out and lined up in the quadrangle to meet him. In a
letter to his father, the Dean described what happened:

> At five he came, and the bells struck up as he entered. He walked to my
> house between two lines of men, who capped him. I went out to meet
> him, and as we entered the house there was a spontaneous cheer. All
> through the streets, which were very full, the people cheered him well.
> Then I took him up to the drawing-room, and entered his name on the
> buttery book. He then retired with his Tutor, Mr Fisher, and put on a
> nobleman's cap and gown in the gallery, and returned to receive greet-
> ings as the first Prince of Wales who had matriculated since Henry V.[5]

The Prince remained at Oxford for two years, living at Frewin Hall,
attending lectures with four or five specially selected men and sometimes dining in Hall. Dodgson, who loved royalty, was very keen to

photograph him, and tried to persuade him to sit. His refusal was a great disappointment to Dodgson, but the prince had been pestered for photographs many times, and saw no reason to indulge this unknown Oxford don. Indeed, the Royal Family had every facility for acquiring photographs, the Queen and her Consort having their own photographic studio at Windsor Castle.

From a literary point of view Dodgson was more active in 1860 than in the preceding year. In January he produced two articles about photography, one of them a humorous essay called 'A Photographer's Day Out', published in the *South Shields Amateur Magazine*, and the other a review of the Photographic Exhibition which shows conclusively that Dodgson's success as a photographer was no accident, but the product of highly developed critical faculties. He contributed poems to *All the Year Round* and *College Rhymes*, and privately published the rules for Court Circular, a card game of his own invention. In addition he brought out two mathematical works, the *Syllabus of Plane Algebraical Geometry*, and a little booklet called *Notes on the First Book of Euclid*, which he published anonymously.

In April 1860 Dodgson went to stay with his Aunt Henrietta Lutwidge at her home in Warrior Square, Hastings. While there he consulted Dr James Hunt, author of *Stammering and Stuttering*. Dodgson's own stammer was far less serious than is often supposed, being mostly no more than a slight hesitancy, which added piquancy to his stories. In the presence of children it disappeared altogether, and he was able to sing and recite in their company, and to speak with confidence before large audiences. But he was extremely sensitive about it, and felt that he benefited from Dr Hunt's method. Nevertheless he felt obliged to advise Mrs Henry Taylor against sending her little girl, a stammerer, to stay with him, as he felt that Hunt's ungentlemanly behaviour might distress her.

It was probably on this visit that Dodgson first met George MacDonald, the novelist, at Dr Hunt's house. The two men had much in common and became lifelong friends. Already MacDonald had achieved literary acclaim with a narrative poem called *Within and Without*, which Tennyson had much admired, and with *Phantastes: a faerie romance* which he had brought out in 1858. Not long after his first meeting with MacDonald, Dodgson met two of his children at the studio of Alexander Munro, the sculptor. Greville, a delightful little boy, was posing for the 'Boy with the Dolphin' in Hyde Park and Mary, then aged about seven years, was there to keep a sisterly eye on him. 'I claimed their acquaintance,' wrote Dodgson, 'and began at once to prove to the boy, Greville, that he had better take the opportunity of having his head changed for a marble one. The effect was that in about two minutes they had entirely forgotten that I was a total stranger, and were earnestly arguing the question as if we were old acquaintances.' In his autobiography Greville MacDonald described their friendship:

> Uncle Dodgson's method was more potent than he knew, and it made him very dear to us. We would climb about him as, with pen and ink, he sketched absurd or romantic or homely incidents, the while telling us their stories with no moral hints to spoil their charm. I clearly remember his urging upon me – and quite in the manner of his 'Alice' fun – the advantage to myself if my head were marble: for then it would never suffer from combing its curls and could not be expected to learn lessons. But he drew for me with his pen one possible consequence, namely that such a head might terrify the sculptor Munro, to whom I was sitting . . .[6]

From Hastings Dodgson travelled to London, where, on the strength of a brief previous introduction, he sent his card to Holman Hunt and was kindly received by the artist, who allowed him a private view of his new picture, 'Christ in the Temple' at the Royal Academy. 'There were few people there, so that I saw it all capitally, and had also the treat of talking to the artist himself about it. It is the most wonderful picture I ever saw,' Dodgson wrote. From London he travelled to Rugby, to meet his youngest brother Edwin, who, with their cousin Jimmy Dodgson, was starting at Rugby School. Dodgson had often, in recent years, deputized for his father in matters affecting his brothers' education, and was well used to interviewing headmasters.

On 12 December 1860 the Queen paid a surprise visit to Oxford. Dodgson gives an account of the event:

> She arrived in Christ Church about twelve, and came into Hall with the Dean, where the Collections were still going on, about a dozen men being in Hall. The party consisted of the Queen, Prince Albert, Princess Alice and her intended husband, the Prince of Hesse-Darmstadt, the Prince of Wales, Prince Alfred, and suite. They remained a minute or two looking at the pictures, and the Sub-Dean was presented: they then visited the Cathedral and Library. Evening entertainment at the Deanery, *tableaux vivants*. I went a little after half past eight, and found a great party assembled – the Prince had not yet come. He arrived before nine, and I found an opportunity of reminding General Bruce of his promise to introduce me to the Prince, which he did at the next break in the conversation H.R.H. was having with Mrs Fellowes. He shook hands very graciously, and I began a sort of apology for having been so importunate about the photograph. He said something about the weather being against it, and I asked if the Americans had victimized him much as a sitter; he said they had, but he did not think they had succeeded well, and I told him of the new American process of taking twelve thousand photographs in an hour. Edith Liddell coming by at the moment, I remarked on the beautiful *tableau* which the children might make: he assented, and also said, in answer to my question, that he had seen and admired my photographs of them. I said that I hoped, as I had missed the photograph, he would at least give me his autograph in my album, which he promised to do. Thinking I had better bring the talk to an end, I concluded by saying that if he would like copies of any of my

photographs, I should feel honoured by his accepting them; he thanked me for this, and I then drew back, as he did not seem inclined to pursue the conversation.[7]

The promised autograph was duly given a few days later, and the Prince accepted about a dozen photographs.

In February 1861 Dodgson wrote to his sister Mary,

As you ask about my mathematical books I will give you a list of my 'works'.
1) Syllabus etc. etc. (done).
2) Notes on Euclid (done).
3) Notes on Algebra (done), will be out this week I hope.
4) Cycle of examples, Pure Mathematics (about 1/3 done).
5) Collection of formulae (half done).
6) Collection of symbols (begun).
7) Algebraical geometry in four volumes (about 1/4 volume one done, doesn't it look grand).[8]

It was indeed an impressive table of work, representing countless hours of painstaking research and analysis. Nos 1 and 2 of this list refer to the two mathematical works completed in 1860, and No. 3 to *Notes on the First Part of Algebra*. No. 5, *Formulae of Plain Trigonometry*, appeared in 1861, and item 4 was published in 1863 after an immense amount of work. Item 6 had to wait until 1866, when it appeared as *Symbols and Abbreviations for Euclid*, though in one volume only, and item 7 was published in the year following under the title *An Elementary Treatise on Determinants*.

On 20 November 1861 Dodgson made his first speech in Congregation, which met to consider the Dean's proposals to increase the stipend of Benjamin Jowett, the Regius Professor of Greek, from the ridiculously inadequate sum of £40 p.a. to the somewhat startling sum of £400. Jowett himself had commented in December of the previous year: 'Dr Stanley has been most kindly and vigorously trying to get an endowment for the Greek Professorship, but has hitherto been "dodged" by the inexhaustible resources of Dr Pusey.'[19] But Pusey was not the only objector. The matter was further complicated by the fact that Jowett was regarded by many as a heretic, as Dodgson explained:

The speaking took up the whole afternoon, and the two points alone, the endowing of the *Regius* Professorship, and the countenancing of Jowett's theological opinions, got so inextricably mixed up that I rose to beg that they might be kept separate. Once on my feet, I said more than I at first meant, and defied them ever to tire out the opposition by perpetually bringing the question on. (Memo.: if ever I speak again I will try to say no more than I had resolved before rising.)[10]

Two days later Dodgson wrote his first major Oxford 'squib' – a notice headed 'Endowment of the Greek Professorship'. Drawing attention to the dual proposals 'That the Corpus element be omitted, and the Professor of Latin be substituted for the Professor of Greek', he wrote:

> Here are two propositions, startling in their novelty, and demanding serious and separate consideration.
>
> The first, 'that the Corpus element be omitted', is a condition never before annexed to a Professorship, and which indicates but too clearly the wide influence which the so-called 'spiritualist' views have attained both in America and in this country.
>
> It may no doubt be desirable that a Professor should be free from the petty cares and distracting influences which are inseparable from our corporeal condition; still, as none but a member of All Souls' can possibly fulfil the stringent requisition here proposed, Members of Convocation are respectfully reminded that to confine this piece of preferment within such narrow limits would be illiberal, if not unjust to other Colleges.
>
> The second portion of the clause quoted above is as novel as the first, but so desirable an innovation, that it cannot be too widely known, or too heartily supported by Members of Convocation. There is no doubt that the substitution of Mr Conington for Mr Jowett would remove one of the most powerful elements of discord in this *'vexata questio'*, and would probably tend to its speedy and peaceful settlement. The question whether Mr Conington himself would consent to the change is one which has no doubt suggested itself to, and been fully considered by, the proposer of these amendments.

The pamphlet was published anonymously, but Dodgson's authorship was an open secret, and Jowett doubtless knew its originator. This could not have helped relations between them when they met at Farringford in April 1862, during the course of Dodgson's stay at Plumbley's Hotel, Freshwater. Tennyson had been ill for a considerable time, and Jowett, who regularly visited him at Christmas and at Easter, had reported in the previous year that the poet was greatly depressed:

> The more I see of him the more I respect his character, notwithstanding a superficial irritability and uneasiness about all things. I have pleasure in repeating this about him, because I find he is greatly mistaken by those who don't know him or only know him a little. No one is more honest, truthful, manly or a warmer friend; but he is as open as the day, and, like a child, tells any chance comer what is passing in his mind. . . . He is the shyest person I ever knew, feeling sympathy and needing it to a degree quite painful. Please not to repeat this to the vulgar, who can never be made to understand that great mental troubles necessarily accompany such powers as he possesses.[11]

But a year later he noted Tennyson's serious illness had passed, leaving him better than ever.

A few days before Dodgson's arrival Tennyson had been summoned to an audience with the Queen at Osborne. Princess Alice had expressed the wish that Tennyson should in some way 'idealize' Prince Albert, whose recent death had left the Queen distraught, but Tennyson wrote to her: 'I was unwilling to attempt the subject, because I felt that I might scarce be able to do it justice: nor did I well see how I should idealize a life which was in itself an ideal'.[12] Instead he decided to dedicate the *Idylls of the King* to the Prince, having inserted some lines on his death. Of his interview with the Queen he wrote: 'I loved the gentle voice that spoke, for being very blind I am very much led by the voice, and blind as I am and as I told her I was, I yet could dimly perceive so great an expression of sweetness in her countenance as made me wroth with those imperfect cartes de visite of Her Majesty which Mayall once sent me.'[13]

Clearly Tennyson was preoccupied, and somewhat to his disappointment Dodgson saw less of him than he had hoped. He lunched at Farringford on 16 April, but Tennyson only turned up for a few minutes at the end. But he saw much more of the two little boys, Hallam and Lionel. He taught them the game of 'elephant hunters', a game well known to the inhabitants of Croft Rectory, told them stories and took them to see Mrs Julia Margaret Cameron. Recently he had received from Mrs Cameron a photograph of Tennyson, in return for which he gave her a copy of *An Index to In Memoriam*, which had just been published by Moxon, Tennyson's own publisher. This interesting little book was compiled at Dodgson's suggestion and under his editorship by his sisters, and includes some three thousand references to Tennyson's elegy to his friend Arthur Hallam, after whom his eldest son was named. With punctilious correctness Dodgson had sought the poet's permission to publish, and by July of that year over five hundred copies had been sold. On the day after the luncheon party Dodgson met the two boys with Harry Taylor, son of Sir Henry Taylor, and Mrs Cameron's two little boys. They were all got up in a sort of uniform, and Dodgson showed them how to represent the Battle of Waterloo. Next day he called at Farringford and got the two little Tennysons to autograph his photograph album, and made a bargain with Lionel to exchange 'The Lonely Moor' for some of Lionel's verses. The subject chosen by Lionel included 'Death of the Prince Consort' and 'The Battle of Waterloo', thus demonstrating beyond doubt that he was a true son of the Poet Laureate. The last verse of the latter reads:

> Bury him in silence, silence, silence.
>   Bury the warrior in his tomb.
> Bury him in great silence, silence,
>   I trust that he goes to bliss.
> Farewell to him, farewell.

'I don't say that the verses were anything remarkable in themselves,' he wrote, 'but I certainly never saw any other child of eight who could write anything half so good.'[14] On 4 June 1859 Dodgson wrote to Mrs

Tennyson regarding the photograph of Hallam which he had taken in September 1857, and another of both Hallam and Lionel taken from a larger group photograph at the same time. His intention was to have them coloured by an artist for presentation to Mrs Tennyson, and with his usual attention to detail went to elaborate lengths to get the colouring accurate. The eyes would present no problem, but he wanted a few strands of hair to get the shade exactly right, and proposed that the hair should be fractionally lighter to allow for the general darkening during the two years that had elapsed since the photographs were taken.

Clearly relationships were still cordial at this stage, but in August 1862 Dodgson made a serious *faux pas* in his friendship with the Tennysons. The Laureate had been greatly vexed by the pirating of his early poems, a copy of which had come into Dodgson's possession. When he heard from the bookseller asking him to return it in view of the poet's objections, he wrote to Tennyson begging to be allowed to keep the book. Any such request was bound to fail with anyone as touchy and irritable as Tennyson, especially as he quite naturally regarded this as a matter of principle. This little episode may have been responsible for a decline in cordiality on the Tennysons' part, for when Dodgson returned to Freshwater for a month in July 1864 he seems to have seen Mrs Tennyson only very briefly, and her husband not at all.

There were compensations, however. Dodgson made several new friends, and greatly improved his acquaintance with Mrs Cameron, outwardly a somewhat strange lady, but highly talented and with great depth and warmth of character. Jowett wrote of her: 'She is a very honest, really kind, enthusiastic person: perhaps she has a tendency to make the house shake the moment she enters, but in this dull world that is a very excusable fault. She is a sort of hero-worshipper, and the hero is not Mr Tennyson – he only occupies second place – but Henry Taylor.'[15] Only three months previously Garibaldi had visited the Tennysons at Farringford, and Mrs Cameron had been introduced to him. 'Mrs Cameron wanted to photograph Garibaldi, and dropped down on her knees before him, and held up her black hands, covered with chemicals,' wrote Emily Tennyson in her diary. 'He evidently thought she was a beggar, until we explained who she was.'[16]

Strangely enough it was the presence of Mrs Cameron, short and squat and untidily dressed in dark shawls, as much as that of Tennyson which created at Freshwater a coterie atmosphere unequalled in England. 'To all who knew her she remains a unique figure, baffling all description,' wrote M. S. Watts. 'She seemed in herself to epitomize all the qualities of a remarkable family, presenting them in a doubly distilled form. She doubled the generosity of the most generous of the sisters, and the impulsiveness of the most impulsive. If they were enthusiastic, she was so twice over; if they were persuasive, she was invincible.'[17] Though she lacked physical beauty in the generally accepted sense, her compulsive charm acted as a magnet. 'The essential work of gathering together the interesting people who were to form the Tennyson Society, the enthusiasm for the hero and for genius in general, was Mrs Cameron's part,' wrote Wilfrid Ward.[18]

Dodgson had seen specimens of Mrs Cameron's work a month before at the Photographic Exhibition, and had remarked, 'I did *not* admire Mrs Cameron's large heads taken out of focus'. But nevertheless he welcomed her invitation to call at her home, Dimbola Lodge, for a mutual exhibition of photographs. 'Hers are all taken purposely out of focus', he wrote to his sister Louisa on 3 August. 'Some are very picturesque – some merely hideous – however, she talks of them as if they were triumphs in art. *She* wished she could have had some of *my* subjects to do *out* of focus – and *I* expressed an analogous wish with regard to some of *her* subjects.'[19]

There were many pretty children on the island and Dodgson regretted having left his camera behind. He called accordingly on Mrs Cameron and asked if she would photograph for him *in* focus the two prettiest, a daughter of Mr Bradley, the Master of Marlborough, and Rosa Franklin, whom his landlady had inaccurately identified as 'Colonel Fonkland's child'. When Mrs Franklin promised him the opportunity of photographing Rosa and the Bradley children, he succumbed to the temptation of sending for his camera. When his photographic apparatus arrived, he took photographs of Mrs Cameron and her sons at Farringford, where with the Tennysons' permission he set up his equipment and worked for six days. But the Tennysons themselves did not appear, and he had to content himself with photographing the house and grounds, and the servants. This latter was rare for Dodgson, who believed that the superior refinement of the upper and middle classes was visible in the features and facial expression, making then better subjects for photographs. The servants attached to the Tennyson household, however, earned a special distinction by their association with the poet. Perhaps, too, Mrs Cameron's interest in servants, whom she often photographed, was briefly infectious. Yet however enjoyable this holiday proved, the lack of contact with Tennyson was a disappointment.

Throughout his life Dodgson approached his problems with strict regard to the rule of formal logic. When one of his cousins offered him a hand-written copy of 'The Lover's Tale', an unpublished poem which Tennyson had written at the age of eighteen, he was mindful of the Laureate's reluctance to allow any unauthorized reading of his work; but here he felt that the circumstances were different and by his standard of logic felt entitled to expect a different response. Whereas the pirated edition was sold for profit without authorization, 'The Lover's Tale' was being passed from hand to hand without payment among a select coterie of Tennyson's admirers. Most people would simply have accepted the manuscript and enjoyed it in secret, but not Dodgson: nothing would satisfy his punctilious code of conduct except the poet's personal permission for him to have the manuscript, and without this he was not prepared even to read it privately. But Tennyson's mind simply did not work in the same way as Dodgson's, and a refusal was inevitable. When it arrived, Dodgson not only complied with Tennyson's wishes, but persuaded his cousin to destroy her copy.

In March 1870 Dodgson wrote again, this time asking permission to keep a manuscript of 'The Window', or 'The Loves of the Wrens', a song cycle which Tennyson had written in 1866. Emily Tennyson retorted curtly:

> Dear Sir,
>   It is useless troubling Mr Tennyson with a request which will only revive the annoyance he has already on the subject and add to it.
>   No doubt the 'Window' is circulated by means of the same unscrupulous person whose breach of confidence placed 'The Lover's Tale' in your hands.
>   It would be well that whatever may be done by such people a gentleman should understand that when an author does not give his works to the public he has his own reasons for it.
>   Yours truly,
>   Emily Tennyson.[20]

This harsh reply was ironically as unnecessary as Dodgson's scrupulousness. 'The Window' was not only circulating widely in manuscript, as Dodgson pointed out, but had actually been published in 1867 with Tennyson's consent at the Canford Manor Press. In fulfilment of a promise, but reluctantly, Tennyson allowed the songs to be published with a musical setting by Arthur Sullivan in December 1870. 'Alfred did not like publishing songs that were so trivial at such a grave crisis of affairs in Europe,' wrote Mrs Tennyson in her diary on 4 November 1870; 'but he had given his promise to Mr Sullivan about them, and "he that sweareth unto his neighbour and disappointeth him not" determined us. So they are to be published with the protest: "I am sorry that my four-year-old puppet should have to dance at all in the dark shadow of these days; but the music is now completed, and I am bound by my promise".'[21]

Dodgson could not countenance Mrs Tennyson's attack on his honour, and wrote two further letters to Tennyson on the subject. He decided to regard Tennyson's reply as a retraction, though it was clearly not an apology, and there were a few trivial items of correspondence later on. But the awe in which Dodgson regarded Tennyson had been finally dispelled, and direct personal contacts were never renewed. It was a sad ending to an acquaintance of which Dodgson had entertained such high hopes.

Preparation for ordination was Dodgson's major preoccupation during the four years covered by the missing diaries. He had already declared his positive intention to begin his preliminary reading programme at the end of 1858. Studies for ordination at that period were centred around Cuddesdon Theological College, which had been opened in 1854 by Samuel Wilberforce, Bishop of Oxford, to combat the imperfect preparation and 'want of clerical tone and religious habits' among candidates presenting themselves for Holy Orders. But in the aftermath of the ferment created by the Tractarian movement there was widespread mistrust of the College, and its first Principal, the Rev. Alfred Potts, wrote that there was a section of the clergy 'who could not divest themselves of the belief that any such institution must lead to the diocese of Oxford being sown broadcast with a body of Romanizing young clergy'.[22]

Dodgson did not enrol as a regular student at Cuddesdon, although he was in due course ordained there. This was in no way indicative of reservations on his part about the validity of its current religious teaching: but with his home background and steady personal conduct, as well as his capacity for private study and excellent past performances in Divinity examinations, he was fully able to prepare himself without breaking with his regular work at Christ Church. He had already consistently supported Cuddesdon activities, attending anniversaries and walking over to the College from time to time. One major incentive was the presence there of his great friend Henry Parry Liddon, who was its first Vice-Principal.

Liddon's spiritual mentor had been Dr Pusey, whose association with Newman and the Tractarian movement caused him to be feared by many. In 1843 Faussett, the Margaret Professor of Divinity, had brought charges against Pusey following a mildly controversial sermon, and as a result he had been condemned unheard and banned for two years from preaching in Oxford. Dodgson had been too young at that time to formulate views of his own on Dr Pusey's conduct, but the matter would certainly have been discussed in the Dodgson household. Archdeacon Dodgson's respect for his old friend Pusey was unabated, and was passed on to young Charles Dodgson.

Before accepting the post at Cuddesdon, Liddon had accepted Keble instead of Pusey as his mentor at his Bishop's insistence, in the hope that distrust would be dispelled. But Victorian Oxford, permanently obsessed by such issues as the number of candles on the altar, continued to harass Bishop Wilberforce with complaints. Repeated attacks on the College were made by the Rev. C. P. Golightly, who claimed to speak for the nobility and gentry of the diocese of Oxford, in condemning 'Romish ornaments and ceremonies' at Cuddesdon. Matters came to a head when Liddon administered Holy Communion to a convict on the morning of his execution. One West country newspaper described Liddon's action as a 'flagrant prostitution of the most sacred of all the ordinances of religion'. With the utmost reluctance Liddon left Cuddesdon at Easter 1859.

An article in *John Bull*[23] set forth the plain conviction that 'nothing was ever practised at Cuddesdon under the authority of the late Principal or Vice-Principal, either in the letter or spirit, that contravened the teaching of the Church', and another, in the *Record*,[24] said, 'The truth is that the polite dismissal of the very man, Mr Liddon, who stamped an impression on Cuddesdon College and made it a success, has turned out a more fatal mistake and a greater loss than was ever anticipated. Many enrolled themselves as alumni for the single and simple privilege of sitting at his feet, for he is verily a Tractarian "Gamaliel".' Liddon did not totally sever his connection with Cuddesdon, but made frequent visits, and was briefly in retreat there in 1860 and again in 1861. Already at the age of thirty Liddon was acknowledged as one of the most brilliant and compelling preachers of his era and Dodgson was supremely fortunate in his friendship with this outstanding young churchman. He often discussed theological matters with Liddon and unburdened himself to him on the vexed question of his fitness for ordination. In his diary Liddon records one such private visit on 11 December 1861, only a few days before Dodgson was due to be ordained.

Of Dodgson's doubts about being ordained his nephew, Collingwood, states: 'He was not prepared to live the life of almost puritanical strictness which was then considered essential for a clergyman, and he saw that the impediment of speech from which he suffered would greatly interfere with the proper performance of his clerical duties.'[25] Yet it is clear that this is no more than a retrospective rationalization of a situation in which Dodgson's major reason to doubt his fitness for ordination is masked. True, his delight in the theatre was something of an obstacle, in view of his bishop's expressed opinion that the 'resolution to attend theatres or operas was an absolute disqualification for Holy Orders'.[26] But from the 1840s the public theatre had cast off its former ill-repute, now making a strong appeal to the upper and middle classes, and the objections of Wilberforce and many others like him were based on the outmoded premise that all public theatres were places of sin and debauchery. Had Dodgson genuinely believed that theatres were intrinsically evil he would have had no difficulty in shunning them; but to him the object of acting was 'to raise the mind above itself', and the stage was 'an engine of incalculable power for influencing society'. His views on this issue, which remained unchanged throughout his life, are admirably set out in a letter to the father of Leslie (sic) Wright, a little girl he met on a train in the latter years of his life:

> The main principle, in which I hope all Christian men agree, is that we ought to abstain from *evil*, and therefore from all things which are *essentially* evil. This is one thing. It is a quite different thing to abstain from anything merely because it is *capable* of being put to evil uses. Yet there are classes of Christians (whose *motives* I entirely respect) who advocate, on this ground only, total abstinence from
> 1) the use of wine
> 2) the reading of novels or other works of fiction
> 3) the attendance at theatres
> 4) the attendance at social entertainments
> 5) the mixing with human society in any form.
> All these things are *capable* of evil use, and are frequently so used, and even at their best contain, as do *all* human things, some evil. Yet I cannot feel it is my duty, on that account, to abstain from any one of them. . . . Novels have been written, whose awful depravity would not be tolerated on the stage, by any audience in the world. Yet in spite of that fact, many a Christian parent would say, 'I do let my daughters read novels: that is *good* novels; and I carefully keep out of their reach the *bad* ones.'
> And so *I* say as to the theatres, to which I often take my young friends, 'I take them to *good* theatres, and *good* plays; and I carefully avoid *bad* ones.'[27]

Throughout his life Dodgson was careful to avoid plays which in any respect gave offence, being known to walk out if he found in any drama material which shocked him. His embargo sometimes extended to performances given in a reverential spirit, as the following extract of a letter to a friend, Helen Fielden, indicates:

> Many thanks for your history of the 'Oberammergau Passion Play', I am very much interested in reading accounts of that play ; and I thoroughly believe in the deep religious feeling with which the actors go through it; but would not like to see it myself. I should fear that for the rest of one's life the Gospel History and the accessories of a theatre would be associated in the most uncomfortable way. I am very fond of the theatre, but I had rather keep my ideas and recollections of it *quite* distinct from those about the Gospels.[28]

Troubled by Wilberforce's objections to theatre going, Dodgson consulted both Liddon and Pusey, who said that the Bishop's ban applied to the parochial clergy only. Liddon added that 'he thought a deacon might lawfully, if he found himself unfit for the work, abstain from direct ministerial duty'.[29]

There was a further problem that troubled Dodgson. He had a curiously naïve belief that others could be converted to his way of thinking if only his arguments were logical enough. His own reasoning processes were startlingly precise, with each thought developing in a seemingly natural sequence from that which preceded it. Yet for all his logic he overlooked one elementary fact: that those with whom he had to deal might be illogical, and not disposed to be converted. If he failed to convince, he was both puzzled and dismayed, blaming himself unreasonably for inadequately conceived lines of argument, and privately going over his points again and again in the hope of finding where he had gone wrong. With infinite patience he exercised his mind in establishing, by a method curiously like his father's, those fundamental religious truths that he felt all men would wish to know. A letter which he wrote many years later to Stuart Collingwood illustrates his reasoning:

> At Eastbourne, last summer, I heard a preacher advance the astounding argument, 'We believe that the Bible is true, because our Holy Mother, the Church, tells us it is.' I pity that unfortunate clergyman if he is ever bold enough to enter any Young Men's Debating Club where there is some clear-headed sceptic who has heard, or heard of, that sermon. I can fancy how the young man would rub his hands, in delight, and would say to himself, 'Just see me get him into a corner, and convict him of arguing in a circle!'
>
> The bad logic that occurs in many and many a well-meant sermon, is a real danger to modern Christianity. When detected, it may seriously injure many believers, and fill them with miserable doubts. So my advice to you, as a young theological student, is: 'Sift your reasons *well*, and, before you offer them to others, to make sure that they prove your conclusions.[30]

The doubt created in his mind by his failure to convince others is brought out in an incident with his own brother described in the diary on 2 February 1857:

> In the evening Wilfred and I had a long argument on college duties, he supporting the theory that each man should judge for himself on each particular college rule, whether he should obey it or not, and ignoring the principle of submission to discipline which would make him obey all alike. My arguments ended as all viva voce arguments seem to do, in returning to the starting point. The subject is worth further consideration, as I have at present no idea of what is the best course to take with one who starts from his premises.
>
> This also suggests to me grave doubts as to the work of the ministry which I am looking forward to – if I find it so hard to prove a plain duty to one individual, and that one unpractised in argument, how can I ever be ready to face the countless sophisms and ingenious arguments against religion which a clergyman must meet with![31]

Yet the real obstacle in Dodgson's mind was not his theatre-going, nor his stammer, nor even his occasional – and to some extent correctible – failure to convince sceptics by sound argument, but a sense of personal unworthiness so strong that it can only be described as obsessive. Knowing himself to be human, and therefore imperfect, he could not content himself with mere striving for perfection; he had actually to achieve it. The absolute impossibility of the task in no way diminished the countless hours of mental anguish that he spent brooding over it. Having to live with the problem was bad enough; but to live with the knowledge of the gulf between his own practice and the ideals which he preached was in his case the ultimate deterrent.

On 6 February 1863 he lists his 'bad habits', at least by implication. They are:

1) Failure to read the Bible and meditate before morning chapel;
2) failure to clear arrears of lecture work every evening;
3) indulging in sleep in the evening, and
4) failing to prepare the outlines of sermons methodically.

Those ominous-sounding sins with which he grapples are, after all, no more than a need of more regular habits.

'There is no surer way of making one's beliefs unreal than by learning to associate them with ludicrous ideas',[32] he once wrote to a friend. In a sermon preached at St Mary's Church, Oxford, towards the end of his life he dealt with the sin of using words of the Bible for jokes, a temptation that he confessed he had known himself. This must have been a particularly difficult sin for Dodgson to resist, for his humour was rooted in his intense preoccupation with the meaning of words, and was an entirely spontaneous reaction. Moreover he knew his Bible thoroughly, and could recite whole chapters from it. Once, without warning, he was asked to read the lesson in Chapel. The light was so bad that he could not make out the words, and confessed that he would have been in serious difficulties, except that he *knew* the whole passage by heart. But that familiarity which was such an asset, could at times prove a disadvantage, especially when, after dark, passages of scripture came crowding into his mind. His method of excluding irreverent thoughts was consciously to channel them into healthier areas of mental activity; indeed it was specifically to encourage others to use this method that in 1893 he published *Pillow Problems*, a set of seventy-two mathematical problems, all of them thought out in the dark.

To imagine that Dodgson adhered to this principle because he looked upon God as a stern, humourless figure, incapable of enjoying his children's laughter, would be a mistake. His motives need deeper analysis, and approximate to the reasons why he never repeated the innocently humorous remarks of children on sacred subjects. He states them fully in a letter to the Duchess of Albany in July 1889:

Is it not a cruelty (however unintentionally done) to tell anyone an amusing story of that sort, which will be forever linked, in his or her memory, with the Bible words, and which *may* have the effect, just when those words are most needed, for comfort in sorrow, or for strength in temptation, or for light in 'the valley of the shadow of death' of robbing those words of all their sacredness and spoiling their beauty.

There are many beautiful texts in the Bible that have been thus spoiled for *me*; and I have never, for years now, repeated any such story, lest I should cause to others the pain I cannot now avoid for myself: for our memories are not under our own command, and we often remember best what we most passionately long to forget.

Imagine some poor widow, in the first agony of grief, opening her Bible to read some of those wonderful words that bring the mourner peace and the hope of life beyond the grave, and finding that some wanton hand has scrawled the page with grotesque caricatures, and you will realize what I mean.[33]

In the late spring of 1861 Dodgson formally notified the Bishop of Oxford of his intention to offer himself at the Bishop's examination in September of the same year, to be ordained Deacon. From Croft, where he spent most of the summer vacation of 1861, he wrote to the Diocesan Registrar for the final details of the necessary formalities, and having passed the Bishop's examination, was ordained Deacon by Bishop Wilberforce at Cuddesdon on 22 December 1861. But ordination did nothing to remove his fears of personal unworthiness.

On 24 July 1862 Dodgson received two requests for sermons. He refused both. 'Till I can rule myself better, preaching is but a solemn mockery,' he wrote. 'Thou that teachest another, teachest thou not thyself? God grant this may be the last such entry I may have to make! that so I may not, when I have preached to others, be myself a castaway.'[34] With these doubts uppermost in his mind, Dodgson consulted Dean Liddell later in the same year to ask whether the terms of his Studentship made it obligatory for him to proceed to Priest's Orders. To his consternation, Liddell not only confirmed that they did, but said that, having been ordained Deacon, he must now consider himself a Clerical Student, and as such compelled to take Priest's Orders within four years of being made MA. Dodgson was dumbfounded, for he had always considered himself a lay Student. It was clearly impossible now for him to enter Priest's Orders within the specified period, since this had already elapsed. The Dean considered the Studentship already forfeited, and spoke of putting the matter before the electors. For a short while the security of his world at Christ Church, on which he so depended, was overturned. Fortunately, on further reflection, Liddell decided to take no action, leaving Dodgson entirely free to decide whether or not to proceed to Priest's Orders.

At the close of the year he had failed in his declared intention to start parochial work, still on account of his supposed unworthiness. 'Vile' and 'Worthless' were the words he used to describe a life that most people would have commended as pious, dutiful and unselfish. His diaries between 1862 and 1867 contain many pious exclamations, all clearly part of a disciplined plan to remind himself of his Christian obligations. By 1865 his doubts had largely diminished, and through-out the year he preached and conducted services frequently. During the course of that year his sermons alone totalled twenty, all different, and all carefully prepared and delivered. The texts were painstakingly noted in the diary to prevent repetition. To the composition of his sermons Dodgson contributed his natural meticulousness, together with that love of precise argument which he had inherited from his father, and which Mr Tate had remarked on during his schooldays at Richmond. He did not care to read his sermons, but sketched for himself an outline in note form, to which he could refer while he preached. But although he preserved by this means the illusion of perfect extempore delivery, his preparation was much more detailed and precise than the brief notes suggest, for he not only worked and reworked his subject matter in advance, but went over the material until he had it very nearly by heart. Always nervous beforehand, he quickly became oblivious to the congregation and thought only of the subject.

An obituary notice in the *Guardian* captures his style of delivery perfectly: 'Looking straight in front of him he saw, as it were, his argument mapped out in the form of a diagram, and he set to work to prove it point by point, under its separate heads, and then summed up the whole.'[35]

On 13 August 1865 he actually made a start by preparing a list of books to read for Ordination in the remaining six weeks of the long vacation. The list reads:

1) Old Testament – begin with Joshua.
2) New Testament – begin with Philippians.
3) Hooker.
4) Pearson.
5) Robertson's Church History.
6) Blunt on the Reformation.

His intention was to monitor his performance so that he could pace himself for his subsequent course of study. But he proceeded no further. A year later the theme of his unfitness recurs: 'Walked back with Jenkins, who told me much of his work as a clergyman among artisans – such work as I feel sadly my unfitness for.' And in April 1867, after an evening of looking at the drafts of Liddon's Bampton Lectures, and offering his services in proof reading, verification of quotations, etc., he finds himself querying his worthiness even to have entered Deacon's Orders: 'To have entered into Holy Orders seems almost a desecration, with my undisciplined and worldly affections.'[36]

To proceed further was now clearly impossible. By the summer of 1867 he had ceased preaching and assisting at services altogether.

Twenty-three years were to elapse before, haltingly and with many doubts as to his stammer and his personal inadequacies, he ventured into the pulpit again. Though he had amply demonstrated his ability to preach fluently, he began to advance his difficulties as a stammerer as the reason for his failure to proceed to Priest's Orders. He repeated the reason so often that it became genuine, and enabled him to conceal even from himself the fact that this was a mere excuse. 'A sermon would be quite formidable enough for me, even if I did *not* suffer from the physical disability of hesitation,' he wrote in 1891, 'but with *that* super-added, the prospect is sometimes almost too much for my nerves'.[37]

These were difficult days for anyone entering the Church. The aftermath of the great flowering of the Tractarian movement was still a powerful factor, and Newman's decision to go over to Rome clouded the issue still more in many people's minds. Max Müller wrote:

> I confess I felt puzzled to see these men, whose learning and character I sincerely admired, absorbed in subjects which to my mind seemed simply childish. I expected I should hear from them some new views on the date of the gospels, the meaning of revelation, the historical value of revelation, or the early history of the Church. No, of all this not a word. Nothing but discussions on vestments, on private confession, on candles on the altar, whether they were wanted or not, on the altar being made of stone or wood, of consecrated wine being mixed with water, of the priest turning his back on the congregation, etc.[38]

Of his own position Dodgson wrote:

> My dear father was what is called a 'High Churchman', and I naturally adopted those views, but have always felt repelled by the yet higher development called 'Ritualism'.
>
> But I doubt if I am fully a 'High Churchman' now. I find that as life slips away (I am over fifty now), and the life on the other side of the great river becomes more and more the reality, of which *this* is only a shadow, that the petty distinctions of the many creeds of Christendom tend to slip away as well – leaving only the great truths which all Christians believe alike. More and more, as I read of the Christian religion, as Christ preached it, I stand amazed at the forms men have given to it, and the fictitious barriers they have built up between themselves and their brethren. I believe that when you and I come to lie down for the last time, if only we can keep firm hold of the great truths Christ taught us – our own utter worthlessness and His infinite worth; and that He has brought us back to our one Father, and made us His brethren, and so brethren to one another – we shall have all we need to guide us through the shadows.[39]

REFERENCES

1   Hallam Lord Tennyson, *Alfred Lord Tennyson: A Memoir*, 1899, p. 347.
2   *Strand Magazine*, May 1901.
3   Ibid.
4   Ibid.
5   H. L. Thompson, *Henry George Liddell: A Memoir*, 1899, p. 177.
6   D.F.C. 18/5/6.
7   Collingwood, p. 83.
8   D.F.C. 18/5/7.
9   Abbott & Campbell (eds.), *Letters of Benjamin Jowett*, 1899, p. 171.
10 Collingwood, p. 91.
11 Abbott & Campbell (eds.), *Letters of Benjamin Jowett*, 1899, p. 172.
12 Hallam Lord Tennyson, *Alfred Lord Tennyson: A Memoir*, 1899.
13 Ibid.
14 D.F.C. 18/5/8.
15 Abbott & Campbell (eds.), *Letters of Benjamin Jowett*, 1899, p. 177.
16 Hallam Lord Tennyson, *Alfred Lord Tennyson: A Memoir*, 1899, p. 418.
17 *George Frederick Watts*, 1912.
18 *The Dublin Review*, January 1912.
19 Helmut Gernsheim, *Lewis Carroll: Photographer*, 1949.
20 Hudson, p. 109.
21 Hallam Lord Tennyson, *Alfred Lord Tennyson: A Memoir*, 1899, p. 501.
22 J. O. Johnstone, *Life of Henry Parry Liddon*, 1904, p. 32.
23 2 June 1860.
24 28 May 1860.
25 Collingwood, p. 74.
26 Ibid., p. 74.
27 D.F.C. 19/8/2.
28 Collingwood, p. 74.
29 Stuart Dodgson Collingwood, *The Lewis Carroll Picture Book*.
30 Collingwood, p. 301.
31 Green, p. 102.
32 John Francis McDermott, *The Russian Journal and other Selections*, New York, 1935, p. 15.
33 D.F.C.
34 Ms. Diaries.
35 Collingwood, p. 70.
36 Ms. Diaries.
37 Hudson, p. 301.
38 Max Müller, *My Autobiography*, 1901, p. 289.
39 Collingwood, p. 340.

7   Tell us a Story

As the spring of 1862 ripened into summer, the sparkling waters of the Isis began overtly to seduce the young men of Oxford, tempting them to abandon the leafy byways, the meadow and the Broad Walk and take to the boats. To Dodgson, revelling in the sound of oars in water and intoxicated by the ripples of children's laughter, those glorious summer days took on a special significance. Yet in spite of the sunlight and the laughter, he remained unaware that fate was propelling him inexorably towards that one golden afternoon when the eager curiosity of three little girls would stimulate his imagination and spur him to scale heights of creativity that he had never before attained. Though his days and nights had been filled with dreams of literary fame, he could scarcely have guessed that he was about to embark on a voyage of literary discovery in a region little explored by the world in general, and never seriously considered by Dodgson himself: the realm of children's books.

He had got into the habit of taking the Liddell children on the river four or five times a year. Their expeditions were carefully planned, and there was almost always a large basket of cakes. Sometimes they took a picnic hamper of cold chicken and salad to eat at Nuneham, where on Tuesdays and Thursdays William Harcourt allowed picnickers to land and dine in his purpose-built picnic huts; and often they would boil a kettle under a haycock and make tea. Now that Harry was away at school, the party usually consisted of the three little girls, Dodgson himself and one other man to help with the rowing: Skeffington or Wilfred perhaps, Southey the photographer, or Robinson Duckworth, always popular with the children because he sang so well. But even more popular than Duckworth's songs were the extempore stories which Dodgson invented for their amusement.

On 14 June Fanny, Elizabeth and Aunt Lucy came to stay in Oxford and three days later Dodgson, his two sisters, Duckworth and the three little girls made an expedition by boat to Nuneham. 'Our first duty was to choose the hut, and then to borrow plates, glasses, knives and forks from the cottages by the riverside', recalled Alice. 'To us the hut might have been a Fairy King's palace, and the picnic a banquet in our honour. Sometimes we were told stories after luncheon that transported us into Fairyland. Sometimes we spent the afternoon wandering in the more material fairyland of the Nuneham woods until it was time to row back to Oxford.'

The presence of the two Dodgson sisters, who seemed stout and elderly to the children, was somewhat inhibiting, and Alice reported that there were no songs or stories on this occasion. And after they had dined and walked in the park they started back; but they had only gone about a mile when they were caught in a heavy downpour which made them abandon the boat and continue on foot. For three miles they walked on through torrential rain and were soaked to the skin when they reached the house in Sandford where Dodgson's friend Ranken lodged. Here Dodgson and Duckworth left the ladies and children with Ranken's landlady, who helped them dry their clothes, while the two men walked on to Iffley and hired a fly to fetch the remainder of the party back to Oxford.

The afternoon having been thus marred, Dodgson made arrangements to take the children on the river again on 3 July; but again it rained, and the expedition was called off. Instead, Dodgson stayed to hear music and singing, and particularly enjoyed the trio's rendering of 'Sally come up', which they sang with great spirit. During the night the rain continued, but by lunchtime on the following day the clouds had cleared completely. After lunch Dodgson and Duckworth exchanged their clerical black for white flannels and boaters; but they retained their black boots, white tennis shoes being at that time unknown. They were now ready to escort the three little girls to Folly Bridge, where they hired a boat. They could not repeat their previous itinerary, for picnickers were not allowed to land at Nuneham on Fridays; so instead they rowed *up* the Isis to Godstowe, a journey which took them about two-and-a-half hours. Dodgson rowed bow, and Duckworth rowed stroke, and Alice and her sisters were stowed away in the stern. Probably, as usual, the children took the sculls which Dodgson laid in the boat for them while he was teaching them to row; but when they tired of this they clamoured for a story.

A quarter of a century later he wrote of that afternoon:

> I can call it up almost as clearly as if it were yesterday – the cloudless blue above, the watery mirror below, the boat drifting idly on its way, the tinkle of the drops that fell from the oars, as they waved so sleepily to and fro, and (the one bright gleam of life in all the slumberous scene) the three eager faces, hungry for news of fairyland, and who would not be said 'nay' to: from whose lips 'tell us a story, please' had all the stern immutability of Fate.[2]

When Dodgson sent his heroine down the rabbit hole he had no formal plan of her adventures in his mind. In adopting the dream convention he was using a literary device whose popularity was firmly established in the English literature of the Middle Ages, when 'Piers the Plowman' fell asleep 'Under a brode banke bi a bornes side' and the dreamers in *Pearl*, *The Dream of the Rood* and *Pilgrim's Progress* slept through visions of overwhelming religious significance. But Dodgson's purpose was not visionary, or moral, or didactic; he was merely adopting a form which gave him maximum flexibility to transport his young audience to a realm where fantasy reigned supreme, and from whose regions he could retrieve his heroine at the flicker of an eyelid. From time to time his inventive powers flagged and his voice grew weak. To earn a little respite he pretended to fall asleep, but always the importunate cries of his youthful crew forced him to rally and proceed.

Alice was now ten years old, three years older than the heroine of the story. There is nothing in Dodgson's existing diaries to indicate that Alice was already his favourite before that golden afternoon when the story of *Alice's Adventures* was first told. Indeed, at the outset, Lorina had stood foremost in his affections. But from that day forward there is no doubt at all that Alice became his dream child. Captivated by her gentle, affectionate nature, and her unfailing courteousness to all, whatever their station in life, he began to look upon himself as a kind of self-elected foster-father; and with her trusting readiness to accept the wildest improbabilities, her eager curiosity and a hint of assertiveness, she inspired him to write as he had never written before. For when, at the end of the day, he took the children back to Oxford, she begged him to write the story out for her, and he was quite unable to refuse her. Next morning, on the 9.02 train from Oxford to London, he began writing out the headings for the book.

Though term had ended, the Liddells lingered on in Oxford, and on 1 August Dodgson and his friend Harcourt, nephew of William Harcourt of Nuneham, called at the Deanery to ask leave to take the three children on the river again. To entertain their visitors, the little girls played a trio and sang a popular song by J. M. Sayles called 'Beautiful Star'. Next day the proposed excursion to Nuneham took place, Harcourt, Dodgson and the three Liddells being joined by Margaret and Ida Brodie, daughters of Sir Benjamin Brodie, the Professor of Chemistry. Afterwards the party adjourned to the Deanery lawn, where they all played croquet.

Four days later the two men took Alice, Lorina and Edith to Godstow, where they had tea. On the way Dodgson tried to interest them in a game called 'The Ural Mountains', but they were determined to hear a further instalment of *Alice's Adventures*, which Dodgson described as his 'interminable fairy-tale'.

On 1 July 1862 Dodgson had taken over from Richard Coles of Pembroke College the editorship of *College Rhymes*, a termly magazine in its third year of publication whose contributors were Oxford and Cambridge men. This had brought him into contact with Shrimpton's, an Oxford fine art and printing firm, who handled the printing of the magazine, and whose artist had been commissioned by Dodgson to colour his photographs of Lorina, Alice and Edith. Anxious for as good a likeness as possible, Dodgson wanted to arrange for the children to have a proper sitting with the artist, and went to Mrs Liddell for permission; but she simply evaded the issue. 'I have been out of her good graces ever since Lord Newry's business'[3] Dodgson commented. Lord Newry, an undergraduate who was a great favourite of the Dean's wife, was very keen to hold a ball which would contravene the general rules of the College, even allowing for the privileges bestowed at Oxford on the aristocracy. In his diary on 25 May 1862 Dodgson had written: 'Talked with Lord Newry about the difficulty the College are in about the ball: the two parties cannot agree on the rules and I am afraid much ill-feeling will result.' But it is unlikely that Dodgson anticipated that his attempt to maintain a consistent policy in college affairs would lead him into difficulties with the children's mother.

On 13 November he went for a walk with his friend Liddon, and on his return met Lorina, Alice and Edith in the quadrangle, where he had a little chat with them – 'a rare event of late' he added rather sadly. But this brief incident stimulated his resolve to compose the book, and later that day he began writing *Alice's Adventures* which he hoped to complete in time to present to Alice at Christmas. A few days later he records, 'Was surprised by a message from Mrs Liddell asking whether the children should come over to me, or if I would go to them. No alternative being offered, I chose the latter, and found that Alice and Edith had originated the idea, that I might put their crests in their books for them. With that, and a game of parlour croquet, I had a very pleasant two hours with them (Ina being in bed with a cold, and Mrs Liddell did not appear).'

By 10 February 1863 *Alice's Adventures* had become sufficiently significant for him to turn back the pages of his diary to mark out the day on which he first told the tale, and to note that he had now finished writing out the text. Perhaps his frequent contact with the children at this period increased his application to the task. But the pictures were nowhere near finished, and soon he borrowed a book of natural history from the Deanery to help him with the animal sketches, which he was determined to make as accurate as possible. The idea of publication had now taken shape and he sent the manuscript to George Mac-Donald and his wife to see how they – and their children – reacted to it.

Meanwhile his association with Alice led him to take up his pen for a different purpose. In his diary he wrote, 'I began a poem the other day in which I mean to embody something about Alice (if I can at all please myself by any description of her) and which I mean to call "Life's Pleasance" I gave up the name "Alice," as I want to put it in *College Rhymes*, and have had a poem sent in with that name.' This was not his first attempt at a commendatory poem addressed to a little girl, for in December 1862 he had addressed a poem to Beatrice Ellison, a beautiful little girl whom he had photographed frequently the previous summer. The poem had appeared in *College Rhymes* in the final term of 1862. But 'Life's Pleasance', the title of which was based on Alice's second name, never appeared in *College Rhymes*. On 20 March Dodgson went for a walk with his friend Fowler, who, as Junior Proctor, shared responsibility for college discipline. He took the opportunity of discussing with Fowler an unspecified 'scrape' which Shrimpton, an undergraduate, had got into, and for which he was likely to be 'discommonsed', that is, expelled. This placed Dodgson in a dilemma, since the Shrimpton family printing firm handled *College Rhymes*. Five days later Dodgson resigned his editorship, returning all the poems, and asking some of the contributors whether they would support a similar magazine under his editorship. The new magazine did not materialize, and 'Life's Pleasance' had to wait until 1871 for publication, when it appeared as a dedicatory poem in *Through the Looking-Glass*.

In April Dodgson was invited to call on the Liddells at Hetton Lawn, Charlton Kings, where they were staying with their grandmother. Although he took a room at the Belle Vue Hotel, Cheltenham, for the duration of his four-day visit, Dodgson spent nearly all his time with the children and Miss Prickett, joining the entire family on excursions and taking most of his meals at Hetton Lawn. It was Easter week, and life was very quiet in Cheltenham, but the *Cheltenham Looker-On*[4] advertised the 'wonderful tricks and sleight of hand' of Herr Döbler, the famous Viennese magician: 'As there are no other public entertainments provided for the amusement of the good people of Cheltenham in the Easter Week,' the article ran, 'they will, doubtless, be glad enough to avail themselves of the opportunity to be afforded them of visiting Herr Döbler's "Enchanted Palace of Illusions".' Dodgson, always fascinated by conjurers, attended a performance with the children and the rest of the house party. These were magical days for him and the three little girls, and it can hardly be doubted that his stories were as much in demand as ever. Perhaps some of them later grew into episodes in *Through the Looking-Glass*. Indeed, the house at Hetton Lawn had a special significance, for it possessed a mirror, still in existence, over the mantelpiece, identical to that portrayed by Tenniel in *Through the Looking-Glass*. Dodgson reported that the children were in the wildest spirits, and this doubtless helped to fire his creative genius.

From Cheltenham Dodgson moved on to Tenby, where a number of his relatives lived, including Menella Smedley. During this visit he called on Horatio Tennyson, brother of the Laureate, returning to Cheltenham eight days later. Owing to a misunderstanding, he missed the Liddells, to whom he had proposed a final excursion, but enjoyed a very merry journey back to Oxford with them. On the following day Harry and the three girls were boating with him, chaperoned by Miss Prickett, by Mrs Liddell's wish. Dodgson did not consider this unreasonable, as he felt that Ina was so tall as to look odd without one. The expedition was only a partial success, for the friend who went along to help with the rowing proved almost useless, while Harry, who sculled by himself, managed to be forever in the way. Four days later he visited Alice, who was laid up with a sprained leg, but commented, 'Alice was in an unusually imperious and ungentle mood, by no means improved by being an invalid'.

A few days later, the party, this time consisting of Harry, the three girls, Miss Prickett, Dodgson and Duckworth, went on the river again, when Dodgson sang to them 'Miss Jones', a song he had composed himself, and set to a cento of popular melodies, with some assistance from one of his sisters.

At about this time a cloud hung over the Deanery. Mrs Liddell had given birth to a son, whose health caused great anxiety. He was hastily baptized on 2 May, 'Albert Edward Arthur', the names chosen by the Prince of Wales, who was Godfather, together with Dr Stanley. But two days later the boy died. And as if this was not enough, vandals by night desecrated the Deanery garden, destroying all the plants and shrubs. Dodgson did his best to take the children's mind off these troubles, spending a great deal of time with them, and teaching them *Croquet Castles*, a game of his own invention, the rules of which he published privately that same year. Some weeks later they made a river excursion to Nuneham, and on this occasion Dodgson had just had the manuscript of his song returned by the singer John Parry, who described it as clever, but unsuitable for his current repertoire.

Oxford, like many communities throughout the country, had celebrated in style the wedding of the Prince of Wales to Princess Alexandra of Denmark on 10 March 1863. To mark the occasion, Lorina, Alice and Edith had publicly planted three trees along the Cherwell, and named them Alexandra, Albert and Victoria. Dodgson and his youngest brother, Edwin, had gone into the Broad Walk to watch the ceremony and hear each of the children pronounce a tiny speech over her tree. Afterwards Dodgson had escorted the children and their grandmother, Mrs Reeve, to see an ox roasted whole near Worcester College – '*not* an exciting spectacle', commented Dodgson. Later they had watched the Torpid race from the barge, where they again met the Liddells, and finally rounded off the day by taking Alice to see the firework display.

In June the royal bride and bridegroom favoured Oxford with a three-day visit. On the day before their arrival, Dodgson was taken over to the Deanery, where he was shown the Royal Chamber, splendidly furnished. Noticing a photograph album with the plume of the Prince of Wales emblazoned on a magnificent onyx, he offered to supply *cartes de visite* from his own collection, and spent a couple of hours filling it. While he was there, he received a note from Lorina, begging him to come and help them with the stall they were setting up in St John's Gardens for a bazaar on the following day. He accordingly spent about four hours with the children, putting up cards and arranging items.

On the day of the royal couple's arrival Dodgson had an excellent view of the proceedings from Bayne's room. Bayne himself was not there, for as Pro-Proctor he was required at the Sheldonian Theatre, but he obligingly broke a pane from his window to accommodate Dodgson's telescope. After accompanying Mrs Bayne to the Sheldonian, Dodgson went on to the bazaar, where he helped the children again, and spoke briefly to the Prince. A banquet in Hall rounded off the day. The following day Dodgson attended Commemoration, followed by an excellent cold collation at All Soul's College and another stint at the bazaar. But this time the Liddell children left the bazaar at four to play croquet at the Deanery with the royal guests. After their departure he went with his friend Harington to see the boat procession, and fell into dispute with the cab driver, who wanted double pay.

The royal party left Oxford the following afternoon. Once again, Dodgson had helped the children at the bazaar, where they had been getting up raffles. A few days later, using a special process in which the collodion was kept moist with treacle, enabling him to transport the plate to his darkroom, he took a photograph of the bedstead in the royal bedchamber at the Deanery, and another external photograph of the Cathedral and Deanery, with Alice and Ina clearly visible at the window of the royal room.

On 9 May the MacDonalds had returned the manuscript of *Alice's Adventures*. They were most enthusiastic and urged him to publish. Greville MacDonald later recalled how his mother read it to her children:

> I remember that first reading well, and also my braggart avowal that I wished that there were sixty thousand volumes of it. Yet I distinctly recall a certain indignant grief that its characters were only a pack of cards; and I still look on that *FINIS* as a blemish upon the sublime fantasy. Doubtless Charles Dodgson felt that a child must never be deceived even by a fairy tale. And he was right; though there would have been little or no risk of this, had he left his immortal narrative just a fairy tale that needed no justifying.[5]

Encouraged by the MacDonalds' response to the manuscript, Dodgson asked his friend Mr Combe, a printer to the University associated with the Clarendon Press, to set up a sample page of it in type. Obviously the first trial page did not suit Dodgson, for on 2 July 1863 he records receiving from Mr Combe a second trial page, larger than the first. Two weeks later he called with his first drawing on wood. Combe was an avid collector of Pre-Raphaelite art who ultimately bequeathed his collecton to the Ashmolean Museum. When Dodgson arrived he found him with Thomas Woolner, one of the original Pre-Raphaelite brethren, who was just starting work on a bust of Combe. The drawing which Dodgson had brought with him was a half-length drawing of his heroine. When Woolner saw it, he immediately condemned the arms, impressing on Dodgson the absolute necessity of working from life. It was a notion to which Dodgson was naturally receptive, and to which he increasingly adhered as time went on. Less than three weeks later Dodgson called on Orlando Jewitt in Camden Town and left with him a block he had drawn, to be cut on wood. Jewitt gave him some useful general advice, and agreed to improve a little on Dodgson's block when he cut it.

During the last few months, Dodgson's meetings with the Liddells had been so frequent as to be almost continuous. But on 12 June 1863 he had written, almost prophetically, 'Not all days are to be marked with white stones'.[6] That summer was to be the last in which he saw the children with any regularity, though there were occasional temporary resumptions of the friendship. During the period February 1863 to May 1864 two major changes of intention revolutionized Dodgson's concept of *Alice's Adventures*, namely, his decisions to double the length of text, and to employ a professional illustrator. Neither decision can be dated exactly, but enough data exist to enable certain conclusions to be drawn.

The book which Dodgson always referred to as the manuscript was in fact the fair copy which he prepared for presentation to Alice Liddell at the time when he had no thought of publication. Though he never mentions any form of rough draft other than the outline chapter headings written out on the London train, his lifelong working methods leave no room for doubt that such a draft once existed. Dodgson was a constant reviser of texts, even after publication, so that his work was always liberally marked with deletions, insertions and rearrangements. Often he would write on the back of used sheets of paper, for in the nineteenth century paper was still costly, and Dodgson, an orderly, methodical man, hated waste. After his death many of his papers were burned, but enough remain to show such items as poetry written on the back of a Punch cartoon, and plans for extending the family house drawn up on the reverse of mathematical notes.

The manuscript fair copy of *Alice's Adventures Underground* contained some 18,000 words, but when the tale was published, it had been extended to 35,000. Possibly the idea of extending the book was suggested by the MacDonalds, or by another friend, Mrs Ottley, who borrowed the manuscript in July 1863. Dodgson may alternatively have taken up the idea in discussion with Combe, or Jewitt, or with Macmillan himself, whom he met at Combe's house on 19 October 1863, and who agreed to print some of Blake's *Songs of Innocence* for him on large paper. On the other hand, he may have taken the decision when he invited Tenniel to do the pictures. The original text had taken about three months to produce, and Dodgson handed the first chapter of his final draft to Macmillan's on 6 May 1864, about three months after asking Tenniel to illustrate it. Thus the time schedule would be roughly consistent with his earlier rate of progress, and would accord well with his later practice of settling the illustrator before starting to write.

The title *Alice's Adventures Underground* was permanently reserved for the presentation manuscript, but Dodgson had second thoughts about the title of the published book, toying with 'Alice's Hour in Elfland' on 9 June 1864. The final version, *Alice's Adventures in Wonderland*, occurred to him on 28 June 1864, though even so he deleted the heroine's name from the title at one stage.

When Dodgson wrote out the presentation manuscript, he left spaces for the insertion of illustrations. The thirty-seven drawings which he eventually provided are uneven in quality, and seem to indicate a development in his ability as a draughtsman as the project proceeded. Certainly he worked hard on the illustrations. In the library at Christ Church there are still several pages of trial sketches, including a picture (not used) of the Mock Turtle signed by his brother Wilfred. The earliest pictures to be inserted can be easily identified. Those which include the White Rabbit appear to pre-date his borrowing the Dean's book of Natural History, for the rabbit is stiff and lifeless, even allowing for the difficulty of the clothes. How much more satisfying is the drawing of Alice leading the curious creatures to the shore. An intermediate stage is seen in the picture of Alice swimming with the mouse, where the mouse is moderately credible (though less lifelike than the curious creatures), while Alice is not well conceived, the face, which is all that is clearly visible, appearing hard and adult, as is the face of her sister in the first drawing in the book.

The illustration which Dodgson showed to Woolner cannot be positively identified, but only one picture in the finished manuscript could remotely be described as a half-length of Alice. There can be no doubt that Dodgson took Woolner's advice and began to draw from life. The question then arises as to who was his model. One fact is clear:

it was not Alice Liddell. For Alice had short, straight dark hair cut in a fringe, while the heroine of the book had long waved hair parted in the middle, of a type dear to the Pre-Raphaelite brethren. Moreover, Alice was already ten years old on the day of that historic expedition to Godstowe, whereas the heroine of the story is only seven. But there was one member of the Liddell family who was ideally suited to sit for the pictures: Edith, two-and-a-half years younger than Alice, with long, luxuriant, waving, Titian-coloured hair parted in the middle; she was also gentle, obedient and well used to posing for Dodgson's photographs, often for relatively long periods. To sit still in Dodgson's company while he entertained her with his marvellous stories and inventions was no hardship to Edith. Though he saw much less of the Liddells between his discussion of the drawing with Woolner and his completion of the pictures at Croft on 13 September 1864, no other models appear possible from the record of the diaries. The only other children with whom he had frequent contact in that period were the MacDonalds, of whom he was very fond. Indeed in January 1864 he commissioned an artist called Darvall to colour in oils a photograph he had taken of Irene MacDonald. But Irene bore no resemblance to Dodgson's drawings, and the other girls can be eliminated on the grounds of their age.

A factor which must be taken into account in any critical appraisal of his drawings is Dodgson's pre-occupation with the visual arts, his growing circle of acquaintances among artists, and essential similarities between Dodgson's drawings and those of the artists whose studios he frequented in this, his most creative period. These artists included Arthur Hughes, Holman Hunt, Millais, Munro, Rossetti, Ruskin, Watts and many others besides. His personal library contained many books about art, and his walls were lined with prints and photographs.

Dodgson made the acquaintance of Dante Gabriel Rossetti in October 1863, and a few days later set up his photographic apparatus in his house in Cheyne Walk, Chelsea. Here he photographed the various members of the Rossetti family, including Dante Gabriel's brother William and sister Christina, severally and in groups. He also looked through a huge volume of Rossetti's drawings, and commented, 'I had never seen such exquisite drawings before'.[7] Twice more he returned during that vacation, on the third occasion spending most of the day photographing Rossetti's drawings.

Jeffrey Stern has pointed out[8] the similarity between Dodgson's drawing of Alice in the White Rabbit's house, and a drawing by Rossetti of Annie Miller, a print of which Dodgson owned. Rossetti, in common with many artists, usually managed to adapt the features of his models to his own idealized concept of the female face. If Edith

Liddell was indeed Dodgson's model, relatively little adaptation would be necessary, for she already possessed the type of beauty, albeit as yet undeveloped, so much beloved by Rossetti and his circle. But by an exaggeration of the melancholy mouth, the soulful eyes and abundant waving hair Dodgson intensifies his drawing in a manner that is truly Pre-Raphaelite.

In the same article Mr Stern points out a certain similarity of pose between one of Dodgson's drawings of Alice and an oil-painting by Arthur Hughes entitled 'The Lady with the Lilacs' which Dodgson bought from Hughes in October 1863, and hung over the mantelpiece in his study.

> The melancholic bittersweetness that gives Hughes' work such power is also a quality never far away in Wonderland. It seems therefore predictable that Carroll liked Hughes' canvas of a melancholic maiden at the moment of imminent decay enough to buy it, proudly hang it on a wall of his study and look admiringly up at it as he illustrated his masterpiece. It seems similarly fitting that Carroll responded to Rossetti's anima image and his world of ultimate beauty. . . . Because portrayal of these emotions was a pressing Pre-Raphaelite concern, Carroll was more than a mere art gallery visitor; he was a Pre-Raphaelite.[9]

At the foot of Dodgson's manuscript he pasted a photograph of Alice Liddell. In 1977 Professor Morton Cohen persuaded the British Museum to remove this temporarily, enabling a photograph to be made of a drawing beneath. What was revealed is the only surviving art portrait made by Dodgson of his young heroine, and although it has less intensity of feeling than the photograph, it is revealed as an acceptable and accurate portrait.

The manuscript of *Alice's Adventures Underground* which was finally presented to Alice on 26 November 1864 as a Christmas gift is still in existence. Alice was an old lady of seventy-six when, in 1928, she finally had the manuscript auctioned at Sotheby's. Her pangs at parting with her treasure could have been only partly eased by the highly satisfactory price of £15,400. The purchaser, Dr A. S. W. Rosenbach, sold it to the American collector Eldridge R. Johnson, for £30,000 only six months later. In 1946, after Johnson's death, Rosenbach bought it back for $50,000. But the then librarian of Congress, Luther H. Evans, felt so strongly that the manuscript belonged in England, that he raised the sum of $50,000 from various private individuals to buy it back, and indeed would have been prepared to go to $100,000. In 1948 he handed it over to the British Museum – 'an unsullied and innocent act in a distracted and sinful world',[10] commented the Archbishop of Canterbury, who accepted the gift on the Museum's behalf.

When Dodgson finally decided to use a professional illustrator for *Alice's Adventures in Wonderland*, it was his friend Tom Taylor of *Punch* who wrote to John Tenniel on his behalf, and gave him a note of introduction. He called on Tenniel for the first time on 25 January 1864 and found him receptive to the idea of undertaking the illustrations, though he would not commit himself definitely until he had studied the manuscript.

Tenniel had spent his childhood in Kensington, where he had been a friend of the sons of John Martin, the painter, who had aroused his interest in drawing. But apart from a few lessons at Academy schools, which he had abandoned in a spirit of dissatisfaction, he had no formal training. Later he studied anatomy and sculpture at the British Museum, and through a Government Commission set up to beautify the Houses of Parliament, went to Munich to study fresco techniques. The result was a failure, for all the artists' frescoes rapidly faded. In 1850 he joined the staff of *Punch*, rapidly achieving a high reputation with his political cartoons, and when Leech died in 1864, succeeding him as leading *Punch* cartoonist. His first book illustrations had appeared in *Hall's Book of British Ballads* in 1842, followed by *Undine* in 1845, *Aesop's Fables* in 1848 and *The Gordion Knot* in 1860. His chief reputation as a book illustrator rested on his drawings for *Lalla Rookh*, published in 1861, and he collaborated with Cruikshank and Leech in *The Ingoldsby Legends*, which were brought out in 1864.

To some extent Tenniel's work suffered because he had failed to appreciate both the possibilities and the limitations of wood block technique. He almost invariably worked in pencil, and his fine lines tended to be lost in reproduction, as his later work on steel indicates. He did not normally use a model, and his animal drawings are his strongest point, which probably explains why Dodgson's book interested him. Ruskin said of him, 'Tenniel has much of the largeness and symbolic mystery of imagination which belong to the great leaders of classic art: in the shadowy masses and sweeping lines of his great compositions, there are tendencies which might have won his adoption into the school of Tintoret.'[11]

On 5 April 1864 Tenniel finally accepted the commission, and on 2 May Dodgson dispatched to him the first galley proofs, which were taken from the beginning of Chapter III. But the manuscript batch of the first chapter, which was largely unaltered from the original, was not sent off to the press by Dodgson until 6 May.

Alice's Adventures Underground contained numerous private jokes. There were references to the wetting the party had got on the earlier excursion to Nuneham, and to their drying off at Sandford; to the song 'Sally come up' that the children had sung with such spirit, and which reappeared as 'Salmon come up'; to their games of croquet on the Deanery lawn, to their lessons, and to little girls known to Alice. For the sake of anonymity, Gertrude and Florence became Ada and Mabel in the new longer version; 'Salmon come up' was omitted, the mouse's tail was improved and the clothes drying session by the fire was replaced with the Caucus Race. Two entirely new chapters, 'Pig and Pepper' and 'A Mad Tea Party' were introduced, and after all the revisions and expansions the book contained a dozen chapters in all. The somewhat trivial Marchioness had disappeared, leaving room for that marvellous virago, the Ugly Duchess, and three new poems, 'Speak Roughly to Your Little Boy,' 'Will You Walk a Little Faster' and ' 'Tis the Voice of the Lobster' had been added.

Of the numerous allusions it should be mentioned that Dodgson and Duckworth appear in the story as the Dodo and Duck respectively, and Lorina and Edith as the Lory and the Eaglet. All three little girls reappear at the bottom of the treacle well, as Elsie (LC, LORINA CHARLOTTE) Lacie (an anagram of ALICE) and Tillie (for MATILDA, Edith's nickname). The Mad Hatter may have been suggested by a *Punch* article[12] entitled 'Mad as a Hatter', which concludes: 'We think we can venture to observe that the madness of a hatter must be, from the nature of his calling, peculiarly one of those things that are said to be more easily *felt* than described', and the caterpillar on the mushroom smoking a hookah may derive from a *Punch* illustration of a frog, similarly seated, smoking two enormous pipes.[13]

The croquet match, obviously the sort of game that royal people played, was a reminder not only of Dodgson's variant, *Castle Croquet*, but of the children's recent game of croquet with the heir to the throne and his bride, though the gentle Princess Alexandra cannot have been the inspiration for the formidable Queen of Hearts. As to Mary Ann, the White Rabbit's maid, Mrs Cameron had a parlour maid called Mary Ann whom she often used to photograph. Dodgson, who had recently returned from Freshwater, had been to her house, and had probably met the girl, who was fifteen years old in 1862. Gloves were the hallmark of good breeding, but to Mrs Cameron, whose hands were permanently blacked with chemicals, they were almost indispensable. Perhaps Dodgson had even heard her call, 'Why, Mary Ann, what *are* you doing out here? Run home this moment and fetch me a pair of gloves and a fan!'

On 20 June 1864 Dodgson called on Tenniel and found, somewhat to his disappointment, that he had not yet begun the pictures. This was perhaps fortunate, for on the following day he called on Macmillan, who convinced him that it would be better to alter the page size and adopt that used for the second edition of Charles Kingsley's book *The Water Babies*. Tenniel readily agreed to the change.

Dodgson was fortunate in finding a publisher as prestigious and experienced as Macmillan to undertake publication for him. But the expenses were to be borne by Dodgson, at his own wish, including the cost of paying the artist. During the next few months he was in constant touch with Tenniel. His own visual concept of the way the book should be illustrated was so firmly established that all he really required from Tenniel was the draughtsmanship that he himself lacked. This made him a difficult and hypercritical taskmaster. Remembering Woolner's advice, he expected Tenniel to use a model for Alice and sent him a photograph of a little girl called Mary Hilton Badcock, a canon's daughter, who would in his view be an ideal model. But except for the long blonde hair, there was no similarity between the little girl and Tenniel's final realization of the heroine.

'Mr Tenniel is the only artist, who has drawn for me, who has resolutely refused to use a model, and declared he no more needed one than I should need a multiplication table to work a mathematical problem!' Dodgson wrote. 'I venture to think that he was mistaken and that for want of a model, he drew several pictures of "Alice" entirely out of proportion – head decidedly too large and feet decidedly too small.'[14] Dodgson was right, of course. Tenniel, a childless widower, had little experience of drawing children, and many of his pictures of Alice portray her as a miniaturized adult rather than as a real child. But for all that the pictures are curiously satisfying. Both men shared a preoccupation with life rather than scenery and Tenniel's backgrounds are rarely more than crosshatching, with total concentration on the characters themselves.

It had been Dodgson's hope that *Alice's Adventures in Wonderland* would be out in time for Christmas 1864; but towards the end of the year Tenniel's mother died, and he wrote to Dodgson in great distress. With characteristic sympathy, Dodgson begged him to put aside his work on the pictures for the time being; a magnanimous gesture, for the Liddells were growing up so fast that he was anxious to press on with publication.

Most authors would have been content to leave matters of detail to the publisher, but not Dodgson. His perfectionism and passion for detail, and his love of gadgetry, particularly when it facilitated the achievement of his own aims, all combined to foster his personal interest in the minutiae of day-to-day publishing business. As early as March 1857 he had entertained the notion of purchasing a small handprinting machine, and had approached his friend Combe to see whether he could tell him where to get one. But Combe advised him strongly against the idea, which he considered was bound to fail, and suggested that it would be better to give any small items he wanted done to a 'job printer'. Dodgson took his advice, but his fascination with the printing process and all connected with it persisted throughout his life. He must have been something of a trial to his publishers, as he himself in later years acknowledged:

The day when they undertake a book for me is a *dies nefastus* for them. From that day till the book is out – an interval of some two or three years on an average – there is no pause in 'the pelting of the pitiless storm' of directions and questions on every conceivable detail. To say that every question gets a courteous and thoughtful reply – that they are still outside a lunatic asylum – and that they still regard me with some degree of charity – is to speak volumes in praise of their good temper and of their health, bodily and mental.[15]

In the event, Tenniel did not hand in the last of the illustrations until 18 June 1865. The Clarendon Press had sent Dodgson the first page, at a cost of two shillings, on 13 May 1865 and Macmillan had forwarded a specimen volume, blank except for the first sheet, bound up in the smooth bright red cloth that the author had chosen for its child appeal. By the end of June two thousand copies had been printed at the Clarendon Press and the first copy, specially bound in white vellum, was dispatched to Alice at the Deanery just in time for the third anniversary of the famous river expedition. Curiously, Dodgson did not record in his diary the receipt of the first copies nor Alice's response, but on 15 July he notes that he called at Macmillan's and inscribed about twenty or so presentation copies of the book. But on 20 July 1865 the blow fell. Tenniel had written to say that he was 'entirely dissatisfied with the printing of the pictures', and Dodgson, fearing that the edition would have to be done again, called on Macmillan to discuss the matter.

For many years Dodgson's hypercritical personal reaction was blamed for his decision to withdraw the first edition and have it done again. But the fact is that Tenniel's criticisms were the deciding factor. Perhaps Tenniel, having suffered Dodgson's criticism with all the patience he could muster, was now over-reacting, consciously or subconsciously, to months of pressure. Probably he did not really expect Dodgson to cancel the entire first issue. But Dodgson felt a dual responsibility, both to his artist, whom he respected, and to the public, to whom he always offered his best. On 2 August he took the decision to withdraw and reprint.

The whole thing seemed likely to Dodgson to represent serious financial disaster. The costs to date had been:

	£
Drawing of pictures	138
Cutting	142
Printing by Clarendon Press	137
Binding and advertising, estimated	80
	£497

The electrotypes for the new edition were to be taken from the original woodblocks, with a few very minor subtractive changes. But he was horrified to find that Clay, the new printer, would charge £240, about double the cost of the work done at the Clarendon Press. By Dodgson's estimate the total financial loss resulting from withdrawal and reprinting was likely to be in the region of £200, though if a second two thousand could be sold, it would cost only £300, against an income of £500, which would cancel out the loss.

In the event the Clarendon Press wrote off £271 1s, and there remained the question of what use should be made of the unbound sheets. Millais, with whom Dodgson was becoming increasingly friendly, advised reserving them for a future edition. The possibilities, as listed by the author in a letter from Croft Rectory to Macmillan were as follows:

(a) reserve them till next year to 'sell in the provinces' (as has been suggested to me) or to send abroad, but keeping the price at 7s 6d.

(b) sell them at a reduced price (say 5s) as being avowedly an inferior edition, stating in the advertisement what the two editions differ in.

(c) get Mr Clay, or some other experienced man, to look them over and select all such sheets as happen to be well printed – use these along with the London-printed copies and sell the rest as waste paper.

(d) sell the whole as waste paper.[16]

Dodgson inclined to course (d), and commented: 'Of these four courses, (a) seems to me scarcely honest.'[17] Finally Dodgson squared his conscience and allowed them to be bound up and sold, with a new title page, to D. Appleton & Co., as the first American edition, published in 1866. W. H. Bond disposed of the theory that minor variants in the title pages of the Appleton *Alice* indicate two distinct issues: 'The Oxford University Press set up the cancel page in duplicate, just as it had previously set up the two leaf preliminary gathering. A thousand impressions (wrongly recorded in the ledger as a thousand titles) of this combined forme would supply titles for the whole edition. There is probably no question of precedence between the two variants.'[18]

Dodgson did his best to get back the forty-eight copies of the book that had already gone out. Most of these were in the hands of close personal friends, several of them children, but some presumably went to newspapers and periodicals for review purposes, for Dodgson would surely not have overlooked this method of making his book known. Thirty-four returned copies were divided up and sent to five hospitals and to his friends Dr Southey and the Rev. Jacobson for similar distribution. Alice's beautiful white vellum copy was removed from its binding, which was reserved for the new presentation copy, and presumably discarded. Probably Clay had at least one, and Dodgson retained two for comparison purposes. Only twenty copies have survived.

The second edition, dated 1866, came out in November 1865, in time for the Christmas market, and Dodgson pronounced it 'very *far* superior to the old, and in fact a perfect piece of artistic printing'.[19] Most people would agree that the second edition was an improvement on the first, particularly in respect of the layout and presswork, the book having been set up from 'a foul case containing a mixture of normal (i.e. narrow) forms of certain characters'.[20] Warren Weaver, an eminent American Carroll collector who conducted a 'Census' of the known surviving copies of the first edition, discovered nine illustrations printed lighter in the earlier edition, nine heavier and twenty-four the same. But the difference could not have been sufficient to justify scrapping the whole edition.

Alice's Adventures in Wonderland was first reviewed on 18 November 1865 in *The Reader*, followed by *The Athenaeum* on 16 December 1865. The latter article reads:

> This is a dream-story; but who can, in cold blood, manufacture a dream, with all its loops and ties, and loose threads, and entanglements, and inconsistencies, and passages which lead to nothing, at the end of which Sleep's most diligent pilgrim never arrives? Mr Carroll has laboured hard to heap together strange adventures, and heterogeneous combinations; and we acknowledge the hard labour. Mr Tenniel, again, is square, and grim, and uncouth in his illustrations, howbeit clever, even sometimes to the verge of grandeur, as is the artist's habit. We fancy that any real child might be more puzzled than enchanted by this stiff, over-wrought story.

The Times had described Tenniel's drawings for *Lalla Rookh* as 'the greatest illustrative achievement of any single hand'. In *The Times* of 26 December 1865 the reviewer barely mentions the author at all, but writes enthusiastically of:

> Mr Tenniel, who has illustrated a little work – *Alice's Adventures in Wonderland*, with extraordinary grace. Look at the first chapter of this volume, and note the rabbit at the head of it. His umbrella is tucked under his arm and he is taking the watch out of his pocket to see what o'clock it is. The neatness of touch may be seen in a dozen other vignettes throughout the volume, the letterpress of which is by Mr Lewis Carroll, and may best be described as an excellent piece of nonsense.

The Spectator[21] predicted that 'big folks who take it home to their little folks will find themselves reading more than they intended, and laughing more than they had any right to expect'. The reviewer in *The Sunderland Herald*,[22] more perceptive than most, wrote, 'This pretty and funny book ought to become a great favourite with children. It has this advantage, that it has no moral, and that it does not teach anything. It is, in fact, pure sugar throughout, and is without any of that bitter foundation which some people imagine ought to be at the bottom of all children's books . . .' This total absence of worthy purpose made *Alice's Adventures in Wonderland* a landmark in children's literature in the same way that *The Lyrical Ballads* had been a landmark in the development of poetry. Before *Alice*, books written for children without a moral or didactic purpose were exceedingly rare, such books as *Holiday House* by Catherine Sinclair[23] and *The Rose and the Ring* by Thackeray[24] being exceptions. The enthusiasm with which Victorian children greeted *Alice's Adventures*, with its absence of such restraints, is a phenomenon scarcely understood in the twentieth century. But another aspect of the book's abiding popularity is the fact that it is crammed from start to finish with memorable lines which seem to adapt to almost any human situation. It is this quality in particular which gives the book its appeal to adults, who return again and again to the book for phrases to apply to real-life situations. Thus it is that the 'Alice' books have become the most quoted books in the English language, except for Shakespeare and the Bible.

The popularity of *Alice's Adventures in Wonderland* led enthusiasts up and down the country to try to link the story in some way to their own local traditions. Llandudno had genuine connections with the real Alice, and also claimed that the proliferation of rabbits there had inspired the character of the White Rabbit. The town was a favourite holiday resort for the Liddells for many years, and in 1861 the Dean built a house called 'Penmorfa' on the slopes of the Great Orme's Head, and not far from property owned by Lord Newry.

Many years after Dodgson's death a curious controversy broke out over his possible connection with Llandudno. Local tradition held that Dodgson stayed with the Liddells in Llandudno, where he told stories to Alice and her sisters, and derived from the local warrens inspiration for his famous White Rabbit. No documentary evidence existed to support the theory, although when Alice was eighty years old she is quoted in the *Daily Dispatch* as saying, 'I remember with great pride Mr Lewis Carroll's visits to Gogarth Abbey, Llandudno, which my father, Dean Liddell, took for several summers, and our games on the sandhills together.' The statement is inaccurate as it stands, for the Dean did not merely 'take' Gogarth Abbey, later known as Penmorfa, but actually bought the land and had it built. The *Daily Dispatch* reporter may therefore have misunderstood Alice's statement. A complication, however, is that H. L. Thompson, Dean Liddell's biographer, erroneously gave 1865 as the date of completion of Penmorfa, so that on the whole the episode has tended to be discounted. The artist W. B. Richmond, for whose picture 'The Three Sisters' Alice, Lorina and Edith posed at Llandudno, claimed that Dodgson was present at the time, but there is no mention of any such visit in Dodgson's extant diaries and correspondence. The people of Llandudno nevertheless stuck to their story, and in 1932, the centenary of Dodgson's birth, Lloyd George unveiled a statue of the *White Rabbit* to commemorate the connection.

However, a new piece of evidence has turned up in support of Llandudno's claim. Alice amassed numerous photographs taken by Dodgson, and in one of her albums is a photograph of Penmorfa. The remaining photographs in the album are all identifiably Dodgson's work, except for views of Penrhyn Castle. The photograph of Penmorfa reveals it as a strangely unattractive Victorian Gothic building, inartistically sited on a barren plot, so that it is not easy to reconcile it with the work of Dean Liddell, whose improvements to Christ Church Cathedral mark him out as a man of architectural taste. There is no signature to the photograph, but carefully posed in true Carrollian fashion on the steps in the foreground are Alice, Lorina and Edith. These tiny but clearly recognizable figures indicate that the photographer was almost certainly Dodgson himself, and that he probably also took the views of Penrhyn Castle to please his little favourites.

There remains the problem of when such a visit could have been made by Dodgson. The ages of the children as photographed suggest 1862 as the most likely date. The extant diaries indicate that Dodgson spent most of the summer at Croft, and though he did not diarize such an event, the gaps in the entries leave sufficient scope for a brief visit. It would have been uncharacteristic of him not to mention it, unless something occurred in his personal relationship with the family to stun him into silence. When his deepest emotions were involved he rarely committed them to paper. But the more likely date is the Easter vacation of 1862, for which the diary is missing. We know that he spent part of the time at Freshwater, but most of the vacation is unaccounted for. Mr Ivor Wynne Jones, by an examination of local archives has proved conclusively that the house was finally completed in 1862, but in the preceding spring the exterior would probably have been sufficiently advanced to give a finished appearance in the photograph. In the absence of any evidence to the contrary, it must be assumed that Dodgson was there and that the people of Llandudno are right.

By 1866 Dodgson had recouped all his losses on the book and the fifth thousand was published. By 1898, the year of Dodgson's death, 160,000 copies had appeared. Warren Weaver sums up much of the special appeal of the book and its heroine:

> I think we ought not to try to explain Alice; we should just be thankful that we have her. Innocence, a tiny but truly patrician courage and a steady determination to get things straight, a movingly sympathetic attitude toward all around her, a demure decency that is as appealing as it is rare – all these belong to Alice. And all these are set for us in a matrix of most deliciously irresponsible humour – a humour that is made all the more enjoyable by the fact that simple Alice, sweet Alice, enchanting Alice, herself never quite catches on.

She belonged to an age that now seems as remote as her own Wonderland. But there are some of us – many of us – for whom frequent revisits to that Wonderland form a pleasure we will never give up. There we recapture some of the far-off flavour of our own childhood. There we hear again, if only for a poignant moment, the fugitive overtones of the clear, high, innocent voices of that magic land where we, too, once lived.[25]

REFERENCES

1   Alice and Caryl Hargreaves, 'Alice's Recollections of Carrollian Days as told to her son, Caryl Hargreaves', *The Cornhill Magazine*, July 1932.
2   Lewis Carroll, 'Alice on the Stage', *The Theatre*, April 1887.
3   Green, p. 188.
4   *Cheltenham Looker-On*, 4 April 1863.
5   *Reminiscences of a Specialist*, 1932, p. 15.
6   Ms. Diaries.
7   Green, p. 204.
8   Article 'Lewis Carroll the Pre-Raphaelite', *Lewis Carroll Observed*, E. Guiliano (ed.), New York, 1976.
9   Ibid.
10   Warren Weaver, *Alice in Many Tongues*, Wisconsin, 1964, p. 21.
11   John Ruskin, *The Art of England: Lectures given in Oxford*.
12   4 January 1862.
13   21 December 1861.
14   *The Annotated Alice*, ed. Martin Gardner, 1970, p. 25.
15   Pamphlet, *The Profits of Authorship*, 1884, as quoted in Collingwood, p. 226, no surviving copy being known.
16   *Letters to Macmillan*, 1967, ed. Simon Nowell-Smith, pp. 71–2.
17   Ibid.
18   Article, 'The Publication of Alice's Adventures in Wonderland', *Harvard Library Bulletin*, Autumn 1956.
19   Green, p. 236.
20   W. H. Bond, 'The Publication of Alice's Adventures in Wonderland', *Harvard Library Bulletin*, Autumn 1956.
21   23 December 1865.
22   25 May 1866.
23   1839.
24   1855.
25   *Alice in Many Tongues*, Wisconsin, 1964, p. 29.

8 A Melancholy Maiden

We shall never know for certain whether that warm, avuncular affection which Dodgson felt for Alice Liddell ever matured to a point where he found himself actually in love with her. What is indisputable is that between the end of June 1863 and the start of the Michaelmas term in mid October something happened to disrupt the even tenor of his friendship with the family at the Deanery.

Relationships could not have been more cordial when, on 25 June, Alice and Edith came to fetch him from his rooms and asked him to arrange an expedition to Nuneham. The party finally consisted of ten people: the Dean, his wife and father; the three little girls and their younger sister, Rhoda; Viscount Newry, Harcourt and Dodgson himself. They hired a four-oar boat, with Dodgson, Harcourt and Lord Newry rowing all the way, and the others manning the stroke oar in rotation. 'We had tea under the trees at Nuneham,' wrote Dodgson, 'after which the rest drove home in the carriage (which met them in the park), while Ina, Alice, Edith and I (*mirabile dictu!*) walked down to Abingdon-road Station, and so home by railway: a pleasant expedition, with a *very* pleasant conclusion.'[1]

Two days later Dodgson wrote to Mrs Liddell urging her to send the children over to be photographed. A minor amendment has been made in the diary in a different hand, to make the paragraph appear complete; but the following – and no doubt highly significant – page has been cut out. The record recommences on 30 June, when the Deanery party departed for Llandudno. Dodgson makes no further reference to the children until 5 December, when he attended the Christ Church Theatricals, performed in the rooms of an undergraduate called Charles Berners. 'Mrs Liddell and the children were there', he wrote, 'but I held aloof from them as I have done all this term.'[2] This tension was eased a fortnight later when Dodgson spent several hours with the children at the Deanery. Although the Dean was absent, Mrs Liddell, then seven months pregnant, was with them for part of the time. But there was to be no return to the old, privileged friendship. On 12 May 1864 he recorded: 'During these last few days I have applied in vain for leave to take the children on the river, i.e. Alice, Edith and Rhoda: but

Mrs Liddell will not let *any* come in future – rather superfluous caution.'
There is no mistaking Dodgson's note of anguish.

In the autumn of 1865 the news leaked out in the family that
Dodgson's younger brother, Wilfred, had fallen in love with Alice Jane
Donkin, and wished to marry her. Alice was a niece of William Fish-
burn Donkin, the Savilian Professor of Astronomy at Oxford. Though
charming and very pretty, she was only fourteen years old. It was by no
means abnormal for young men to pay court to girls of her age, or even
younger, for the Victorian era was one of long engagements, with the
man having to establish himself to maintain the wife of his choice in
appropriate style. Wilfred, who had taken his BA degree at Christ
Church in 1860, could not at that stage be said to have progressed far in
his chosen career of real estate. On 7 October 1865 Dodgson records:
'Wrote Wilfred a long letter on the subject of Alice Donkin, as things
are not on a satisfactory footing at present and urged on him the
wisdom of keeping away from Barnby Moor [the Donkin family home]
for a couple of years.'[3] Wilfred's reply indicated that he saw his present
position altogether differently. When Dodgson broke his journey from
Croft to Oxford at Milford Junction five days later, he hoped that
Wilfred would meet him there, but he was disappointed. 'I doubt if I
can do any good just now by volunteering further advice,'[4] he concluded. Wilfred persevered in his suit, but it was several years before he
and Alice Donkin were finally married, on 9 August 1871.

Wilfred's problem continued to trouble Dodgson and he also had
difficulties of his own to consider. In October Uncle Skeffington, who
emerged more and more as a personal confidant as time went on,
arrived in Oxford, and on two successive evenings Dodgson dined with
him. 'On each occasion we had a good deal of conversation about
Wilfred, and about A.L. It is a very anxious subject,'[5] Dodgson wrote.
This close association of his anxieties about Wilfred's romantic affairs
and his own relationship with Alice Liddell is one of the strongest
arguments for concluding that he was romantically attached to the
Dean's daughter and wished to marry her.

If these two situations were indeed romantic parallels, Charles
Dodgson's reactions were the reverse of his brother's, though it is only
fair to say that the obstacles that Charles had to contend with were
greater than in Wilfred's case. The age gap was wider between Charles
and Alice Liddell, and it is scarcely conveivable that she would have
wished in later years to perpetuate her childish affection in marriage.
The Dodgsons were socially well connected; but the Dean's father was
brother to an earl, and understandably enough he and his wife hoped
for splendid matches for their beautiful and talented daughters.

Whether Dodgson ever actually asked for Alice's hand, however
tentatively, remains a mystery. Oxford rumour claimed that he had,

and that he had been rejected. This might, of course, have been idle speculation, based on his long association with the children, and his immortalization of Alice both in prose and in verse. Far more significant is the belief among Alice's own descendants that an offer was made and rejected. It is also impossible to overlook the length and strength of his attachment, which goes far beyond that which normally attached to his child friendships, and which is not altogether explained away by the sentimental link with his fictional heroine. And more than a decade later, when he was writing *The Hunting of the Snark*, his old grievance against the Dean and his wife showed through. What is absolutely certain is that he would never have continued to address Alice herself on the subject of matrimony without her parents' consent, and this he clearly did not have. Dodgson, moreover, believed that looks and gestures of love should never be exchanged between a man and a woman before the parental terms had been met. Once he rebuked Ellen Terry, who was playing the part of Portia in *The Merchant of Venice*, for indicating in her by-play that Portia was already in love with Bassanio before he had legitimately won her hand by choosing the right casket. If he could take this line with a mere stage play, how much more punctiliously must he have clung to this notion in real life. It was not absolutely impossible for a man of Dodgson's scholastic attainments to become acceptable as a prospective husband for Alice; headmastership of a large public school, or a bishopric, even a canonry might have tipped the scale in his favour. But he was already in his thirties, and showed no likelihood of attaining any of these. His inhibitions about taking Priest's Orders were indeed an effective bar to ambitions of this kind. True, in 1865, as we have seen, he began again positively reading for ordination; but personal motives could never have prevailed with Dodgson. Perhaps the abandonment of this, his final attempt at ordination, also marked the point at which he finally buried his hopes of Alice Liddell; but he never fully recovered from the pain that accompanied the severance of their relationship; and though eventually other child friends took over, for years he went on dedicating the fruits of literary labours to her and her alone.

It appears that Dodgson was never in love with anyone else in his entire life, though one of his sisters suspected at one time that he was in love with Ellen Terry. Ever since he had seen the little nine-year-old child making her stage debut as Mamilius he had wanted to meet her, but it was not until 21 December 1864 that his wish was finally fulfilled. Any hopes Dodgson might have entertained in relation to Ellen Terry had been irrevocably demolished before he even met her, for in January 1864, at the age of only sixteen years, she had married the artist G. F. Watts. Her childlike innocence at the time of her marriage is emphasized in a letter which she wrote many years later to George

16   Alice's drawing of
Christ Church Cathedral,
Oxford

17   The Prince and
Princess of Wales in the
Deanery garden. Mrs
Liddell has Rhoda on her
knee; the Dean is seated
right

Christ Church Cathedral Oxford 1858   Alice Pleasance Liddell

18　Lewis Carroll's own illustration of Alice in the White Rabbit's house for *Alice's Adventures Under Ground*

19　Print of a Rossetti drawing entitled 'Miss Miller', from Lewis Carroll's photograph album

20　Antoinie Zimmerman, who translated *Alice* into German. From Alice's own album

21   Photograph by Carroll of a
drawing by D. G. Rossetti

22   Arthur Hughes, 'Girl with
Lilacs', painted for and once owned
by Lewis Carroll

23 Charles Dodgson. Photograph by Reginald Southey

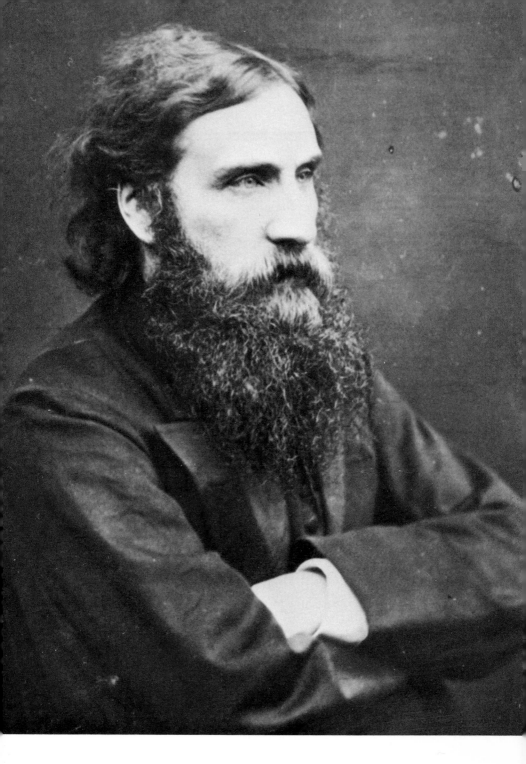
24   George MacDonald. Photograph by Lewis Carroll

25 Prince Leopold. He fell in love with Alice. Photograph by Lewis Carroll

26 Oil painting of Alice, by her sister Violet in 1886

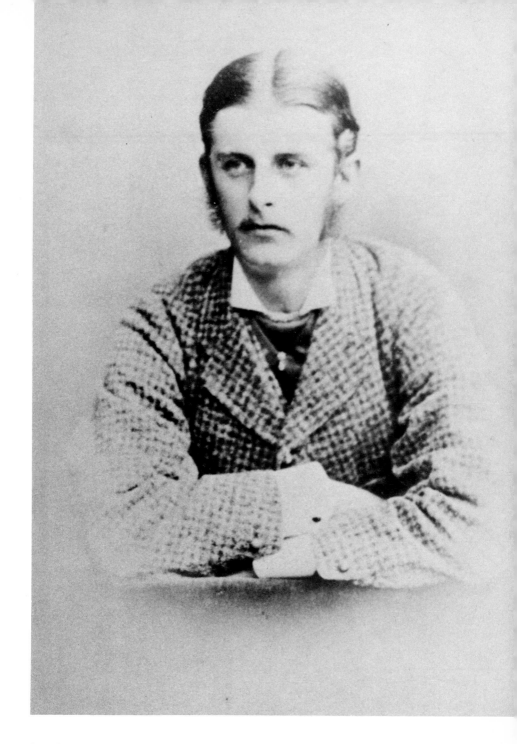

27 Reginald Hargreaves. Alice married him in 1880

28   Lorina Liddell, Alice's elder sister. Believed by Lewis Carroll

Bernard Shaw: 'Mr Watts kissed me in the studio one day, but sweetly and gently, all tenderness and kindness, and then I was what they call "engaged" to him and all the rest of it, and my people hated it, and I was in Heaven for I knew I was to live with those pictures. "Always", I thought, and to sit to that gentle Mr W. and clean his brushes, and play my idiotic piano to him, and sit with him there in wonderland (the studio).'[6] But later when Ellen was taken ill and had to stay at his home, Little Holland House, Watts kissed her again somewhat differently. Ellen nursed the secret of that kiss for two whole weeks, and finally confided to her mother: 'I told her I *must* be married to him *now* because I was going to have a baby !!!! *and she* believed me!! Oh, I tell you I thought I knew everything then, and I was nearly 16 years old then, – I was *sure THAT* kiss meant giving me a baby!'[7]

At the time he met Ellen, Watts was living at Little Holland House with Mrs Thoby Prinsep, mother of Val Prinsep, and sister of Mrs Julia Margaret Cameron. With the genial acquiescence of her husband, unkindly called 'dog Thoby' by some, she was attempting to establish a *coterie* there similar to that which her sister had created at Farringford. Watts' motives in marrying Ellen were no less naive and remote from reality than hers in accepting him. The ethereal quality which he saw in her could not stand the test of everyday domesticity. Mrs Prinsep, with whom they continued to live, treated Ellen like a naughty child; Ellen was bored and rebellious.

In July 1864 Dodgson had been introduced by Alex Munro, the sculptor, to Val Prinsep, who in turn gave him a note of introduction to Watts. Besides showing Dodgson pictures of Tennyson, Henry Taylor and Garibaldi, Watts let him see a large negative by Mrs Cameron of Ellen Terry in 'Choosing' and promised to bring his young wife over two days later so that Dodgson could photograph her. But as an afterthought Dodgson wrote suggesting that instead he bring his camera to Little Holland House to photograph him and his friends, whereupon Watts replied that he would have to consult Thoby Prinsep first. Nothing ever came of this.

It is possible that Dodgson learned of the disharmony between Watts and his wife from Mrs Cameron, whom he met at Freshwater a few days later, or from his friend Tom Taylor, who had been a witness at the Watts' wedding. On 13 August Tom Taylor wrote to him at Freshwater that the Terry family were back at 92 Stanhope Street, their London home, and enclosed a note of introduction. With this note of hand Dodgson called on Mrs Terry as soon as he returned from Freshwater, and tentatively arranged with her that he would return in October and photograph them all, including Mrs Watts. In the event, although his friendship with Mr and Mrs Terry rapidly developed, he did not meet Kate Terry until 20 December 1864. Against the diary record of that meeting he copied out *The Times* review of Kate's debut as Arthur in *King John*. 'Here and there marks of training might be traced in this little girl,' the reviewer wrote, 'but she was much more easy and natural than is usually the case with juvenile performers.'[8]

His first meeting with Ellen, whom he described as 'the one I have always most wished to meet',[9] took place on the following day. He had already had a long chat with Tom Taylor about her, and presumably her separation from Watts had been discussed. It was a very domestic scene, with Ellen cuddling her new brother, who was only two weeks old. She was 'lively and pleasant, almost childlike in her fun, but perfectly ladylike'.[10] If Dodgson was a little in love with her, he could surely be forgiven. 'Her charm held everyone, but I think pre-eminently those who loved pictures,' wrote her friend of later years, Graham Robertson. 'She was *par excellence* the Painter's Actress and appealed to the eye before the ear; her gesture and pose were eloquence itself . . .'[11] Yet hers was not a stereotyped, conventional beauty. Charles Reade wrote of her, 'Ellen Terry is an enigma. Her eyes are pale, her nose rather long, her mouth nothing particular. Complexion a delicate brickdust, hair rather like tow. Yet somehow she is *beautiful*. Her expression *kills* any pretty face you see beside her.'[12]

Of her relationship with Dodgson, Ellen Terry wrote, 'He was as fond of me as he could be of anyone over the age of ten,'[13] and this in many ways sums up Dodgson's problem. All the indications, and these increase as his life progresses, are that Dodgson would have been perfectly able to form a normal marriageable relationship with a mature woman, had he only known where to begin. Although his shyness did not prevent his enjoying the society of other people, includ-ing women, it inhibited him from embarking on a relationship of intimacy with a marriageable and desirable young woman. His only hope was of growing into such a relationship as an automatic develop-ment of a friendship with a child. Ironically, the older he got, the older the children were with whom he spent his leisure hours. But the more he developed, the greater was the age-gap between himself and his young protégées. At the same time, the older he grew, the more he fostered that extreme protectiveness that is the role of the father rather than that of lover, with the result that he became almost incapable of treating his childhood friends as adults with a mind of their own. It is remotely possible that he could have married Ellen Terry, had she been free, for he had known her from afar in childhood, and easily slipped into friendship with her. Children, and ultimately grandchildren of his own would have satisfied his urgent need for someone to protect and shelter. But had he attained that goal, the world might never have had Lewis Carroll.

By his standards, though separated, Ellen Terry was strictly unavailable, and remained so even after her divorce in 1877. For Dodgson's personal code of conduct was so strict that, while sympathetic to those who felt otherwise, he himself considered widowers were wrong to remarry. This being the case, marriage with a woman whose first husband was still living would be even worse. He was certainly never likely to allow his emotions to sway his judgment in matters of the heart. Once, when discussing the question of insurance with his father, he put forward the view that insurance policies were of no advantage to those without concrete intentions of matrimony. The only disadvantage of failing to insure was the risk that 'a life which might have been insured at 20, may be precarious at 30 from disease or accident, and so it may be impossible then to insure it, but I do not give much weight to this because I think that the very fact of life having become precarious would render it inadvisable to marry.' Duty, with Dodgson, was always after all bound to prevail.

Ellen Terry was not only beautiful, talented, and representative of a great romantic ideal, but she and indeed her entire family shared Dodgson's love of the theatre. Dodgson was interested in the entire range of dramatic art, but his greatest interest was in child performers. Having been brought up to the theatre, Ellen Terry was an invaluable adviser on all aspects of the drama, and had a special sympathy for the feelings of little actresses, or would-be actresses. In January 1866 Dodgson decided to try his hand at writing a play for Ellen Terry and Percy Roselle, then aged about eighteen years, but able to pass himself off as a boy of eight. A week after seeing Roselle in *Little King Pippin*, Dodgson devoted several hours to writing out an extended synopsis of his play, which he decided to call *Morning Clouds*. The hero (Percy Roselle) was to be stolen from his widowed mother (Ellen Terry) by his father's younger brother. On a cold winter's night the boy passes the house where his mother lives. She hears him singing outside, and opens the window, but too late. Finally the villain dies miserably, and the boy is reunited with his family. The play ends with the boy singing his old grandfather to sleep. It seems almost incredible that, while Dodgson was engaged in writing his timeless classic, he could sink to producing this maudlin Victorian plot.

Dodgson sent his synopsis to Tom Taylor, who reacted favourably and promised to find out if Percy Roselle was likely to be available. He also undertook to show it to Ellen Terry; but finally their joint opinion was that the play would be impracticable, and lacked the sensationalism that public taste demanded. The final obstacle was the fact that Percy Roselle was not to be had. Dodgson thereupon decided to abandon the project.

His disappointment was temporarily abated when Mr Coe, who ran a company of talented child performers, and who allowed Dodgson to watch rehearsals from the prompter's box and mingle freely with the little actors and actresses, expressed an interest in *Morning Clouds*. He suggested that Dodgson try a little dialogue, and also encouraged him to consider the possibilities of a dramatization of *Alice's Adventures in Wonderland*; but he advised against using it as a pantomime, as he considered the text too good for such treatment. But the stage version of *Alice* was deferred for many years, and *Morning Clouds* was never completed.

In May 1867 the staff of Punch, shocked by the death of their illustrator Charles Bennett, who had illustrated Dodgson's 'The Path of Roses' for *The Train* in May 1856, staged a benefit for his widow and eight children. 'His facile and singular sublety of fancy were, we hoped, destined to enrich these pages for many a year,' wrote Shirley Brooks, then editor of *Punch*. 'It has been willed otherwise, and we lament the loss of a comrade of invaluable skill, and the death of one of the kindliest and gentlest of our associates, the power of whose hand was equalled by the goodness of his heart.'[14]

The benefit took the form of a theatrical performance of *Box and Cox*, some glees and madrigals, and Tom Taylor's one-act play, *A Sheep in Wolf's Clothing*. Quintin Twiss, whom Dodgson had photographed as a Christ Church undergraduate, and Du Maurier took the leading roles in the first play. In the interval Dodgson joined the Terry party, Tom Taylor, and Arthur Lewis, Kate Terry's fiancé, in their box. Tom Taylor, Mark Lemon, Shirley Brooks, Burnand and Tenniel all took part, and were joined by Kate, Ellen and Flo Terry. 'Tom Taylor was good, but a little tame,' wrote Dodgson. 'Mark Lemon was first rate; Burnand good (he showed some presence of mind, when he could not open the door to admit Kinke, while the locksmith was examining the cupboard, in extemporizing: 'Simon Zoyland, bring thy tools here and open this door!'); Tenniel seemed nervous and was hardly audible; Miss Terry was, in parts, *very* pathetic, and reduced poor Polly to floods of tears.'[15] The benefit raised about £650. Despite Tenniel's nervousness, he was immensely popular in his role as Colonel Lord Churchill of the Lifeguards, and when the benefit was taken to Manchester, he was warmly cheered.

Though Dodgson's intimacy with the Terry family continued uninterrupted, he broke off his friendship with Ellen Terry in 1868, when she went to live with Edward Godwin, an architect, by whom she had two children. 'I felt that she had so entirely sacrificed her social position that I had no desire but to drop her acquaintance,' wrote Dodgson later. It was a sharp and unwavering judgment. Yet his attitude was basically more sympathetic than would at first appear.

> I honestly believe her position was, from her point of view, this. 'I was tied by *human* law to a man who disowns his share of what ought to be a

mutual contract. He never loved me and I do not believe, in God's sight, we are man and wife. Society expects me to live, till this man's death, as if I were single and to give up all hope of that form of love for which I pine and shall never get from *him*. This other man loves me as truly and faithfully as any lawful husband. If the marriage ceremony were *possible* I would insist on it before living with him. It is *not* possible and I will do without it.'

I allow freely that she was headstrong and wild in doing so; and her only real *duty* was to accept the wreck of her happiness and live (or if necessary die) without the love of a man. But I do not allow that her case resembled *at all* that of those poor women who, without any pretence of *love*, sell themselves to the first comer. It much more resembles the case of those many women who are living as faithfully and devotedly as lawful wives without having gone through any ceremony and who are, I believe, married in God's sight though not in Man's.[16]

Dodgson's bright angel of the footlights was now tarnished. He continued to pity, and in a sense, to love her, but his unyielding code of conduct prevented further association with her as long as she continued in these circumstances, just as it would have forbidden him to yield to impulses of love for this lonely, beautiful young woman. That code which gave him so much inner strength was also a formidable barrier between himself and womankind in general, and as time went on it became increasingly unlikely that he would ever cross over it.

REFERENCES

1   Green, p. 199.
2   Green, p. 208.
3   Ms. Diaries.
4   Ibid.
5   Ibid.
6   Christopher St John, *Ellen Terry and George Bernard Shaw: a Correspondence*, 1931, p. 111.
7   Roger Manvell, *Ellen Terry*, 1968, p. 47.
8   *The Times*, 10 March 1852.
9   Green, p. 225.
10   Roger Manvell, *Ellen Terry*, 1968, p. 129.
11   Ibid.
12   Ibid, pp. 84–5.
13   *Ellen Terry's Memoirs*, p. 142.
14   George Somes Layard (ed.), *A Great Punch Editor: Shirley Brooks*, 1907, p. 297.
15   Green, p. 259.
16   Roger Manvell, *Ellen Terry*, 1968, p. 237.

9 Head of the Family

'They are very blunt and reserved to strangers, which makes them appear unsociable; but they are hospitable, sincere and generous, when known. They are likewise remarkable for silent curiosity, cool observation, and patient perseverance, which make them successful in scientific pursuits. You must all take care to preserve this good character which I have given you as Englishmen.'[1]

Dodgson had read these words as a small child. In 1867, for the first and only time in his life, he allowed the world at large to put his character as an Englishman to the test by taking a foreign tour. His companion was his friend Liddon, who was greatly interested in the Russian Orthodox Church. Liddon had long wished to visit Russia, and to make contact with men of religion there as a kind of antidote to accusations of Romanizing tendencies among the English clergy. On 4 July 1867 Liddon wrote in his diary: 'Proposed to Dodgson that we should go together to Russia. He much taken by the idea.' Six days later he visited Oxford, dined in Hall and made the final arrangements with Dodgson for starting to Russia. Next day, the very eve of their departure, Dodgson's passport arrived, and on 12 July the two men travelled separately to Dover, where they spent the night at the 'Lord Warden'. Next morning they boarded the boat, where they hired a private cabin, a great comfort, as it was raining heavily. 'After two trains had been emptied into it [the boat] and a very successful imitation of the Great Pyramid had been made on deck, to which interesting work we were proud to contribute a couple of portmanteaus, we got under weigh,' wrote Dodgson. 'The pen refused to describe the sufferings of some of the passengers during our smooth trip of 90 minutes: my own sensations – it was not for *that* I had paid my money.'[2]

In Calais they took a stroll about the market place, which was 'white with the caps of the women, and full of their shrill jabbering', before boarding the train for Brussels. The monotony of the journey was broken between Lille and Tournai by the company of a French-speaking couple and their two little children, aged about six and four, the younger of whom greatly interested Dodgson. 'She pulled her father's whiskers, and moustaches, got on his back, tried on his specs, etc.'[3] wrote Liddon. Dodgson drew a picture of her, and as they finally left the carriage the mother sent her back to say 'Bon soir' and to be kissed.

In Brussels they broke their journey and put up for two nights at the Hotel Bellevue, where they took dinner, 'très-simple, and therefore consisting of only seven courses'.[4] Later they strolled into the park, where they sat at a table under the trees for an hour or more listening to orchestral music by lamplight. Next morning they attended the Sunday service at the church of St Gudule; but although Dodgson praised the music and the picturesque swinging of the incense censers by two boys in scarlet and white, he condemned the lack of real participation by the congregation. Afterwards they witnessed the annual procession of the 'Host' through the town, watched by an orderly crowd of many thousands. In the procession were choirboys with banners, strewing coloured paper as they went; little girls in white, with long veils; priests, and even a troop of cavalry. Despite the visual effect, Dodgson considered it theatrical and unreal. Later, while Dodgson toured the Grande Place and the Hotel de Ville, Liddon called at the home of Prince Orloff, whom he had recently met in Oxford. He had hoped to get from him some letters of introduction, but unfortunately the Prince was away, although he later forwarded the letters to them at St Petersburg.

Next day they moved on to Cologne. Although Dodgson reported that the journey was without incident, Liddon commented, 'Great difficulty in saving the train at Verviers owing to Dodgson's delay about the tickets'. 'We spent about an hour in the cathedral, which I will not attempt to describe further than by saying it was the most beautiful of all churches I have ever seen, or can imagine,' wrote Dodgson. 'If one could imagine the spirit of devotion embodied in any material form, it would be in such a building.' This brief mention typifies his habit of understatement where his deepest feeling were involved. Liddon's diary reads, 'Dodgson was overcome by the beauty of Cologne Cathedral. I found him leaning against the rails of the choir, and sobbing like a child. When the verger came to show us over the chapels, he got out of the way. He said that he could not bear the harsh voice of the man in the presence of so much beauty.'[5] Next morning they toured several churches, including ' "The Church of St Ursula and of the 11,000 Virgins," whose bones are stored away in cases with fronts of glass, through which they are hardly visible'. What impressed him most in every church he visited was the way in which women and children wandered into the church to pray quietly, and then departed, though he remarked on the almost total absence of men and boys.

Overnight they moved on by rail to Berlin, where they spent the day at picture galleries and strolling along the *Unter den Linden* to the

Brandenburg Gate, and round to St Peter's Church, where they attended evening service. According to Liddon, they spent the greater part of the following morning looking round the shops for photographs for Dodgson, who regrettably had not brought his photographic apparatus with him. In the afternoon they paid a second visit to the picture gallery of the Musée, where the pictures, mainly religious, were arranged by the great art critic, Waagen. Liddon took most pleasure in the Italian school, and in particular in the work of Ghirlandajo; but Dodgson's favourite was a triptych by Van Weyden representing scenes after the death of Jesus, including one in which Mary's tears are detailed hemispheres.

The following day was devoted mainly to the Royal Palace, and to the palace at Charlottenburg. But Liddon noted: 'In the late evening Dodgson insisted on our going out in quest of the New Jews Synagogue which we found. . . . A discussion with him on our way home as to the duty of maintaining the rule of saying the Daily morning and evening service.'[6] They returned to the Synagogue next morning and stayed for the service, but on the way back resumed the argument of the previous night about the obligation of the daily service, 'an obligation which he [Dodgson] fiercely contended', commented Liddon. Of their six-hour expedition to Potsdam during which they saw the rooms of Frederick the Great in the New Palace, Dodgson wrote:

> The amount of art lavished on the whole region of Potsdam is marvell-ous; some of the tops of the palaces were like forests of statues, and they were all over the gardens, set on pedestals. In fact, the two principles of Berlin Architecture appear to me to be these. On the house-tops, wher-ever there is a convenient place, put up the figure of a man; he is best placed standing on one leg. Wherever there is room on the ground, put either a circular group of busts on pedestals, in consultation, all looking inwards – or else the colossal figure of a man killing, about to kill, or having killed (the present tense is preferred) a beast; the more pricks the beast has, the better – in fact a dragon is the correct thing, but if that is beyond the artist, he may content himself with a lion or a pig. The beast killing principle has been carried out everywhere with a relentless monotony, which makes some parts of Berlin look like a fossil slaughter-house.[7]

Both men were impressed by the Cathedral at Danzig, and admired its rigidly preserved Pre-Reformation ornaments, and in particular a magnificent figure of Christ over the entrance to the chancel. From Danzig, where they spent a single night, they moved on to Königsberg, where extremes of temperature – it was 88 degrees on the journey, and at night gusts of wind in a thunderstorm broke the windows of his bedroom – contributed to a temporary breakdown in Liddon's health. He was so ill with diarrhoea that shortly after midnight Dodgson sent for the doctor, who applied blotting paper soaked in spirits of mustard, and gave him morphia powder and camomile tea. By the following afternoon he was ready to dine on mutton chops and accompany Dodgson to the Bösse-Garten to listen to military music. Dodgson's interest in the theatre was so great that on the following day he went to the theatre, where he could understand very little of the plot, but where one of the characters was an English journalist, who was a sort of butt of the other characters, and ended his career by falling into a drum.

When they moved on to St Petersburg it was Dodgson's turn to fall ill during the night; but his sickness was insufficient to curtail his sightseeing. He was impressed by the width of the streets, even the secondary ones being broader than anything seen in London, and by the gigantic blue and gold domed churches. At Sunday service he was impressed by the unaccompanied chants, but remarked that the congregation's participation was confined to bowing and crossing themselves, and to kneeling and touching the ground with their foreheads. 'The more one sees of these gorgeous services, with their many appeals to the senses, the more, I think one learns to love the plain, simple (but to my mind far more real) service of the English Church,'[8] he remarked.

Liddon remarked on the atmosphere, redolent of the fourth century, and on the devotion of people of all classes. But afterwards he had a long theological dispute with Dodgson, presumably about the validity of the ritual they had witnessed. 'Today I feel for the first time in my life I stand face to face with the Eastern Church,' wrote Liddon. 'To the outward eye she is at least as imposing as the Roman. To call her a petrifaction here in Russia would be simple folly. That, on the other hand, she reinforces Rome in the cultus of the Blessed Virgin Mary and other matters is too plain to be disputed.'[9]

Predictably Dodgson was enthusiastic about the magnificent art treasures in the Hermitage, commenting particularly on the rooms devoted to Titian and to Murillo, and on Raphael's circular painting of the Holy Family. He also enjoyed a steamer excursion down the tideless Gulf of Finland to the Peterhof:

> At every corner, or end of an avenue or path, where a piece of statuary *could* be introduced with effect, there one was sure to find one, in bronze or in white marble; many of the latter had a sort of circular niche built behind, with a blue background to throw the figure into relief. Here we found a series of shelving ledges made of stone, with a sheet of water gliding down over them; here a long path, stretching down slopes and flights of steps, and arched over all the way with trellises and creepers: here a huge boulder, hewn, just as it lay, into the shape of a gigantic head and face, with mild, Sphinx-like eyes, as if some buried Titan were struggling to free himself; here a fountain, so artfully formed of pipes set in circles, each set shooting the water higher than those outside, as to form a solid pyramid of glittering spray; here a lawn, seen through a break in the woods below us, with threads of scarlet geraniums running over it, and looking in the distance like a huge branch of coral; and here

and there long avenues of trees, lying in all directions, sometimes three or four together side by side, and sometimes radiating like a star, and stretching away into the distance till the eye was almost weary following them.[10]

But even the splendours of Leningrad were eclipsed by those of Moscow:

a city of white and green roofs, of conical towers that rise one out of another like a foreshortened telescope; of bulging gilded domes, in which you see, as in a looking-glass, distorted pictures of the city; of churches which look, outside, like bunches of variegated cactus (some branches crowned with green prickly buds, others with blue, and others with red and white) and which, inside, are hung all round with Eikons and lamps, and lined with illuminated pictures up to the very roof; and finally of pavement that goes up and down like a ploughed field, and drojky-drivers who insist on being paid thirty per cent extra to-day, 'because it is the Empress's birthday.' After dinner we drove to the 'Sparrow Hills'[11] whence we had a grand panoramic view of the forest of spires and domes, with the river Moskva winding in front – the same hills from which Napoleon's army first caught sight of the city.[11]

From Moscow they travelled to Nijni Novgorod, sleeping on the floor of the railway carriage, and having to get off and walk about a mile in torrential rain, crossing a river by a temporary footbridge, because the railway bridge had been washed away. Their hotel was 'a truly villainous place', where meals were good and everything else bad. But the excitement of the world's fair compensated for all the discomforts.

It was a wonderful place. Besides there being distinct quarters for the Persians, the Chinese, and others, we were constantly meeting strange beings, with unwholesome complexions and unheard-of costumes. The Persians, with their gentle, intelligent faces, the long eyes set wide apart, the black hair, and yellow-brown skin, crowned with a black woollen fez something like a grenadier, were about the most picturesque we met. But all the novelties of the day were thrown into the shade by our adventure at sunset, when we came upon the Tartar mosque (the only one in Nijni) exactly as one of the officials came out on the roof to utter the muezzin cry, or call to prayers. Even if it had been in no way singular in itself, it would have been deeply interesting from its novelty and uniqueness, but the cry itself was quite unlike anything I have ever heard before. The beginning of each sentence was uttered in a rapid monotone, and towards the end it rose gradually till it ended in a prolonged shrill wail, which floated overhead through the still air with an indescribably sad and ghostlike effect; heard at night, it would have thrilled one like the cry of the Banshee.[12]

Back in Moscow they had an interview with Bishop Leonide, whose gentle, winning manner put them instantly at ease. He was deeply interested in English Church matters, but was unhappy at the warm welcome given by the British Government to the Sultan of Turkey, who had arrived in London on the day they began their tour, and whose reception seemed to him 'a national repudiation of the Name and Authority of Jesus Christ'.[13]

A few days later they travelled by train and by tarantas, a kind of long barouche without springs, to the village of Eriniyo, where they visited a Russian monastery. En route they applied at a peasant's cottage for bread and milk, as a pretext for seeing what it was like inside. Dodgson regretted having no camera, but sketched the interior, and a group of six little boys and a girl outside. At the monastery Dodgson found a monk who spoke English, and who conducted them to the 'Church of the Holy Sepulchre', said to be an exact copy of the one in Jerusalem. Bishop Nikon, who built it, had lived the life of a hermit in a small house with innumerable tiny rooms about six feet square. In one of these was the Bishop's stone bed, only five feet nine inches long, and with a stone pillow. 'The Bishop's life must have been one of continual mortification, only to be surpassed by that of his domestics, who lived in a tiny cellar entered by a door about four feet high, and with only a glimmer of daylight admitted,'[14] Dodgson wrote.

The two men had extended their stay in Moscow to be present at the jubilee of Archbishop Philaret at Troitska. But Bishop Leonide, whom they had expected to meet, did not appear, and the morning was something of a failure, for although they went along to the Church of the Assumption and got inside the Iconostasis, after a while they were turned out. 'Dodgson made his way round to the other side of the church, and so into the very sanctuary itself,' wrote Liddon, 'but I was drifted about in the nave, and saw and heard little or nothing, except the choir. The robes of the Bishops in the distance seemed very gorgeous; and the final blessing was most touching.'[15] Philaret, by whom Liddon was received, had an income of about £7000 a year, of which he gave away all but about £200. 'His life is evidently modelled on a sterner and grander type than we are familiar with – one which would, perhaps, be impossible in England, but which secures to the Church here an unbounded influence over the people,'[16] Liddon commented.

Two days later they left Moscow for Leningrad, where they spent a few more days before beginning the first stage of their leisurely return home, visiting first Warsaw and then Breslau. Here they came unexpectedly upon the playground of a girls' school, 'a very tempting field for a photographic camera', Dodgson remarked; 'after the Russian children, whose type of face is ugly as a rule, and plain as an exception, it is quite a relief to get back among the Germans with their large eyes and delicate features.'[17]

Their next call was at Dresden, where they spent three days. Wishing to attend Sunday service, Dodgson looked on the map and found three churches listed as 'the English Church', and concluded that two of them were probably dissenters, so he went to none of them, although it was Sunday. Liddon went to the Roman Catholic Church, where Dodgson briefly joined him for the sake of the music; but in the evening there was some dissension between the two men about the validity of the service. 'He thought the Roman Catholic Church like a concert room – a wash out. Disliked the name Catholic because it connected it with Rome',[18] noted Liddon.

After overnight stops at Leipzig and Giessen, they moved on briefly to Ems, which Dodgson found delightful:

> The really unique feature of the scenery was the way in which the old castles seemed to grow, rather than to have been built, on the tops of the rocky promontories that showed their heads here and there among the trees. I have never seen architecture that seemed so entirely in harmony with the spirit of the place. By some subtle instinct the old architects seem to have chosen both form and colour, the grouping of the towers with their pointed spires, and the two neutral tints, light grey and brown, for the walls and roof, so as to produce buildings which look as naturally fitted to the spot as the heath or the harebells. And like the flowers and the rocks, they seemed instinct with no other meaning than rest and silence.[19]

Finally, they somewhat reluctantly took the Rhine steamer to Bingen, before making their final run, to Paris. 'I wonder no more that Parisians call London "triste",'[20] commented Dodgson, who was impressed by the beautiful parks and open spaces. The Paris Exhibition, concerts, theatre visits and last-minute shopping occupied most of his six days in the city. In all, his tour had lasted two months when at 2 a.m. on 14 September 1867 he embarked at Calais:

> We had a beautifully smooth passage, and a clear moonlight night to enjoy it in – the moon shining out with all its splendour, as if to make up for the time lost during the eclipse it had suffered four hours earlier – I remained in the bow most of the time of our passage, sometimes chatting with the sailor on the look-out, and sometimes watching, through the last hour of my first foreign tour, the lights of Dover, as they slowly broadened on the horizon, as if the old land were opening its arms to receive its homeward bound children – till they finally stood out clear and bold as the two light-houses on the cliff – till that which had long been merely a glimmering line on the dark water, like a reflection of the Milky Way, took form and substance as the lights of the shoreward houses – till the faint white line behind them, that looked at first like a mist creeping along the horizon, was visible at last in the grey twilight as the white cliffs of old England.[21]

Shortly before he embarked on his Russian tour, Dodgson had begun writing a story for *Aunt Judy's Magazine*, and soon after he returned to Christ Church in October 1867 he sent the completed manuscript to the editor, Mrs Alfred Gatty. *Bruno's Revenge*, as he called it, tells how fairies can be seen, and what can be done to help them, and how a naughty little boy called Bruno can be changed into a well-behaved and willing child, to the delight of his angelic sister Sylvie. Mrs Gatty's response was enthusiastic. She published it in December 1867, and urged Dodgson to write more. 'You may have great mathematical abilities, but so have hundreds of others,' she wrote. 'This talent is peculiarly your own, and as an Englishman you are almost unique in possessing it. If you covet fame, therefore, it will be (I think) gained by this. Some of the touches are so exquisite, one would have thought nothing short of intercourse with fairies could have put them into your head.'[22] The tale was accompanied by an illustration by F. Gilbert, which Dodgson condemned in a letter to Harry Furniss almost twenty years later: 'They both look grown-up, and something like a blacksmith and a ballet-dancer.'[23]

Dodgson found the lecturing work more than he could cope with that term, and had to arrange for Bartholomew Price to take up to eight of his pupils, for which Dodgson paid him £50 a term. Even so, he was almost as busy in the following term, remaining so until after Easter, when his old friend and rival Bosanquet took up a vacant position as Reader in Mathematics. Dodgson's responsibilities were further increased when, on Bayne's nomination, he was made Pro-Proctor, with an active part in College discipline. This left him little opportunity for writing in term-time. However, he had several projects on hand. As early as August 1866 he had begun to consider French and German editions of *Alice*. Although Macmillan had reacted favourably, the consensus of opinion was that the heavy reliance on puns, parodies and poems made the book untranslatable. But Dodgson's Aunt Caroline introduced him to a language teacher called Antoinie Zimmerman, who set to work on the German translation. Meanwhile, in April 1867, Dodgson had located a French translator in Oxford. Henri Bué was then completely unknown, but he worked with amazing speed and translated the entire book in about two months. While the son was engaged on the translation, Dodgson was taking lessons from the father to improve his own standard of French, enabling him to appraise the text more competently himself. He even felt confident enough later to venture into the field of French verse composition, and his friend Bayne recorded one of Dodgson's verses in his diary:

> On sort, on crie;
>   C'est la vie.
> On crie, on sort,
>   C'est la mort.

But despite the improvement in his own critical standard, he relied heavily on the judgment of others, and on 31 October 1867 he sent the songs for the French *Alice* to George Du Maurier, the artist, for criticism. In January 1868, while at Ripon, he also informed Macmillan that he wished to produce a very small edition of a book of poems for adults. 'My idea is to do all for it that type and paper will do, and to use broad leads – I think none but the very best poetry will stand close printing and cheap paper,' he wrote. The volume was to be entitled *Phantasmagoria and other Poems*, the focal point being a previously unpublished, whimsical poem in seven cantos, about a friendly ghost who expounds 'Hys Fyve Rules' for haunting, and points out that the things ghosts do are by no means enjoyable. The book was ultimately divided into two parts, the first comprising thirteen humorous poems, including the title poem, and the second consisting of thirteen serious ones. Of the twenty-six poems only six were previously unpublished, the remainder having already appeared in magazines. Those not previously published include an acrostic on the names Lorina, Alice and Edith, and 'Christmas Greetings', written at Christmas 1867, and later included in the facsimile edition of *Alice's Adventures Underground*, and separately published in 1884. Dodgson's original intention was to produce an edition of six hundred copies of *Phantasmagoria*, of which only two hundred would contain *The Elections to the Hebdomadal Council*, which deals with an Oxford matter. But when the edition came out in January 1869, all copies had this item. By 7 January 1869 Macmillan had already sold three or four hundred copies to the trade, and had secured Dodgson's permission to print a further thousand.

The volume had no illustrations. His ripening friendship with the Du Maurier family had encouraged him to think that Du Maurier might illustrate it and he asked the artist to draw a specimen illustration for him. But when Dodgson called on the family in April 1868, he learned that Du Maurier had developed an eye condition which forced him to defer the project.

Meanwhile Dodgson's mathematical writings had been rapidly developing. In December 1867 he had brought out *An Elementary Treatise on Determinants*, which he had written in the space of a month, and in the first two weeks of January 1868 he had written almost the whole of *The Fifth Book of Euclid treated Algebraically*, a thirty-eight page booklet published later in the year. He was also continuing with his manuscript on Geometric Conic Sections, and a few months later he published anonymously an eight-page pamphlet entitled *Formulae in Algebra for Responsions*. More importantly, he had written a few more pages of what he described as 'the second volume of Alice', better known as *Through the Looking-Glass*. But what now exercised his mind was not the text of the book, but who should illustrate it. Tenniel did his best to avoid taking it on, by pleading that he could not begin work on it until 1870, if then. Dodgson next decided to try Sir Noel Paton, and his friend Goerge MacDonald wrote, at his request, to the artist, inviting him to undertake the commission. But he was too ill to do it, and urged

Dodgson strongly to approach Tenniel again, as he was clearly the man for the job. Fortunately, Dodgson took his advice, this time offering to pay Tenniel's publishers for five months of his time; and finally, in June 1868 Tenniel undertook the commission, on the understanding that he would have to fit it in as and when his commitments allowed. Dodgson gratefully accepted.

On 21 June 1868 Dodgson's father died. He had been somewhat indisposed, but not sufficiently so to cause alarm. The end came suddenly. According to *The Church Times*[24] 'The Archdeacon had been out within a day or two, but was seized with a severe attack of diarrhoea, which carried him off in a few hours.' His daughters who had nursed him with every care, and had kept a log of the progression of his illness and his changes of temperature, were stunned by his death. Dodgson was at Oxford when the news came. Almost thirty years later he described his father's death as 'the greatest blow that has ever fallen on my life'.[25] And in a letter to a friend, he wrote, 'In those solemn days, when we used to steal, one by one, into the darkened room, to take yet another look at the dear calm face, and to pray for strength, the one feature in the room that I remember was a framed text, illuminated by one of my sisters, "Then are they glad, because they are at rest; and so he bringeth them into the haven where they would be." That text will always have for me, a sadness and a sweetness of its own.'[26] The same words were carved on the tombstone shared by the Archdeacon and his wife, and the illuminated text always hung in Dodgson's bedroom in the family home.

Dodgson spent the first seven weeks after his father's death at Croft. He was now head of the family. None of his brothers and sisters was married. Skeffington had taken Priest's Orders and would need a suitable living within easy reach of the family. Edwin, at twenty-two years of age, was not definitely settled in a career. At this point Wilfred was the only member of the family, apart from Charles, whose future was already mapped out. The rectory would have to be vacated for Mr Law, the new incumbent, so that a home would have to be found, and surplus furniture and effects were to be sold at the auction which he had arranged for early September. The family was to move out on 1 September, and he, Elizabeth and Caroline were to go into lodgings while the rest went to relatives at Whitburn and Scarborough. It was a heavy load of responsibility. 'May God help me to be a real comfort to the dear ones around me!'[27] he wrote.

By 9 August he was able to report that the family's plans were firmer, and that their ideas of a home were inclining to Guildford. This was a major step, for the Dodgsons had always lived in the north of England, and had close family ties there still. In some ways it might have been expected that Dodgson would have taken the opportunity of establishing his sisters in the Oxford area, both for the sake of convenience, and also to widen their circle of acquaintances to include more cultured, eligible bachelors; but perhaps he felt that close proximity might have ruptured the sense of privacy and personal freedom that he had come to value so much. Guildford had excellent rail connections with London and was within easy reach of Oxford. The population was under ten thousand, though by the turn of the century it had risen to thirteen thousand, but the reasons why the family chose it remain obscure. An old school friend from Dodgson's Rugby days, called George Portal, was rector at Albury, but the friendship was not sufficiently close to constitute a reason for moving near him.

However, Dodgson may have known that his artist friends Mr and Mrs Anderson were looking for a suitable property in the area. He enjoyed their company, and admired their work, particularly their paintings of children. He also applauded Mrs Anderson's perspicacity in engaging as a servant Elizabeth Turnbull, Hughes' model for 'Girl with Lilacs', which resulted in her being permanently available to sit for her, while at the same time being unavailable for other artists. The Dodgson sisters, like Charles Dodgson, had inherited their father's love of art, and the Andersons would have been ideal social contacts. In the previous year Dodgson had submitted to Mrs Anderson for criticism a photograph of 'Minnie Morton' which his sister Mary had coloured. Mrs Anderson had indicated that the face was too blue and that the hair ended too abruptly, like a wig. At that period Mary was keenly interested in the colouring of photographs and Mr Anderson suggested a change in techniques: that after the photographs had been made transparent with mastic varnish the colour be applied by laying oil paint at the back in masses, which would show through and give a very rich effect. This he said could be heightened by adding a few touches at the front.

On 14 August 1868 Dodgson arrived in Guildford on a house-hunting expedition and, by a stroke of great good fortune, met Mr Anderson and went on a 'voyage of discovery' with him. Dodgson quickly found two houses which would suit the family: 'The Chestnuts', with an excellent view, almost two hundred yards from Guildford High Road, and another with an even better view and a much better garden, but less conveniently situated in the village of Merrow. Next day, Dodgson went to look at two houses near Dorking, but found the town inferior to Guildford. Three days later he took Fanny and Aunt Lucy to 'The Chestnuts', and they liked it so well that the matter was settled without their bothering to visit the other houses. The lease was taken out in Charles' name.

'The Chestnuts' looks like a late Georgian building, but in fact it was built in 1860, as part of the development of land near Guildford Castle which took place after the removal of the country gaol in 1853. It had stood empty for eight years and the Dodgsons were its first occupants. Although it had four storeys, including a semi-basement, and eight bedrooms, it was only just adequate for a family of eight women, their brothers when at home, and the servants. There was constant movement in a family of that size, with frequent reciprocal visits to relatives, and the house was so crowded with visitors that Dodgson himself on his frequent visits often had to put up at the White Lion or the White Hart.

Dodgson's tendency to withdraw from society in the latter years of his life makes it easy to overlook the essential gregariousness of his nature. His eagerness for social links for himself and his family is clearly demonstrated in his early visits to Guildford. Perhaps his new status as head of the family increased his self-confidence, for within three days he had not only met up with the Andersons, but had called three times on the Portals at Albury, met Sir Benjamin Brodie and his daughter Ethel and been invited to dinner, established contact with Robert Trimmer, the Vicar of St Mary's, Guildford, and met the granddaughters of Sir Henry Austen, of Shalford House, near Guildford. When the family took possession of 'The Chestnuts' shortly afterwards, social contacts were already well established. Some of these contacts were permanently recorded by Dodgson little more than a year later in a pamphlet, now exceedingly rare, called *The Guildford Gazette Extraordinary*, in which he celebrated a private theatrical performance which he attended on 28 December 1869 at the house of his friend, William W. Follett Synge. Anthony Trollope, the novelist, and his wife were present, together with other friends. To what extent Dodgson's enjoyment of the evening was due to the presence of a number of young ladies is a matter for conjecture, but he described Alice Shute's singing as '*the* treat of the evening', and wrote, 'we can only say that if Cupid's darts were not flying thick as hail, it was not for want of bright eyes to rain them down'.[28] Both Edwin and Wilfred Dodgson had speaking parts in the theatricals, and Charles himself played the part of an MD in a charade in dumb-show. At the end of the performance Mrs Trollope and their host danced an Irish jig. 'So brilliant was the performance of each in this most spirited of dances, that it is scarcely possible to award to either the palm of superiority: all we can say is, that all the previous Terpsichorean feats of the evening were fairly overtopped and thrown into the shade, and that the spectators applauded with an unbounded enthusiasm this richest, most comical, and most memorable gem of their evening's entertainment,'[29] Dodgson wrote.

Within a few months of his father's death, Dodgson's life had resumed its normal pattern, though he still had much work to do in connection with the drawing up of the executors' accounts. He had seen his brothers Skeffington and Edwin settled professionally, the former in a curacy near Chertsey, and the latter in the Post Office. His sister Mary became officially engaged in the autumn of 1868 to the Rev. Charles Collingwood, whom she had met at Whitburn in the early days after her father's death, and whom she married in April 1869.

In October 1868 Dodgson moved into the suite of rooms, formerly occupied by Lord Bute, on the first and second floors of the north-west corner of Tom Quad. Reputedly the best suite in the College, it consisted of a large sitting room with two turretted alcoves overlooking St Aldate's, a smaller sitting room or study, two bedrooms and an entrance lobby. Permission was also given to him to erect a photographic studio on the top, which replaced one he had rented at £6 a year in the yard of Badcock the builder. His dark-room was a large closet on the upper floor of his suite. Many years afterwards, Alice Liddell recalled the excitement of his dark-room:

> What could be more thrilling than to see the negative gradually take shape, as he gently rocked it to and fro in the acid bath? Besides, the dark-room was so mysterious, and we felt that any adventure might happen there! There were all the joys of preparation, anticipation, and realization, besides the feeling that we were assisting at some secret rite usually reserved for grown-ups![30]

Many child friends recalled in later years the strong smell of photographic chemicals that pervaded Dodgson's rooms. A clear picture emerges, too, of the large sitting room, with its green wallpaper and turkey carpets, its red brocade curtains and matching red sofa and chair covers. His dining table and writing desk were of mahogany, and he had a reading stand at which he stood writing into the early hours of the morning. The walls were lined with books, pictures and photographs, including some taken by Dodgson himself of favourite child friends.

In spite of the spaciousness of his College apartment, Dodgson still felt the need of additional accommodation. In 1890 he took over the lease of a house belonging to Christ Church at 6 Brewer Street, Oxford. The following letter, dated 28 February 1890, to his niece Edith, enclosing £5 for her to buy educational books, tells her about his new house.

> You see one is so cramped in one's tiny College rooms: but, by having a house in Brewer Street *as well*, one really has enough room to swing a cat.

> He took a second-storey flat
> In which you could not swing a cat.
> But such was never his intent:
> His only object was low rent:
> And to swing cats he never meant.[31]

But Dodgson's tenure was short-lived, for less than two years later the house was demolished to make way for Christ Church Choir School.

REFERENCES

1   Peter Parley (i.e. Samuel G. Goodrich), *Tales about Europe*, p. 16.
2   John Francis McDermott (ed.), *The Russian Journal and other Selections*, New York, 1935, p. 73.
3   Liddon, Ms. Diaries.
4   John Francis McDermott (ed.), *The Russian Journal and other Selections*, New York, 1935, p. 73.
5   Liddon, Ms. Diaries, 15 July 1867.
6   Liddon, Ms. Diaries.
7   Collingwood, pp. 98–9. (N.B. Collingwood's account differs marginally from that in *The Russian Journal*, but Collingwood does not actually state his source, and may be quoting from a letter. Dodgson often used his journal as a basis for his letters.)
8   *Russian Journal*, p. 87.
9   Liddon, Ms. Diaries.
10   *Russian Journal*, pp. 91–2.
11   Ibid, p. 93.
12   Ibid, pp. 96–7.
13   J. O. Johnstone, *Life of Henry Parry Liddon*, 1904, p. 104.
14   *Russian Journal*, p. 106.
15   Liddon, Ms. Diaries.
16   J. O. Johnstone, *Life of Henry Parry Liddon*, 1904, p. 108.
17   *Russian Journal*, p. 115.
18   Liddon, Ms. Diaries.
19   *Russian Journal*, p. 118.
20   Ibid, p. 119.
21   Ibid, p. 121.
22   Collingwood, p. 109.
23   *The Lewis Carroll Handbook*, 1970, p. 42.
24   28 June 1868.
25   Collingwood, p. 131.
26   Ibid.
27   Ms. Diaries, 2 August 1868.
28   *The Guildford Gazette Extraordinary*, 29 December 1869, p. 3.
29   Ibid, p. 14.
30   *Cornhill Magazine*, July 1932, Alice and Caryl Hargreaves, 'Alice's Recollections of Carrollian Days. As told to her son, Caryl Hargreaves.'
31   E. H. Courville, *Autograph Prices Current*, vol. iv, August 1918–July 1919 (drawn to my attention by R. B. Shaberman.)

10 Through the Looking-Glass

In January 1869 Dodgson sent the first chapter of Behind the Looking-Glass to Macmillan: the title *Through the Looking-Glass* was later suggested by Liddon. The German translation of *Alice's Adventures* was brought out in February 1869 and the French one four months later. Specially bound copies of each were sent, with the Queen's permission, to Princess Beatrice. But there was now no mention in the diaries of the Liddell children, while, as if by way of compensation, a variety of other child friends filled his leisure and kept his camera busy. In the summer vacation he spent a week at Torquay with the Rev. Marsham Argles, Canon of Peterborough, and his family. It was an enjoyable time for Dodgson, with long walks amid the beautiful coastal scenery and plenty of opportunities for photography. He took some excellent pictures, and was especially pleased with one of a child called Laura Smith, on a tiger skin. On the journey home he wrote a double acrostic called 'Babbacombe Friendship' for Edith Argles. He also took some excellent photographs at Guildford, and on 5 October noted, 'some of the prettiest photographs I have done for some time have been of May and Edith Haydon in their seaside dresses, tunics and knickerbockers – but they do not surpass those I took today of the little Watsons'. This was a 'white stone' day for Dodgson.

In January 1870 Dodgson visited Tenniel in London and saw rough sketches of about ten pictures for *Through the Looking-Glass*. Two months later he called again and spent a couple of hours with the artist. Together they arranged about thirty pictures, the first three having already been sent to be cut. In its final form the book contained twelve chapters and fifty illustrations, though in early 1870 Dodgson was still working on the basis that there would be only forty-two pictures and eleven chapters: indeed, the text was far from complete at this stage. Yet by 15 April 1870 Dodgson had already seen and criticized a trial title page which Macmillan had had set up for him; and though it is tempting to dismiss as hyper-critical, Dodgson's complaints of bad spacing and misplaced commas, there is no doubt that the title page in its final form was far superior to the original.

Commemoration, on 22 June 1870, was of more than ordinary

interest to Dodgson, for Lord Salisbury was installed as Chancellor of the University, and Liddon was given the honorary degree of DCL. Dodgson attended the ceremony with his Guildford friend Synge, who was his guest. Afterwards Liddon applied to Lady Salisbury on Dodgson's behalf for permission to photograph the children, as a result of which Dodgson was very cordially received by Lady Salisbury. 'I fancy *Wonderland* had a great deal to do with my gracious reception,' he wrote afterwards. Next day Lord Salisbury and the children came to his rooms, and he took negatives of Lord Salisbury alone, and with his two little boys in the robes they had worn as his train-bearers. In the afternoon Lady Salisbury brought the children again, and looked at pictures, including the first seven illustrations for *Through the Looking-Glass*. When she departed to make some calls, she left the children with Dodgson, and he took two more photographs, one of Lady Gwendolen and Lady Maud Cecil, and the other of all four children. Two weeks later he dined at Lord Salisbury's London home, and next day photographed the four children again at the home of his artist-friend Henry Holiday, where he had set up his camera for a few days. There were two further visits from the children that summer, and on 28 July he noted that lately he had been writing verse riddles for them, a style of composition that was new to him. Some of these, under the title 'Puzzles from Wonderland', found their way into *Aunt Judy's Magazine* in December 1870.

During the summer of 1870 his sister Louisa's health had given serious cause for concern, and in mid August he went down to the coast to find a suitable place for a recuperative holiday. He chose Margate, and spent five weeks there with Louisa, Fanny, Margaret and Miss Goode, daughter of the former Dean of Ripon, who had been a firm friend of the Dodgson sisters, despite the controversy between their fathers over Mr Dodgson's sermon *Ritual Worship*. Dodgson met many pleasant people at Margate, chiefly through their children, but commented: 'Very few turned out to be above the commercial class – the one drawback of Margate society.'[1]

Back at Oxford, Dodgson wrote to the Dean and suggested that as his friend Sampson was now to be a Lecturer, he himself should take the Pass-work only, leaving all the Class-work to Sampson. He had previously given up £150 of his salary of £500 for help with this work, but now offered to divide it equally in order to buy extra time for his literary pursuits. In November he received a copy of the *Songs from Alice's Adventures in Wonderland*, with music by William Boyd of Worcester College. He had added a further two lines to the second stanza of the song ''Tis the voice of the Lobster', which he amended and expanded even further in 1886 for Savile Clarke's *Alice* operetta.

Towards the close of 1870 he received two invitations to spend a few days with Lord and Lady Salisbury at Hatfield House; the first he declined because it clashed with the election of Senior Studentships at Christ Church, and the second for 31 December 1870 to 3 January 1871 he accepted; but in the event he could not go, because he had a severe cough. Despite his reluctance to face a railway journey in his poor state of health, he had travelled to Guildford on Christmas Eve, and after a single night at 'The Chestnuts' had moved into the White Lion as the family home was overcrowded. He found the solitary leisure enjoyable, and decided that he would do no work other than draw up examples for lectures. Clearly he did not regard *Through the Looking-Glass* as work, for on 4 January 1871 he finally finished the manuscript and sent it to Macmillan. On 13 January he received the slips for all except the verses at the end from Clay the printer, and next day he dispatched them to Tenniel. He still had hopes of getting the book out for Easter, but everything now depended on the artist.

Early in 1871 Dodgson was faced with a problem which he felt could best be resolved by approaching a number of his friends to obtain a consensus of opinion. The matter concerned Tenniel's drawing of the Jabberwock, which had been proposed as the frontispiece, but which Dodgson feared might prove too terrifying for nervous children. He accordingly wrote to about thirty mothers asking them to exhibit the picture to any children they thought fit, and to indicate which of the following three courses they could recommend:

1)   To retain it as the frontispiece.
2)   To transfer it to its proper place in the book (where the ballad occurs which it is intended to illustrate) and substitute a new frontispiece.
3)   To omit it altogether.

'The last-named course would be a great sacrifice of the time and trouble which the picture has cost, and it would be a pity to adopt it unless it is really necessary,'[2] he added. In the event course No. 2 was chosen, and a picture of the White Knight was substituted for the Jabberwock as the frontispiece. Few people would dispute that this was the right choice.

As always, Dodgson was an exacting critic of the illustrations, and constantly asked for minor amendments. He disliked the crinoline, and insisted that the suggestion of crinoline in Alice's costume be modified; he complained that the White Knight should not look too old, and demanded that he be shorn of his whiskers. But Tenniel, too, was capable of criticism, often of a constructive nature, the most important of all his objections leading to the omission of an entire chapter. The portrayal of a wasp in a wig was in his view 'beyond the appliances of art'. 'Don't think me brutal,' Tenniel wrote, 'but I am bound to say that the *wasp* chapter doesn't interest me in the least, and I can't see my way to a picture. If you want to shorten the book, I can't help thinking – with all submission – that *there* is your opportunity.'[3] It was at Tenniel's suggestion that Dodgson made a textual alteration to 'The Walrus and the Carpenter', and omitted an elderly lady from the third chapter of the book. Whether or not these amendments and omissions improve the book is debatable, but they indicate the value set by Dodgson on the opinions of others, and of his artist in particular.

As the year progressed and the work on the book continued, family matters continued to claim Dodgson's attention. In April 1871 his brother Wilfred secured the agency of Lord Boyne's estates in Shropshire, an important event which enabled him to go ahead with his plans for his long-hoped-for marriage to Alice Jane Donkin. Soon afterwards Wilfred visited Oxford, and Dodgson gave dinner parties for his future sister-in-law and her family. These dinner parties sparked off in Dodgson one of the countless minor ingenuities which were so characteristic of him. Irked by the necessity of explaining which gentleman would escort each lady in to dinner, and who was to sit where, he devised a series of cards indicating the seating arrangements, and bracketing each gentleman with the lady he was to escort. The master card could then be kept as a permanent record, and would help the host on future occasions by reminding him which guests got on well together. Dodgson toyed with the idea of publishing such cards. In the late autumn he tried the idea out on a friend, Mrs Bradley, and was delighted with her favourable reaction. But when he discovered that his friend Harcourt believed the idea to be his, his enthusiasm waned, and he abandoned all thought of publishing the notion.

In the long vacation Dodgson visited 'The Moor', Wilfred's future home, which was being refurbished ready for the young couple, and pronounced it a capital house with large gardens. The wedding took place in August. A month later Dodgson went to Bo'ness to visit his father's step-sister Mary and her husband William Wilcox, who, like Dodgson's father, was a grandson of the Bishop of Elphin. He spent five days with them, and described them as 'the heartiest of hosts and hostesses'. Another highlight of the vacation was Dodgson's visit to Sir Noel Paton on the Isle of Arran, where he was most kindly received, and taken on a sailing expedition to see the laying and taking in of a 'long sea line', 700 yards long, with a thousand hooks. Later Sir Noel took him to see the Hermit's Cave on Holy Island, after which Dodgson spent the evening with the family and their friends. By the end of the day Dodgson was a friend of everyone there, but particularly of Sir Noel's daughter Mona, and enjoyed himself so well that he went back for two or three hours with them a few days later. When he left, he carried with him a note authorizing him to look over the portfolios in Sir Noel's studio. Availing himself of this privilege, he described the experience as 'such a treat as I do not remember *ever* having had in any one day. The drawings are perfectly exquisite, and almost come up to *my* highest ideals of beauty,'[4] – an indication that he realized how exacting he was as an art critic. In Edinburgh and Glasgow his companion for a week was Uncle Skeffington, newly recovered from a freak accident when he was struck on the head by a stone flung at the train he was travelling in.

When the term began Dodgson was still preoccupied with family matters. His youngest brother Edwin had finally decided to abandon the post office and study for Priest's Orders, and to this end now began his first term at Chichester Theological College. His Aunt Lucy, who had had to consult an eye specialist in the summer, had an operation on both eyes in September, and afterwards went to stay with her brother Skeffington in Onslow Square, where Dodgson visited her. Concerned for the future of the family, Dodgson now made his will.

On 11 October 1871 Dodgson received five finished sheets of *Through the Looking-Glass* and noted that the book was printing off rapidly. Of the Liddells there was still no word in the Diaries – until 16 November 1871, when Dodgson records meeting the party from the Deanery at a reception given in the new Common Room by Sidney Owen, a tutor and Reader in Law and Modern History at Christ Church. He took in Edith Liddell to dinner, and found her a very pleasant neighbour; but they were so far estranged that he had to break the ice first, and of Alice there is no mention.

On 21 November Dodgson telegraphed to Clay his authority to electrotype all the rest of *Through the Looking-Glass*, and followed it up with a couple of postal corrections. Meanwhile, he had sent his cousin Menella Smedley the text of a little address in pamphlet form entitled *To all Child-Readers of Alice*, which she approved in a letter Dodgson received on 22 November. He then had it printed as a four-page pamphlet to be inserted in copies of *Through the Looking-Glass*, and presumably, in *Alice's Adventures in Wonderland* also.

On 30 November Macmillan informed him that preliminary orders already accounted for 7500 copies of *Through the Looking-Glass*. As only 9000 copies had been printed, they decided to print a further 6000. The first complete copy reached Dodgson on 6 December 1871, and two days later he received three copies bound in morocco, and a hundred in cloth.

Alice's personal copy was to have had a mirror incorporated in the cover, but the notion proved impractical, and finally Dodgson decided on morocco. Her book was despatched with cloth-bound copies for Lorina and Edith to the Deanery before any others were sent out. He then sent out ninety-six more cloth-bound copies, and morocco-bound copies to Florence Terry and Tennyson, making a total of a hundred given away in a single day. The book then went on sale to the public in time for the Christmas market, though the imprint of the first edition was 1872.

Of the reactions of the family at the Deanery and of the numerous other friends who thus received copies, he wrote absolutely nothing. From 7 to 18 December he was confined to his rooms with a chill and a cough which troubled him at night, but he was not too ill to take an active interest in the progress of the printing of the additional copies. Tenniel had complained about inequality of printing in a further batch of 3000 copies of *Alice's Adventures in Wonderland*. Dodgson thought these imperfections due to pressing the sheets between blank leaves to accelerate the drying process. He accordingly wrote to Macmillan on 17 December 1871:

> I have now made up my mind that whatever be the *commercial* consequences, we must have no more artistic 'fiascos' – and I am stimulated to write *at once* about it by your alarming words of this morning. 'We are going on with another 6000 *as fast as possible.*' My decision is, we must have *no more hurry*: and *no more sheets must be pressed under blank paper*. It is my *particular desire* that all the sheets shall in future be 'stacked' and left to dry naturally. The result of this may possibly be that 6000 will not be ready for sale till the end of January or even later. Very well: then fix that date in your advertisement: say that 'owing to the delay necessary to give the pictures their full artistic effect, no more copies can be delivered until the end of January.'
>
> You will think me a lunatic for thus wishing to send away money from the doors; and will tell me perhaps that I shall thus lose thousands of would-be purchasers, who will not wait so long, but will go and buy other Christmas books. I wish I could put into words how entirely such arguments go for nothing with me. As to how many copies we sell I care absolutely nothing: the one only thing I *do* care for is, that all copies that *are* sold shall be artistically first-rate.[5]

In 1865 Dodgson's motive in withdrawing the first edition of *Alice's Adventures in Wonderland* had been his sense of duty towards his artist, and though this continued to be an important factor it was now clearly reinforced by his feeling of moral responsibility towards the British public. Tenniel had cause to be grateful to Dodgson for his care in the matter of printing standards. Though the *Alice* books were Tenniel's crowning achievement, and owed as much to Dodgson's close personal supervision of the project as to his own artistic talent, he privately resolved never to work for him again. Many years later, when declining a request from Dodgson to illustrate another project, he wrote, 'It is a curious fact that with *Through the Looking-Glass* the faculty of making drawings for book illustrations departed from me, and notwithstanding all sorts of tempting inducements, I have done nothing in that direction since.'

The success of *Through the Looking-Glass* was immediate. On 27

January 1872, his fortieth birthday, Dodgson heard from George Lillie Craik of Macmillan's that 15,000 copies had been sold, and that there were orders for 500 more. Like *Alice's Adventures in Wonderland*, the book was essentially dramatic in presentation, with heavy emphasis on dialogue. Opinions vary as to which of the books is the better. Some people admire the tighter structure of *Through the Looking-Glass*, while others prefer the greater spontaneity of *Alice's Adventures*. But both contain a wealth of effervescent dialogue, memorable songs and unforgettable characters, and are so well matched that to many readers the two books merge to become simply *Alice*. They are as evenly balanced as Dodgson could make them. Each contains twelve chapters; and surely it is not a coincidence that added and (appropriately in that land where everything is back to front) reversed they make forty-two. This 'magic' number permanently intrigued Dodgson, and he included it in many of his works: Rule 42 in the Trial Scene in *Alice's Adventures in Wonderland*, Rule 42 in the preface to *The Hunting of the Snark*, and the age of the narrator in *Phantasmagoria*.[6]

Just as the Liddell children's preoccupation with croquet had offered a focal point in *Alice's Adventures in Wonderland*, so their later interest in chess provided the framework for its sequel. The moves in the game are not worked out in correct sequence according to the rules of modern chess, for Dodgson's interest lay in the implications of the moves rather than in the game itself. Alexander Taylor aptly noted this:

> He based his story, not on a game of chess, but on a chess lesson or demonstration of the moves such as he gave to Alice Liddell, a carefully worked-out sequence of moves designed to illustrate the queening of a pawn, the relative powers of the pieces – the feeble king, the eccentric knight and the formidable queen whose powers include those of rook and bishop – and finally a checkmate. That is to say, he abstracted from the game exactly what he wanted for his design, and expressed that as a game between a child of seven-and-a-half who was to 'be' a White Pawn and an older player (himself) who was to manipulate the other pieces.[7]

Most remarkable of the poems in *Through the Looking-Glass* is *Jabberwocky*, which takes as its first and last verse the 'Stanza of Anglo-Saxon Poetry' which he had composed at Whitburn in 1855 and copied into *Mischmasch*. In January 1868 he was already concerned about the technicalities of producing the verse in mirror fashion, back to front, and wrote to Macmillan about it; but although Macmillan confirmed that it was technically possible, Dodgson decided to print only the first stanza in reverse, in order not to weary the reader. The poem demonstrates Dodgson's total ignorance of Anglo-Saxon language and poetic tradition. He is totally unaware not only of basic vocabulary, but also of inflexions and word order. An Anglo-Saxon poet would have used unrhymed qualitative verse, i.e. sprung rhythm, as exploited by Gerard

Manley Hopkins, and to a limited extent by Coleridge and Swinburne. But though Hopkins was a contemporary of Dodgson's, his poetry was not published until 1918, and in Victorian England the experiments of Coleridge and Swinburne in this field were not fully understood or appreciated. Dodgson's poem was in quantitative verse, with rhyming quatrains throughout. The test of an Anglo-Saxon poet's skill was the extent to which he could 'vary his words' by elaborate metaphors and so forth. Dodgson varied his words not by metaphors but by portmanteaux and other nonsense words, occasionally interspersed with archaisms, but he retained the basic structure of modern English.

This ignorance of Old English was irrelevant to the success of the poem, both among the general readership, and in academic circles where the critics could be assumed to possess a degree of expertise. *Jabberwocky* immediately intrigued Dodgson's scholarly contemporaries, and as early as February 1872 Dr Robert Scott, co-author with Liddell of the *Greek Lexicon*, wrote an excellent German translation of the poem which he claimed was the original, of which Dodgson's was a translation. To Dodgson himself Scott wrote:

> Are we to suppose, after all, that the Saga of Jabberwocky is one of the universal heirlooms which the Aryan race at its dispersion carried with it from the great cradle of the family? You must really consult Max Müller about this. It begins to be probable that the *origo originalissima* may be discovered in Sanscrit, and that we shall by and by have a *Iabrivokaveda*. The hero will turn out to be the Sun-God in one of his Avatars; and the Tumtum tree the great Ash *Ygdrasil* of the Scandinavian mythology.[8]

The translation was discussed shortly afterwards in *Once a Week*:[9]

> Macmillan (No. 148) perpetuated a little hoax, not to be expected in such a staid magazine, in an article, 'The Jabberwock traced to its true source; by Thomas Chatterton.' This source was said to be the German of Hermann von Schwindel. By many readers it was taken in sober earnest. Overlooking the ominous names of Chatterton and Schwindel, they were completely taken in. . . . 'Macmillan' was about the last print in the world in which one would have expected to find the editor poking such fun at his readers. Of course, most of them could not read German. One good German scholar, however, was so far taken in by the verses 'De Jammerwoch' as to write to Heidelberg, to a savant there, to learn something more about them, under the impression for the moment, that they were written in some patois of the tongue of the Fatherland.

In March 1872 Augustus Vansittart, Fellow of Trinity College, Cambridge, translated *Jabberwocky* into Latin elegiacs under the title *Mors Iabrochii* for Trinity College Lecture Rooms. Here, as in many colleges, it was the practice once a week to set an English passage to be translated into Greek or Latin. Afterwards a 'model' translation by one of the fellows was handed out.[10] Dodgson's friend Bayne pasted a copy of the Latin page into his scrap-book. The popularity of this Latin version is indicated by the fact that in 1881 Vansittart published it in pamphlet form.

In *Through the Looking-Glass* it is Humpty Dumpty who interprets the meanings of the hard words in the first stanza of *Jabberwocky*. These words had already been defined in *Mischmasch*; but now in the dialogue between Humpty Dumpty and Alice the definitions have been polished and improved, thus revealing that the words acquired a specific meaning for Dodgson only after he had invented them. 'When *I* use a word . . . it means just what I choose it to mean – neither more nor less,' says Humpty Dumpty. It was a principle to which Dodgson returned often in his later writing. 'Any writer of a book is fully authorized in attaching any meaning he likes to any word or phrase he intends to use,' Dodgson wrote. 'If I find an author saying, at the beginning of his book, "Let it be understood that by the word *black* I shall always mean *white*, and that by the word *white* I shall always mean *black*, I meekly accept his ruling, however injudicious I may think it".'[11] Humpty Dumpty is the vehicle by means of which Dodgson conveys many of his ideas about language and logic. Of Dodgson's general system of semiotic theory, Robert D. Sutherland writes:

> It is highly unlikely that he ever developed a coherent and consistent scheme of linguistic theory. The principles to be inferred from his illustrations should not be regarded as scattered parts of a fossil skeleton, only requiring our articulation to form a reconstructed whole. One cannot hope to assemble a complete skeleton, for none is present. Over a period of years Carroll desposited these bones at random in a sedimentary matrix from which they must be extracted, and he did this without self-conscious plan or any expectation that a paleontologist would come seeking a complete skeleton. He was not a systemizer of linguistic theory. He was not a trained linguist. He was a logician and humorist who used his largely intuitive insights into the nature of language as a vehicle for a sophisticated kind of play.[12]

The character of the White Knight is in some respects even more interesting than that of Humpty Dumpty. William Empson remarks that he stands for the Victorian scientist, modestly and patiently labouring at absurd but fruitful conceptions. At the same time, with his parody of Wordsworth's 'Resolution and Independence' he also represents the poet. 'The Knight has the same readiness to accept new ideas and ways of life, such as the sciences were imposing without ceasing to be good and in his way sensible, as Alice herself shows for instance when in falling down the rabbit-hole she plans a polite entry into the Antipodes and is careful not to drop the marmalade onto the inhabitants,' Empson writes. 'It is the childishness of the Knight that lets him combine the virtues of the poet and the scientist, and one must expect a creature so finely suited to life to be absurd because life itself is absurd.'[13]

Although the White Knight was an entirely spontaneous creation not based on the character of any particular person, it is impossible to overlook certain similarities between the Knight and Dodgson himself. Such parallels as exist may be wholly coincidental, or they may have been subconscious. Certainly there is an allegorical significance in the journey with Alice almost to the edge of the brook which she must cross to become a queen. The moments leading up to their parting have a peculiar poignancy:

> Years afterwards she could bring the whole scene back again, as if it had been only yesterday – the mild blue eyes and kindly smile of the Knight – the setting sun gleaming through his hair, and shining on his armour in a blaze of light that quite dazzled her – the horse quietly moving about, with the reins hanging loose on his neck, cropping the grass at her feet – all this she took in like a picture, as, with one hand shading her eyes, she leant against a tree, watching the strange pair, and listening, in a half-dream, to the melancholy music of the song.

Tenniel was surely not unaware of the parallel between the character of the White Knight and the author. Carrying the notion one step forward, he turned the physical appearance of the White Knight into a self-portrait of the artist.

The excised 'Wasp in a Wig' chapter, which Dodgson omitted following Tenniel's objections, was missing for over a century. But in July 1974 it reappeared suddenly in Sotheby's Sale Rooms in the form of six galley proofs amended in the hand of the author and bearing his instruction to the printer to leave it out. The chapter was finally published for the first time on 4 September 1977. Its place in the book is after the parting with the White Knight and on the very brink of the brook which Alice must cross to become a queen. Hearing a sigh from the rheumaticky old man with the face like a wasp, and aware that once over the brook she will be powerless to help, Alice returns to talk to him. His peevish response offends her but, significantly, she reflects, 'Perhaps it's only pain that makes him so cross'.

Morton Cohen, in 'Alice: The Lost Chapter Revealed'[14] notes how the galleys reveal much of Dodgson's art and consistently high level of invention:

> The narrative is strong, the incidents develop well and, in a short space, we get an amount of characteristic Carrollian word play. Dodgson furthermore creates a truly believable character in the old wasp, who, however crotchety, elicits our sympathy. And the author shows his heroine, who, as we know, can be testy and impatient, in a generous, charitable light. Not least creative of Dodgson's concoctions here is a newspaper from which Alice reads aloud, printed for and about wasp society. Recalling that this is an early crude draft, still lacking Dodgson's final polish, we must concede it to be a remarkable accomplishment.

There is little doubt that the farewell to the wasp, like the farewell to the White Knight, symbolizes Alice's farewell to Dodgson. To this extent it is repetitive. It has less emotional appeal than the White Knight chapter, and its inclusion would have weakened the effect of this, the artistic, though not the structural, climax of the book. Some of the references, especially those about the relationship between pain and peevishness, seem particularly personal, and could be interpreted as Dodgson's apology for the aloofness he had adopted when his relationship with Alice Liddell broke down. On the whole Dodgson's decision to omit the chapter seems to have been the right one.

Such was the appeal to the imagination made by *Through the Looking-Glass* that, as with *Alice's Adventures*, those who knew Dodgson personally wished to identify in some way with the author and his books. After Dodgson's death many people came forward with stories about him, and in sifting through them it is clear that with the passage of time the memory of what had actually happened had lost something of its sharpness of focus. By far the most important of the stories about *Through the Looking-Glass* came from Alice Theodora Raikes, a remote connection of Dodgson's by marriage. Alice, who was born in 1862, was the eldest daughter of Henry Cecil Raikes, Member of Parliament and ultimately Postmaster General. The family lived at 95 Onslow Square, just a few doors away from Uncle Skeffington, and all the houses backed on to a communal garden. Sixty years after *Through the Looking-Glass* was published, Alice Raikes (then Mrs Wilson Fox) recalled meeting Dodgson in that garden:

> One day, hearing my name, he called me to him saying, 'So you are another Alice. I'm very fond of Alices. Would you like to come and see something which is rather puzzling?' We followed him into the house which opened, as ours did upon the garden, into a room full of furniture with a tall mirror standing across one corner.
> 'Now,' he said, giving me an orange, 'first tell me which hand you have got that in.' 'The right,' I said. 'Now,' he said, 'go and stand before that glass, and tell me which hand the little girl you see there has got it in.' After some perplexed contemplation, I said, 'The left hand.' 'Exactly,' he said, 'and how do you explain that?' I couldn't explain it, but seeing that same solution was expected, I ventured, 'If I was on the other side of the glass, wouldn't the orange still be in my right hand?' I remember his laugh. 'Well done, little Alice,' he said, 'the best answer I've had yet.'[15]

Since Dodgson rarely failed to call on Uncle Skeffington when in London, he could have met Alice Raikes on any of a number of visits. But his first recorded meeting with her did not take place until 24 June 1871, when he noted in his diary that he met her on the lawn, and that she took him in and introduced him to her father. Since the book was already advancing 'pretty well' in December 1867, when Alice Raikes was only five years old, and since in any event the nature of the question indicates that Dodgson was already preoccupied with the subject, the importance of this episode has to be kept strictly in perspective. Nevertheless, the incident is an intriguing one. Dodgson was certainly attached to Alice Raikes, and continued to call on her even when she was a married woman with a daughter of her own.

Despite its charm and humour, *Through the Looking-Glass* is intensely preoccupied with the transience of beauty, with decay, death and loss of maidenhood. Dodgson had a special reverence for maidenhood, a kind of awe which he once likened in a sermon to one aspect of man's love of God.[16] The introductory poem sets the theme:

> Come, hearken then, ere voice of dread,
>   With bitter tidings laden,
> Shall summon to unwelcome bed
>   A melancholy maiden!

The mood is of romanticized melancholy, closely akin to the emotions idealized by the Pre-Raphaelite Brotherhood, with which Dodgson was artistically in sympathy. The passage is capable of dual interpretation and no doubt Dodgson was fully conscious of this. While he could claim to speak metaphorically of mortality, he could equally well be referring literally to the 'arranged' marriage. Linked as it is so closely with sentiments of nostalgia, it is the nearest Dodgson ever comes to mourning his rejection publicly. For by this time he seems to have given up all hope of winning Alice's hand. He was now nearing his fortieth birthday, she her twentieth. They were 'half a life asunder', and he must have realized it would be only a matter of time before an eligible suitor claimed her hand. At around this period Dodgson's opposition to the Dean reached a peak. He may indeed have entertained hopes of marrying into the Dean's family, but his conduct was never modified on that account. Over the years he must have been a constant source of irritation to Liddell and it is remarkable that he was tolerated by the Dean and his wife for so long.

For an understanding of Dodgson's participation in College affairs, it is necessary to examine briefly what happened when Christ Church, which had had no statutes at all for over three centuries, suddenly received two sets within less than ten years. In 1850 a Royal Commission had been set up to look into Oxford matters. In making its report the Commission's principal intention was to transfer power to the Professors. But it failed to note that Christ Church was unique in its dual nature as both college and cathedral. The Dean and Chapter were powerful, prestigious and wealthy. They administered the vast College estates, distributing two-thirds of the annual income amongst themselves. The Professorial Canons were compelled to be resident, to deliver their statutory lectures, but the remaining Canons could, and often did, live elsewhere. But the Dean was constantly in residence during the term, and acted as a bridge between the Students and Chapter. The Students had no say in the government of the College, and the Dean and Chapter were reluctant to relinquish the immense power which they wielded.

Chief Architect of the Oxford Act of 1854 was Gladstone, then Member of Parliament for the University. By setting up a Royal Commission to interpret the Act he reduced direct interference by Parliament in University affairs to a minimum. The Act was a failure at Christ Church because it allowed the Students no voice in the government of the College, and thus did not secure for them the rights of Fellows in other Colleges. Its result was to split the College into two factions, on the one hand the Dean and Chapter, and on the other the Students. As a Student, Dodgson was therefore automatically at odds with the Dean on this issue. It was not until 1857 that the Students were consulted about the draft of the Ordinance, but when they were, Dodgson made his views on points of detail known to the Commission in letters which are still preserved in the Public Record Office. But at that time he was a very junior Student, and although his arguments were clearly and logically set out, they carried very little weight with the Commission.

Though Dodgson had opposed the Dean in the raising of Jowett's salary, the first recorded occasion on which he clashed openly with him on an individual basis was in January 1864, when the Dean's notice about the award of six Junior Studentships appeared in *The Times*. In Dodgson's view the right of the Electors to choose the person most fit in every respect was undermined by the Dean's statement that one of the Studentships would go to 'the candidate who shows the greatest proficiency in Mathematics'. As the probable mathematical assessor, Dodgson set out his reservations in a letter to the Dean. The latter considered his objections 'hypercritical and unnecessary', but agreed to modify the wording of future notices. This, however, was insufficient to satisfy Dodgson, who replied that it did not affect his objection to the present notice. When Liddell refused to amend it, Dodgson declined to act as assessor until such future time as the notice had been altered. Dodgson described their correspondence on the subject as rather 'disagreeable'.

On 1 February 1864, Dodgson, with a few suggestions from Bayne, composed a squib in thirteen rhyming couplets on the following day's division in convocation about the new Examination Statute. The voters are arranged alphabetically, with the names left blank, but Bayne's personal copy, still in Christ Church Library, reveals the identities. Bayne himself is not among them, but Dodgson is represented:

> I am the author, a rhymer erratic . . .
> J is for Jowett, who lectures in Attic:

K is for Kitchen, than attic much warmer,
L is for Liddell, relentless reformer! . . .
U's University, fractiously splitting,
V's the Vice Chancellor, ceaselessly sitting.
W's Wall, by Museum made frantic,
X the Xpenditure, grown quite gigantic.
Y are the young men, whom nobody thought about . . .
Z is the Zeal that this victory brought about.

Next day, by 281 votes to 243, Convocation passed the new Examination Statute introducing the third class degree in any school. Foreseeing in this the beginning of 'grievous changes' in the University, Dodgson wrote a letter to the Vice Chancellor announcing his resignation from the Examinership. He also had it printed in pamphlet form for distribution in the College, and it subsequently appeared in the *Morning Post*.[17] His objections were two-fold: first, that allowing students to abandon the study of classics in the latter half of their residence was a step towards 'a total surrender of the principle, hitherto inviolate, that the classics are an *essential* part of an Oxford education', and that the introduction of the new 'Fourth Class' would lower the status of 'Honours' graduates and degrade both Classics and Mathematics.

Dissatisfaction with the inferior status of Students at Christ Church was at its highest when, on 11 February 1865, a historic meeting was called in the rooms of T. J. Prout. Dodgson reported that there was agreement on the need for Students to be raised to the position of Fellows in the College. He himself seconded Prout's motion that this involved 'the admission of the Students into the Corporation of The House, with a due share of the administration of the revenues and in the government of the same, and also the possession of such other rights and privileges as commonly attach to the Fellows of other Colleges.'[18]

Three days later the Chapter decided to raise the salary of Benjamin Jowett, the Regius Professor of Greek, from £40 p.a. to £500, and until or unless some other means could be found to defray the cost by a proportionate levy on the means of the Dean and Canons. Pusey saw that this might be regarded as a precedent for requesting the increase of other salaries at the personal expense of the Dean and Chapter, and regarded it as 'inconvenient'. In view of the level of dissatisfaction among the Students, the Chapter also appointed a Committee composed of the Dean, Sub-Dean, Treasurer and Dr Pusey to look into their grievances and suggest remedies to the Chapter. For their part the Students appointed Prout, Sandford and Harcourt to confer with the Committee, and added the proposition that all Students should have a voice in the election of Students. At the same time Dodgson had raised the question of wages for college servants, another issue on which feelings ran high, and which publicly erupted in November 1865 in the so-called 'Bread and Butter Row'. For the servants were not paid a wage, and had to subsist by grossly overcharging the men for the compulsory food which established their being 'in residence'. The price charged for bread and butter, for instance, was 60 per cent higher than the normal purchase price. The management of the entire internal economy of the College was called into question, and somewhat unfairly some of the blame fell on Dodgson's Rugby contemporary, Walter Shirley, who had succeeded to the Canonry vacated by Arthur Penryn Stanley in 1864, and was appointed Treasurer early in 1865. There was a good deal of anonymous correspondence about the 'Bread and Butter Row' in *The Times*, which devoted a leader to the question. One 'Tutor of Christ Church', probably Osborne Gordon, wrote, 'It is hoped that in the course of the next year the government of Christ Church may be placed in the hands of those interested in it as a place of education – the Students, as distinguished from the Chapter. Were this done such abuses as those complained of would not last for a single day, and the noble revenues of Christ Church would be applied to their proper object – the cheapening of education.'

On 15 February 1865, at the height of the furore, Dodgson conceived the notion of producing *American Telegrams*, a squib embodying current Christ Church proceedings in the form of mock American news. Dodgson's device was topical, for the American Civil War was then in progress. President L . . . is, of course, Liddell. Both General Grant and General Butler are Henry Grant, the Butler of Christ Church, and the 'blot' is Alfred D. Blott, the Christ Church Under Treasurer. The Confederate 'Platform' is Dodgson's interpretation of the demands of the Students for alteration to the constitution and financial affairs of the College. The Dean had recently altered the hour of morning Chapel from 7 a.m. to 8 a.m., hence the remarks about General Early. 'Martial law' is a reference to the Examiner George Marshall, and 'Gold 200' to the value of a Senior Studentship. In view of its rarity, the text is given in full:

AMERICAN TELEGRAMS. – (SUMMARY.)

The interview which has just taken place, between President L and the Confederate Commissioners, has resulted in a proposal from the President that three representatives from each of the contending parties shall meet to arrange conditions of peace. The following is said to be the Confederate 'platform':

(1.) That the almost dictatorial power, held by General Grant, shall be largely curtailed, if not altogether abolished. It is understood that the President himself is so entirely under his influence as to be a free agent in name only: a state of things which, it is urged, cannot but be highly prejudicial to the Union.

(2.) That the enormities perpetrated by General Butler shall meet with their due reward. The document from which we quote urges that 'he has cost his country more in battels [*sic*] than any other known in our time,' and that 'the interests of the few magnates, whose wealth he has augmented, cannot be suffered to outweigh those of the Commons he has so wantonly sacrificed.'

(3.) That the Treasury shall be placed under the control of Confederates and Federals alike: the Confederates urge that their party is 'inadequately represented under the present administration,' and that the Secretary in particular 'would be a blot in any conceivable system of government.'

(4.) That the forces at present in occupation of Confederate territory be withdrawn. 'We can discuss no terms of peace,' say the Confederates, 'with an armed foe. It is unworthy the dignity of a nation to be thus dictated to by the roar of the canons [*sic*].'

2

Other minor propositions may, it is understood, be presented to the Federals for consideration. One is, 'that the services which General Early has rendered to his country be rewarded by advancement in the course of the ensuing summer. This proposal, however, is said to be distasteful to the Federals, and the President himself is so opposed to the very idea of Early rising, that there is little hope of its being agreed on. Various charges are brought against this unpopular general, of which his abandonment of 'Pillow' (the Federals' strongest fort) is one of the gravest.

———————

Gold 200, at which price it occasionally excites a brisk competition.

The difficulties of transit from place to place are enhanced by the insufficiency of public conveyances, and most of the travelling is done by means of private coaches. So much of the country, however, is still under martial law, that passes are not easy to obtain: in some instances they have been refused altogether.

The officers continue to send in long lists of sick and missing: much of this illness is supposed to be feigned for the sake of avoiding active service.

With a view to improving the condition of the lower classes, it is understood that collections will shortly be set on foot, under the authority of the President: this will probably have the effect of drawing attention to their number and wretchedness, but, beyond this, it is not anticipated that any great results will be derived from this measure.

Feb. 17, 1865.

C. L. Dodgson
Ch.Ch.

A fortnight later Dodgson conceived the idea of writing a sham mathematical paper on the controversy over Jowett's salary. The notion occurred to him of using π as the symbol of Jowett's remuneration and of hanging his problem on the most appropriate method of evaluating π. The squib is called *The New Method of Evaluation as Applied to π*, and in it he examines five methods: Rationalization, the Method of Indifferences, Penrhyn's Method, the Method of Elimination, and the Method of Evaluation under Pressure. The first required 'the breaking up of U [the University] into its partial factions', and the method was

abandoned when it *appeared* that all the Ys were on one side. In the
second he investigated the locus of EBP [Pusey]:

> This was found to be a species of Catenary, called the Patristic Catenary,
> which is usually defined as 'passing through origen, and containing
> many multiple points.' The locus of HPL [Liddon] will be found almost
> entirely to coincide with this. Penrhyn's Method involved 'transforming
> (AP) S [Arthur Penrhyn Stanley] into a new scale of notation: it had
> hitherto been, through a long series of terms, entirely in the senary, in
> which scale it had furnished many beautiful expressions: it was now
> transformed into the denary.'

As to the Elimination Method. Dodgson wrote, 'In an earlier age of
mathematics J would probably have been referred to rectangular axes,
and divided into two unequal parts – a process of arbitrary elimination
which is now considered not strictly legitimate.' Evaluation under
Pressure, the method finally chosen, was said to be 'taken from the
learned treatise *Augusti de fallibilitate historicorum* and occupies an entire
Chapter'. The relentlessness with which Dodgson pursues his objective
through the series of pseudo-mathematical examples makes this one of
the best of all his Oxford squibs.

Dodgson was now in the vein for writing squibs, and the Oxford
elections of 13–18 July 1865 formed the subject of *The Dynamics of a
Parti-cle*. A staunch Conservative like his father, Dodgson took a
sufficient interest in party politics to record the results of elections and
to return in vacation-time to exercise his right to vote. Occasionally,
when issues such as the Reform Bill and the Disestablishment of the
Irish Church, which particularly interested Dodgson, were being
debated he went to the House of Commons to listen to the proceedings.
He had a profound mistrust of Gladstone, who represented the University from 1847 for eighteen years. But in July 1865 Gladstone was
opposed by Sir William Heathcote and by Gathorne Hardy, who
ultimately became the first Earl of Cranbrook. Two members had to be
chosen.

Archdeacon Clerke, the Sub-Dean, was Chairman of Gathorne
Hardy's campaign committee. Samuel Wilberforce, Bishop of Oxford,
complained of this in the words of Samson, 'They Plough with my
heifer'. Liddell, on the other hand, was among Gladstone's staunchest
supporters. It was he who nominated Gladstone on 17 July 1865, and
personally led the way to the poll. Sir John Mowbray, a supporter of
Hardy, wrote in his diary on the first day, 'We leave off ten ahead, 385
to Gladstone's 375. This of course reveals nothing. At 3 o'clock we were
50 ahead, but then they began to pour in voting papers. The Dean of
Christ Church in particular has polled a large number against us.'
Polling went on till 19 July, but the final results were Heathcote 3236,
Hardy 1904 and Gladstone 1724, giving Hardy a majority of 180 over

Gladstone. Afterwards Hardy wrote, 'This was the crowning triumph of my life, unsolicited and unexpected, but I always feel that Gladstone misrepresented the constituency, and proved it by declaring himself unmuzzled when defeated – not a very honest outbreak!'[19] Lygon, who later became Earl Beauchamp, sent Gathorne Hardy a copy of *The Dynamics of a Parti-cle*, describing it as 'the only squib worth having, and indeed the only one which exists in an existent shape'.[20]

Dodgson's pamphlet is in three chapters. The first contains parodies, mainly political, on the definitions, postulates and axioms of Euclid, e.g.:

> Plain Superficiality is the character of a speech, in which any two points being taken, the speaker is found to lie wholly with regard to those two points. . . . When two parties, coming together, feel a Right Anger, each is said to be COMPLEMENTARY to the other, (though, strictly speaking, this is very seldom the case).

Chapter II deals in the main with the contest between Gladstone and Hardy, with some satire on miscellaneous subjects, e.g.:

> Prop. I Pr.
> 'To find the value of a given Examiner.'
> *Example.* – A takes in ten books in the Final Examination, and gets a third Class: B takes in the Examiners, and gets a Second. Find the value of the Examiners in terms of books. Find also their value in terms in which no Examination is held.
> Prop. II Pr.
> 'To Estimate Profit and Loss.'
> *Example.* Given a Derby Prophet, who has sent three different winners to three different betting men, and given that none of the three horses are placed. Find the total Loss incurred by the three men (a) in money, (b) in temper. Find also the Prophet. Is this latter generally possible? . . .
> Prop. VI Pr.
> To remove a given Tangent from a given Circle, and to bring another given Line into contact with it

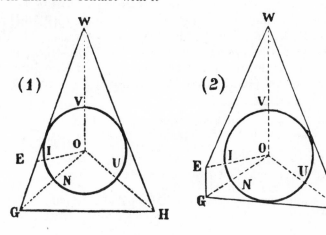

Let UNIV be a Large Circle, whose centre is O (V being, of course, placed at the top) and let WGH be a triangle, two of whose sides, WEG and WH, are in contact with the circle, while GH (called 'the base' by liberal mathematicians,) is not in contact with it. (See Fig. 1.) It is required to destroy the contact of WEG, and to bring GH into contact instead. . . .

The final chapter is a reprint of *The New Method of Evaluation as Applied to* π.

The Elections to the Hebdomadal Council which Dodgson included in *Phantasmagoria* was written at the close oi 1866. Although it did not specifically attack the Dean, it constituted an assault on the Oxford Liberals. On 20 October 1866 when the election to the Hebdomadal Council took place the Conservatives overthrew the former Liberal majority. This so disturbed Goldwin Smith that he wrote to Sandford, the Senior Censor, suggesting a number of 'remedies', including 'The exclusion [from Congregation] of the non-academical elements which form a main part of the strength of this party domination', and even the abolition of the Hebdomadal Council. Dodgson's pamphlet was a poetic parody of the letter:

> My scheme is this: remove the votes of all
> The residents that are not Liberal –
> Leave the young Tutors uncontrolled and free,
> And Oxford than shall see – what it shall see.
> What next? Why then, I say, let Convocation
> Be shorn of all her powers of legislation.
> But why stop there? Let us go boldly on –
> Sweep everything beginning with a 'Con'
> Into oblivion! Convocation first,
> Conservatism next, and, last and worst,
> 'Concilium Hebdomadale' must,
> Consumed and conquered, be consigned to dust!

The Deserted Parks, a parody of Goldsmith's *Deserted Village*, was Dodgson's anonymous response to the decree of April 1867 that the University Parks should be partly given over to cricket. The extent to which Dodgson's pamphlet, which was dated May 1867, influenced matters is uncertain, but the decree was rejected on 6 June. Having once taken up his pen, Dodgson could not resist another attack on Jowett:

> A man he was to undergraduates dear,
> And passing rich with forty pounds a year.
> And so, I ween, he would have been till now,
> Had not his friends ('twere long to tell you how)
> Prevailed on him, Jack-Horner-like, to try
> Some method to evaluate his pie,
> And win from those dark depths, with skillful thumb,
> Five times a hundredweight of luscious plum.

In January 1868 Professor R. B. Clifton sent a letter to Sandford, the Senior Censor, detailing the needs of the Department of Natural Science. This was the subject of a parody called *The Offer of the Clarendon Trustees*, in which Dodgson set out the requirements of the Department of Mathematics for 'roofed buildings' in which a variety of Mathematical occupations could be carried out. The list of requirements included 'A room for reducing Fractions to their Lowest Terms. This should be provided with a cellar for keeping the Lowest Terms when found, which might also be available to the general body of Undergraduates for the purpose of "keeping Terms"', and 'A narrow strip of ground, railed off and carefully levelled for investigating the properties of Asymptotes, and testing practically whether Parallel Lines meet or not: for this purpose it should reach, to use the expressive language of Euclid, "ere so far".' He added, 'This last process, of "continually producing the Lines", may require centuries or more: but such a period, though long in the life of an individual, is as nothing in the life of the University.'

On 23 November 1868 a Conservative, Henry Barnett, defeated the Liberal candidate, George Broderick, in the Woodstock election, and on the following day a letter giving an account of it appeared in the *Oxford Chronicle*. Dodgson described the letter, from a Liberal, as 'charmingly candid as to the brutal behaviour of the Liberal electors', and wrote a letter on the subject to the *Oxford University Herald*, which published it on 28 November. Signing himself 'A Liberal of the Liberals', Dodgson praised the hoots and execrations with which the Liberal supporters greeted the successful candidate.

> Though Tory tricks, aristocratic art, and the brute force of numerical superiority, had turned the day against that noble and enlightened minority, I seemed to hear in those voices the knell of a dying monster, the crashing downfall of the rotten fabric of Conservatism! The Liberal candidate's speech was listened to in perfect silence. What! that a set of electors with lungs in their bodies and breath in their lungs, should listen to a political opponent *'in perfect silence.'* It is too mean, too pitiful for belief. . . . But we have not yet reached the depths of this abyss of infamy. The successful candidate, we are told, '*had to be escorted at every appearance in public by twenty or thirty policemen, and even then seemed hardly secure from personal violence*'. This is as it should be: else what are fists meant for in 'Merrie England? . . . it is a thick skull indeed that is insensitive to a brickbat!' [After deploring the cowardice of the Conservative supporters in allowing their opponent to walk unmolested through the crowd.] . . . 'What is demonstration to a dig in the ribs? Is there any reasoning like rotten eggs?' . . . he goes on, 'So long as Woodstock is degraded by a voiceless, heartless, Conservative majority, who can neither hoot, pelt nor execrate their foes, we must with shame confess that Mr Barnett only too truly represents them.'

REFERENCES

1 Green, p. 290.
2 S. H. Williams and Falconer Madan, *A Handbook of the Literature of the Rev. C. L. Dodgson (Lewis Carroll)*, Oxford 1931, p. 44.
3 Collingwood, pp. 148–9.
4 Green, p. 305.
5 Hudson, pp. 180–1.
6 Noted by Selwyn H. Goodacre, *Jabberwocky*, Spring 1972.
7 Alexander L. Taylor, *The White Knight*, 1952.
8 Collingwood, p. 143.
9 15 June 1872.
10 Selwyn H. Goodacre, 'The First Separate Edition of Jabberwocky', *Jabberwocky*, Spring 1975.
11 *Symbolic Logic*, p. 166.
12 *Language and Lewis Carroll.*
13 *Some Versions of Pastoral.*
14 *Daily Telegraph*, 11 September 1977.
15 *The Times*, 22 January 1932.
16 Rev. N. C. Roberts, *The Times*, 29 January 1932.
17 4 March 1864.
18 A. Hassall, *Christ Church, Oxford*, 1911, p. 42.
19 A. E. Gathorne Hardy, *Gathorne Hardy, First Earl of Cranbrook: A Memoir*, 1910, p. 179.
20 Ibid, p. 180.

11   Squibs and Suitors

Initially Dodgson's squibs had in the main touched only indirectly on the Dean; but Dodgson now entered on a phase in which he began deliberate attacks on Liddell's activities. In about 1871 the governing Body decided to create a direct approach to the Cathedral from Tom Quad by constructing a double archway, known to its critics as the Tunnel, and to remove the bells from the Cathedral tower, relocating them over the staircase of the Hall. The bells were cut free from the stonework by means of a 'trench', and housed in a plain wooden case. To Dodgson the subject was irresistible, and in 1872 he published *The New Belfry at Christ Church, Oxford: A Monograph by D.C.L.* The transposition of his initials would have left nobody in doubt as to his identity. The title page contains an 'illustration' of the belfry – a simple square labelled 'East view of the new Belfry, Ch.Ch., as seen from the Meadow', and various theories are offered as to who conceived the shape, including the Mathematical Lecturer (Dodgson himself) who found it in the Eleventh Book of Euclid. Fastening upon the surname of Sir George Scott, the architect first appointed, Dodgson wrote: 'The head of the House, and the architect, feeling a natural wish that their names should be embodied, in some conspicuous way, among the alterations then in progress, conceived the beautiful and unique idea of representing, by means of the new Belfry, a gigantic copy of a Greek Lexicon.' A footnote adds: 'No sufficient reason has been adduced why a model of a Greek Lexicon should in any way "embody" the names of the above illustrious individuals.' The text continues: 'But, before the idea had been reduced to a working form, business took them both to London for a few days, and during their absence, somehow (*this* part of the business has never been satisfactorily explained) the whole thing was put into the hand of a wandering architect, who gave the name Jeeby', This name was a pun on GB, i.e. George Bodley, Scott's pupil, who produced the final design for what Dodgson now described as the 'tea-chest'. Of 'the impetus given to Art in England by the new Belfry' Dodgson wrote, 'Already an enterprising maker of bonnet-boxes is advertising "the Belfry pattern": two builders of bathing machines at Ramsgate have followed his example: one of the great London houses is supplying "bar-soap" cut in the same striking and symmetrical form: and we are credibly informed that Borwick's Baking Powder and Thorley's Food for Cattle are now sold in no other shape.' And at the next Christ Church banquet, each guest was to be presented with 'a portable model of the new Belfry, tastefully executed in cheese'. The Bread and Butter row and the affair of Jowett's salary were again brought in by Dodgson, who was unable to let pass any opportunity to press his points home.

In a short parody based on a conglomeration of Shakespeare plays, the Dean is represented both as Hamlet and Lear, and Jeeby appears as the fool in cap and bells. Morton's farce *Box and Cox* is briefly introduced, with the Belfry appearing as 'Box', and the scene concludes with a parody of Ariel's Song:

> Full fathom five the Belfry frowns;
>   All its sides of timber made;
> Painted all in greys and browns;
>   Nothing of it that will fade.
> Christ Church may admire the change –
> Oxford thinks it sad and strange.
> Beauty's dead! Let's ring her knell.
> Hark! now I hear them – ding-dong, bell.

On 19 March 1873, the day on which the new 'Tunnel' to the Cathedral was revealed, Dodgson began writing *The Vision of the Three T's; a Threnody by the Author of 'The New Belfry'*. The Three T's are the Tunnel, Trench and Tea-Chest and the squib is a dramatic parody of *The Compleat Angler*. An angler, a hunter and a professor converge on the pond in the centre of Tom Quad and in the intervals of angling read 'The Ballad of The Wandering Burgess'; the Burgess is Gladstone who, after his defeat in the Woodstock election, became Member of Parliament for South Lancashire, and in 1868 was elected Member for Greenwich. Many of the Dean's projects, architectural and cultural, are satirized, even to his introducing a performance of Bach's Passion in the Cathedral before a congregation of 1200. This had offended Dodgson's sense of propriety, for he thought that churches should not be used for such purposes. 'A Bachanalian Ode', beginning 'Here's to the Freshman of bashful eighteen' is a direct reference to the Bach music. The last verse reads:

> Here's to the Governing Body, whose Art
>   (For they're Masters of Art to a man, Sir!)
> Seeks to beautify Christ Church in every part,
>   Though the method seems hardly to answer!
>   With three T's it is graced –
>   Which letters are placed
> To stand for the names of Tact, Talent and Taste!

On the whole the satire is good humoured and without malice, but one passage gave much offence at the Deanery. Describing the fish in the Christ Church pond, Dodgson writes:

> The Common kinds we may let pass: for though some of them be easily Plucked forth from the water, yet are they so slow, and withal have so little in them, that they are good for nothing, unless they be crammed up to the very eyes with such stuffing as comes readiest to hand. . . . I will say somewhat of the Nobler Kinds, and chiefly of the Gold-fish, which is a species highly thought of, and much sought after in these parts, not only by men, but by divers birds, as for example the King-fishers.

Tolerant though the Dean and his wife had been in the past, they could scarcely have been expected to put up with these attacks, not only on the Dean, but also on Mrs Liddell, the King-fisher seeking Gold-fish – perhaps royal ones at that, and presumably not merely as undergraduates, but as potential sons-in-law.

In *The Blank Cheque, A Fable*, published in 1874, Dodgson took the offensive again. His subject on this occasion was the decision of Convocation on 28 November 1873 to build the new Examination Schools on the site of the Angel Inn and to leave the matter entirely in the hands of a nine-man executive committee, who would choose a plan, obtain approval of the estimates from the Curators of the Chest and put the work in hand without further consultation. This squib takes the form of an imaginary conversation between Dodgson himself – Mr De Ciel, a cryptogram for DCL, the transposed initials he used in *The New Belfry* – and 'Mrs Nivers,' who at least outwardly stands for U-Nivers-ity. But the reader is left with a strong suspicion – almost a certainty – that Mrs Nivers is also Mrs Liddell. Her 'broad, good-humoured face' and dominance over her husband's affairs are reminiscent of *The Masque of Balliol*, which equates the couple to the University, and by its metre encourages the separation of the word 'Nivers'.

> I am the Dean, and this is Mrs Liddell;
> She is the first, I am the second fiddle.
> She is the Broad, I am the High.
> We are the University.

The story centres round the inability of the Nivers family to agree on a suitable new school for their daughter Angela and a watering place for the season. They settle the matter by leaving it all to the maid, and handing her a blank cheque to pay for it. It is surely no coincidence that the maid has the same Christian name as Susan Prickett, the Liddell children's governess, who did indeed sometimes decide the children's holidays. There are references to the election of 1865; to Gladstone – 'Mr Prior Burgess . . . as liberal as could be' and his successor, Gathorne Hardy, who would have to be 'more hardy in his notions, or I could warrant him we shouldn't suit each other'. Jowett features as Benjy, 'a nice boy, but I daren't tell you what he costs us in pocket money!' – a direct reference to the fact that Jowett's increase in salary was at the personal expense of the Dean and Chapter.

The moral, which is tipped to a stub at the end of most copies, explains the purpose of the Squib. 'Is it really seriously proposed – in the University of Oxford, and towards the close of the nineteenth century (never yet reckoned by historians as part of the Dark Ages) – to sign a Blank Cheque for the expenses of building New Schools, before any estimate has been made of those expenses – before any plan has been laid before the University, from which such an estimate could be made – before any architect has been found to design such a plan – before any Committee has been elected to find such an architect?' Dodgson's satire had its effect, for on 20 April 1874 Convocation repealed the decision to leave matters entirely to the executive committee. Similarly a small serious pamphlet entitled *Objections, submitted to the Governing Body of Christ Church, Oxford, against certain proposed alterations in the Great Quadrangle* resulted in modifications to the proposals, and a letter which he sent to the Pall Mall Gazette on 3 November 1874 was partly responsible for the decision not to build cloisters in Tom Quad.

Despite Dodgson's justification for taking up these points, his attacks on Mrs Liddell were both cruel and unnecessary. But the year 1874 saw the birth of an Oxford squib from another hand in which Dodgson, as well as the Dean and his wife, is lampooned. The author was the Rev. John Howe Jenkins, an undergraduate. Dodgson, as a Student, was relatively immune from disciplinary action, but Jenkins was not, and was sent down when his authorship became known. His squib was called *Cakeless*.

On 7 February 1874 Lorina had married William Baillie Skene, DL, younger son of Patrick George Skene, of Hallyards, Fife. *Cakeless* hints that Skene was not wealthy enough to please the Dean and his wife (Apollo and Diana) and centres round the triple marriage of Ecilia, Rosa and Psyche (Alice, Edith and Rhoda) to more acceptable suitors. Ecilia announces that she wishes to marry:

> You always wished that I should marry one
> Or Prince, or peer, or else a member's son.
> The last have I at length securely trapped,
> And in the toils of courtship firmly wrapped.

Her bridegroom is revealed as Yerbua (Aubrey Harcourt, grandson of the Earl of Sheffield) whereupon Diana exclaims:

> My blessings on you daughter! would that she
> Who's gone before had made a match like thee.

Later, at the wedding breakfast, Apollo raises a toast:

> Another bride before them went;
> Her money must be well-nigh spent.
> May these for ever moneyed be.

The bridegroom assigned to Rosa is Rivulus, 'a noble lord of high degree', easily identified as Lord Brooke, an undergraduate, who later became Earl of Warwick. Psyche does even better:

> I've trapped a Prince, the youngest of his race;
> Of tender flesh, but yet of handsome face.

When the marriage is about to begin, Kraftsohn (Dodgson) interrupts. The British Museum copy has a pencilled contemporary note that Dodgson had been rejected, i.e. as a suitor.

	I do protest against this match, so let me speak.
Apollo (Irate)	Strip, strip him, scouts! this is the knave we seek.
Kraft	By circles, segments and by radii, Than yield to these I'd liefer far to die.
Romanus (waving his hood)	Arm, arm, ye brave! and rush upon the foe, Who never did to early temple go, Nor taste in lordly hall the luscious steak, Nor would his frugal luncheon e'er forsake.

(Scouts advance, throwing their 'perquisites' at the head of Kraftsohn, who takes refuge in the cloisters.)

Rosa	Take him through trench and tunnel to the chest, Nor ever leave the cursed fiend at rest. Leave him in Wonderland with some hard-hitting foe, And through the looking-glass let him survey the blow; Confine him in the belfry, not in Peck, And make him sign at pleasure your blank cheque.

There is no suggestion that John Howe Jenkins was making serious predictions about the future of the Dean's daughters, but there was enough in them to whet the appetites of the Oxford gossip-mongers. All the Liddells were exceptional for their good looks and talent, and it is natural that the girls should attract the attention of the men of the University. Alice did not marry Aubrey Harcourt, though it is very possible that in 1874 he was already haunting the Deanery. But it was on Edith that his choice ultimately fell, and in 1876 he became formally engaged to her. Tragically the marriage never took place, for in June 1876, at the age of twenty-two, she died of peritonitis, following measles. Dodgson was deeply grieved by her death; six months later Mrs Liddell came to his rooms to see the photographs he had taken of her between 1858 and 1860, and accepted several of them, sending him two recent cartes of her in return.

Jenkins' prophecies about a royal suitor were nearer the truth than he probably realized. Queen Victoria had been so pleased with the Prince of Wales' education at Oxford that in 1872 she resolved to send her fourth and youngest son, Prince Leopold George Duncan Albert, to Christ Church also. Leopold had always been somewhat delicate in health, and when he was born at Buckingham Palace on 7 April 1853 it seemed doubtful whether he would survive. As he grew up he developed a taste for academic pursuits. He loved literature, and in particular Shakespeare and Scott; but his greatest aptitudes were for music and modern languages. Arthur Penrhyn Stanley was one of his religious teachers; the other was Dodgson's old friend Robinson Duckworth, who became Chaplain in Ordinary to the Queen in 1870, and Canon of Westminster five years later. On 27 November 1872 Prince Leopold matriculated at Christ Church, and went into residence with his private tutor, Robert Hawthorne Collins. He lived at Wykehan House, St Giles, near the parks, and put on the gown of a gentleman-commoner. The lecturers he attended were history, political science, poetry, music and fine art. At the Oxford Museum he studied science, and at the Taylorian Institution he studied modern languages. The consensus of opinion was that he was an admirable young man, pleasant in private and in public alike. He was particularly noted as a graceful and effective public speaker, and his linguistic capability seemed likely to enhance his position in international circles.

When he met Alice Liddell she was twenty years old. Attractive children often lose their looks as their features mature, but Alice had fulfilled all the promise of beauty that she had offered as a child of seven. Wit and intelligence animated her delicate features and her hair was long and luxuriant. She loved music and singing, and that compelling element of romanticism that Dodgson had observed in her as a child had prompted Hubert Parry to dedicate to her his nostalgic setting of Shelley's 'Lament'. The Dean's passion for Greek and Latin naturally communicated itself to his family, but in the case of his daughters greater emphasis was placed on modern languages, which they learnt from private tutors. Mrs Liddell was fluent in French, a language often heard in the Deanery. The Dean's artistic talents were also passed on to his children. In later years Violet, the youngest daughter, developed a gift for portraiture, and her portrait of Alice still exists (Plate 26). Rhoda preferred wood as a medium of artistic expression, and her work included a carved wooden screen for the cathedral, a fine carved table, and mirror frames. Alice, however, excelled in drawing, and many of her sketches survive to prove her ability. Many well-born young ladies had drawing lessons in her day, for it was an accepted part of Victorian education for girls; but Alice's drawing master was John Ruskin, and her level of achievement amply repaid the trouble he took with her.

In short, Alice was beautiful, gifted, and possessed a range of talents that corresponded with Prince Leopold's own. They met and, almost inevitably, they fell in love. Of this romance Dodgson makes no comment, though he must have been aware of it, and he would have felt anxieties on Alice's behalf. For the romance was bitter-sweet, doomed from the outset to heartache and disappointment. Leopold was fourth in line of succession, and life was precarious in the Victorian era. The Queen was determined that all her sons should marry princesses. Though he came of age in April 1874, and was made a member of the Privy Council with an annuity of £15,000, Prince Leopold knew that he would never be able to marry against the Queen's wishes. And far from acting the 'King-fisher', Mrs Liddell was too sensible of the trust the Queen had placed in her and the Dean to give any encouragement to romantic notions of marriage between these two young people. She was in any event even more concerned about the state of the Prince's health, for in the winter of 1874–5 his life hung in the balance when he went down with a severe attack of typhus fever, from which he fortunately recovered.

On 24 May 1875, Dodgson wrote to the Prince's tutor asking whether Prince Leopold would be willing to sit for a photograph. He not only assented, but also invited Dodgson to lunch at Wykeham House on 26 May. Six people sat down to lunch, and Dodgson was delighted to find himself treated as the senior guest, with the honour of sitting next to the Prince. He described him as 'particularly unassuming and genial in manner', and added, 'I do not wonder at his being so universal a favourite'.[1] Afterwards they adjourned to a large tent in the garden for coffee and cigars (though Dodgson himself did not smoke) and the Prince looked through a selection of Dodgson's photographs. A week later he called alone at Dodgson's rooms and spent nearly an hour and a half there, being joined later by Collins, his tutor. Dodgson took two photographs of him, though neither was free from movement, and gave him a selecton of photographs of the Prince's own choice. In his diary account of the visit Dodgson gives no indication of which he chose, and it is interesting to consider whether any portraits of Alice were included, and if so, what Dodgson's reactions and feelings were. His last recorded photograph of her had been taken in 1870, when she was eighteen years old.

In 1876 Prince Leopold received the honorary degree of DCL and left Oxford, establishing himself first at Boyton House, Wiltshire, and moving to Claremont in Surrey three years later. Alice accepted the inevitable and did her best to put the young prince out of her mind.

Eventually she found love and happiness elsewhere. Reginald Gervis Hargreaves was a Christ Church graduate whose father had made his fortune in the mills in the north of England. He was an attractive, energetic and very likeable young man who was fond of outdoor sport. Golf and sailing were among his favourite pastimes; he was a fine shot and played cricket for Hampshire. He was deeply in love with Alice, and the elation he felt when she accepted him is amply demonstrated in this intriguing letter to a friend:

> Wed. 7th.
> Junior Carlton Club,
> Pall Mall, S.W.

> My dear Ribsy,
> You will be glad to hear that you have succeeded in saying a clever thing at last and that I am engaged to Alice Liddell. I don't think I need say any more, as from what you know I think you will be able to form some idea of my happiness, it is worth all I have suffered a good many times over – Ah how I wish you cld be happy in the same way. It was settled yesterday and the next letter I am going to write is the one we had talked about to my cousin to throw him over for the 12th, I hope at that time to be at Cowes, 'Sailing on the summer seas' with her. I am afraid I shall not see you now before I leave town, wh. will be abt. the 22nd but I shall expect a letter, wh I know will be full of good wishes for me, before then.
> By the Bye you need not repeat what I told you abroad – I don't think Lewie's example in that matter is a desirable one to follow.
> Yrs ever,
> Reginald Hargreaves.[2]

Alice was still in Prince Leopold's thoughts when, on 15 September 1880 she married Reginald Hargreaves. As a wedding present he sent her a ruby and diamond horseshoe brooch. The young couple settled into the family estate at Cuffnells, in Hampshire, which boasted some of the tallest trees in England, and raised three sons, Alan Kynaston, born on 25 October 1881, Leopold Reginald, named after the young prince, born on 8 January 1883, and Carryl Liddell, born on 19 November 1887. Tragically Alan was killed leading an attack on Fromelles in 1915, and in the following year Leopold was killed leading the troops in an assault on Les Boeufs.

When Alice's second son was born, she invited Dodgson to be godfather, but he refused. When thirteen years earlier his sister Mary had approached him with a similar request, he had replied, 'Though I am fully intending to decline, in all *other* directions, any additions to my quite sufficient family of godchildren, I cannot possibly refuse to gratify *your* wish in such a matter.' One is tempted to ask how he could have found it in his heart to refuse Alice.

Prince Leopold did not choose a bride until several months after

Alice's marriage. He was created Duke of Albany, Earl of Clarence and Baron Arklow in 1881, and a few months later met Princess Helene Frederica Augusta, daughter of His Serene Highness George Victor, Prince of Waldeck-Pyrmont. Europe now contained very few eligible princesses, and Queen Victoria gave her consent to the marriage, which took place at St George's Chapel, Windsor on 27 April 1882. But ill health continued to trouble Prince Leopold, and in the spring of 1884 he went to Cannes to recuperate. Here he suffered a nasty fall which resulted in an attack of epilepsy and he died tragically on 28 March 1884 at the Villa Nevada, at the age of thirty. He left one daughter, Princess Alexandra, and his son Leopold, born posthumously on 19 July 1884, succeeded him as Duke of Albany.

On the subject of Alice's engagement and marriage, Dodgson preserved absolute silence. Perhaps he had already thrust the beautiful, accomplished young woman into the background of his thoughts, remembering only the dreamchild in the boat, the laughter and bright water. Or perhaps the old wound still festered and, like his father's death, was too painful to be written or spoken about.

If Dodgson was unhappy in his relationship with Alice Liddell, he had learned to conceal it. Child friendships too numerous to recount provided the relaxation he needed. Among the most important child friends of the early 1870s were Julia and Ethel, daughters of Thomas Arnold, and granddaughters of the great Arnold of Rugby. Julia eventually married Leonard Huxley, later editor of the *Cornhill* Magazine and was the mother of Aldous and Julian Huxley. Julia in particular was a favourite photographic sitter and was first photographed by Dodgson in his new studio above his rooms in Christ Church. In later years Ethel described a party of girls with their governess meeting Dodgson, a tall black clerical figure swinging along with brisk, almost jerky steps. The children joined hands to stop him from passing and Dodgson charged the line with his umbrella:

> The line broke in confusion, and the next moment four of the little band were clinging to such portions of the black-coated figure as they could seize upon. Two little people, however, hung back, being seized with shyness and a sudden consciousness of their audacity, a sudden awe of this tall, dignified gentleman in black broadcloth and white tie. But in a moment he had shaken off the clinging, laughing children, and before the two little strangers had time to realize what had happened, they found themselves trotting along on either side of him, a hand of each firmly clasped in the strong, kind hands of Lewis Carroll, and chatting away as if they had known him all their lives.[3]

Dodgson's friendship with Julia and Ethel continued for many years and it was he who introduced Ethel to Ellen Terry and her family on a 'Terryble' day in 1883. He also invented games and puzzles for their amusement, and dedicated his word game *Doublets* to them when he published it in 1879.

Three sisters who acted as a spur to Dodgson's creativity in the early 1870s were Mary, Ina and Harriet Watson, whom he called by the omnibus name 'Harmarina'. When he first learned their ages and birthdays, he wrote to Mary: 'By careful calculation I find you are just two years and two months older than me (I mean the three of you).'[4] In a birthday letter to Ina he claimed to have called at her house: 'I had just time to look into the kitchen, and saw your birthday feast getting ready, a nice dish of crusts, bones, pills, cotton-bobbins, and rhubarb and magnesia. "Now," I thought, "she will be happy!" and with a smiling face I went on my way.'[5] In 1924 a selecton of Dodgson's letters, puzzles and poems addressed to the Watson children was privately printed under the title *Some Rare Carrolliana*. Dodgson was still in correspondence with them in the 1890s.

Even stronger creative stimuli were provided at that period by Lady Maud and Lady Gwendolen Cecil, the daughters of Lord Salisbury. For besides seeing them in London, he continued to receive periodic invitations to join the family at Hatfield House, where he usually found himself pressed into the role of storyteller. One such occasion occurred in 1872–3, when he stayed there for four days over the New Year. The children were already familiar with the story of 'Bruno's Revenge', which he had published in *Aunt Judy's Magazine* in 1867. On the afternoon of his arrival he exhausted a couple of regular favourites, 'Pixies', a story of his own, and a Russian tale called 'The Blacksmith and the Hobgoblin'. Two days later he was pressed into another session in the Gallery, and wrote: 'I gave them a new chapter of Sylvie and Bruno, which I devised since the story-telling on Tuesday, and which I must write out before I forget it.' On the following day he continued, 'The appetite of the party for stories is insatiable. Luckily I had thought of a few more incidents for *Sylvie and Bruno*, and gave them another chapter, which took nearly an hour.'[6] Clearly these were large sections of the book; but although *Sylvie and Bruno* eventually ran into two substantial volumes, crammed not only with wit and invention, but with his personal philosophy also, one vital element was missing: there was no Alice Liddell to beg him to write it out, with the result that the book took more than twenty years to write.

At around this period illness and death overtook some of the older members of Dodgson's family. On 9 November 1872 he received a telegram telling him of the death of his much-loved aunt, Henrietta Lutwidge. The only comforting feature was that Aunt Lucy, as residual legatee, inherited her house at 9 Wellington Square, Hastings, where Dodgson quite rightly assumed that the Guildford party would like to stay from time to time. Other frequent visitors at Hastings were Mary's two little boys, Stuart and Bertram, and Wilfred with his wife and baby. On 21 May 1873 an even worse catastrophe occurred. Uncle Skeffington was visiting Salisbury in his capacity as commissioner for lunacy when he was struck by a lunatic and seriously injured. Dodgson responded instantly to the telegram summoning him to his uncle's bedside in Salisbury, and consulted Sir James Paget as well as the local surgeon. When his uncle rallied, Dodgson returned to Oxford. But on 28 May he had a relapse, and although Dodgson hurried back with Sir James Paget, his uncle died a few minutes before their arrival.

Death in the elderly may bring grief, but at least it conforms to the rightful order of things. It is much more difficult to watch the young struggling against incurable disease. In the summer of 1874 Dodgson's cousin Charlie Wilcox, stricken with tuberculosis, was staying at 'The Chestnuts'. Charlie was the seventh son of Dodgson's father's step-sister Mary, and her husband William Wilcox of Whitburn. When Charlie was born in 1852, Dodgson stood as his godfather and there was in consequence a special bond between them. Superficially it is perhaps surprising that Charlie should have left his own family at such an advanced stage of his illness, but it is possible that the seriousness of his condition was not realized until after his arrival. His father, a sea-captain, had business problems, which might have prevented him from offering him the comforts he now needed, and it would have been impractical for his London physician, Dr Sibson, to attend him in Whitburn.

When on 30 June 1874 Dodgson went to Guildford for a two-day visit, he gave Charlie's presence at 'The Chestnuts' and his illness no more than a cursory mention. But it appears that shortly afterwards the young man suffered a setback, and on 14 July Dodgson wrote to his sister Fanny, offering to share the nursing. He accordingly returned to Guildford on 17 July, where he sat up with Charlie most of the night.

Next day Dodgson escaped for a long, solitary walk over the Surrey Downs:

> I was walking on a hillside, alone, one bright summer day, when suddenly there came into my head one line of verse – one solitary line – 'For the Snark *was* a Boojum, you see.' I knew not what it meant, then: I know not what it means, now; but I wrote it down: and some time afterwards, the rest of the stanza occurred to me, that being its last line: and so by degrees, at odd moments during the next year or two, the rest of the poem pieced itself together, that being its last stanza. And since then, periodically, I have received courteous letters from strangers, begging to know whether *The Hunting of the Snark* is an allegory, or contains some hidden moral, or is a political satire: and for all such questions I have but one answer, 'I don't know!'[7]

Morton Cohen advances the convincing theory that the flash of inspiration which carried him to a world of nonsense was Dodgson's

personal defence against the tragedy being acted out at 'The Chestnuts': 'Out of the nightmare of Charlie's illness, perhaps, Dodgson
built a fun-giving work of art: perhaps it was his way of demonstrating a
superior logic, the logic of artistic survival.'⁸ But it is also possible that
in his long nocturnal vigil Dodgson's thoughts had naturally turned to
his many happy hours with the Wilcoxes at Whitburn, where the first
stanza of his other great nonsense poem, *Jabberwocky*, had been his
response to a simple family game.

Dodgson never liked to proceed far without settling on an illustrator
for his books, and this time he already had an artist in mind. He had
known Henry Holiday since 1870, but of late the friendship had
deepened. On 15 January 1874 he had visited the Holidays and looked
at some drawings of groups of two nude girls which Holiday had been
producing for him. The idea was that Dodgson would then arrange
similar groupings of nude children and photograph them. Next day he
returned and suggested to Holiday that he might illustrate a children's
book for him. 'If *only* he can draw grotesques, it would be all I should
desire – the grace and beauty of the pictures would quite rival Tenniel,
I think.'⁹ On 4 February he received from Holiday five drawings of
children, plus a drawing for *Sylvie and Bruno*. Three months later Holiday
came to stay with him at Oxford for several days, and on 18 May took
Xie Kitchin to Dodgson's studio to be photographed. Xie was the
daughter of Dodgson's old friend, the headmaster of Twyford School.
She was a beautiful girl and was Dodgson's favourite child model, Alice
Liddell excepted, for she was a relaxed and patient sitter and an ideal
photographic subject. On this occasion Dodgson produced a picture
which he considered the best he had ever taken of her; but it was
Holiday who arranged her lying full-length on the sofa in a long
nightgown.

As the summer advanced, Charlie Wilcox became 'decidedly con-
valescent', and the Dodgsons bore him off to the Isle of Wight, where
they were joined by innumerable Wilcoxes. But despite all their devotion, they could do no more than make his last months more pleasant,
for on 11 November 1874 he died there.

In the interim Dodgson had built upon his original nonsense line,
and invited Holiday to submit three illustrations. His original intention
was that the poem should be incorporated, under the title 'The Boojum', in *Sylvie and Bruno*, but since the book was not likely to be out for a
considerable period, he was toying with the idea of printing it separately for private circulation. The poem was to be in three 'fits', and we
can deduce from Holiday's account of the earliest illustrations that
these were 'The Landing', 'The Hunting' and 'The Vanishing'.
Despite Dodgson's assertion that he did not know whether the poem
contained any hidden significance, it is impossible to ignore certain

references to the subjects of his recent Oxford squibs, most of which in 1874 had been published together under the title *Notes by an Oxford Chiel*. The Baker, so absentminded that he loses his boxes, and even forgets his own name, can only bake 'bridecake', a reminder that, in *Cakeless*, John Howe Jenkins refers to the non-arrival of the wedding cake, which Diana (Mrs Liddell) had forgotten to order. Perhaps this was a reference to a real incident at Ina's wedding, which took place on 7 February 1874, though it appears also to refer to regulations about bringing food into the College. And it is also surely impossible to ignore the reference to the Banker drawing a blank cheque.

Dodgson had been somewhat discouraged when on 23 November 1874 Ruskin called at his request to discuss the pictures and expressed the view that Holiday would be unable to illustrate the book satisfactorily. After some anxious reconsideration, however, he decided to go ahead and back his own judgment. He had been delighted with two of the first three illustrations and the shipboard scene had already been cut on wood. But Holiday's picture of the disappearance of the Baker was rejected because it contained a picture of a Boojum. 'Mr Dodgson wrote that it was a delightful monster, but that it was inadmissible,' Holiday wrote. 'All his descriptions of the Boojum were quite unimaginable, and he wanted the creature to remain so. I assented, of course, though reluctant to dismiss what I am still confident is an accurate representation. I hope that some future Darwin, in a new *Beagle*, will find the beast, or its remains; if he does, I know he will confirm my drawing.'[10]

On 29 September 1875 Dodgson met Gertrude Chataway for the first time on the beach at Sandown, and she was to become one of his most important child friends. He delighted in her unselfconscious freedom as she played bare-legged on the sand in a sailor's jersey and bathing drawers, a costume which he later borrowed for other child friends. Years later, Gertrude recalled their friendship:

> Next door there was an old gentleman [Dodgson was forty-three!] – to me at any rate he seemed old – who interested me immensely. He would come on to his balcony, which joined ours, sniffing the sea air with his head thrown back, and would walk right down the steps on to the beach with his chin in the air, drinking in the fresh breezes as if he could never have enough. I do not know why this excited such keen curiosity on my part, but I remember well that whenever I heard his footstep I flew out to see him coming, and when one day he spoke to me my joy was complete. . . . We used to sit for hours on the wooden steps which led from our garden onto the beach, whilst he told me the most lovely tales that could possibly be imagined, often illustrating the exciting situations with a pencil as he went along.
> One thing that made his stories particularly charming to a child was that he often took his cue from her remarks – a question would set him off on quite a new trail of ideas, so that one felt that one had somehow helped

to make the story, and it seemed a personal possession. . . . To *me* it was
of course all perfect, but it is astonishing that *he* never seemed either too
tired or to want other society. I spoke to him once of this since I have
been grown up, and he told me it was the greatest pleasure he could have
to converse freely with a child, and feel the depths of her mind.[11]

Dodgson left Sandown on 11 October, but thoughts of Gertrude still
haunted him, and thirteen days later he wrote to Holiday and to
Macmillan announcing his intention of publishing the poem as a
Christmas book, incorporating a dedicatory acrostic on Gertrude
Chataway. On the following day he finished the acrostic and sent to
Mrs Chataway for consent to publish it. He now resolved to call the
poem *The Hunting of the Snark*, and to preface it with a tipped-in greeting
to his 40,000 child readers; in its final form this was the 'Easter
Greeting', that John Henry Newman said was 'likely to touch the
hearts of old men more than those for whom it is intended'.

Perhaps fortunately, Swain, the engraver, needed three months to
complete the blocks, only one being finished already. Dodgson thought
of going ahead, using the single illustration as a frontispiece, but when
he abandoned this idea, the text was expanded until it contained 141
four-line stanzas in eight 'fits' of varying lengths. On 26 January 1898
Dodgson wrote to Holiday saying how pleased he was with the proofs.
'They seem to me *most* successfully cut, and I agree with you in thinking
the head of 'Hope' a great success; it is quite lovely.' But a problem had
arisen, for the gorgeous cover design submitted to Macmillan would
cost 1s 4d a copy. They therefore needed to reduce the cost of 5d–6d a
copy in order to peg the retail price at 3s:

> My idea is this, to have a simpler cover for the 3s copies, which will, no
> doubt be the ones usually sold, but to offer the gorgeous covers also at 4s,
> which will be bought by the rich and those who wish to give them as
> presents. What I want you to do is to take 'Alice' as a guide, and design
> covers requiring about the same amount of gold, or, better, a little less.
> As 'Alice' and the 'Looking-Glass' have both got grotesque faces outside,
> I should like *these* to be pretty, as a contrast, and I don't think we can do
> better than to take the head of 'Hope' for the first side, and 'Care' for the
> second; and, as these are associated with 'forks' and 'thimbles' in the
> poem, what do you think of surrounding them, one with a border of
> interlaced forks, the other with a shower of thimbles? And what do you
> think of putting a bell at each corner of the cover, instead of a single line?
> The only thing to secure is that the total amount of gold required shall be
> rather less than on the cover of 'Alice'! All these are merely suggestions:
> *you* will be a far better judge of the matter than I can be, and perhaps may
> think of some quite different, and better, design.[12]

Dodgson eventually ordered a hundred copies in red and gold,
twenty in dark blue and gold, and two in white vellum and gold. He also
introduced an important innovation – the dust-wrapper: 'The advantage will be that it can stand in bookstalls without being taken out of

paper, and so can be kept in cleaner and more saleable condition.'[13] Publication date was 1 April 1876 – the date Dodgson thought it fittest for it to appear, and on 29 March he went to London and autographed eighty presentation copies. The first edition consisted of 10,000 copies, and despite poor reviews the first reprint was in May of the same year. A second reprinting in December 1876 brought the total to 19,000, though most of the second reprint may have been issued in 1877 and the following years. In 1879 Dodgson instructed Macmillan not to print any more copies, as he proposed to incorporate the whole, pictures and all, in *Rhyme? and Reason?*, which he published in 1883.

The Hunting of the Snark and the Oxford squibs were by no means Dodgson's entire literary output between 1874 and 1876. There were two pamphlets about election methods, *Suggestions as to the Best Method of Taking Votes, Where More Than Two Issues are to be Voted On*, published in 1874 under the initials CLD, and a refined version anonymously published in 1876. Voting methods were of great interest to Dodgson, some of his suggestions being taken up at Oxford, and it was a subject to which, as we shall see, he returned a few years later. He produced three mathematical works in this period, all under his real name. The first, entitled *Examples in Arithmetic*, was clearly printed off in some haste, for there are a number of striking omissions and inconsistencies. No solutions are given to the examples, though the author's personal copy in the Parrish Collection contains the answers written in his own hand. The second was called *Euclid, Book V Proved Algebraically so far as it Relates to Commensurable Magnitudes, to which is Prefixed a Summary of all the Necessary Algebraical Operations, Arranged in Order of Difficulty*. This was very different from the pamphlet which he had published under a similar title in 1868. The use of algebraic methods must have constituted a considerable improvement on the original. The third was *Euclid, Books I and II* which was printed in March 1874 and circulated among his mathematical friends. But the volume as set up contained four blank pages and was headed 'not yet published'. Dodgson's intention in writing this book was to set it before the public with as few alterations to the original as was consistent with nineteenth-century usage. The published edition did not come out until 1882, and is much amended.

Dodgson never kept animals, although Croft Rectory was not without household pets. These included Dido, the family dog, and various pet rabbits. His sister Henrietta was very fond of cats, and when she set up home independently for herself at Brighton, always kept several cats, and could not resist taking in and caring for the strays that found their way to her. But though Dodgson had no pets of his own, he could not bear to see animals ill treated. While staying at Sandown in September 1875, for instance, he found a kitten with a fish-hook stuck fast in its mouth, and took the animal to Dr Mears, the local surgeon, who extracted the hook. Years later Tommy, the Common Room cat, who had lived to an almost legendary old age, became so feeble that it was decided to put him out of his misery. Dodgson accordingly went to a great deal of trouble to find out from Sir James Paget the most humane means of doing this, and saw to it that his recommendations were scrupulously carried out.

In February 1875 Dodgson read a letter in *The Spectator* which seemed to suggest the question 'How far may vivisection be regarded as a sign of the times, and a fair specimen of that higher civilization which a purely secular State education is to give us?' He responded with a lengthy letter published in the *Pall Mall Gazette* in which he asks:

> Is the anatomist, who can contemplate unmoved the agonies he is inflicting for no higher purpose than to gratify a scientific curiosity, or to illustrate some well-established truth, a being higher or lower, in the scale of humanity, than the ignorant boor whose very soul would sicken at the horrid sight? For if ever there was an argument in favour of purely scientific education more cogent than another, it is surely this – 'What can teach the noble quality of mercy, of sensitiveness to all forms of suffering, so powerfully as the knowledge of what suffering really is? Can the man who has once realized by minute study what the nerves are, what the brain is, and what waves of agony the one can convey to the other, go forth and wantonly inflict pain on any sentient being?' A little while ago we should have confidently replied, 'He cannot do it'; in the light of modern revelations we must sorrowfully confess, 'He can.' And let it never be said that this is done with serious forethought of the balance of pain and gain; that the operator has pleaded with himself, 'Pain is indeed an evil, but so much suffering may fitly be endured to purchase so much knowledge.' When I hear of one of these ardent searchers after truth giving, not a helpless dumb animal, to whom he says in effect, '*You* shall suffer that *I* may know,' but his own person to the probe and to the scalpel, I will believe in him as recognizing a principle of justice . . .[14]

He took up the theme again in *Some Popular Fallacies About Vivisection*, which was published in *The Fortnightly Review*, expressing his concern about the unnecessary infliction of pain for mere academic interest, and about the brutalizing effect of such activities on the vivisector.

A further pamphlet published in February 1876 under the title *Professorship of Comparative Philology* dealt with an issue to be voted on in Convocation. The proposal before Convocation was that Professor Max Müller should be allowed to pursue his Indian studies uninterrupted, and that a Deputy be appointed to do his work on half the salary, the Deputy being in effect a new professor, and Müller a pensioner without obligations to the University. Dodgson's great concern was for the unfair treatment of the Deputy. There were separate issues of his pamphlet in the days leading up to the meeting, the third being prefaced by the motto 'Be just before you are generous', and when the matter came before Convocation he had copies handed out at the door as the voters went in. His intention was to remain silent during the proceedings, but wrote that the advocates of the Decree praised Max Müller, and ignored the half-pay of the Deputy, so that eventually he got up and asked them to stick to the point. Despite his efforts to prevent a patent injustice, the Decree was carried by ninety-four votes to thirty-five.

Dodgson's relationship with Max Müller had in the past been very cordial. Social visits had been exchanged, and the family had been photographed. But although Dodgson had done his best to make it clear that his objections in no way reflected on Müller, and that his prime concern was to see fair play by the Deputy, Müller appears to have taken it personally, and the old familiarity was not resumed. But shortly afterwards Dodgson produced an extraordinary poem in which he launched an attack on 'little men of little souls' who valued money above learning. Vivisectors, too, receive a share of the general condemnation in this surprisingly vitriolic verse, which he called *Fame's Penny Trumpet:*

> Go, throng each other's drawing-rooms,
>   Ye idols of a petty clique:
> Strut your brief hour in borrowed plumes
>   And make your penny-trumpets squeak:
>
> Deck your dull talk with pilfered shreds
>   Of learning from a nobler time,
> And oil each other's little heads
>   With mutual Flattery's golden slime:
>
> And when the topmost height ye gain,
>   And stand in Glory's ether clear,
> And grasp the prize of all your pain –
>   So many hundred pounds a year –
>
> Then let Fame's banner be unfurled!
>   Giving paeons for a victory won! . . .

The poem was rejected by the *Pall Mall Gazette*, *Punch*, and *The World*, and Dodgson therefore decided to go ahead with private publication, calling himself 'An Unendowed Researcher'. He must have been particularly keen to see it in print, for as he was away on a visit to his old friend Ranken he allowed his friend Bayne to handle the printing order for him – a rare honour indeed. But despite its anonymity, Dodgson's authorship, as usual, was probably an open secret, and the poem is likely to have aroused considerable hostility towards him in some quarters. But Dodgson seemed not to care. He was already beginning to retreat into a private world which he barricaded effectively against the outside world in general; all the world, that is, except a few close relatives and friends, and the ever-increasing number of child friends.

REFERENCES

1 Green, p. 339.
2 Jeffrey Stern, *Jabberwocky*, Spring 1973.
3 *The Atlantic Monthly*, June 1929.
4 Hatch, p. 117.
5 Ibid, p. 116.
6 Green, p. 317.
7 'Alice on the Stage', *The Theatre*, April 1887.
8 'Hark the Snark', *Lewis Carroll Observed*, Edward Guiliano (ed.), New York, 1976, p. 95.
9 Green, p. 326.
10 'The Snark's Significance', *The Academy*, 29 January 1898.
11 Collingwood, p. 380.
12 'The Snark's Significance', *The Academy*, 29 January 1898.
13 Dr Selwyn Goodacre, 'The Hunting of the Snark – A History of the Publication', *Jabberwocky*, Autumn 1976.
14 *Pall Mall Gazette*, 12 February 1876.

12 Favourite Dress of 'Nothing'

At around this time of his life Dodgson began to withdraw more and more into the world of his numerous child friends. Every summer he spent several weeks at the seaside, keeping a careful note of every child he met there. His standard for measuring the success of his holiday had once been the number of new acquaintances he had made, and if the list included famous people, so much the better. Now the test was more specifically the number of *child* friends he had made, and his hope each year was to meet a mixture of old friends and new, so that the list of children was continually growing. In a sense he 'collected' little girls as eagerly as some people collect antiques or first editions. After the holiday was over, there was hardly any limit to the distance he was prepared to travel to renew the acquaintance. The Isle of Wight had long been a favourite holiday resort for Dodgson, though after his break with the Tennysons he had abandoned Freshwater for Sandown. But in July 1877 Dodgson went to Eastbourne, and after three weeks at 44 Grand Parade, moved to 7 Lushington Road, which was to become his permanent seaside lodging for the next nineteen years. The proprietors were Mrs Dyer, and her husband, who was at the local post office, and Dodgson's accommodation consisted of a pleasant first floor sitting room with a balcony and a bedroom adjoining, to which an additional bedroom on the floor above was added a few years later.

At the end of each holiday he listed meticulously the names of the child friends he had made. Dodgson's diary entry of 2 August 1877 was typical of many over the years:

> It is time to record the various beginnings (or pseudo-beginnings) of child friendships here. Last Sunday a handsome little brunette, about 11 years old, asked me about the service at Trinity: since then we have recognized one another once or twice: she has a sister of 13 or 14, and two little brothers, all good-looking.
>
> This afternoon I shared a bench on the Marine Parade with a gentleman and his wife, and a nice little girl, about 10 (Barber), to whom I showed some puzzles: a pleasant child, though not very bright. But this evening, on the pier, I have made friends with quite the brightest child, and nearly the prettiest, I have yet seen here – 'Dolly' (Edith Rose Blakemore), about 5 years old, realizes Coleridge's 'little child, a

limber-elf', etc. She seems to be on springs, and was dancing incessantly
to the music: in face she reminds me of Bessie Slatter [an earlier child
friend] as a child, and her eyes literally glitter. The father is from
Birmingham, evidently in business: there was also the mother, quiet and
pleasant, and a boy of about 10. Dolly is fascinating, and I hope to see her
again.[1]

Dodgson's hope was fulfilled, but not his expectation, for Dolly was a
very shy child and unused to conversation outside the family circle.
Mrs Blakemore was rather put out by Dodgson's suggestion that Dolly
would be better for less petting, and it seemed that the attempt at
friendship would have to be abandoned. But after a chance meeting on
the Parade, Dolly not only spoke to him without crying, but invited him
to go with them. After much patient encouragement, Dodgson was able
to record, 'The small person is now as friendly as possible'.[2] When the
Blakemores left Eastbourne, Dodgson paid them a farewell visit and
told Dolly the story of the little foxes, which eventually became Chapter
15 of *Sylvie and Bruno Concluded*. Dolly Blakemore became a lifelong
friend, and their letters in adult life dealt with intimate matters which
illustrated a very special rapport between them.

His attempted friendship with Janie, Nellie and Lottie Williamson
proved entirely abortive. He wrote to their mother explaining how he
had met her children and seeking her approval for the friendship, but
she replied declining the acquaintance. Stung by this rare rebuff,
Dodgson replied undertaking not to *speak* to them, but that he could not
undertake to *avoid* them. But on 20 August he made an important new
friendship with the Hull family, with whom he remained on intimate
terms for the rest of his life. Mr Hull was a barrister in the Temple
whose father had been at Westminster School with Dodgson's father
and Uncle Hassard. He and his wife had four daughters and a son, and
Dodgson loved them all. He was charmed with little Jessie, who used to
trot along to his rooms and wake him out of bed in the mornings, an
innocent freedom which delighted Dodgson and was wholly new to
him. But his favourite was Agnes, whom he sketched on the beach, and
for whom Gertrude Chataway lent him her fisherman's jersey.

When Dodgson was back at Oxford, he wrote to Agnes claiming that
he had succeeded in forgetting her after a course of six lessons in
forgetting from 'Professor Gnome Emory'. 'After three lessons I forgot
my own name, and I forgot to go for the next lesson. So the Professor
said I was going on very well; "but I hope," he added, "you won't
forget to pay for the lessons." I said that would depend on whether the
lessons were good or not.'[3] Dodgson kept a special notebook for the
acrostics, riddles and poems that he wrote for Agnes, visiting the family
often, and writing to Agnes in ever-increasing terms of familiarity. As
time went on he began to address her as 'My Darling Aggie' and once

playfully as 'My Own Aggie (though, when I think of all the pain you have given me, I feel inclined to put the syllables in another order and say "My Agg own ie!")'.[4]

In December 1877 Dodgson wrote to Agnes, 'Oh! child, child! why have you never been over to Oxford to be photographed? I took a first-rate photograph only a week ago, but then the sitter (a little girl of ten) [May Forshall, for whom Dodgson wrote a madrigal on 24 December 1874] had to sit for a minute and a half, the light is so weak now.'[5] He had to wait almost a year for the chance to photograph Agnes, but in October 1878 Mrs Hull brought both her and her sister Alice to Oxford, and Dodgson took six photographs of them.

Although Dodgson had given up taking his photographic equipment to the seaside, he was still as keenly interested in the art of photography as ever. Besides taking straightforward portraits, he loved to dress up his child models, and had assembled a large quantity of costumes for the purpose. Mrs Coote, mother of Lizzie, Bertie and Carrie Coote, three little stage children in whom Dodgson was particularly interested, was a great help in supplying him with discarded costumes, and even made a new prince's outfit for him on one occasion. For he delighted in taking pictures of girls bare-legged, or dressed as boys. Such subjects, albeit innocent, were regarded by Victorian England as somewhat risqué, as were photographs of children in nightgowns, however voluminous, and scenes which incorporated a bed.

Dodgson had long earnestly wished to photograph children in the nude, but it was not easy to arrange. On 27 June 1879, however, he met a young lady who was able to smooth the way for him. Dodgson had seen and admired some fairy drawings by E. Gertrude Thomson and at the close of December 1878 had written to say that he would like to see more of her work. Her publisher, who had supplied her address, wrote at the same time to let her know that Dodgson and Lewis Carroll were the same person. Miss Thomson already had a copy of both *Alice* books, but she now received autographed matching copies in white and gold. The accompanying note read:

> I am sending you 'Alice' and 'the Looking-Glass' as well. There is an incompleteness about giving only one, and besides the one you bought was probably in red and would not match these. If you are at all in doubt as to what to do with the (now) superfluous copy, let me suggest your giving it to some poor sick child. I have been distributing them to all the hospitals and convalescent homes I can hear of, where there are children capable of reading them, and though, of course, one takes some pleasure in the popularity of the books elsewhere, it is not nearly so pleasant a thought to me as that they may be a comfort and relief to children in hours of pain and weariness. Still, no recipient *can* be more appropriate than one who seems to have been in fairyland herself . . .[6]

After some months of correspondence they arranged to meet in the South Kensington Museum. Dodgson had two child friends, Beatrice and Maud Fearon, with him. Miss Thomson wrote:

> The room was fairly full of all sorts and conditions as usual and I glanced at each masculine figure in turn, only to reject it as a possibility of the one I sought. Just as the big clock had clanged out twelve, I heard the high vivacious voices and laughter of children sounding down the corridor. At that moment a gentleman entered, two little girls clinging to his hands, and as I caught sight of the tall, slim figure, with the clean-shaven, delicate, refined face I said to myself, 'That's Lewis Carroll.' He stood for a moment, head erect, glancing swiftly over the room, then bending down, whispered something to one of the children; she, after a moment's pause, pointed straight at me. Dropping their hands he came forward, and with that winning smile of his that utterly banished the oppressive sense of the Oxford don, said simply, 'I am Mr Dodgson; I was to meet you, I think?' To which I as frankly smiled and said, 'How did you know me so soon?' 'My little friend found you. I told her I had come to meet a young lady who knew fairies, and she fixed on you at once. But, *I* knew you before she spoke.'[7]

Not long afterwards Dodgson wrote to her again: 'Are you sufficiently unconventional (I *think* you are) to defy Mrs Grundy and come down to spend the day with me in Oxford? Write and ask permission of your father.'[8] Despite the unconventionality of his own approach to Miss Thomson, it seems curious that he still expected this adult woman of nearly thirty to obtain parental consent to her day out. Her visit was one of many days spent together in artistic pursuits. Before long he wrote and invited her to come and photograph 'human fairies'. After his death she described what these photographic sessions were like:

> His photographic studio, on the roof of the college, was a big place filled with all sorts of properties, costumes, &c. He dressed up the children in a variety of quaint costumes, and 'took' them in all sorts of attitudes; intervals for refreshment and play being very frequent. The magic cupboards were opened and there issued forth a marvellous procession. Mechanical bears and wrestlers, rabbits, monkeys, and other uncouth and delightsome beasts. We would group together on the floor, Lewis Carroll, the fairies, the beasts and myself, and gay indeed were the hours we spent. How his laugh would ring out like a child's!
>
> And the exquisite nonsense he talked! It was like pages out of the *Alices*, only more delightful, for there was his own voice and smile to give the true charm to it all. I used to try to recall and record it. It was impossible – as impossible as to catch the gleam of colour on sunlit water, or to grasp a drifting rainbow. It was a mystic, intangible, gossamer-like thing, that, to chain it down in the words with which we should have translated it would have been to crush out all life and grace – to destroy it altogether . . .
>
> For many years there was a delightful interchange of visits. I would go down to Oxford for the day to photograph or draw portraits of his

child-friends for him. The children would return home, sometimes after lunch; in the afternoon Mr Dodgson and I would each bury ourselves in a luxurious armchair and talk, or look over sketches I had brought for him to see, or go through part of his vast collection of photographs of famous people taken long years before. Many of Gabriel Rossetti and his sister Christina, Ruskin, the Millais children, the Terry family. I remember one of Ellen Terry, taken when she was about eighteen; she happened to laugh at the moment, and she looked one of the loveliest young creatures imaginable. Then he would make the afternoon tea himself, all in his deft and dainty fashion, and this would bring the happy visit to its close.

A lady friend of Mr Dodgson's – a good woman, eminently practical and steeped to the lips in conventions – once took me to task. We had spent the morning at her house sketching her children; at least, I sketched while he talked 'Alice'. He left before lunch, and after this meal was over she sent the children away, and, taking up her sewing, sat down in front of me.

'I hear that you spent the other day in Oxford, with Mr Dodgson?'

'Yes, it was a most delightful day.'

'It's a very unconventional thing to do.'

'We are both very unconventional.'

'Mr Dodgson is not a ladies' man.'

'He wouldn't be my friend if he were.'

'He is a confirmed bachelor.'

'So am I; and, what is more, he is old enough to be my father.'

She steadfastly regarded me for a moment, and then said, 'I tell you what it is, Mr Dodgson doesn't think of you as a "young lady" or anything of that kind, he looks upon you as a sort of "old child".' I laughed delightedly. 'I don't mind if Mr Dodgson looks upon me as a sort of old grandmother if only he will ask me down to Oxford.' But I was deeply offended. Our pure and beautiful friendship seemed hurt somehow by this coarse handling.[9]

On 4 July 1879 Dodgson called on Sir Frederick Leighton who showed him some unfinished pictures, including one of a female figure standing, with a child kissing her. This was painted from two sisters, and Sir Frederick recommended the child for Miss Thomson, who needed a model. A fortnight later Miss Thomson brought one of Sir Frederick's models to Oxford, where Dodgson took six nude studies and one ordinary photograph. He recorded that Miss Thomson was a great help to him in arranging the model. Dodgson rarely photographed children unclothed without a chaperone, and was always solicitous for the welfare of his sitters, both as regards their feelings and their physical well being. Once when Miss Thomson engaged a child model to come to her studio and sit for him, he expressed alarm that the child had travelled across London unaccompanied. The child was well used to this, but Dodgson wrote, 'I don't quite like the idea of that small and pretty child going all that way alone on my account. If she got lost or stolen I should feel an awful responsibility in having caused her to run the risk. I fear such beauty, among the very poor, is a very dangerous possession.'[10]

On the very next day two children called Annie and Frances Henderson came with their mother to Dodgson's studio. Mrs Henderson was willing in principle that the children should pose in the nude, but Dodgson was concerned about how they would react to the idea, and said that he would not even ask for bare feet if they were shy. But to his delight they were ready for any amount of undress, and revelled in the privilige of being allowed to run about naked. 'It was a great privilege to have such a model as Annie to take,' Dodgson wrote. 'A very pretty face, and good figure. She was worth any number of my models of yesterday.'[11] Three days later Miss Thomson came again, and this time little Frances posed, and Dodgson photographed her lying on the sofa in 'her favourite dress of "nothing".' On 29 July Mrs Henderson brought Annie again and Dodgson's photographs of her included one lying on a blanket, 'naked as usual'. Dodgson now had enough nude studies to be able truthfully to say that this was a kind of photography that he had often done lately, and that very afternoon, perhaps reassured that this was now a practised artistic pursuit, Mrs Hatch brought Beatrice, Ethel and Evelyn over to be photographed, although only Evelyn posed in the nude.

In July 1880, suddenly and without explanation, Dodgson gave up photography for good. In May and June he had had several photographic sessions with the Henderson children, some in fancy dress but mostly nude. He spent a great deal of time at the end of term sorting and mounting photographs and erasing some of his negatives, as the number on hand was far too great. Various theories have been advanced as to the reasons why Dodgson gave it up, one of them being the gossip caused by his nude studies. But Dodgson was all his lfe indifferent, in the final analysis, to the opinion of others, the true arbiter in every case being his own conscience. Certainly in the closed community of Oxford he could not have hoped to keep his activities a secret for long; but although he gave up photography, he continued to draw nude studies, and it was in fact the frequent visits to his rooms in his later years of unchaperoned young ladies that gave most exercise to the wagging tongues of Oxford.

Another theory is that he may have given up because of the advancing popularity of dry plate photography. 'All "dryplate" photography is inferior, in artistic effect, to the now abandoned "wetplate" ', he once wrote, although he conceded that it was invaluable as means of making 'memoranda of attitudes'. 'If I had a dryplate camera,' he wrote to Miss Thomson, 'and time to work it, and could secure a child of a really good figure, either a professional model, or (much better) a child of the upper classes, I would get her into every pretty attitude I could think of,

29 Lewis Carroll's father, the Archdeacon, photographed by Carroll's favourite uncle, Skeffington Lutwidge

30 'The Two Alices'. Lewis Carroll's sister-in-law (seated) and her cousin of the same name

31   The Deanery, Christ Church. Believed by Lewis Carroll

32   Liddell family group, about 1885. Alice is seated in the foreground, with her arm on the Dean's knee

33 Mary Anne, Mrs Cameron's maid (second left). Was she the
White Rabbit's Mary Ann? (page 134)

34 Beatrice Hatch, dressed as a Turk. Photograph by Lewis Carroll

35 Xie Kitchin posed by Henry Holiday and photographed by Dodgson

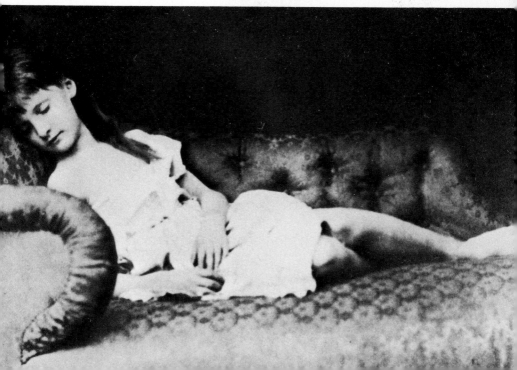

36 Performers in the Charles Bennett
'Benefit' include Ellen and Kate Terry, Tom
Taylor (seated right) and Sir John Tenniel
(second row, in white trimmed hat)

37 Sketch by Lewis Carroll for *Sylvie and
Bruno*

38 Autographed photograph sent to Dodgson in 1890 by Princess Alice and the Duke of Albany, children of Prince Leopold

"I DO not believe GOD means us to divide life into two halves—to wear a grave face on Sunday, and to think it out of place to even so much as mention Him on a week-day. Do you think He cares to see only kneeling figures, and to hear only tones of prayer and that He does not always love to see the lambs leaping in the sunlight, and to hear the merry voices of the children, as they roll among the hay? Surely their innocent laughter is as sweet in His ears as the grandest anthem that ever rolled up from the "dim religious light" of some solemn Cathedral? And if I have written anything to add to these stores of innocent and healthful amusements that are laid up in books for the children I love so well, it is surely something I may hope to look back upon without shame and sorrow (as how much of life must then be recalled!) when my turn comes to walk through the valley of shadows."

From "An Easter Greeting." by Lewis Carroll.

I am the Resurrection and the Life.

Charles Lutwidge Dodgson
(Lewis Carroll),
Fell asleep Jan. 14, 1898.

and could get, in a single morning, 50 or 100 such memoranda. Do try this, with the next pretty child you get as a model, and let me have some of the photos.'[12] Here then was a real clue as to his reasons – time. For despite his obvious reservations about the new method, the means were always available for him to continue with the old, had he wished. Nor had his interest in the subject as an art form declined. But he now reached a point in his life when he felt a compulsion to work at his literary projects before it was too late. With the passing of various relatives – and in 1880 Aunt Lucy died, mercifully, for her faculties of communication had begun rapidly to desert her – he felt that it was his Christian duty to carry through as many projects as he could, especially where the themes were didactic. He took no decision to abandon photography immediately – if indeed it was ever a conscious resolution – but such evidence as exists seems to suggest that, having failed to find time to resume, as usual, when the brighter weather arrived, he somehow lost the habit. For on 25 September 1880 he met and sketched on the beach a child called Helen Cowie, who had the loveliest legs he had ever seen at Eastbourne. Three days later he met her uncle and aunt, made a more careful sketch of Helen, and urged them to bring her to Oxford to be photographed.

As late as March 1883 Dodgson called to see the mother of a child of eleven-and-a-half years called Nellie May, who had sat for a number of artists of his acquaintance for nude studies. His idea was to try and arrange for her and perhaps one of her sisters to sit for nude photographs for him; but when he saw the child, he wrote, 'She is very pretty, and no doubt an artist can make *very* pretty pictures of her, but I doubt her being a good photographic subject for a "nude" study, I should guess her to be too fat, at present, though she is 11½: in another year or two she might be more graceful.' This remark, and others similar, indicate that Dodgson certainly did not lose interest in the nude child who had reached puberty. Later he expressed considerable interest in the figure of an eighteen-year-old girl who performed publicly in a sort of aquarium, and was so delighted with her grace and beauty that he returned to see her again.

The boundary of Dodgson's relationships with the opposite sex appears to some extent to have been defined by what was attainable. He was an attractive man, whose face remained tranquil and unlined as the years advanced, and whose thickly curling grey hair lent him added appeal. In congenial company he was witty and entertaining; he was kind, compassionate, and comfortably circumstanced. What he sought was a mixture of delicate, refined beauty animated by intelligence and education. His relationship with Miss Thomson was an interesting one. Despite her protestation of confirmed bachelorhood, it seems very probable that she was in love with Dodgson, whom she clearly idolized.

She was herself by no means unattractive, having a generous, sensual mouth and thoughtful eyes, but her bone structure was a little heavy for Dodgson's taste. Although he clearly enjoyed her company, it is difficult to escape the feeling that his main interest in her was that she could, and did, arrange child nude models for him. Her talent would not have been sufficient to interest him had she not sketched nude children, and although he made several attempts to commission work from her, she rarely completed what she undertook.

But there was never any doubt of Miss Thomson's devotion to him. After his death she painted a fine miniature of him, which was shown at the exhibition put on in Columbia University in 1932 to mark the centenary of Dodgson's birth; and among the many wreaths at Dodgson's funeral was one inscribed, 'To the sweetest soul that ever looked with human eyes'. This was from E. Gertrude Thomson.

Dodgson's literary output had not been great between 1876 and 1880. Perhaps business and family commitments had occupied him more than usual. Early in 1878 his youngest brother, Edwin, having been duly ordained at Chichester Theological College, left to be a missionary in Zanzibar; but before the year was out he had to return for medical reasons. Dodgson also had heavy financial losses. He had invested heavily in steamships, mainly to accommodate his cousin, Herbert Wilcox, but in 1878 Herbert Wilcox failed for £13,000, and had to sell his ship the *Corsica* at a loss. In all Dodgson was £1340 out of pocket. New management was appointed to the shipping line, but there were continual problems, with ships running aground, and at one stage there was talk of deliberate grounding, presumably for purposes of fraudently claiming insurance. Bayne, a prudent man at all times, had invested in the same shares and also lost heavily. But Dodgson did not finally sell out his shares until 1890. By this time one of the ships, the *Tartessus*, had been condemned after running aground in Bilbao, and the sale of his shares in the remaining three steamships fetched £1450. 'I am heartily glad to be out of it,'[13] he commented.

In the main Dodgson's publications consisted of letters and pamphlets, on subjects as varied as Oxford examinations, vote-taking and vaccination. The latter took the form of three letters to the *Eastbourne Chronicle*, criticizing the misuse by 'that well-meaning, but most mischievous association, the "Anti-vaccination League".' Dodgson's argument is summarized in his second letter:

> The statistics so constantly quoted by the opponents of vaccination, namely, the percentage of vaccinated persons among small-pox patients, prove nothing, when taken alone, as to vaccination increasing or diminishing the liability to take small-pox; in order to prove anything, they must be compared with other statistics, namely, the percentage of

vaccinated persons among the whole population; and, when so compared, they prove that vaccination diminishes that liability.[14]

Word Links, published in 1878, was an earlier version of the game *Doublets*, which came out in the following year, and which had been invented to relieve Julia and Ethel Arnold from boredom. An item which brought together two distinct interests was *Memoria Technica* (1877), which Dodgson produced with the 'electric pen' he bought from Parker's on 20 June 1877. The pen operated by making a series of minute holes, and an inking process enabled numerous copies to be run off, rather in the manner of modern duplicating.[15] After some practice, in which he modified his personal handwriting style, Dodgson mastered the technique, and found it exceedingly useful, particularly in Christ Church business. The system of *Memoria Technica* was one of a number devised by Dodgson over the years. The method certainly worked, for he used it himself, but it is doubtful whether many people would find the complicated process any advantage over learning by rote.

The most important publication was *Euclid and his Modern Rivals*, an attack on those presumptuous enough to rewrite Euclid, which he brought out in 1879. His object in writing the book was to establish the advantage of teaching and examining elementary geometry from a single textbook, and the superiority for the purpose of Euclid over all other manuals. The book is presented dramatically, being set in a College study, where Minos, an examiner, is distracted by the difficulties of marking examination papers in which substitutes for Euclid are offered. He consults his fellow examiner, Rhadamanthus, and then falls asleep to dream of a visitation by the ghosts of 'Professor Niemand', Euclid, Archimedes, Pythagoras, etc., who argue the merits of the various textbooks. The popularity of the book was due almost entirely to its dramatic structure, and to its light and humorous style.

Dodgson now had a number of literary projects in mind, and being anxious to increase his output in the years that remained to him, had been toying for some time with the notion of resigning his Mathematical Lectureship, though still retaining his Studentship. For his own part, he had been in a position to retire for some years, and his chief motive for hanging on had been to provide money for others. In 1880, when his lecturing work was lighter than usual, he voluntarily took a cut in salary of £100 for that year; but his normal salary was £300 p.a., and he now calculated that he could make this up by additional book-writing.

He had almost decided on his resignation on 14 July 1881, but cautiously hesitated for a little longer, perhaps waiting to see how much work he would get through in his ten weeks at Eastbourne. He travelled down there on 20 July, and four days later had arranged all his books and papers and drawn up a list of the work he expected to get through. His intention was to work on revisions for *Euclid, Books I and II*, which ultimately ran into eight editions, *Euclid and his Modern Rivals*, 2nd Edition, and 'Limits of Circle-Squaring – or some such name'. He proposed to finish the second edition of *Phantasmagoria*, for publication at Christmas, and hoped to make progress with *Sylvie and Bruno*. He also intended to improve his French and German, arranging to have French conversation lessons twice a week, and to do some 'double translation' from George Sand's *La Petite Fadette* – presumably from French into German. Shakespeare and Birk's *Difficulties on Belief* were noted for revision, and he intended to try out his newly conceived 'writing on subjects' plan. This entailed writing all he knew about a given subject, studying the subject for a month, writing all he knew about it again and comparing the two versions to establish his progress. The subject he chose for his first experiment was physiology, but at the end of his holiday he had not even begun it, though he had read four Shakespeare plays and dabbled in French and German. Nor had he done anything on *Euclid and his Modern Rivals*, *Phantasmagoria* or *Sylvie and Bruno*. He had, however, nearly finished *Euclid, Books I and II*, the first published edition of the book he had privately circulated in 1875, revised fairly extensively and with an introduction and appendices. Also well advanced was 'Limits of Circle-Squaring', sparked off by correspondence he had had in July with a 'circle-squarer', which Dodgson had judiciously ended until such time as the 'circle-squarer' should acquire the elements of algebraical geometry. Ultimately, though the first manuscript chapter still survives, most of this was absorbed into *Curiosa Mathematica. Part 1. A New Theory of Parallels*, which he published in 1888. The preface is humorous and Dodgson, who never wasted anything, even managed to work in a parody which he had sung to Archbishop Longley some thirty years earlier, when Longley was Bishop of Durham and on which, according to Bayne's diary, Longley complimented him:

> I have wandered, I have pondered
> I have squandered many a boon;
> In the gladness, in the sadness
> In the madness of the moon.
> Seek thy pillow near the billow
> Where the willow doth not weep;
> Few will wonder who lies under
> Hearing thunder fast asleep.

But despite the humour which Dodgson introduces, the book is a serious critical appraisal of the controversial Twelfth Axiom of Euclid. Tony Beale writes:

In a sense. Dodgson joined the 'Modern Rivals', but on closer examination reveals that he had only accepted that the Axiom was not intuitively true. He wriggled out of the difficulty by dividing the whole class of theorems needing proof 'into two sub-classes – one including those which are *absolutely* true: the other those which are only *approximately* true – the error, if any, being *infinitesimal* when compared with the Magnitudes with which the Theorem is concerned'. He further suggested that if Euclid had realized the defect in his Axiom, 'it is possible that he may have thought fit to ignore it, on the ground that, when Finite Magnitudes differ only by an Infinitesimal, they are for all *practical* purposes, equal.' There must be many pure mathematicians who would squirm at such a justification.[16]

On 18 October 1881 Dodgson wrote to the Dean notifying him of his intention to resign his Lecturship at the end of the year. The concept of himself as a elderly man is traceable back to the publication of *Through the Looking-Glass* and his fortieth birthday, and with every year that passed he became more obsessed with the notion of working while life yet remained. In January he would be fifty years old, and he would have held the Lectureship for exactly twenty-six years. 'I shall now have my whole time at my own disposal, and, if God gives me continued health and strength, may hope, before my powers fail, to do some worthy work in writing – partly in the cause of Mathematical Education, partly in the cause of innocent recreation for children, and partly, I hope (though so utterly unworthy of being allowed to take up such work) in the cause of religious thought.'[17] Three days later Dodgson noted that the Dean had written to him expressing regret at losing his services, although acknowledging that he had earned his retirement. A month later Dodgson attempted a partial retraction by offering to go on with the Euclid lectures for £50 a year, but the Dean rejected his offer, saying he had already offered it to Sampson, and could not retract. Only two men out of nine attended his last lecture, the remainder opting to absent themselves as it was a saint's day.

Dodgson had much to occupy his new-found leisure. He had written to Macmillan in February 1881 suggesting a 'Nursery Edition' of *Alice*, larger and thinner than the original, with a selection of text and pictures printed on colours, to retail at about 2s a copy. This, he thought, would not interfere with sales of the 6s edition, as it would have an entirely separate market. Macmillan was doubtful about the idea. But Dodgson reported that he was more receptive on 6 January 1882 when he called on him in London and broached the subject again. Macmillan, however, had other ideas for extending the market. On 10 February he wrote drawing Dodgson's attention to the new 6d edition of *Tom Brown's School Days* which he was preparing to meet the apparent demand for good books at very cheap prices. The object was to print 150,000 copies, which should sell very quickly, and then let the edition go out of print. He believed that this cheap edition would act as an advertisement both to itself and to good literature in general, and since its existence was to be only temporary, it would not injure sales of the regular edition. As advance orders had already exceeded 100,000 copies, the scheme seemed likely to succeed.

Macmillan now sought Dodgson's agreement to a similar edition of 100,000 copies of the *Alice* books, on payment of £200 down, and the right to print 50,000 more at £2 per thousand. In principle Dodgson was as anxious as anyone to see his books reach a wider readership than was possible at 6s a copy, but he was seriously concerned at the economics of the thing. This led him to question the whole basis of the returns received by authors. He had a large specimen quarto page set up in double column with a picture of the Queen of Hearts in the centre, by Clay the printer, through Macmillan; but the first did not satisfy him as to the printing, and he ordered another version in slightly larger and clearer type. This meant a slight loss of words to the page, but he estimated that the whole could be done in forty-seven pages. He was convinced that it ought to be possible to do the job more cheaply, and sent Clay's copy to the Clarendon Press for an estimate. Curiously, for all his experience of publishing detail, Dodgson entertained the naive belief that the 'compactness' of the proposed edition – i.e. forty-eight pages only – should make it cheaper, even though there was just as much typesetting to be done, and the overall quantity of paper was undiminished. When he sent to the Clarendon Press for an estimate, his old friend Bartholomew Price, writing from the Secretary's room, on 9 March 1882, disabused him. 'The compactness is but a small matter: the most important are the paper and the Press work, and mainly the former of that two. Acting on your instructions on the mode of charging, with discounts and deferred payment and with paper of the quality you have sent, we find that we could print and deliver in London covered and sewn the first 50,000 at 2 pence per copy: the second 50,000 at one and seven eighths of a penny (1⅞d) per copy.'[18] He added that if he could use paper of the same quality needed in the 6d editions, it might be possible to negotiate a more favourable rate with a papermaker.

Careful scrutiny of the figures satisfied Dodgson that the publisher's charges were not exorbitant. The blame, he felt, lay with the booksellers. He had already in 1876 sent Macmillan an analysis of the profits of 40,000 copies of *Alice's Adventures in Wonderland*, and proposed to cut booksellers' discounts. Macmillan had replied that to attempt to formulate by figures the respective share of the profits of all parties was impossible, and added, 'You remember the old story of Robin Hood and someone else who tried to split the willow wand with him. The rival hits it on the side. Robin says, "Well shot, but you did not allow for the wind." This not allowing for the wind is the fault of all abstract calculators of mercantile results from Alcashar with his basket down to Ruskin and his FORS – and his fish.'[19]

Nevertheless, Dodgson was determined to make a stand against the booksellers, and in 1883 the following notice began to appear in his books: 'In selling Mr Lewis Carroll's books to the Trade, Messrs Macmillan & Co. will abate 2d in the shilling (no odd copies), and allow 5 per cent discount within 6 months, and 10 per cent for cash. In selling them to the Public (for cash only) they will allow 10 per cent discount.' This provoked a letter from 'A Firm of London Booksellers' published in *The Bookseller* on 4 August 1883, which read: 'Rather than buy on the terms Mr Lewis Carroll offers, the trade will do well to refuse to take copies of his books, new or old, so long as he adheres to the terms he has just announced to the trade for their delectation and delight.' Receiving a copy of the letter from Macmillan, Dodgson commented in his diary: 'I mean at once to write a letter, or pamphlet, or both, to tell the public what booksellers' profits really are, and that I am trying to reduce their monstrous proportions'. The pamphlet was *The Profits of Authorship*, published in 1884. So far from being deterred by the response of booksellers, Dodgson continued to include the notice, and it appeared in the first edition of *Rhyme? and Reason?* which came out in December 1883.

This book was a new and more sophisticated version of the illustrated edition of *Phantasmagoria* that Dodgson had once intended to publish. *Rhyme? And Reason?* comprised the whole of *The Hunting of the Snark* with Holidays's illustrations, a selection of humorous poems from *Phantasmagoria* including the title poem, plus *Fame's Penny Trumpet*, which had been privately printed, and 'Tema Con Variazioni', which as 'The Dear Gazelle' had appeared in the *Comic Times* of 1855. The dedicatory poem is the acrostic for Gertrude Chataway which prefaced *The Hunting of the Snark*.

But although the text was in the main a collection of previously published items, the book was enlivened by a series of brilliant new drawings to illustrate those portions of the text which had previously appeared without pictures. With his usual care Dodgson had considered a number of illustrators. Du Maurier had again been approached, as had Linley Sambourne, Walter Crane and E. Ralston, but the arrangement fell through in every case. Various friends had suggested possible artists and Dodgson had sent for specimens of their work. Among these were E. Fairfield, who had drawn two sketches of the Jabberwock, and his brother A. F. Fairfield, F. W. Lawson, whose woodcuts interested him, and M. Hendschel, who lived in Frankfurt. Ruskin was asked over to look at the drawings of the Fairfield brothers, but though he thought the drawings of E. Fairfield 'very comic', and the faces by his brother 'very pretty, and some of his figures good', he considered both brothers amateurish and unfinished in style. Lawson's woodcuts pleased Ruskin most, and Dodgson, who had already invited the Fairfields to submit an illustration of a poem from *Phantasmagoria*, toyed with the idea of inviting Lawson to do likewise, but was so taken with Hendschel's work, and so disappointed with a fresh batch of Lawson's woodcuts, that he dropped the idea. Finally, however, it was an American artist, Arthur Burdett Frost, who provided the sixty-five illustrations, twenty-four of which were full page. Frost's reputation in the main rested on his fine paintings of sporting subjects; but his illustrations for *Rhyme? and Reason?* are conceived and executed with wit and polish, doing much to enliven the poems. Brian Sibley has noted Frost's uncanny ability to see illustrative possibilities in seemingly un-illustratable poems, including *Fame's Penny Trumpet*, and 'Melancholetta', and of the spectacular troupe of ghosts in *Phantasmagoria*, too ludicrous to terrify. He writes:

> He captures their translucent wraithe-like forms perfectly: the phantom swaying from side to side before the gothic window, the moonlight streaming right through him; and the Inn-Spectre, resting his ghostly, gouty foot on the parlour table, and clutching the neck of a bottle of more earthly spirits! There is something frightfully menacing about the indescribable grotesquerie, howling on the rain-soaked battlements; and in the hand-standing ghost who confronts the fisherman (surely one of them is Holiday's Banker?), with its dreadful coach-lamp eyes and gleaming buck teeth. But the other spirits are simply puckish creatures, totally lacking in any decent ghostly terror, as they drill through the wainscoting, munch their sandwiches a-top the garden wall, pass their platter for more duck, and eye the quality of their glass of bitter beer.[20]

Other minor publications of the period included a poem which he contributed under protest to *The Garland of Rachel*, a small anthology produced by her father to mark the first birthday of Rachel Daniel, and the finest and most illustrious of the Daniel Press publications; and *Lanrick*, a complicated board game that never achieved real popularity. This may have been intended as an item for 'Original Games and Puzzles' which Miss Thomson had agreed to illustrate for him. His failure to publish this book was almost certainly due to Miss Thomson's not supplying the promised pictures. On 28 July 1893 he wrote to her:

> I wonder if you have any idea how long my two books have been on hand? The 'Serious Poems' came first. Your letter, agreeing to illustrate them, came July 24, 1885: so that I have been waiting just over *8* years for the pictures. Of which I have not, as yet, seen *one*. The 'Games & Puzzles' you undertook in Mar./'86, more than 7 years ago. As the text is still very unfinished, I am in no particular hurry; even if you got a sufficient lot of pictures (say 25) done this year, I do not think I could spare the time necessary for getting it out next Christmas. But the

'Serious Poems' have been ready all the time, and could have been published, any Christmas from 1885 onward, if the pictures had been done.

His pamphlet *Lawn Tennis Tournaments* argues on a statistical basis that knock-out competitions in which all those beaten in the first round are eliminated, and so on, while ensuring that the best man wins, do not guarantee that the second man gets second prize. The odds, he points out, are only 16–31 in favour of this, and are 12–1 against the four best finally coming out in the right order. But his alternative scoring method is too complicated to be generally practicable, and in any event assumes that the right order is necessarily the prime consideration; such elements as surprise and excitement are overlooked. However, his objections are now catered for in the modern 'seedings' system at Wimbledon and elsewhere.

Of far greater significance are *Parliamentary Elections* and *The Principles of Parliamentary Representation*, both published in 1884. Of the second, Duncan Black writes: 'Carroll's model of the political system is unmatched in its logical rigour and it will be found possible to alter some of its assumptions . . . so as to bring the model into closer contact with political reality. The booklet, neglected for almost a century, seems to me to present the way to new development in Political Science.'

At the time when Dodgson was writing, the political system operated in this country was for all practical purposes a two-party one. Elections took place over about a week; ballot boxes were not sealed and information as to the state of the poll was at all times readily available. In *Parliamentary Elections* Dodgson based his scheme on the following axioms:

1) That each Member of Parliament should represent approximately the same number of electors.
2) That the minority of the two parties into which, broadly speaking, each district may be divided, should be adequately represented.
3) That the waste of votes, caused by accidentally giving one candidate more than he needs and leaving another of the same party with less than he needs, should be, if possible, avoided.
4) That the process of marking a ballot-paper should be reduced to the utmost possible simplicity, to meet the case of voters of the very narrowest mental calibre.
5) That the process of counting votes should be as simple as possible.

In *The Principles of Parliamentary Representation* Dodgson uses statistics, algebra and logic to support his argument in favour of proportional representation. Looking at the multiple seat constituency, he pointed out that if a constituency had five seats and each elector were given one vote, on the average of an infinite number of elections 61 per cent of the voters will be represented by the five members winning the seats; but if each elector gets only one vote in a five member constituency, 84 per cent of the voters will be represented by the five members chosen. Dodgson makes the assumption that each party will know its own supporters, and will be able to direct the way they vote. He also assumes that each party will choose its strategy to maximize the number of seats that it fills, and that the opposing party will adopt the most effective counter-strategy. Duncan Black writes:

> The argument has a mathematical structure and has all the rigour of mathematics without the mathematics appearing, save in a few pages where it emerges as a simple equation or an algebraic inequality. In fact the argument throughout is based on the 2-person zero-sum game, and it could have been put into mathematical form only after 1928 when the first exposition of the 2-person zero-sum game was given by John von Neuman. This astonishing feature may be taken to indicate that the booklet incorporates something of Carroll's genius. Dodgson also deserves credit for drawing attention to the possible effect that knowledge of the state of the poll may have on the electors, who may give way to a psychological desire to be on the winning side, whichever that may be. 'It surely would involve no practical difficulty', he wrote, 'to provide that the boxes of voting papers should be sealed up by a government official and placed in such custody as would make it impossible to tamper with them; and that when the last election had been held they should be opened, the votes counted, and the results announced.'[21]

On a personal level Dodgson's life changed little after the resignation of his lectureship. He continued to live at Oxford during term time, and to spend most of the summer holiday at Eastbourne. His visits to London were frequent, as also were his visits to Guildford. He maintained close links with his cousins, the Wilcoxes, and paid annual visits to Brighton to see Barclay, his friend of undergraduate days. Although he toyed with the idea of going to board in Paris in order to learn French conversation, nothing came of it. However, he bought a velociman, a kind of clumsy tricycle, and after having several modifications made to the design, used it to cycle around the outskirts of Oxford. He was now spending a great deal of time with Theo Heaphy, daughter of an old friend, Thomas Heaphy, whose interests in religion and in psychic research Dodgson shared. After the death of her father, Dodgson was a great support to Theo, arranging for her and her mother to stay in Oxford, and getting her away for a holiday when she seemed in danger of a breakdown in health.

Meanwhile, problems had arisen in his friendship with the Hull children. He had begun to feel that he was being 'used', and that the pleasure he took in their company was much greater than theirs in his. His distress at their behaviour was considerable; he had known them for exactly five years, and now he resolved not to call again unless he had some definite indication that he was welcome. But a week later Agnes called to make friends again. It was a great relief to him no longer to feel estranged, and he marked it as a 'dies cretâ notandus'. This relief was only temporary, for less than a month later Jessie declined to accompany him to a concert in the park, and Mrs Hull said that she did not wish her to go to the park with him again. This seemed extraordinary behaviour to Dodgson, who recalled that only a year before Evelyn and Jessie had been his guests at Oxford, when Mrs Hull had actually proposed that they should sleep in College! The tenor of Dodgson's reply to Mrs Hull led him to expect a prolonged estrangement, but he felt that the vexation he had suffered would not be in vain if the girls learnt from it to treat friends in some sort of self-sacrificing spirit. He described his feelings as 'desolate', and was very pleased when a few days later he received a very friendly letter from Mr Hull. But when he sent Agnes and Jessie some photographs and drawings he was hurt that both their letters of thanks began 'my dear' instead of 'dearest' and ended 'affte' instead of 'loving'. 'The love of children is a fleeting thing,' he commented. But perhaps he took some comfort from the visit of Margie Dymes to Oxford in November 1883. The Dymes family were at that time in severe difficulties, the father being threatened with bankruptcy. He had a wife and eight children. In December of that year Dodgson wrote a circular letter to 180 friends asking for help to get the family on their feet again. Margie's visit lasted a week, and she stayed with Miss Lloyd, an old friend of Dodgson's. During her visit he had a tête-à-tête dinner with Margie, the first time he had ever had such a meal in the College.

After his brief period in Zanzibar, Dodgson's brother Edwin had gone in 1881 to Tristan da Cunha, where he was priest in charge. The population of the island was only about a hundred, and the inhabitants had lived well enough as long as the whalers had called at the island for fresh meat and vegetables. But the whales deserted the area, with the result that no ships now called there, and to make matters worse, the rats which swarmed on the islands were eating all the crops. The result was that the islanders were now on the verge of starvation. When Edwin wrote home about it, Dodgson suggested that the only solution was to remove the entire population to the Cape, or Australia, a plan with which Edwin heartily concurred. Over the next four years Dodgson campaigned actively towards that end. The multitude of people he approached in the cause included the Governor and Prime Minister at the Cape, the permanent secretary to the Admiralty and the permanent under-secretary to the Colonial Office. On 25 November 1883 he was visited by Sir George Baden-Powell, who had heard about Dodgson's proposals, and who suggested that as Australia was anxious for immigrants, it should be possible to give the islanders land, so that the only cost would be that of a passage, and the only difficulty that of transporting the cattle; but if the latter could be got to the Cape, they could be sold. He then arranged a further interview with Sir Paul Samuel, who suggested that the islanders and cattle be got to the Cape, whereupon he could arrange for them to go at £6 a head to New South Wales as labourers. Dodgson took the opportunity of asking whether the Dymes family could go, but found it would cost about £30 a head.

Matters had reached a deadlock when, in June 1885, Lord Salisbury became Prime Minister. In December of that year, when Edwin decided to come to England to press the cause personally, Dodgson wrote to Lord Salisbury, who agreed to interview them both. A number of minor benefits accrued. The Admiralty allowed Edwin a free passage and sent some essential stores, including potatoes, but no other progress was made. He wrote again in February 1887 to report that fifteen men from the island had recently been lost at sea, leaving only eleven able-bodied men among a population of ninety. But all Dodgson's efforts were in vain, for nothing was done, and Edwin was ultimately transferred to Zanzibar.

REFERENCES

1   Green, pp. 364–5.
2   Ms. Diaries, 10 September 1877.
3   Hatch, p. 132.
4   Ibid, p. 145.
5   Ibid, pp. 132–3.
6   *The Gentlewoman*, 29 January 1898.
7   Ibid.
8   *The Gentlewoman*, 5 February 1898.
9   Ibid.
10 Ibid.
11 Ms. Diaries, 18 July 1879.
12 D.F.C. 27/5/2a.
13 Ms. Diaries, 15 November 1890.
14 *Three Letters on Anti-Vaccination*, Lewis Carroll Society, 1976.
15 See Article, Morton Cohen, *Illustrated London News*, Christmas 1976.
16 Article, 'C. L. Dodgson, Mathematician', *Mr Dodgson: Nine Lewis Carroll Studies*, Lewis Carroll Society, 1973, p. 31.
17 Green, p. 400.
18 Christ Church Library, Ms. C. 14.
19 Simon Nowell-Smith, *Letters to Macmillan*, 1967, p. 76.
20 Article, 'Ten degrees of Frost', *Jabberwocky*, Spring 1976.
21 Duncan Black, 'Evaluating Carroll's Theory of Parliamentary Representation', *Jabberwocky*, Summer 1970.

13 Nine Years in a Curatorship

On 30 November 1882 Bayne resigned the Curatorship of the Common Room, which he had held for twenty-one years. The Common Room was in effect a kind of exclusive social club for Christ Church graduates, and the Curator an honorary Steward. His resignation sparked off a controversial meeting a few days later at which J. Barclay Thompson accused Bayne of extravagance and obstinacy. In some quarters Dodgson was considered a difficult person to deal with; but if Dodgson was difficult, Barclay Thompson was impossible. Though entitled to membership of the Common Room, he held no office at Christ Church and was not resident, though he chose to exercise his rights to the full. Dodgson did his best to rebut the accusations against his old friend, but then found himself elected in Bayne's place. Fresh powers were at the same time given to the Wine Committee. Although Dodgson accepted the Curatorship he was not without misgivings, for he realized that it would take a great deal of time to make it work satisfactorily. Nevertheless, he felt the work would take him out of himself a little, which would be beneficial; for he felt that his life was becoming too much that of a selfish recluse.

As Curator, Dodgson was responsible for the purchase and storage of food and wines, coal, newspapers, stationery, furniture, etc., as well as for the hire and payment of the servants. He quickly found that improvements were needed in certain areas, particularly in the accounting system and in the stock-control of the wine cellar. These were areas which he tackled almost immediately, and in February 1883 he made a map of the wine-cellar, so that instant assessments could be made of the stocks in hand. In December 1886 he analysed the stock, which totalled 28,210 bottles, and by comparing it with four years' average rate of consumption worked out that the 420 bottles of best claret constituted fifteen years' supply, the 550 bottles of best sherry ninety years' supply, while the 5420 bottles of brown sherry would last for thirty-five years.[1] Despite the earnestness of his application to the task, Dodgson's sense of humour never deserted him. In *Twelve Months in a Curatorship*, which he published in 1884, he wrote:

One curious phenomenon I wish to call attention to. The consumption of Madeira (B) has been, during the past year, zero. After careful calculation, I estimate that, if this rate of consumption be steadily maintained, our present stock will last us an infinite number of years. And although there may be something monotonous and dreary in the prospect of such vast cycles spent in drinking second class Madeira, we may cheer ourselves with the thought of how economically it may be done.

Clashes between Dodgson and Barclay Thompson were almost inevitable, and Thompson's comments in the book of 'Libri Desiderati' were carping and often caustic. He objected that olives and preserved ginger were not provided on Sundays, to which Dodgson replied that they were not *always* provided, though the same might be said of almost any other article. But every effort was made to provide a 'good, sufficient and sufficiently varied' dessert, and he doubted whether the charge of 3d a head covered the cost. Thompson next complained that a terribly ugly and vulgar screen now occupied the fireplace in Common Room, and asked the Curator to replace it with 'something a little less hideous'. Dodgson replied, 'Opinions apparently differ as to shavings, which have been used in the fireplaces in Hall for at least 30 years. Personally, I like their appearance, and only think them vulgar in the sense that English is "the vulgar tongue".' But he agreed to replace them. When new easy chairs were being ordered, Dodgson obtained a sample and invited comments, to help him decide whether to order more. Thompson suggested 'that the Mathematical Tutor assisted by the Canons and attended by the Education Staff be requested to determine how long it will take the present Curator to furnish (throughout) an ordinary sentry-box, given, that 5 months are required to buy two chairs'.

Dodgson was not insensitive to Barclay Thompson's criticisms. On 15 November 1883 he wrote in his diary: 'Have been working six or eight hours a day at Common Room ledgers and have received a series of letters from J. B. Thompson reprimanding me for my conduct as Curator. It would be very disheartening work if it were more than a single individual who did this.'[2] But to Thompson himself he wrote expressing the earnest wish 'that no difference of *views* may affect our *personal* friendship, and that the "odium theologicum" may have no place in Common Room matters or between Christ Church men'.[3]

But the main issue between them was a dispute concerning the relative functions of the Wine Committee, of which Barclay Thompson was a member, and of the Curator. His complaints were, broadly, that Dodgson did not always consult the Wine Committee before acting, and sometimes modified their orders; and that he purchased special orders for individual members with Common Room monies. Dodgson ventilated the points at issue in *Twelve Months in a Curatorship*, which he insisted was 'not a plagiarism – as its name might suggest – of *Five Years in Penal Servitude*. Nor again is it meant to traverse precisely the same ground as *Six months on the Tread Mill*'. Thompson had written: 'It is obvious that the sober imagination of the Curator has been morbidly excited by the presence of so large a number of unsold Liqueurs in his rooms.' Dodgson, who described the growth of the Wine Committee from a simple amoebic organism to a complex structure whose rules were too tight for comfort, set out the rules and listed the ways in which he had broken them:

Rules for the Wine Committee.

(Agreed upon December 8, 1882.)

1) There shall be a Wine-Committee, consisting of five persons, including the Curator, whose duty shall be to assist the Curator in the management of the Cellar.
2) The members of the Committee, other than the Curator, shall be elected at the annual audit.
3) A meeting of the Committee *shall be held in the second week of each Term*, on a day to be fixed by the Curator, *who shall give notice* of the meeting *in the preceding week*. Other meeetings of the Committee may be summoned by the Curator, *a week's notice being given*. The Curator shall summon a meeting of the Committee, when required to do so by three members thereof.
4) All questions relating to the selection, purchase, except as hereinafter provided (see Rule 6) keeping, serving and sending out of wines shall be decided by a majority of the Committee at a meeting.
5) *No business* shall be transacted unless *at least three members* of the Committee shall be present, of whom the Curator shall be one.
6) No expenditure of money shall be made by the Committee without the concurrence of the Curator.

Dodgson then lists ways in which he has interpreted the rules on a broader but more practical basis, and draws the conclusion:

Thus it appears that I have broken every portion of the Code which it was possible for me to break by myself: the excepted portion being the last clause of Rule 5. But here, just as it began to seem inevitable that this portion of the Rules would survive unbroken, my friends the Members of the Committee gallantly came to the rescue. On Friday November 9 three Members of the Wine Committee assembled themselves together, *the Curator not being present*, but what was then done has been repeatedly referred to by them, as business transacted at a real meeting.

Does the reader expect to learn that I resented this unconstitutional conduct on the part of the Committee? Not I! I was a very lamb on the occasion – a sucking dove. Whether or no I laughed in my sleeve is another question, which I do not propose to enter on further than to remark that the sleeve of the 'M.A.' gown is peculiarly adapted for that purpose, the quadrantal excavation at the lower corner being apparently exactly fitted for concealing a mouth when on the broad grin.

Of Barclay Thompson's correspondence he wrote: 'These letters are, I suppose, meant to "aid" me: but I feel inclined to say, with the man who was aided by an officious bull in surmounting a fence, "you have assisted me: yet it was not precisely the form of assistance I desired".' Of Rule 1 of the Wine Committee Dodgson noted, 'logically it is the bounden duty of the Curator "to assist himself". I decline to say whether this clause has ever brightened existence for me – or whether, in the shades of the evening, I may ever have been observed leaving the Common Room cellars with a small but suspicious-looking bundle, and murmuring, "Assist thyself, assist thyself!".'

Two years later Dodgson followed this up with *Three Years in a Curatorship* which he prefaced:

> A Curator who contents himself with simply *doing* the business of the Common Room and puts out no statistics, is sure to be distrusted. 'He keeps us in the dark!' men will say. 'He publishes no figures. What does it mean? Is he assisting himself?' But, only circulate some abstruse tables of figures, particularly if printed in lines and columns, so that ordinary readers can make nothing of them, and all is changed at once. 'Oh, go on, go on!' they say, satiated with facts. 'Manage things as you like! We trust you entirely!'

The pamphlet is about ventilation, light and furniture – 'Airs, Glares and Chairs' – with accounts and a statement of the wine stock, which then stood at about 20,000 bottles.

Voluminous letters and notices indicate the immense amount of trouble that Dodgson went to on behalf of his colleagues. All correspondence with tradesmen was conducted in the third person without salutation; business was always conducted in writing, and personal callers were firmly discouraged. The following from the Common Room Manifold book is a fair sample:

> To Messrs. Barrett & Clay   June 25th 1883.
>   The Curator of the Common Room (the Rev'd C. L. Dodgson) will be much obliged if Messrs Barrett & Clay would give him the benefit of their advice on 2 or 3 points in the treatment of wine, about which he finds much difference of opinion exists.
>   1)   What amount of damp is desirable in a wine cellar?
>   2)   Is ventillation desirable?
>   3)   Should light be admitted?
> He would thank them if they would fill in the enclosed paper, as to particular temperature needed etc.
>   Mr Dodgson takes this opportunity of mentioning that he understands from the previous Curator, Mr Bayne, that the wine-merchants, or representatives of them, are in the habit of calling periodically on the Curator. This practice he hopes he may, without giving offence, request may be discontinued. He cannot undertake to remember accurately any information given by word of mouth, to lay it before the Committee who manage the details of the wine. It would be necessary to have it all in

writing, and any such information, in the form of letters, price lists, etc. will be very acceptable.

Moreover, Mr Dodgson has his time very fully occupied, and such interviews, without giving him any information he could use, would be a serious tax on time already wanted for other purposes.[4]

Common Room orders for food and wine represented a considerable turnover of business, and there was ample scope for the Curator to acquire perquisites from the local tradespeople. Nevertheless Dodgson was above all this. When he received a box of Portugal fruit from Messrs Snow, the wine merchants, he returned it promptly, with a letter stating firmly that as it was his duty to get the best goods, he could not possibly accept presents from the tradespeople concerned. Indeed, as he pointed out, 'any repetition of such attentions may seriously affect their position as wine merchants dealt with by the Common Room'.[5]

Occasionally Dodgson became aware of accidental overcharging. Such an instance occurred in 1890, when Dodgson discovered that he had accidentally charged 10d a bottle too much for category 'B' Champagne. Scrupulously he went back over the records and repaid the balance to the men concerned, and so was able to rectify this simple error. A more serious matter came to light on 4 February 1888 when he accidentally learnt from Bayne that the system used for getting annual subscriptions from new MAs was to name the fee as a necessary expense of taking the MA, no choice being given to what Bayne called 'beings incapable of choice'. Bayne then said that his reason for resigning the Curatorship had been the dropping of the old rule that new MAs should call automatically on the Curator, which led to a falling off of income. Dodgson wrote, 'I learned this with pain and shame', and called the process by the plain name of 'cheating'. He could not now rest until he had put matters right, and accordingly he sent a circular to about seventeen members paying Quarterage, pointing out that the entrance fee and annual quarterage were optional, and asking whether they wished to withdraw from membership. Fourteen replied that they had entered under false impressions, and eight asked to withdraw. In 1889 Dodgson produced a printed paper which he placed before a meeting of the Common Room, asking approval to repay the £50 back money levied from these eight men. It is a tribute to Dodgson's skill in administration that he succeeded in managing Common Room affairs at a time when it was admitted that revenues had declined.

During Dodgson's Curatorship an important bequest was made to the Common Room by Dodgson's old friend and colleague, Scoltock. Almost the last entry in Scoltock's diary records a walk with Dodgson. His gift was in the form of three oil-paintings, 'Garrick', by Gainsborough, 'Cattle', by Cuyp, and 'A Woman', by Franz Hals, all of them valuable acquisitions. It also fell to Dodgson's lot to receive on behalf of the Common Room a splendid polished wooden table made from a fallen tree, and to advise on a suitable commemorative plate.

From time to time Dodgson used to pin up notices in the Common Room on personal matters. When his brother Skeffington, now married with a rapidly increasing family, began making large quantities of marmalade for his own requirements, he offered to obtain jars at 9d or 10d each for anyone who would like some. He also advertised his brother-in-law's need of an extra curate, and his cousin's need of a 'Locum Tenens' to look after his parish for a few weeks while he recovered from a serious illness.

In 1889 Dodgson tendered his resignation when he was defeated in proposals about the use of the Drawing Room in the evening, and minor adjustments to the servant's wages. But he was persuaded to withdraw his resignation when it was unanimously decided to leave all questions of the wages in the Curator's hands. There was in any event no natural successor. But in 1892, after he had held office for nine years, T. B. Strong let it be known that he would be willing to succeed him as Curator. To mark the occasion he distributed a circular headed 'Nonumque prematur in annum' '*And let him be oppressed until the ninth year*', in which he gracefully tendered his resignation. The office had in some respects been very pleasurable. 'I have thoroughly enjoyed the opportunities thus afforded me, by the frequent practice of placing a guest next to the Curator, of coming into contact with many interesting strangers,' he wrote. He had not begrudged the time while there was nobody else to do it, but now that a successor had appeared he was glad to revert to the position of an ordinary member.

Dodgson also published a booklet called '*Curiosissima Curatoria*' by 'Rude Donatus' in which he recorded some of the business of his nine years' Curatorship. Characteristically, though factual, it was not without humour: 'An enthusiastic computer of Averages will discover . . . that the average time spent by a Common Room Librarian in not completing a Library Catalogue is 29 years, . . . by a Picture Committee in not commencing a Picture Catalogue, is two years . . . by a Smoking Committee in drawing up a report is three years . . . by a Hot Dishes Committee in not drawing up a report is six years.'

It has often been suggested that Dodgson's work as Curator prevented him from spending more time on his literary projects; but there is no evidence to support this. His output was not significantly higher before or after his period as Curator. Those nine years had certainly not been devoid of literary projects. Indeed, on 29 March 1885 he recorded in his diary that he had never had so many literary projects on hand at the same time. He listed them as follows:

1) Supplement to Euclid and Modern Rivals.
2) 2nd Edition of Euclid and Modern Rivals.

3) A book of Mathematical curiosities, which I think of calling 'Pillow Problems, and other Mathematical Trifles.' This will contain Problems worked out in the dark, Logarithms without Tables, Sines and angles ditto, a paper I am now writing on 'Infinities and Infinitesimals', condensed Long Multiplication, and perhaps others.

4) Euclid V.

5) 'Plain Facts for Circle-Squarers' which is nearly complete, and gives actual proof of limits 3. 14158, 3. 14160.

6) A symbolical Logic, treated by my Algebraic method.

7) 'A Tangled Tale.'

8) A collection of Games and Puzzles of my devising, with fairy pictures by Miss E. G. Thomson. This might also contain my 'Mem. Tech.' for dates; my 'Cypher-writing' scheme for Letter-registration, etc. etc.

9) Nursery Alice.

10) Serious poems in *Phantasmagoria*.

11) 'Alice's Adventures Underground.'

12) 'Girl's Own Shakespeare.' I have begun on 'Tempest'.

13) New edition of 'Parliamentary Representation'.

14) New edition of Euclid I, II.

15) The new child's book, which Mr Furniss is to illustrate. I have settled on no name as yet, but it will perhaps be 'Sylvie and Bruno'.

On 1 March 1885 he had recorded in his diary 'sent off two letters of literary importance, one to Mrs Hargreaves [the former Alice Liddell], to ask her consent to my publishing the original MS. of *Alice* in facsimile (the idea occurred to me the other day); the other to Mr H. Furniss, a very clever illustrator in *Punch*, asking if he is open to proposals to draw pictures for me.' The letter to Alice ran as follows:

My Dear Mrs Hargreaves:

I fancy this will come to you almost like a voice from the dead, after so many years of silence, and yet those years have made no difference that I can perceive in *my* clearness of memory of the days when we *did* correspond. I am getting to feel what an old man's[6] failing memory is as to recent event and new friends (for instance, I made friends, only a few weeks ago, with a very nice little maid of about twelve, and had a walk with her – and now I can't recall either of her names!), but my mental picture is as vivid as ever of one who was, through so many years, my ideal child-friend. I have had scores of child-friends since your time, but they have been quite a different thing.

However, I did not begin this letter to say all *that*. What I want to ask is, Would you have any objection to the original MS book of 'Alice's Adventures' (which I suppose you still possess) being published in facsimile? The idea of doing so occurred to me only the other day. If, on consideration, you come to the conclusion that you would rather *not* have it done, there is an end of the matter. If, however, you give a favourable reply, I would be much obliged if you would lend it me (registered post, I should think, would be safest) that I may consider the possibilities. I have not seen it for about twenty years, so am by no means sure that the illustrations may not prove to be so awfully bad that to reproduce them would be absurd.

There can be no doubt that I should incur the charge of gross egoism in publishing it. But I don't care for that in the least, knowing that I have no such motive; only I think, considering the extraordinary popularity the books have had (we have sold more than 120,000 of the two), there must be many who would like to see the original form.

Always your friend,
C. L. Dodgson.[7]

Alice gladly gave her consent, and Dodgson began to prepare for the edition, writing the Preface on 13 July 1885. Several of the other projects on Dodgson's list were well advanced or even completed at this stage. The *Supplement to Euclid and his Modern Rivals* came out in April 1885, and the second edition of *Euclid and his Modern Rivals* was published a few months later. *A Tangled Tale* did not have an altogether smooth passage. The book consisted of ten puzzles or 'knots' which had already been published by Charlotte M. Yonge in the *Monthly Packet*, with the answers, between April 1880 and March 1885. Illustrations for the book were by Arthur Burdett Frost, who had illustrated *Rhyme? and Reason?* But Dodgson had objected to some of the pictures, and Frost had declined to draw them again. Dodgson therefore purchased them all, as agreed, but used only six, five being full page. The dedication was to Edith Rix, whose name is found by taking the second letter of each line of the acrostic poem. Edith was nineteen when the book came out. She was an able mathematician, taught by Dodgson, with whom she carried on an intimate correspondence in adult life, mainly on the subjects of religion and mathematics. Dodgson complained that the first thousand had been dried too quickly, and it is possible that these never went on sale. The edition of 2000 copies issued on 22 December 1885 was almost certainly the second and third thousand, and the fourth thousand was printed in 1886. The critics were not enthusiastic about the book. On 27 March 1886 Dodgson wrote to Macmillan, 'Many thanks also for the long series of notices, condemnatory of *Tangled Tale*. I feel rather tempted to send a few of them to Miss Yonge (at whose request it was written) and say "and this blighted reputation I owe to your baneful influence". 'Spite of this chorus of blame, it is selling pretty well, don't you think?'

The Game of Logic, which was first printed in December 1886 and withdrawn, is an attempt to explain formal logic by a board and counter method. Very few children would be able to make anything of it, for it was intended for older scholars or adults, but the humorous approach and the absurdity of the propositions make it entertaining reading. The latter include 'All hungry crocodiles are unamiable', 'No exciting books suit feverish patients', 'No nightingale drinks wine', 'No lobsters are selfish', and many more besides. The dedicatory poem, an acrostic using the second letter of each line, is to Climene Mary Holiday, niece of the illustrator of *The Hunting of the Snark*. Dissatisfied with the standard of printing, Dodgson had the book done again by Clay in 1887.

Alice's Adventures Under Ground was also finally brought out in facsimile in December 1886. The publication of the edition had been incredibly complicated, as the following letter to Alice indicates:

My Dear Mrs Hargreaves:

Many thanks for your permission to insert 'Hospitals' in the preface to your book. I have had almost as many adventures in getting that unfortunate facsimile finished *above* ground, as your namesake had *Under* it!

First, the zincographer in London, recommended to me for photographing the book, page by page, and preparing the zinc-blocks, declined to undertake it unless I would entrust the book to *him*, which I entirely refused to do. I felt that it was only due to you, in return for your great kindness in lending so unique a book, to be scrupulous in not letting it be even *touched* by the workmen's hands. In vain I offered to come and reside in London with the book, and to attend daily in the studio, to place it in position to be photographed, and turn over the pages as required. He said that could not be done because 'other authors' works were being photographed there, which must on no account be seen by the public'. I undertook not to look at *anything* but my own book; but it was no use: we could not come to terms.

Then he recommended me a certain Mr Noad, an excellent photographer, but in so small a way of business that I should have to *prepay* him, bit by bit, for the zinc-blocks: and *he* was willing to come to Oxford, and do it here. So it was all done in my studio, I remaining in waiting all the time, to turn over the pages.

But I daresay I have told you so much of the story already.

Mr Noad did a first-rate set of negatives, and took them away with him to get the zinc-blocks made. These he delivered pretty regularly at first, and there seemed to be every prospect of getting the book out by Christmas, 1885.

On October 18, 1885, I sent your book to Mrs Liddell, who had told me your sisters were going to visit you and would take it with them. I trust it reached you safely?

Soon after this – I having prepaid for the whole of the zinc-blocks – the supply suddenly ceased, while twenty-two pages were still due, and Mr Noad disappeared!

My belief is that he was in hiding from his creditors. We sought him in vain. So things went on for months. At one time I thought of employing a detective to find him, but was assured that 'all detectives are scoundrels'. The alternative seemed to be to ask you to lend the book again, and get the missing pages re-photographed. But I was most unwilling to rob you of it again, and also afraid of the risk of loss of the book, if sent by post – for even 'registered post' does not seem *absolutely* safe.

In April he called at Macmillan's and left *eight* blocks, and again vanished into obscurity.

This left us with fourteen pages (dotted up and down the book) still missing. I waited awhile longer, and then put the thing into the hands of a solicitor, who soon found the man, but could get nothing but promises from him. 'You will never get the blocks,' said the solicitor, 'unless you frighten him by a summons before a magistrate.' To this at last I unwillingly consented: the summons had to be taken out at —— (that is where this aggravating man is living), and this entailed two journeys from Eastbourne – one to get the summons (my *personal* presence being necessary), and the other to attend in court with the solicitor on the day fixed for hearing the case. The defendant didn't appear; so the magistrate said he would take the case in his absence. Then I had the new and exciting experience of being put into the witness-box, and sworn, and cross-examined by a rather savage magistrate's clerk, who seemed to think that, if he only bullied me enough, he would soon catch me out in a falsehood! I had to give the magistrate a little lecture on photozincography, and the poor man declared the case was so complicated he must adjourn it for another week. But this time, in order to secure the presence of our slippery defendant, he issued a warrant for his apprehension, and the constable had orders to take him into custody and lodge him in prison, the night before the day when the case was to come on. The news of *this* effectually frightened him, and he delivered up the fourteen negatives (he hadn't done the blocks) before the fatal day arrived. I was rejoiced to get them, even though it entailed the paying a second time for getting the fourteen blocks done, and withdrew the action.

The fourteen blocks were quickly done and put into the printer's hands; and all is going on smoothly at last: and I quite hope to have the book completed, and to be able to send you a very special copy (bound in white vellum, unless you would prefer some other style of binding) by the end of the month.

Believe me always,
Sincerely yours,
C. L. Dodgson.[8]

Besides the new introduction, the book contains 'An Easter Greeting' and 'Christmas Greetings from a Fairy to a Child'. There is one alteration to the body of the text; Dodgson had originally attempted to draw a small portrait of his heroine within the last line of the book. Dissatsified with his attempt, he had cut out a small portrait of Alice Liddell aged seven years from one of his own photographs, and had pasted it over the drawing. But Dodgson decided to omit this from the published version, and had to rewrite the last line accordingly.

The problems of *Alice's Adventures Under Ground* did not end with publication. On 23 January 1887 Dodgson wrote to Macmillan:

A letter which I received from Messrs Burn and Co. on the 20th about *Alice Under Ground* contains a sentence I do not like *at all*. It is this: 'It [the book] was bound in a very great hurry.' This I suppose was done in order to get it out before Christmas.

I believe I have expressed my wishes on this point, but, as I do not seem to have made them fully understood, I may as well repeat that I *do not care* in the least for any book of mine being brought out at any particular season: it matters nothing to me in what week, or month – I may even say year – the book appears. What *does* matter to me, very seriously, is that it should be done with all the leisure necessary to produce the *best* results that we can give the public for their money. You may say, 'the sale would have been less if it had been delayed.' By all means. *Let* it be less: I am quite willing it should be so.

I have laid it down as a fixed principle that I will give the public (profit or no profit) the *best* article I can: I consider that any 'very great hurry' involves very serious risk on the article *not* being the best I can give: and I shall be really much obliged if you will take measures to prevent any such hurry on future occasions.

On the same subject a week later he wrote: 'Please understand (that we may not quarrel about it when the time comes) that, if a similar thing happens in future, I will have no mercy at all, but shall come to town and myself examine the whole impression, and cancel all spoilt copies, and decline to reckon them as part of my order.'

Dodgson's object in publishing this facsilime edition was not financial, for the profits were to go to children's hospitals. This was only one of numerous similar acts of charity on his part. These had begun in a relatively small way with the recalled copies of the first edition of *Alice's Adventures in Wonderland*. In 1872 he had produced a 'Circular to Hospitals' offering copies of the *Alice* books for the use of sick children. In May 1876 he had approached Macmillan's for an estimate for five hundred of each of the *Alice* books on cheap, but not thin paper, in a strong, gay colour without gilt edges or ornament specifically with the idea of donating them to hospitals. In the event he published three hundred of each, and produced circular letters to hospitals in July 1876 and again a year later offering copies. This became standard practice on Dodgson's part when (as was frequently the case) he discovered 'imperfections' and withdrew copies of his books. Later, Mechanics' Institutes and village reading rooms also benefited in this way.

Meanwhile, Dodgson had not forgotten the idea of a coloured edition of *Alice* for small children, first suggested to Macmillan in February 1881, and went ahead with the illustrations. These were mechanically enlarged from twenty of Tenniel's original drawings with minor amendments, and coloured by Tenniel himself. Cover pictures were to be produced by Miss Thomson. Dodgson rewrote the text completely in an embarrassingly patronising picture-show style and completed it by 20 February 1889. His intention was to publish in time for Easter, but, as ever, Miss Thomson was late with her pictures. Edmund Evans, whom he chose as his colour printer, was the foremost colour printer of children's books in the 1880s, and was notable for his excellent work for such famous illustrators as Crane, Caldecott and Kate Greenaway. Besides engraving the wood blocks, Evens undertook the printing. His process was a complex one of transferring the drawing photographically on to the 'key' block, and reproducing wet impressions of this on separate plain blocks for each of the colours – in this case, seven. These were then engraved also.

Surprisingly, Dodgson did not see the proofs of the illustrations before printing, but when, in June 1889, he received a copy of the printed sheets, he was bitterly disappointed with them. 'The pictures are far too bright and gaudy, and vulgarize the whole thing. *None must be sold in England*: to do so would be to sacrifice whatever reputation I now have for giving the public the *best* I can. Mr Evans must begin again and print 10,000 with Tenniel's coloured pictures before him: and I must see all the proofs this time: and then we shall have a book really fit to offer to the public.'[9] This would seem to suggest that Dodgson himself had taken back the original drawings after the blocks were cut.

Although he had originally rejected the notion of American sales, Dodgson now urged Macmillan to bind five hundred copies, send them to America, and try to persuade them to buy the lot. For some reason this idea fell through, and Dodgson, using the third person he normally adopted with tradesmen, wrote to Roberts Bros of New York: 'Mr Lewis Carroll . . . has had 10,000 copies printed: but the colours have come out brighter than he likes, and he does not wish to have them sold in England. . . . He is willing to sell them to American Booksellers, at 2 shillings and three pence a copy: but, if any one likes to buy the whole 10,000, he may have them at two shillings.' He estimated that the latter course would enable Roberts Bros to make £500 profit. But when Dodgson sent a sample copy, they rejected it as 'not bright enough'. Eventually Macmillans sold 4000 copies of the 1889 printing to America, and a new edition of 10,000 copies was prepared for sale in this country by Easter 1890.

Of the justification for the rejection of the first printing, Selwyn Goodacre writes:

> If the two printings (1889 and 1890) are set side by side, it becomes immediately apparent that the second is quite clearly superior. The paper of the 1890 copies is a purer white, the 1889 copies are printed on a cream-coloured paper. The second feature of the 1890 copies is that the print of both text and pictures is a darker brown. These two features produce the effect of clearer and sharper pictures, plainly evident throughout the twenty illustrations. The other essential difference is in the tone of the colour, and here we can perhaps see why Dodgson says the pictures are too bright, although I suggest 'heavier' would be the better word. He also uses the word 'gaudy', so it is apparent that he found difficulty in describing just what the defect was. In fact the defect in the 1889 illustrations I think is due to an over-preponderance of red. . . . What is particularly significant is that the 1890 versions of the pictures are *very* much closer to the original Tenniel painting.[10]

The Dedication of *The Nursery Alice*, whose name is revealed in the second letter of every line of the introductory acrostic poem, is Marie

Van der Gucht, a friend of Climene Holiday. She was eleven years old when Dodgson first met her on 24 July 1885, and in September of the following year she went to stay with him at Eastbourne. A few weeks later, he sought her mother's permission to use her as model for Furniss' illustrations of Sylvie in *Sylvie and Bruno*, but Furniss later claimed that he had used his own daughter instead. Nine years later, when she was twenty-one years old, she spent another week with him at Eastbourne. 'Her week has been very pleasant, to both of us, I think', he wrote.

The rejection of the first printing left Dodgson without copies to give away, and these he was most anxious to have. He therefore instructed Evans to print fourteen copies in brown ink only. Of these, two copies were bound in morocco. The first, naturally, went to Alice Hargreaves. Dodgson had met Reginald Hargreaves for the first time two months before beginning *The Nursery Alice* and had written in his diary: 'It was not easy to link in one's mind the new face with the olden memory – the stranger with the once-so-intimately known and loved "Alice", whom I shall always remember best as an entirely fascinating little seven-year-old maiden.'

It has been suggested that Marie Van der Gucht was the other recipient of a morocco-bound copy of the brown ink edition; but a more probable recipient was Princess Alice, the six-year-old daughter of the late Prince Leopold. In June 1889 Dodgson had been staying for a lengthy period at Hatfield House, and while he was there had been delighted with the little Princess and her five-year-old brother, Prince Leopold Charles, Duke of Albany. He had also fallen into conversation with their mother, the Duchess of Albany, and on 1 July 1889 wrote to her: 'In sending the book I promised for the little Princess and one also which (as I understand from Miss Maxwell) I am permitted to give to the little Duke of Albany, I am bold enough to hope that your Royal Highness will honour me by accepting one more book as well, which will follow in a few days.' As a postscript he adds, 'I send the *Nursery Alice* in brown ink only, because the *coloured* edition has turned out a failure, and will have to be printed again. The new edition will be out by Christmas, I hope, and I will then send a copy to the little Princess – trusting that she will not object to possessing both kinds!'[11]

One hundred copies of the 'condemned' printing were sold to Australia, leaving a balance in hand of 5900 copies. These Dodgson called the 'People's Edition' and sold at 2s a copy. The precedent for doing this was the publication, in 1887, of the 'People's Edition' of the *Alice* books at 2s 6d each, or 4s 6d for the two in one volume. When advertising the 'People's Edition' of *The Nursery Alice* Dodgson wrote, 'If not quite artistic enough for your own children, you will find them well suited to give to invalid children among the poor. . . .'[12]

Over the years Dodgson's interest in the theatre had continued as strong as ever. In 1879 (as mentioned earlier) he had renewed his friendship with Ellen Terry, which he had broken off when she went to live with the architect Godwin. G. F. Watts had divorced her in 1877, presumably out of compassion, for he did not himself remarry until nine years later. Godwin, by whom she had had two illegitimate children, had left her in November 1875 and three months later had married his twenty-one-year-old student, Beatrice Phillips. In March 1878 Ellen married Charles Wardell, an actor who used the stage name Charles Kelly, and, after a decent interval had elapsed, Dodgson approached Mrs Terry to inquire whether Ellen would be willing to resume their friendship. Ellen assented, and they remained close friends until Dodgson's death. They had more than just the theatre in common, for they were both filled with the desire to help others, and each appreciated the other's generous heart. Almost invariably accompanied by a child friend – and the definition of 'child' had broadened to include young women as Dodgson's life progressed – he haunted the theatre, and often took stage-struck girls backstage to see her in her dressing room. Always before introducing child friends, he told their mothers Ellen's history and sought approval for the meeting. One such friend was Dorothea (Dolly) Baird, a keen amateur acturess who graduated to the professional stage, became a leading lady and eventually married Sir Henry Irving's son Harry. To her mother he wrote of Ellen Terry:

> I have now introduced to her four of the daughters of my friends of ages between eighteen and twenty-five; but in every case, *before* doing so, I told the mother the history . . . and if, knowing it, you still wish Dolly to be introduced, I am quite satisfied. . . . The other question is, may Dolly come and dine with me? I ask this, not knowing your views on 'Mrs Grundy'. And you may be sure I shall not feel in the least hurt if you think it best to say 'No.' It is only in these last two or three years that I have ventured on such unique and unconventional parties.[13]

Dolly was then nineteen years old. The introduction took place on 26 May 1894, and afterwards Dodgson wrote to Ellen Terry:

> I want to thank you, as heartily as words can do it for your kindness in letting me bring Dolly behind the scenes to you. You will know without my telling you what an intense pleasure you thereby gave to a warm-hearted girl, and what love (which I fancy you value more than mere admiration) you have won from her. Her wild longing to try the stage will not, I think, bear the cold light of day when once she has tried it, and has realized what a lot of hard work and weary waiting and 'hope deferred' it involves.[14]

Dodgson's proposed expurgated Shakespeare for girls aged ten to seventeen years, concerning which he once wrote a circular letter to his friends, never came to fruition, although he ventilated his views on Shakespeare, and indeed on stage production in general, fairly frequently. One of his letters to Ellen Terry actually contains a passage of Shakespeare which he had rewritten, and although he advances the theory tongue-in-cheek, his criticism of Shakespeare's plot-structure is genuine enough. The letter reads:

> Now I'm going to put before you a 'Hero-ic' puzzle of mine, but please remember I do not ask for your solution of it, as you will persist in believing, if I ask your help in a Shakespeare difficulty, that I am only jesting! However, if you won't attack it yourself, perhaps you would ask Mr Irving some day how *he* explains it?
>
> My difficulty is this: – Why in the world did not Hero (or at any rate Beatrice on her behalf) prove an 'alibi' in answer to the charge? It seems certain that she did *not* sleep in her room that night; for how could Margaret venture to open the window and talk from it, with her mistress asleep in the room? It would be sure to wake her. Besides Borachio says, after promising that Margaret shall speak with him out of Hero's chamber window, 'I will so fashion the matter that Hero shall be absent.' (*How* he could possibly manage any such thing is another difficulty, but I pass over that.) Well then, granting that Hero slept in some other room that night, why didn't she say so? When Claudio asks her, 'What man was he you talked with yesternight out at your window betwixt twelve and one?' why doesn't she reply: 'I talked with no man at that hour my lord. Nor was I in my chamber yesternight, but in another, far from it, remote.' And this she could, of course, prove by the evidence of the housemaids, who must have known that she had occupied another room that night. But even if Hero might be supposed to be so distracted as not to remember where she had slept the night before, or even whether she had slept *anywhere*, surely *Beatrice* has her wits about her! And when an arrangement was made, by which she was to lose, for one night, her twelve-months' bedfellow, is it conceivable that she didn't know *where* Hero passed the night? Why didn't *she* reply:
>
> But good my lord sweet Hero slept not there:
> She had another chamber for the nonce.
> 'Twas sure some counterfeit that did present
> Her person at the window, aped her voice,
> Her mien, her manners, and hath thus deceived
> My good Lord Pedro and this company?
>
> With all these excellent materials for proving an 'alibi' it is incomprehensible that no one chould think of it. If only there had been a barrister present, to cross-examine Beatrice!
>
> 'Now, ma'am, attend to me, please, and speak up so that the jury can hear you. Where did you sleep last night? Where did Hero sleep? Will you swear that she slept in her own room? Will you swear that you do not know where she slept?' I feel inclined to quote old Mr Weller and to say to Beatrice at the end of the play (only I'm afraid it isn't etiquette to speak across the footlights):
>
> 'Oh, Samivel, Samivel, vy vorn't there a halibi?'

Dodgson's interest in the theatre was heightened when the popularity of the *Alice* books encouraged people to think in terms of a stage version. He was somewhat alarmed at the possibility of losing control over the copyright, and as early as November 1872 he had asked Macmillan to engage a couple of copying-clerks to write out the text in dramatic form, being careful to include all the speeches and speakers, and giving stage directions as to exits and entrances. As soon as completed, they were to be registered as dramas under the same title as the books. There was never any intention of actually acting them in this form. In 1876 he sanctioned a production based on *Alice* at the Polytechnic, though he insisted that all extraneous material be cut out, and in 1880 and 1882 freely gave permission to Mrs K. Freiligrath-Kroeker to publish the stories in dramatic form.

For some time he toyed with the idea of writing an *Alice* operetta and even approached Sir Arthur Sullivan to see if he would write the musical score. Sullivan was interested in the idea, but confessed himself defeated by the metre of the songs. Finally, on 2 September 1886, Dodgson gave permission to Henry Savile Clarke to go ahead and produce his own version. But he did not give him carte blanche, and no less than ninety-seven letters were sent by Dodgson to Savile Clarke and Miss Kitty Clarke. The operetta opened on 23 December 1886 at the Prince of Wales' Theatre, and Dodgson saw it for the first time a week later. The lead was played by Phoebe Carlo, a young actress to whom Dodgson was much attached, and whose song and dance with the Cheshire Cat Dodgson particularly enjoyed. On the whole he approved the play, which was based on both the *Alice* books.

The operetta was revived in December 1888, and when Dodgson went to see it he wrote an immediate letter of protest to Savile Clarke: 'The white king, this afternoon, fell flat on his back with his feet towards the audience who (at any rate all in the stalls) were thus presented with a view of him which – which I leave to your imagination.' The red king, too, had indulged in stage business of a kind which Dodgson found objectionable, having pulled up his shirt to dance 'the regular abominable ballet dancing style'. The nature of Dodgson's objection was strangely illogical: 'I don't say he was not fully clad in tights, beneath that shirt, and I don't say he needed the skirt: nor that there would have been any indecency in appearing without the skirt: but I do say that having the skirt on, it was *distinctly* indecent to pull it up.'[15]

Dodgson's interest in the theatre led him to write a number of articles connected with stage matters. In January 1882 he had sent a circular letter to a number of his friends, including Lord Salisbury, enclosing a copy of a pamphlet passed on to him by his friend Augustus Dubourg, the dramatist, advocating the institution of a school of dramatic art. He contributed two articles to *The Theatre*, 'Alice on the Stage',[16] which describes the origin of the *Alice* books and *The Hunting of the Snark*, and details his idea of the characters of Alice, the White Queen, and so on, and 'Stage Children',[17] in which he advocates licensing child actors, limiting the number of weeks worked every year and compulsory schooling to agreed minimum standards; (he also felt that children under ten should not act, but felt that to prohibit this would bring serious deprivation on many a poor family). He also published the following letter in the *St James Gazette* of 16 July 1887:

> I spent yesterday afternoon at Brighton where for five hours I enjoyed the society of three exceedingly happy and healthy girls, aged twelve, ten and seven. We paid three visits to the houses of friends: we spent a long time on the pier, where we vigorously applauded the marvellous under-water performances of Miss Louey Webb, and invested pennies in every mechanical device which invited such contributions and promised anything worth having, for body or mind, in return: we even made an excited raid on headquarters, like Shylock with three attendant Portias, to demand the 'pound of flesh' – in the form of a box of chocolate drops, which a dyspeptic machine had refused to render. I think that anyone who could have seen the vigour of *life* in those three children – the intensity with which they enjoyed everything, great or small, which came their way – who could have watched the younger two running races on the Pier, or could have heard the fervent exclamation of the eldest at the end of the afternoon, 'We *have* enjoyed ourselves!' – would have agreed with me that here at least was no excessive 'physical strain', nor any *imminent* danger of 'fatal results'!
>
> But these, of course, were *not* stage children? They had never done anything more dangerous than Board school competition? Far from it: all three are on the stage – the eldest having acted for five years at least, and even the tiny creature of seven having already appeared in four dramas!
>
> But, at any rate it is their holiday time, and they are not at present suffering the 'exceedingly heavy strain' of work on the stage? On the contrary. A drama, written by Mr Savile Clarke, is now being played at Brighton; and in this (it is called *Alice in Wonderland*) all three children have been engaged, with only a month's interval, ever since Christmas: the youngest being 'Dormouse', as well as three other characters – the second appearing, though not in a 'speaking' part – while the eldest plays the heroine, 'Alice' – quite the heaviest part in the whole play, and, I should think, the heaviest ever undertaken by a child: she has no less than 215 speeches! They had been acting every night this week, and *twice* on the day before I met them, the second performance lasting until half past ten at night – after which they got up at seven next morning to bathe. . . .

Naturally enough, Dodgson's lifelong preoccupation with stage children became even more sharply focused on the juvenile cast of the *Alice* operetta. In the summer of 1887 the company put on *Alice* again in Brighton, and Dodgson pronounced the cast much improved. He travelled from Eastbourne to Brighton several times to see the performance, which as before starred Phoebe Carlo as Alice, and to enjoy the spectacle of an eighteen-year-old girl called Louey Webb swimming in a tank. 'As she is beautifully formed, the exhibition is worth seeing, if only as a picture,'[18] Dodgson wrote. His sister Henrietta, who was now living permanently at Brighton, often entertained Dodgson and his young friends. On one occasion she even went with him to see the *Alice* operetta, thereby breaking the taboo against theatre-going instituted among the Dodgson sisters by their father.

On 17 August 1887 Dodgson brought Irene Barnes, who later achieved fame as the actress Irene Vanbrugh, to Eastbourne to spend a week with him. *Alice* was now being staged at the Devonshire Park Theatre in Eastbourne, and Dodgson had bought tickets for the afternoon of her arrival; but shortly before the performance began, he received a letter telling him that his cousin, Margaret Wilcox, had just died. In view of this news, he did not attend the performance.

His next guest that summer was Edith Lucy, of whom Dodgson wrote: 'Edith will be sixteen next December, and "Mrs Grundy" will be much more offended than in the case of Irene Barnes.'[19] But her visit was a great disappointment, for Edith was so wretchedly homesick that she had to be returned to her mother after only seventeen hours. Dodgson was as pleased to part with her, as she was to be back with her mother. Edith was replaced by Edith Barnes, Irene's sister, who stayed for five days, and she in turn was replaced by Katie Lucy, Edith's sister, who stayed for six days.

So pleased was Dodgson with the performance of the cast of *Alice*, that in September he went to Macmillan's where he signed forty-one presentation books for the children who had acted in the play. On the way back he stopped at the studio of the son of Julia Margaret Cameron, Henry Hay Cameron, a professional photographer from whom he bought photographs of Phoebe and Dorothy Carlo, and others from the cast, in costume. He also took the opportunity of discussing with him a young lady of thirteen years, who had played a minor role, and who had attracted Dodgson's notice: Isa Bowman.

On the strength of this conversation Dodgson contacted Isa's mother and arranged for her to bring Isa to meet him in London. After taking her to Mr Cameron's studio for a portrait, which Isa declared made her look a dreadful sight, he escorted her to an exhibition of paintings, had lunch with her, and finally took her home to Stratford, where he met the rest of the family. Isa was the eldest of four girls and a boy, all of whom were on the stage. Thus began one of the most significant of Dodgson's friendships. A few days later he whisked her off to Eastbourne for a week, during which he arranged many treats for her benefit; but in addition they read the Bible together every day, and he taught her three propositions of Euclid. When she left he noted with satisfaction that she seemed stronger and better than when she came.

In July 1888 Dodgson called on Savile Clarke to discuss a revival of the *Alice* operetta, suggesting that this time Isa should play the lead. It was duly staged in London at the Globe Theatre, commencing 26 December 1888, and Isa acted the part of Alice, dressed in a frock of cream-coloured Liberty silk that Dodgson had chosen and had had made up especially for her. Charlie, her brother, played the White Rabbit, and her sister Emsie was the Dormouse.

Meanwhile Dodgson had seen Isa frequently in Oxford, London and Eastbourne. On 11 July 1888 Dodgson collected her from London and took her for a week's holiday in Oxford, where she stayed at a nearby house and took her meals in Dodgson's rooms. To commemorate her visit he gave her a 'diary' of her holiday entitled *Isa's Visit to Oxford, 1888*, a charming account of the daily activities of Isa and the A.A.M. (Aged, Aged Man, i.e. himself). The following are fair samples of the contents:

> On Saturday Isa had a music lesson, and learned to play on an American Orguinette. It is not a *very* difficult instrument to play, as you only have to turn a handle round and round: so she did it nicely. You put a long piece of paper in, and it goes through the machine, and the holes in the paper make different notes play. They put one in wrong end first, and had a tune backwards, and soon found themselves in the day before yesterday: so they dared not go on, for fear of making Isa so young she would not be able to talk. The A.A.M. does not like visitors who only howl, and get red in the face, from morning to night. . . .[20] [They] looked at a lot of dresses, which the A.A.M. kept in a cupboard, to dress up children in, when they came to be photographed. Some of the dresses had been used in Pantomimes at Drury Lane: some were rags, to dress up beggar-children in: some had been very magnificent once, but were getting quite old and shabby . . .'[21]

Of Dodgson's rooms in Christ Church Isa wrote, 'I do not think there was ever such a fairy-land for children'.[22] She described his wonderful collection of musical boxes, and what happened when one of them went wrong: 'Uncle used to go to a drawer in the table and produce a box of little screw-drivers and punches, and while I sat at his knee he would unscrew the lid and take out the wheels to see what was the matter.' With his rather large but deft fingers he always managed to get them working again. Just as remarkable as the musical boxes was 'Bob the Bat', a toy which could fly about the high ceilinged room. Once it flew right out of the window into the garden, where a frightened scout dropped and broke a bowl of salad. 'I was always a little afraid of this toy because it was too lifelike,'[23] Isa wrote.

Shortly after the visit to Oxford, Dodgson took Isa to Eastbourne, where she spent five whole weeks with him. He was deeply attached to her and even allowed her the rare privilege of calling him 'Uncle Charles'. When she eventually went home, he wrote, 'Life feels rather lonely without Isa. Cold weather has suddenly set in . . .' Perhaps the chill in the air was partly psychological. Next year Dodgson repeated the experiment, fetching Isa to Eastbourne from London on 17 July. Three days later, as a surprise for Isa, he brought her sister Nellie to stay too. Dodgson's sisters Louisa and Margaret, with his sister-in-law Alice and her three youngest children were staying in Eastbourne also at that time, and sometimes took Isa and Nellie off his hands, so that he could get on with his literary work. They both danced for the Dodgson sisters, listened to Dodgson's stories and swam in the sea instead of the Baths, so that he could watch them. He arranged swimming lessons for them, and took them on a boating expedition. Now he referred to them proudly as 'my children' and even engaged a French teacher for them. And when they were due to return home, Mrs Bowman wrote to say that Emsie had scarlet fever, so Isa and Nellie stayed with him until 27 August.

Shortly afterwards the Bowmans went to New York, and remained there until May 1890; but Dodgson and Isa kept in touch by letter, and in September Isa joined him for another week at Eastbourne. She had now been confirmed, and they were able to take Communion together. 'It was a real pleasure to have this new and yet closer link between us,'[24] Dodgson wrote. Isa was now sixteen years old.

Though Isa was a fine actress and a graceful dancer, her singing was her weak point, and in the *Alice* operetta the critics had noted that her voice was hardly strong enough to do justice to the songs. But in 1891, shortly after her fifth and last visit to Eastbourne, Dodgson arranged for her to have singing lessons from Mademoiselle Victoria de Bunsen, a relative of the singer Ernest de Bunsen, who a quarter of a century before had graced the parties at the Deanery. He also approached Ellen Terry about an elocution teacher for Isa, and to his great delight she actually offered to coach Isa herself. But Isa was now beginning to drift away from him. She spent a few days with him at Oxford in 1892, and in the following summer he made inquiries about a gold watch which he planned to send her; but the demands of her stage career made it increasingly difficult for her to keep up the friendship. In May 1895 Isa called on him unexpectedly to announce her engagement. This was the last recorded meeting between them. Eighteen months later he heard rumours that she had married.

REFERENCES

1   Christ Church Ms. C.R. 59.
2   Ms. Diaries.

3   Hudson, p. 246.
4   Christ Church Ms. C.R. 55.
5   Hudson, p. 250.
6   Carroll was then fifty-three years old.
7   Collingwood, p. 237.
8   Ibid, pp. 256–7.
9   Dr Selwyn Goodacre, '*The Nursery Alice* – A Bibliographical Essay', *Jabberwocky*, Autumn 1975.
10 Ibid.
11 D.F.C.
12 *The Lady*, 24 March 1892.
13 Roger Manvell, *Ellen Terry*, New York, 1968, pp. 235–6.
14 Ellen Terry, *The Story of my Life*, pp. 358–9.
15 Mary Breasted, 'Collection of Lewis Carroll Moves on to N.Y.U. Library', *The New York Times*, 19 March 1975.
16 April 1887.
17 September 1889.
18 Green, p. 452.
19 Ibid, p. 451.
20 Isa Bowman, *Lewis Carroll as I knew him*, 1972, p. 48.
21 Ibid, pp. 51–2.
22 Ibid, p. 21.
23 Ibid, p. 22.
24 Ms. Diaries, 14 September 1890.

14 Sylvie and Bruno

The evolution of *Sylvie and Bruno* fell into three quite distinct phases. The first phase, which occupied approximately eight years, began in June 1867 with his writing the story of *Bruno's Revenge*, as published by Mrs Gatty in *Aunt Judy's Magazine*, and continued with the telling of fairy stories to groups of children at Hatfield House and elsewhere. Of the second phase, which lasted about a decade, Dodgson wrote, 'I jotted down, at odd moments, all sorts of odd ideas and fragments of dialogue, that occurred to me – who knows how? – with a transitory suddenness that left me no choice but either to record them then and there, or to abandon them into oblivion.'[1] This left him with the enormous task of 'classifying these odds and ends sufficiently to see what sort of a story they indicated: for the story had to grow out of the incidents, not the incidents out of the story'.[2] Finally, between 1885 and 1893, when the second volume, *Sylvie and Bruno Concluded*, was at last completed, he had connected these fragments into a unified whole.

Dodgson was never happy in his written work until the matter of an illustrator was settled. In his search for an artist Dodgson had considered his old friend Henry Holiday, Arthur Burdett Frost, and Walter Crane. But in the event it was Harry Furniss who finally landed the contract. 'When I, a little, a very little boy in knickerbockers, first enjoyed the adventures of Alice and worshipped the pen and pencil which recorded them, I little thought I would some day work hand in hand with the author,' Furniss wrote.[3] Dodgson called on him for the first time on 13 April 1885, and discussed with him the drawings for 'Peter and Paul', a long poem in *Sylvie and Bruno* centred round an April Fool's joke and whose connection with the main plot was tenuous. The drawings were quickly executed and on 20 April reached Dodgson, who immediately commissioned Furniss for the entire work.

Of his acceptance of the commission Furniss wrote:

> When I told Tenniel that I had been approached by Dodgson to illustrate his book, he said, 'I'll give you a week, old chap; you will never put up with that fellow a day longer.' 'You will see,' I said. 'If I like the work, I shall manage the author.' 'Not a bit of it; Lewis Carroll is impossible,' replied Tenniel. 'You will see that my prophecy will come true.' It was

therefore in a way, as the acceptance of a challenge that I undertook the work. Carroll and I worked together for seven years, and a kindlier man never lived. I was always hearing of his kindness to others. He was a generous employer, and his gratitude was altogether out of proportion to my efforts.[4]

At £20 for a full-page illustration and £15 for a three-quarter page illustration, Dodgson's scale of payment to Furniss was handsome. But Furniss found him a captious critic, whose practice was to examine a square inch of drawing under a magnifying glass, and compare the number of fine lines per square inch with those on a square inch of Tenniel's *Alice* work. He was also irritated by Dodgson's use of mathematics for the purpose of criticizing proportions. The following extract from one of Dodgson's numerous letters to Furniss indicates the line this took: 'I will venture to say that I think Sylvie's face too small both for her head and for her figure. The "mathematical statistics" (which you think so irrelevant, but which I think you will find all great figure painters observe to a hair's breadth) say that the eyes should come half way between the top of the head and the point of the chin.'

At one stage Dodgson sought permission from Mrs Van der Gucht for Furniss to use Marie, the dedicatee of *The Nursery Alice*, as the model for Sylvie; but although her mother agreed, the idea came to nothing. Instead, Dodgson used to send Furniss photographs of children who possessed some feature that he wanted incorporated in his heroine. A complication was that the fairy child Sylvie and the grown-up Society Lady Muriel were counterparts. The following extract from one of Dodgson's letters suggesting a suitable child model and enclosing a set of photographs illustrates his extreme preoccupation with the features of his heroine:

I must confess that Nora has a deeper and more prominent chin than I like. I don't want my heroine to have the small receding chin which is said to show a weak character: but I certainly would like Nora's chin a little reduced. If you take No. 3 and cover the chin up to one-third of the way from its point to the mouth you will see the face I admire most. She is a very sweet-natured girl with plenty of life and good abilities I should think. All that would do well for Lady Muriel. But I am not intimate with her and do not know if she has all the depth of thought (especially of religious thought) that I imagine Lady Muriel to have. But photo No. 4 looks to me quite the expression I should like Lady Muriel to have while discussing some serious subject. And No. 1 would do capitally for her face when enjoying a joke or talking nonsense, as I mean her to do in some parts of the book. On the whole I doubt if you could have a better guide for the head of Lady Muriel than No. 4. It is to my mind sweet and thoughtful and practical and thoroughly refined. I like her hair very much, too, especially the fringe . . .'[5]

Unlike Tenniel, Furniss always used a model, and as it became clear that he did not use the children he suggested, Dodgson did his best to discover who the models were. The truth never struck him, despite his frequent visits to the Furniss home: 'Sylvie' was the artist's own daughter, and 'Bruno' his second son.

Dodgson was as much preoccupied with the characters' clothes as with their features. As Sylvie and Bruno were not to be fairies throughout the book, their style of dress was something of a puzzle. 'They mustn't have *wings*: that is clear', wrote Dodgson. 'And it mustn't be *quite* the common dress of London Life. It should be as fanciful as possible, so as *just* to be presentable in Society. The friends might be able to say "What oddly-dressed children!", but they oughtn't to say "They are not human!" ' And once he confessed, 'I *wish* I dared dispense with *all* costume; naked children are so perfectly pure and lovely, but Mrs Grundy would be furious – it would never do. Then the question is, how little dress will content her? Bare legs and feet we *must* have, at any rate. I so entirely detest that monstrous fashion *high heels* (and in fact have planned an attack on it in this very book), that I cannot possibly allow my sweet little heroine to be victimized by it.'[6]

Of Bruno he wrote, 'Don't draw a podgy boy – a great eater of pudding – but give us a little acrobat, a boy that can run and jump . . .'[7] The result was a compromise, for Furniss' Bruno is engagingly plump. Here again, clothes were a problem and Dodgson complained that Bruno was 'much too naked. Excuse my using coarse language (I don't know how to put it more euphemistically), but a picture exhibiting the naked posteriors, even of a very young boy, cannot possibly go into the book.'[8] This was not, he explained, a question of art, but of suitability to his book. But Furniss very quickly grasped Dodgson's concept of Sylvie's costume. Dodgson wrote, 'I am charmed with your idea of dressing her in *white*; it exactly fits my own idea of her; I want her to be a sort of embodiment of Purity. So I think that, in Society, she should be wholly in *white* – white frock ("clinging" certainly; I *hate* crinoline fashion): also I *think* we might venture on making her *fairy* dress transparent. Don't you think we might face Mrs Grundy to *that* extent? In fact I think Mrs G would be fairly content at finding her *dressed*, and would not mind whether the material was silk, or muslin, or even gauze.'[9] But when Furniss gave Lady Muriel a fashionable gown suitable for London Society, Dodgson wrote, 'Could you cut off those high shoulders from her sleeves? Why should we pay any deference to a modern fashion that will be extinct a year hence? Next to the unapproachable ugliness of the "crinoline", I think those high-shouldered sleeves are the worst things invented for ladies in our time. Imagine how horrified they would be if one of their daughters were *really* shaped like that!'[10]

Though Dodgson liked Furniss' interpretation of the Chancellor, he insisted on a change of attitude in one of the drawings. 'Please don't let him clasp his hands under his coat-tails. It is the regular low-comedy "business" in which the actor always manages to show a little more of the least beautiful part of his figure than is quite seemly. I don't want to have an atom of playing for the gallery! They can be under his "gown" by all means, which may float about as wildly as you like.'[11] But his final verdict on Sylvie was one of delighted satisfaction: 'Sylvie is just delicious, just the face and figure I want, and what a pretty pair of legs you've given her!' It was a comment he could never have made of Tenniel's drawings of Alice, whose legs were mere cardboard representations. The same was true of Dodgson's personal illustrations of *Alice's Adventures Underground*; even when he was making his most earnest efforts at realism, his attempts stopped strictly short at the heroine's hemline. Only in his later years was he able to overcome this particular Victorian inhibition.

In their seven-year collaboration, despite personal eccentricities on both sides, author and artist got along famously together, mainly because each was willing to make concessions to the other. Dodgson was anxious to press on with the work quickly, for he was very conscious of the uncertainty of life. Once he wrote to Furniss: 'It is now just a year and eight months since you undertook the illustrating of my new book, and only four pictures are as yet delivered: at which rate it would take more than thirty years to finish the book.' But his concessions to Furniss were made not only from a desire to conclude matters quickly, but from a genuine respect for his artist's abilities. Sometimes concessions on one side led to withdrawal of objections on the other. In one letter to Furniss offering to replace 'Albatross' with another trisyllable, such as 'cormorant' or 'dragon-fly', Dodgson wrote, 'I made the very same offer to Mr Tenniel when he remonstrated against the walrus and the carpenter as a hopeless combination and begged to have the carpenter abolished. I remember offering "baronet" and "butterfly" (which by the way might suit you) but he finally chose carpenter.'[12]

But on 26 August 1889 Dodgson heard the disastrous news that Furniss declined to complete the book because Dodgson had refused to use (although he was prepared to pay for) two of the pictures. In one of these, of 'Sylvie helping beetle', the heroine was eight heads high, which outraged Dodgson's sense of mathematical proportions. Despite his obvious distress, Dodgson wrote at one to Alice Havers (Mrs Norman), the artist who illustrated Mrs Hodgson Burnett's *Little St Elizabeth*, and asked her to do all the Sylvie and Bruno pictures. Nevertheless he still expressed the hope that Furniss would finish the grotesques, and was overjoyed when Furniss revoked his decision. At this point both men decided to concede: Dodgson to accept the pictures unaltered and Furniss to draw them again. But one picture by Alice Havers, of the magic locket, was incorporated in the book. By Dodg-

son's fine-lines-per-square-inch method of criticism this could not be
faulted, but it is a very ugly illustration unfit for comparison with
Furniss' superb drawings.

Dodgson's motivation for writing the *Alice* books had been simply
that of entertaining a child he loved; but he approached *Sylvie and Bruno*
with a set of objectives that were much more complex. He now entertained 'the hope of supplying, for the children whom I love, some
thoughts that may suit those hours of innocent merriment which are the
very life of childhood; and also in the hope of suggesting, to them and to
others, some thoughts that may prove, I would fain hope, not wholly
out of harmony with the graver cadences of life.'[13]

By 30 November 1888 Dodgson realized that the huge quantity of
material he had amassed would fill two large volumes. He had also
temporarily dropped the name *Sylvie and Bruno* in favour of the tentative
title 'Four Seasons'. On one issue he was firmly resolved: that the
project should be completely different from the *Alice* books. 'Anything
which would have the effect of connecting the book with "Alice" would
be absolutely disastrous,' he wrote. 'The thing I wish above all to avoid
in this new book is the giving of any pretext for critics to say "this writer
can play only one tune: the book is a réchauffé of Alice." I'm trying my
very best to get out of the old groove, and to have no "connecting link"
whatever.'[14]

Dodgson hinges his story on an intricately worked-out series of
hypotheses. First, that besides the world in which we live there exist
two others: its counterpart, called Outland, whose society is a kind of
burlesque of the real world, and Fairyland as we all understand it.
Second, that human beings, unseen and in a state of trance, may
observe people and events in Outland, and that in another state, which
Dodgson describes as 'eerie', they may participate in adventures in
Fairyland, without losing consciousness of events in the real world.
Thirdly, time may reverse or stand still, and fairies may assume human
form. The links between Outland and the real world are the narrator,
who passes back and forth between the two, and Sylvie and Bruno,
alternately appearing in fairy form or as human children.

The 'real world' plot centres around Lady Muriel Orme and a young
and impecunious doctor, Arthur Forester, with whom she is in love.
Arthur is inhibited from a declaration of feeling by his lack of fortune.
For her part, Lady Muriel is similarly inhibited by an understanding
that has grown up over the years between herself and her cousin, Eric
Lindon. Though she is in a sense repulsed by Eric's lack of religious
principles, she is also tied to him by a desire to lead him to true
Christianity. When Arthur learned that he had inherited a fortune, he
was still inhibited from speaking by his firm conviction that Lady
Muriel was in love with Eric. An army promotion meanwhile enables

Eric to propose to Lady Muriel, who becomes engaged to him, and Volume I concludes with Arthur's decision to go to India.

Inability to reconcile herself to Eric's lack of religious conviction induces Lady Muriel a few months later to speak to Eric, who releases her unconditionally. Arthur returns and marries her, but almost immediately goes to the rescue of a village ravaged by plague. Soon his heroic death is recorded in a newspaper article; but Eric discovers him still alive, and in a new spirit of religious conviction returns him to his bride. Edmund Miller sums up the deficiencies in the plot: 'The sophisticated modern reader is almost bound to be unhappy with such a qualitative resolution of plot. He has nothing against love, but he would rather see it growing out of plot than magically justifying the most agreeable but unlikely developments. The resurrection of Arthur is like something out of Mrs Radcliffe. But Carroll obviously did not see it that way. There is certainly a moral purpose behind his vision. And this sort of plot manipulation was a common feature of the Victorian novel.'[15]

Closely interwoven with this is the account of affairs in Outland, where a state of political confusion reigns. The Vice-Warden puts out false reports of the death of his brother, the wise and saintly Warden, and usurps his authority. The fairies, Sylvie and Bruno, are the Warden's two children, and when the Vice-Warden seizes power he sets aside Bruno's right of succession in favour of Uggug, his own objectionable son. When the Warden returns as the Elf King, his brother is filled with remorse, but is left in possession of the throne to become a wiser ruler for the future.

Dodgson considered the fairy duet sung by Sylvie and Bruno the best poem he had ever written, but it is marred by a tripping measure altogether unsuitable to its serious intention. Brian Sibley writes of it:

> 'A Song of Love' is Carroll's paean in praise of the greatest of St Paul's three abiding truths; it is a perfectly scanned lyric, whose sentiments would be unbearable if it weren't so overtly sincere. For the poem is the key to the unlocking of many of the mysteries of *Sylvie and Bruno*, and the quintessence of Carroll's religious thinking. Carroll's vision of love as the embodiment of the Spirit of God, symbolizing the origins and aims of Life: strength, hope, faith and peace – those same facets of human spiritual endeavour reflected in the lives of the novels' central characters.[16]

The pace of the book is leisurely, with scope for poems and tales. There is much discussion of religious and moral issues, of politics, education and a host of the inventions that exercised the mind of the author. If many of the characters, as they are introduced, seem already familiar, it is because Dodgson consciously introduces correspondences between them. Thus Lady Muriel in the real world is the counterpart of Sylvie, and Arthur of Bruno. The narrator, an aged man, is clearly

Dodgson himself. Significantly perhaps he casts himself in the role of
unsuccessful suitor from the moment when Lady Muriel enters his
railway compartment: ' "A young and lovely lady!" I muttered to
myself with some bitterness. "And this is, of course, the opening scene
of Vol. I. *She* is the Heroine. And *I* am one of those subordinate
characters that only turn up when needed for the development of her
destiny, and whose final appearance is outside the church, waiting to
greet the Happy Pair!" ' And there is an interesting scene in which the
Narrator urges Arthur not to wait too long before speaking to Lady
Muriel of his love, for fear that another man might engage her affections. Arthur replies, ' "If she loves another better than me, so be it! I
will not spoil her happiness. The secret shall die with me. But she is my
first – and my *only* love!" "That is all very beautiful *sentiment*," I said,
"but is it *practical* . . ." "I *dare* not ask the question whether there is
another!" he said passionately. "It would break my heart to know it!"
"Yet is it wise to leave it unasked? You must not waste your life upon an
'if'!" '17

Of the broad spectrum of ideas and personal philosophies incorporated in the book, the most important are those appertaining to love
and religion. The first volume contains a criticism of ritualism and of
lack of participation by the congregation in church services. In the
preface to *Sylvie and Bruno Concluded* he refers to many objections to the
severity of his language:

> While freely admitting that the 'Ritual' movement was sorely needed,
> and that it has effected a vast improvement in our Church-Services,
> which had become dead and dry to the last degree, I hold that, like many
> other desirable movements, it has gone too far in the opposite direction,
> and has introduced many new dangers. For the Congregation this new
> movement involves the danger of learning to think that the Services are
> done *for* them; and that their bodily *presence* is all they need contribute.
> And, for Clergy and Congregation alike, it involves the danger of regard-
> ing these elaborate Services as *ends in themselves*, and of forgetting that
> they are simply *means*, and the very hollowest of mockeries, unless they
> bear fruit in our *lives*.18

Even more interesting than Dodgson's attitude to the controversies
surrounding ritualism in his day are his concepts of sin. The theory
advanced by Arthur is that environment must be taken into account in
assessing the severity of a sin. He puts forward the paradoxical claim
that a common thief committing a major crime may be less at fault than
his social superior who gives way to undetectable minor unfair dealing,
since the social training of the superior ought to make him less vulnera-
ble to temptations of this kind. Lady Muriel is alarmed at the way in
which this theory seems to widen the possible area of sin in the world;
but Arthur expresses joy 'that the millions whom I had thought of as

sunk in hopeless depths of sin, were perhaps, in God's sight, scarcely sinning at all'.

Though he still found room for plenty of nonsense-writing, the serious thought is much more concentrated in the second volume than in the first. Perhaps this indicated an increasing desire to get his religious and other serious ideas across while life remained to him. But he was mildly concerned lest he give offence by the juxtaposition of nonsense and religion. 'I hope I have not offended many . . . by putting scenes of mere fun, and talk about God, into the same book,'[19] he wrote. But by the sparkle of his wit in the lighthearted passages and the elegance of his prose style throughout, he succeeded in elevating the book to a level at which the inclusion of serious thoughts appears neither intrusive nor profane. He confessed that he worked hard at his prose style, and he was meticulous at improving and polishing it, as he was about anything that he considered worth doing. 'I think *newspapers* are largely responsible for the bad English now used in books,' he wrote to his sister Mary. 'How few novels of the day are written in correct English. To find any such, you must go back fifty years or more. That is one reason why I like reading *older* novels – Scott's, Miss Austen's, Miss Edgeworth's, etc. – that the English is so perfect. We have one living novelist whose English is *lovely* – Miss Thackeray. I have brought a volume of hers with me, to read a bit, now and then, and get my ear into tune before going on with *Sylvie and Bruno Concluded*.'[20]

The first volume of *Sylvie and Bruno* was dedicated to Isa Bowman. When the book came out in December 1889 the Bowman family were acting in New York, and although Dodgson had a copy specially bound for Isa, he did not send it to her until she returned in May 1890. 'I really didn't dare to send it across the Atlantic – the whales are so inconsiderate,'[21] he wrote. Although Isa should have been well used to Dodgson's penchant for acrostic verse, she failed to notice that her name was incorporated not once, but twice, in the dedicatory poem. Her name is found both by taking the first letter of each line, and also by taking the first three letters of each stanza. 'She was so long, without finding it out, that I've had to give her a hint, and I don't know whether she has found out that it comes in in two different ways,' Dodgson wrote.

Sylvie and Bruno Concluded was not published until 29 December 1893, thereby just missing the Christmas market. His checks to the working-off of the book had occupied most of his time from the end of July to late November 1893, but with Dodgson's past record it was hardly to be expected that the book could be got through the press without some sort of major disaster. Selwyn Goodacre summarizes the calamities that had befallen previous major works:

> In 1865 he rejected the first edition of *Alice's Adventures in Wonderland*. In 1885 he found fault in *A Tangled Tale*; in 1886 he rejected the first private

edition of *The Game of Logic*, and in 1889 the first printing of *The Nursery
'Alice'*. *Through the Looking-Glass*, first published in 1871, initially survived
unscathed. Trouble started in 1878, when Dodgson found that the kings
were missing from the Chess diagram in the 42nd thousand: 'They are in
the proper places in a copy I referred to of the tenth thousand: but in
which thousand the misprint first appeared I have not the means to
discover.' In fact they were first missing in the 26th thousand, 1872.
They promptly reappeared on a redesigned board on the 45th thousand,
1878.[22]

Much more serious was the problem which arose over the printing of
Through the Looking-Glass when, on 21 November 1893, Dodgson
received six copies of the sixtieth thousand. On examining the fifty
pictures, he discovered twenty-six were overprinted, of which eight
were very bad. Luckily they had been done as a separate batch, and
only sixty had gone out. He gave immediate instructions that the
remaining 940 copies were to be destroyed, and that the working-off of
Sylvie and Bruno Concluded was to be stopped, despite the risk of heavy
financial loss to himself through missing the Christmas market. Four
days later, after discussions with Frederick Macmillan and an assurance that Clay the printer would guarantee this would not happen
again, he decided not to have the sheets destroyed, but to have them
bound up in plainer bindings for donations to Mechanics' Institutes
and so on. In *The Times* of 2 December 1893 he published the following
advertisement:

> Mr Lewis Carroll, after having for over 25 years made it his chief object
> with regard to his books that they should be of the best workmanship
> attainable at the price, is deeply annoyed to find that the last issue of
> Looking-Glass, consisting of the 60th Thousand, has been put on sale
> without its being noticed that most of the pictures have failed so much in
> the printing as to make the book not worth buying. He requests all
> holders of copies to send them to Messrs Macmillan and Co. of 29 Bedford
> Street Covent Garden with their names and addresses, and copies of the
> next issue shall be sent to them in exchange. Instead, however, of
> destroying the unsold copies, he proposes to utilize them by giving them
> away to Mechanics' Institutes, village school libraries, and similar
> institutions where the means for purchasing such books are scanty.
> Accordingly he invites applications for such gifts, addressed to him 'c/o
> Messrs Macmillan'. Every such application should be signed by some
> responsible person, and should state how far they are able to buy books
> for themselves, and what is their average number of readers. He takes
> this opportunity of announcing that, if, at any future time, he should
> wish to communicate anything to his readers, he will do so by advertising
> in the 'Agony' column of some of the daily papers on the first Tuesday in
> the month.

A similar advertisement on an octavo leaf was inserted in *Sylvie and
Bruno Concluded* when it eventually came out. 'This *Looking-Glass* fiasco
has stopped things for exactly a week,'[23] Dodgson commented of the

progress of *Sylvie and Bruno Concluded*. But further disappointments were to come. On 2 December he received two finished sheets of *Sylvie and Bruno Concluded* and pronounced them *faded* by the standards of Volume I. Five days later he learned that this was because the sheets had been rolled too soon. It was not till 12 December that he received corrected sheets and telegraphed Clay the printer to go ahead.

Sylvie and Bruno Concluded was dedicated to Enid Stevens, a little girl whom he had first met on 27 February 1891. She was a beautiful child, with large dreamy eyes and lovely dark curly hair, at that age very like Furniss' drawings of Sylvie. In later years she often wondered whether it was her similarity to his heroine that attracted Dodgson to her, although he himself said that what he liked most was her ability to converse, rare in a child of her years. Although she was not the model for Sylvie, the first volume having been published before she met Dodgson, she had distinct recollections of two occasions when a large bearded man, very like Furniss, sketched her in Dodgson's rooms. 'I remember them so clearly, even now – even to seeing the large bearded man squatting in a corner drawing me on your uncle's knee,' she wrote half a century later to Miss Violet Dodgson. 'And what could be more natural than that having found a child that looked like the pictured Sylvie, your uncle should invite the artist to have a look at her?'[24] This does indeed sound most probable: though the only artist known to have drawn Enid Stevens for Dodgson was Miss Thomson, who had no beard. Her portrait of Enid hung over the fireplace in Dodgson's study for the rest of his life, and Dodgson showered Enid with love and affection.

Dodgson composed the dedicatory acrostic to Enid Stevens on a three-and-a-quarter hour walk to Beachy Head, very reminiscent of his composing the last line of *The Hunting of the Snark* on a long walk. He was unaccompanied, but Enid recalled many delightful walks with him when he was in a mood for versifying: 'It . . . [*Useful and Instructive Poetry*] reminds me most vividly of walks with him, when he suddenly became inspired, and began to pour forth similar verses – apparently quite effortlessly – instead of continuing to talk in ordinary prose. . . . Believing him (as I did) to be quite different from anybody else at all, it never surprised me, and I used to try (very unsuccessfully) to reply in similar vein!'[25]

In the preface to *Sylvie and Bruno* Dodgson had listed a number of literary projects that he intended to pursue. First of these was a Child's Bible, consisting of selected passages illustrated with Biblical pictures by the world's great masters. 'Religion should be put before a child as a revelation of *love* – no need to pain and puzzle the young mind with the history of crime and punishment,' he wrote. Secondly he proposed a book of extracts from the Bible which people could learn by heart; for he felt that such extended passages could often be called to mind when brief texts could not. A third project complementary to the last would be a collection of prose and verse from sources other than the Bible; and finally, he proposed a 'Shakespeare for Girls' suitable for people aged ten to seventeen years. Thereafter he thought the need to edit the material available to young women ceased, but he felt there was a great need for such a book. Answering the question whether the Bowdlerized version did not meet this need, Dodgson wrote, 'Bowdler's is the most extraordinary of all: looking through it, I am filled with a deep sense of wonder, considering what he has left in, that he should have cut *anything* out.' None of these schemes came to anything, though as early as June 1882 Dodgson had invited readers of the *Monthly Packet* to list about fifteen of the plays considered most suitable to be issued in an expurgated Shakespeare. Though he began work on *The Tempest* in March 1885, he made no headway.

The two volumes of *Sylvie and Bruno* were such a drain on his creative resources that Dodgson published very little else in the four years that separated the publication of these two books. There was *Circular Billiards*, a pamphlet dated 1890 which describes the rules for playing billiards on a round table with cushions but no pockets or spots. The table was actually made and used, but the game never caught on. More important was *Eight or Nine Wise Words About Letter-Writing* and the Wonderland Stamp Case, devised by Dodgson and made up by his sister Louisa. The Stamp Case contains little stitched pockets for twelve stamps of values from ½d to 1s. The case and its cover both have pictures of Alice. When the case is pulled out, the picture of Alice holding the baby changes to Alice holding the pig. Similarly, the Cheshire Cat on the reverse is replaced by the grin alone. *Eight or Nine Wise Words About Letter-Writing* was advice from a real expert. On 1 January 1861 Dodgson had started a letter register in which he recorded every letter he wrote or received, with a précis of its contents, and a cross-referencing system enabling him to trace a complete series of correspondence, even if it extended through several volumes of the register. The last entry was numbered 98,721. Dodgson's letters were all beautifully set out, and he selected the size of paper so as to fit the length of the letter. Usually he composed the letter and then made a fair copy. He once worked out his rate of copying material in his diary at twenty words a minute, or seven-and-a-half minutes a page. With such a quantity of letter-writing it was not surprising that his working list of outstanding letters usually ran into some seventy or eighty items. Replies to letters were often delayed by months, even years. Besides the ever-increasing volume of letters from child friends – many of them now grown-up – there were business and family matters, plus a large quantity of correspondence sparked off by his books. Where these were genuine queries about points in his texts, he liked to reply personally, but he steadfastly refused to gratify autograph hunters, and in 1890 he produced the 'Stranger Circular', which was designed to ward off inquiries from people who wrote to the Rev. C. L. Dodgson about the works of Lewis Carroll. The text of the second edition read:

> Mr Dodgson is so frequently addressed by strangers on the quite un-authorized assumption that he claims, or at any rate acknowledges the authorship of books not published under his name, that he has found it necessary to print this, once for all, as an answer to all such applications. He neither claims nor acknowledges any connection with any pseudonym, or with any book that is not published under his own name. Having therefore no claim to retain, or even to read the enclosed, he returns it for the convenience of the writer who has thus misaddressed it.

In 1893 Dodgson brought out *Syzygies and Lanrick*, two word games of his own invention, both of which had appeared separately, and as magazine articles in *The Lady* and the *Monthly Packet* respectively. Much more important was *Pillow Problems, Thought out During Sleepless Nights*, which formed the second part of *Curiosa Mathematica*, and which con-tained seventy-two problems, most of them in algebra, plane geometry or trigonometry. All the problems were invented and solved in the dark and not committed to paper until next morning. In the second edition, 'Wakeful Hours' was substituted for 'Sleepless Nights' to abate the fears of his friends that he had become a chronic insomniac. Though the problems are not beyond the scope of most mathematicians of reason-able ability, given pencil and paper, they need tremendous concentra-tion if they are to be done in the dark.

But one of the problems, if we can assume that his intention was serious, exposed his limitations as a mathematician. The problem is: 'A bag contains 2 counters, as to which nothing is known except that each is either black (B) or white (W). Ascertain their colours without taking them out of the bag.' Warren Weaver explains:

> In his attack on this problem (which as stated cannot actually be solved) he makes two dreadful mistakes. First, he assumes, incorrectly, that the statement implies the probabilities of BB, BW, and WW (the three possible constitutions of the bag) are 1/4, 1/2, and 1/4 respectively. Then he adds a black ball to the bag, calculates that the probability of now drawing a black ball is 2/3 and makes his fatal error in concluding that the bag must now contain BBW. His line of reasoning thus leads him to the conclusion that the two original balls were 1B and 1W! . . . It has been pointed out that if one applies Dodgson's argument to a bag containing three unknown balls (black or white), he can now come out with the conclusion that it was impossible for there to have been three balls at all.[26]

During the period 1886–92 when he gave lectures to the pupils at Lady Margaret Hall and the Oxford High School for Girls Dodgson also published a series of papers on logic. Ethel Rowell, a pupil at the Oxford High School, gave an account of Dodgson's lectures: 'When Mr Dodgson stood at the desk in the sixth-form room and prepared to address the class I thought he looked very tall and seemed very serious and rather formidable. . . . As he proceeded I think the facts became more fanciful and the fancies more fantastic; nevertheless Logic had them all in hand, and it appeared that skilful manipulation of the little red and grey counters was adequate to any situation.' Finding Ethel a promising pupil, Dodgson offered to give her private lessons. 'By his own real wish to know what I was thinking Mr Dodgson compelled me to that arduous business of thinking, and to an independence of thought I had never before tried to exercise. . . . And then Mr Dodgson gave me his affection – the reflection, in our own particular relation, of his great-hearted concern for all children.'[27]

To *The Lady* Dodgson contributed a number of items in 1891–2, most intriguing of which was his invention for writing in the dark, which he originally called the Typhlograph and later he renamed the Nyctograph. This consisted of a grating of sixteen squares, cut in card, and an alphabet of which each letter could be made by drawing lines along the edges of the squares, and dots at the corners. The system was an improvement on his earlier method of writing within oblongs of cardboard, which he rejected because he found that the result tended to be illegible. He invented the Nyctograph to spare himself the unpleasant task of getting out of bed and striking a light when he wanted to commit an idea to paper; but although he found it answered the purpose well, most people would consider it too complicated and far more trouble than getting a light.

The intricacies of the Nyctograph give an indication of the sheer complexity of Dodgson's mind, and of that delight in novelty and invention that characterized him from childhood to the end of his life. His inventions were remarkable for their diversity. Several were connected with the postal services, and included not only the postage stamp case, but a new form of money order in duplicate containing a key number which had to be quoted by the recipient on encashing it; a special cape and mail basket for postmen to use in wet weather, and paper gummed on both sides for fastening envelopes or mounting items in albums. He devised his own modifications to heating, lighting and air-conditioning systems, and produced a series of alterations to his velociman, all backed up with detailed drawings. He thought up new methods for all sorts of activities, from maintaining letter-registers and filing data to systems of reading and study. Orderliness was a passion, and everything had to be neatly stacked in its proper place. And besides his own inventions, he made liberal use of the inventions of others. He called Edison's Phonograph 'the new wonder of the day, just as I

remember Photography was about 1850', and regretted not being able
to use it in fifty years, when he believed it would have achieved its
perfect form.

Jean Gattégno aptly summarizes Dodgson's character:

> Not only is he a pedagogue, anxious to convey knowledge in the most
> attractive manner possible; not only is he a mathematician, a man of
> reasoned thought, of logical steps and demonstration; he is, first and
> foremost, a real *inventor*, for whom the joy of discovery is one of the
> greatest delights life has to offer. . . . A joy of discovery, of invention; this
> is an element we must be very careful never to forget in any effort to
> capture the personality of Lewis Carroll.

REFERENCES

1 *Sylvie and Bruno*, 1889, p. ix.
2 Ibid, p. x.
3 *Confessions of a Caricaturist*, 1902.
4 Harry Furniss, *Some Victorian Men*, 1924, p. 77.
5 Beatrice and Guy Mackenzie, 'Lewis Carroll Shown in a New Light', *The New York Times Magazine*, 24 August 1930.
6 Harry Furniss, *Confessions of a Caricaturist*, 1902.
7 Beatrice and Guy Mackenzie, 'Lewis Carroll Shown in a New Light', *The New York Times Magazine*, 24 August 1930.
8 Ibid.
9 Harry Furniss, *Confessions of a Caricaturist*, 1902.
10 Ibid.
11 Beatrice and Guy Mackenzie, 'Lewis Carroll Shown in a New Light', *The New York Times Magazine*, 24 August 1930.
12 Ibid.
13 *Sylvie and Bruno*, 1889, p. xiii.
14 Beatrice and Guy Mackenzie, 'Lewis Carroll Shown in a New Light', *The New York Times Magazine*, 24 August 1930.
15 Article, 'The Sylvie and Bruno Books as Victorian Novel'.
16 Article, 'The Poems of Sylvie and Bruno', *Jabberwocky*, Summer 1975.
17 *Sylvie and Bruno*, p. 189.
18 p. xix.
19 Collingwood, p. 309.
20 D.F.C. 18/5/16
21 Isa Bowman, *Lewis Carroll as I knew Him*, 1972.
22 Article, 'Lewis Carroll's Rejection of the 60th Thousand of *Through the Looking-Glass*', *The Book Collector*, Summer 1975.
23 Green, p. 504.
24 D.F.C. 19/4/2a.
25 D.F.C. 14/4/1.
26 Article, 'Lewis Carroll: Mathematician', *Scientific American*, April 1956.
27 Article, 'To me he was Mr Dodgson', *Harper's Magazine*, February 1943.

15 'Death is Over Now'

On 19 September 1893 Gertrude Chataway came to stay with him in Eastbourne. Dodgson once claimed that he had defied 'Mrs Grundy' more often than anyone else in Christ Church. Inevitably such freedoms invited gossip. Gertrude's visit prompted Dodgson's sister Mary Collingwood to write and warn him of the risks of provoking adverse comment. In his reply he said that he regarded the opinion of people in general as worthless as a test of right and wrong. His own conscience before God, and the full approval of the parents of his young friends were the only standards he now applied. '*Anybody* who is spoken about at all, is *sure* to be spoken against by *somebody*,' he wrote. '. . . if you limit your actions in life to things that *nobody* can find fault with, you will not do much.'[1]

His interest in drawing children from life had continued unabated. In January 1888 he recorded drawing from life a fourteen-year-old child called Ada Frost at the home of a friend, Mrs Shute. He described it as a quite new experience, and added that the only nude drawings he had made before had been of children aged about five years. Ada had already had nine years' experience as a model, and Dodgson was impressed by her quiet dignity and modest demeanour. 'I think a spectator would have to be really in *search* of evil to have any other feelings about her than simply a sense of beauty, as in looking at a statue. She has a fairly pretty face, and a quite lovely figure. . . . It was a real enjoyment to have so beautiful an object to copy.'[2]

Though Dodgson never achieved the fine draughtsmanship he so desired, he was an expert appraiser of the work of others, and based his criticism on careful reasoning. The following extract from a letter to E. Gertrude Thomson indicates his excellent eye for proportions:

> Though I like the horizontal figure (if only her arm were a little shorter): and the other one, down to the waist (if only *her* arm were shorter), I cannot say I like the rest of her. The curve, from the inbend of the back to the inbend of the knee, is almost an exact semicircle, and I *don't* admire it at all. The position of the legs is uncomfortable – suggestive of her slipping down the bank. The effect of the foreshortening is to make the upper part of her left leg look too short, as compared with the lower and

the outline of her right leg is a smooth elliptic arc, giving no hint of a *knee* anywhere. I don't see how the legs *could* be made to look graceful . . .[3]

This apparently refers to a rejected drawing which had been meant for *Three Sunsets. Original Games and Puzzles* and *The Valley of the Shadow of Death*, both to be illustrated by Miss Thomson, were advertised in *Sylvie and Bruno Concluded*; but they were never published, apparently because of Miss Thomson's failure to produce the drawings. Even *Three Sunsets* was not published until after the author's death. Of all the artists who worked for Dodgson, Miss Thomson was the only one whose pictures bore no relation to the text. He was happy to include her nude children thinly disguised as fairies just because he thought them pretty.

On the whole Dodgson's health was excellent throughout his life and he took sensible precautions to preserve his physical fitness. His bout of whooping cough at Rugby seems possibly to have led to secondary bronchiectasis, and the coughs and chills from which he often suffered in the winter months were probably all mild exacerbations of this.[4] His diaries do tend to give an impression of unnecessary invalidism at such times, but there were no antibiotics to take care of any sudden complications, and his precautions were probably standard among those who could afford to be ill.

On 31 December 1885 while staying at 'The Chestnuts' he suffered what his doctor described as an 'epileptiform' attack. This left him with a headache and a general malaise for a week or so. There was no repetition of any such attack until 6 February 1891. Writing on 26 April 1891 to his former child friend Dolly Blakemore, who was now a schoolteacher in Birmingham, he described what happened:

> I woke up one morning from an uneasy dream, saying to myself 'how very uncomfortable the pillow is!' and found myself lying on the floor up in the stalls of the cathedral. I wouldn't believe it at first, but thought I was *still* dreaming: but in a few moments I was broad awake, and found it really was so. I was lying in a pool of blood, having bled profusely from the nose, which no doubt had received a heavy blow in my fall (in that the doctor said the bones were loosened, and would take several weeks to get set firmly again), and had been lying there exactly an hour.[5]

Dodgson remembered the service clearly until a few words before the end. When the congregation filed out, the two tutors who went out last noticed that he was still on his knees, but assumed that he was praying privately.

Next day Bayne called on him and found him revived. He reported, 'Dr Brooks enjoins quiet for some days, and that before morning chapel he should have a little milk and a mouthful of bread and butter.'[6] Two days later he walked with Dodgson for about an hour, and on 26 February noted that he had walked in the meadow before lunch with Dodgson, who had been told to get fresh air in the morning as well as in the afternoon. These two attacks worried Dodgson a great deal, for in both cases the doctor treating him thought they might have been epileptic. His nephew's mild epileptic attacks in childhood made him fear that it was in the family. It seems unlikely that Dodgson had epilepsy as this does not normally develop in men of his age (fifty-five years) except as a symptom of severe intracranial disease. Though Dodgson suffered from severe headaches in his later years, such disease in his case was unlikely, since he survived the first attack by twelve years. In any event other usual features of epilepsy appear to have been absent. Nevertheless, Dodgson himself seems to have been uncertain, and referred to them as epileptic attacks. On 5 December 1891 he wrote, 'Both my epileptic attacks have been in the *winter*, and the first (end of /85) was ascribed partly to a cold day in London.' He knew a good deal about epilepsy, for when he was twenty-three years old he had caught a sufferer as he fell in a fit, and though he rendered sensible first-aid till the doctor's arrival, he felt that ignorance had made him helpless. Three days later he bought a book called *Hints for Emergencies*; and from that time onwards, by a strange coincidence often found himself in situations where his medical knowledge proved useful.

His medical expertise was to some extent a disadvantage, for he often succumbed to the temptations of self-diagnosis, despite the limitations of his knowledge. In August 1891 he had referred to a heart condition: 'I don't feet at all justified in counting on many more years of life – in that last attack it might so very easily have happened that the heart (it *is* weak, I know) might simply have ceased to beat, and my waking up might have been in that strange region we all look forward to seeing and know so little about!'[7] No positive evidence survives to indicate whether or not he did in fact suffer from a weak heart; but several active and energetic years still remained to him, and indeed he later rejoiced in renewed health and vigour which he devoted in the main to literary output. There was a curious tendency among Victorians to romanticize heart conditions, and it is perhaps significant that the narrator in *Sylvie and Bruno* had a similar heart ailment.

Yet the fund of medical knowledge that he built up over the years was indeed far above the average. As a young man of twenty-three he had gone to observe an operation for the amputation of a leg in order to be satisfied that he could rely on himself in an emergency. He had an excellent collection of books on anatomy, physiology and pathology, and these were the only items dealt with separately in his will, being left to his nephew Bertram Collingwood, who entered the medical profession. A human skull and the skeleton of a hand and foot were among his personal effects at his death, as well as two Whitely exercisers, which he bought a few months before his death and used every day, and two pairs of dumb-bells, which indicate his interest in preserving and strengthening his own physique. Homeopathy had fascinated him from an early age, and in his early family magazine, *The Rectory Umbrella*, he had referred to 'the evils of homeopathy'. But his 'conversion' to homeopathy seems to date from around December 1877, when his Oxford friend Shuldham settled as a homeopathic doctor near Guildford. Thereafter he regularly kept a supply of homeopathic remedies by him, wherever he went, and made such good use of them in treating the Hull children at the seaside that he found, to his amusement, that they regarded themselves as his patients. Two boxes of homeopathic medicines were in his possession when he died; but although he consulted a homeopath, he always called in a conventional medical practitioner when necessary.

Dodgson loved walking and records that it used to take him about five-and-a-half hours to do his favourite Besilsleigh round, a distance of some eighteen miles. Several contemporaries referred to his somewhat stiff and jerky gait, which could well have been due to the synovitis of which he complained off and on in the last decade of his life. The term 'synovitis' as it stands is fairly meaningless, and the condition was more probably a degree of osteo-arthrosis.[8] In 1891 the attack was so bad that he was laid up for nearly four months, and could not go home for Christmas. Initially Dodgson hoped that rest, bandaging and painting with iodine would cure it, but on 16 December 1891 Bayne wrote, 'Sat awhile with Dodgson, who is at last taking heed of his doctor, Brooks, though putting the knee in splints does not seem to succeed.'[9] On 9 February 1892 Dodgson noted that Dr Brooks was trying massage, but still the knee did not respond. Finally he resorted to iodine again, and moderate walking, which apparently did the trick.

When this illness set in the Duchess of Albany was staying at the Deanery and sent little Princess Alice and Prince Charlie over to see him. He taught them how to fold paper pistols, a trick he had learned from 'Piffy', the son of Coventry Patmore, with whom he occasionally exchanged visits. There was something of a stir at the Deanery, for the Dean had announced his intention of retiring at Christmas, and, somewhat to his annoyance, for Lord Salisbury had not consulted him in the matter, Paget had been appointed to succeed him. Dodgson was delighted to receive his first-ever visit from Violet and Rhoda Liddell, who came to tea and insisted on waiting on him. The sensitivity of his relationship with the Deanery is underlined by his failure to cultivate the acquaintance of the two youngest Liddell daughters, who by their age, wit and beauty would have seemed natural successors to Lorina, Alice and Edith. There is also a marked contrast between Dodgson's absence from the Deanery and Bayne's warm relationship with the family, as he accompanied Violet on the piano, or looked at her pictures, or admired Rhoda's woodwork.

On 3 December 1891 Mrs Liddell herself called, bringing Lorina (Mrs Skene) with her. A few days later Dodgson heard that Alice herself was at the Deanery and invited her to tea. 'You would probably prefer to bring a companion, but I must leave the choice to you', he wrote.[10] She could not come, but called on him for a short time instead, bringing Rhoda with her. It was the last time he ever saw Alice.

Probably it was only his illness that kept him away from the farewell and presentation ceremony to the Dean; but it is curious that among the many names of the Dean's Oxford friends, in his splendid blue morocco presentation volume, there is no mention of C. L. Dodgson.

In the last few years of his life Dodgson threw off the habit of making those endless rounds of social calls that were part of the Victorian way of life. His reasons were twofold: first, a desire to avoid being lionized, which he abhorred, and second, an urgent desire to get through as much writing as possible, while health and strength remained. From 5 May 1884 he refused all invitations to dine out in Oxford, and from May 1886 he accepted no more invitations to friends' houses. But though he gave up paying lip-service to convention, he kept up those friendships which gave him real pleasure. 'He was always completely at ease with women and children, and I fancy he was happier with them than in the company of men,' wrote Ethel Rowell.

Nevertheless he continued to value the friendship of old colleagues, like Liddon and Bayne. The diaries of all three men indicate that they continued to seek out each others' company. Occasionally there were disagreements, of course. Once Bayne records a long discussion with Dodgson, apparently about College affairs, and added, 'It needs not be said that we agree as to no single thing'. But such matters did not disturb the even tenor of their friendship. Bayne was usually treated to a preview of Dodgson's work, and continued to receive copies of his publications. It is to his zeal in collecting such items together that Christ Church owes its fine collection of rare pamphlets by Dodgson, for Bayne never doubted his friend's genius, nor the value to posterity of his minor publications. For Dodgson's part, that warm affection he had for his old childhood friend extended to Mary Anne Bayne, his widowed mother. Had she been one of those child friends whom he loved so much, Dodgson could not have treated this old lady with more kindness, courtesy and consideration. Even until her death on 2 December 1888 at the age of eighty-three, he rarely failed to call on her when in London, and often took her out to art exhibitions.

The diaries of both Dodgson and Bayne record frequent walks together, and dinners, mostly in the Common Room, but occasionally *tête-à-tête*. Only rarely did they record the subjects of their conversation, but they had much common ground. Though Bayne could not match his friend's genius, he was highly intelligent and cultured and his warmth and kindliness endeared him to many. Like Dodgson he was unmarried; he prospered, but was not without regrets. On 6 March 1888 he recorded in his diary that he walked with Dodgson through a 'Slough of Despond'. The cause of their despondency is not mentioned: but among Bayne's personal papers was a scrap of paper on which Dodgson had written a poignant verse from 'Winifreda' in Percy's Reliques:

> And when, with envy Time, transported
>   Shall think to rob us of our joys,
> You'll in your girls again be courted,
>   And I'll go wooing in my boys.[11]

Life had offered much to these two ageing bachelors, but one vital element was missing: neither had a wife to share his old age; neither had children.

Perhaps it was because he had no children that Dodgson was able to treat his own family with such open-handed generosity. His benevolence extended not only to his sisters and brothers, nephews and nieces, but to his cousins, who could rely on him not only for interest and advice in their problems, but in the case of serious need, for discreet financial help. To his nephews and nieces he was a 'watchful' uncle, ready to give a gold watch when the children reached the appropriate age, take an interest in their education and act 'in loco parentis' in Oxford. Many were the holidays provided at his expense; whenever expert medical advice was needed he was ready to summon the best available, and quietly take care of the bill. His kindness and patience with the sick were phenomenal. His visits to his brother-in-law's niece Loui Taylor when she was lying helpless on her side in Cowley Hospital without hope of recovery were a prime example. For her he ordered a special reading stand so that she could read despite her inability to adopt a normal posture, and went to infinite trouble to get her transferred to a more suitable hospital.

Nor were his own relatives the only people to benefit from his generosity. His child friends and their relatives all formed part of a wide adoptive 'family' who reaped abundant benefits from their friendship with him. Gifts of books – not necessarily his own – were only one item of his prodigality. Besides outings and meals, which countless children over the years enjoyed, there were holidays for some with all expenses paid; and his giving was so tactfully and gracefully done that the recipients could not have felt embarrassed. Dodgson enjoyed a comfortable income; he was a moderate man whose personal needs were not great, and it is impossible not to compare his estate at the time of his death with that of his friends Liddon and Bayne. Liddon was by no means insensible of the need to practise Christian charity, but was not prepared to impoverish himself for the sake of his fellow man. His remarks about Bishop Philaret during his Russian tour with Dodgson put his views into perspective: 'Philaret has about £7000 a year, all of which he gives away except about £200. His life is evidently modelled on a sterner and grander type than we are familiar with – one which would, perhaps, be impossible in England. . . .'[12] Liddon travelled widely and lived in reasonable comfort. He died on 9 September 1890, aged sixty-one years, and on 13 November 1890 *The Times* announced that his estate was £47,226 0s 10d. The size of Bayne's estate was even more remarkable. He had inherited no fortune from his parents, yet at his death his friends were astonished to learn that his estate amounted to £138,000. By contrast, Dodgson's estate amounted to only £4004 9s 4d, to be divided equally between his brothers and sisters, with the exception of the medical books left to his nephew Bertram Collingwood.

During his lifetime Dodgson published ten books of mathematics and logic, and forty-eight booklets and papers on these subjects; these included nearly two dozen texts for students of arithmetic, algebra, trigonometry, plane geometry and analytical geometry. His works in mathematics and logic comprised approximately one-fifth of the items he published during his lifetime. Besides his published works he had an immense quantity of mathematical notes. At his death sixty-two packets of methodically arranged papers were found, containing 1787 individual sheets. Warren Weaver, who examined the sheets in depth, writes: 'One has ample evidence of Dodgson's industry and of his meticulous habits. But one is also forced to realize that the more elementary aspects of calculus represented the upper limits of Dodgson's mathematical flights, and that even in calculus he had such vague and inaccurate notions about infinitesimals that one must confess that he lagged behind the best knowledge of his times.'[13] Instead of occupying himself with understanding and extending fundamental principles, he concentrated on trivial problems, which he solved with all the panache of a magician pulling a rabbit out of a hat.

While this habit of looking at his work as a kind of game was a hindrance to serious mathematical advance it was a positive asset in his logic work. The success of *The Game of Logic*, which he had produced in 1886, encouraged him to expand and develop it into a book two hundred pages in length called *Symbolic Logic: Part 1, Elementary*. On 1 February 1893 he wrote to Macmillan of the project, 'I have been at the book for twenty years or more.'[14] It was first published in February 1896, and was Dodgson's attempt to popularize formal logic, chiefly through the use of diagrams. The style he adopted was humorous, and he used all his powers of invention to make the propositions as intriguing as possible; but he did not extend the work beyond syllogisms and sorites, being content to reserve further exploration for a later volume. In May 1896 he wrote a new preface and added a postscript to the advertisement: 'I take the opportunity of giving what publicity I can to my contradiction of a silly story, which has been going the round of the papers, about my having presented certain books to Her Majesty the Queen. It is so constantly repeated, and is such an absolute fiction, that I think it worth while to state, once for all, that it is false in every particular: nothing even resembling it has ever occurred.' The story to which he referred was that after reading *Alice* the Queen had asked for his next work, which turned out to be *Condensation of Determinants*.

Dodgson's declared intention in writing *Symbolic Logic Part I* was to provide mental recreation of a kind he considered essential for our mental health. 'Once master the machinery of Symbolic Logic, and you have a mental occupation always at hand, of absorbing interest, and one that will be of real *use* to you in *any* subject you may take up,' he wrote. 'It will give you clearness of thought – the ability to *see your way* through a puzzle – the habit of arranging your ideas in an orderly and get-at-able form – and, more valuable than all, the power to detect *fallacies*, and to tear to pieces the flimsy illogical arguments, which you will so continually encounter in books, in newspapers, in speeches, and even in sermons, and which so easily delude those who have never taken the trouble to master this fascinating Art.'

In the eighteenth century a Swiss, Leonhardt Euler (1707–83), had devised a diagrammatic method using interlocking circles for solving logical problems. But the real pioneer of modern logic was George Boole (1815–64), who used algebra for the same purpose. Dodgson was familiar with Boole's work, and owned a copy of his most important book, *Laws of Thought*. By a process consisting fundamentally of continual dichotomy of the class terms in his propositions, Boole could solve problems whose complexity had been beyond the range of previous logicians. John Venn, of Gaius College, Cambridge, with whom Dodgson corresponded, collated the methods of Euler and Boole. Yet Venn realized the limitations of Euler's circle. Venn produced three important books on logic, *The Logic of Chance* (1866), *Symbolic Logic* (1881), and *The Principles of Empirical Logic* (1889). By adding to the diagrammatic method of inclusive and exclusive circles the new device of shading segments of the circle he was able to represent possibilities excluded by the propositions; but as an innovator he could not compete with Dodgson's untrammelled imagination.

Dodgson's great breakthrough came when he devised the box diagram method, whose advantage was its extreme simplicity and its capability of registering examples requiring ten attributes or more, whereas the interlocking circle method, despite its complexities, was incapable of registering more than six. Though Venn was undoubtedly familiar with Dodgson's method, he could not or would not concede its superiority.

Dodgson had studied Aristotelean logic even in his Rugby days, but he had come to the conclusion that the use of Aristotle's method had many pitfalls. It was to him 'an almost useless machine, for practical purposes, many of the conclusions being incomplete, and many quite legitimate forms being ignored'.[15] Nevertheless he adhered to the Aristotelean belief in the existential import of universal propositions, or 'all' statements, believing that the statement 'All men are mortal' equated to two statements, 'Some men are mortal' as well as 'No men are not-mortal'. Had he accepted the modern concept that the existence of its subject-term is not implicit in the universal proposition, his work could have been both subtler and simpler.

In the main Dodgson worked on his logic in isolation, but a certain amount of correspondence arose out of his logic publications. His only regular contact on matters of logic was John Cook Wilson, an Oxford professor of logic, whose stimulus to Dodgson's work was a negative one, since he disapproved of Dodgson's innovations. In attracting Wilson's disapproval Dodgson was in good company; when, in 1910, Bertrand Russell and Alfred North Whitehead published their *Principia Mathematica*, which revolutionized twentieth-century study of logic, Wilson expressed his astonishment that they could find a publisher, for he considered Russell's work 'contemptible'.

One of Dodgson's disputes with Wilson was permanently recorded in *A Disputed Point in Logic*, which was written out by Wilson and published by Dodgson in pamphlet form. This takes the form of a dialogue between Nemo and Outis, two pseudonyms meaning 'Nobody' and representing Dodgson and Wilson respectively. Two months later it was completely recast and republished with improved clarity by Dodgson, who finally published the paradox in *Mind*, the same philosophical journal which later included *What the Tortoise said to Achilles*.

As originally planned, Dodgson's *Symbolic Logic* was scheduled to appear in three volumes; but death intervened, and he only succeeded in publishing Vol. I. Though he was known to have been working on Vol. II in the period immediately leading up to his death and to have reached virtual completion, the text was thought to have been lost. Faced with voluminous private papers as well as numerous personal effects, his executors had fought in vain to sort and set aside all that was valuable, and much that might have interested posterity was burned. But in 1977 *Symbolic Logic Part II* was published under the title *Lewis Carroll's Symbolic Logic* by W. W. Bartley III, who had identified some of the work in slip form in Christ Church Library. But the bulk of the galleys were discovered by Morton Cohen in the library of J. H. A.

Sparrow, the warden of All Souls College, Oxford, who had acquired them from A. S. L. Farquharson, editor of the posthumous papers of John Cook Wilson. Dodgson had posted the papers to Wilson on 6 November 1896 and Wilson had retained them. In rescuing the work from oblivion, Professor Bartley made available work which Dodgson knew by an unerring instinct was of major importance, as this letter, written in 1896 to one of his sisters indicates:

> I am beginning to think that, if the *books* I am still hoping to write are to be done *at all*, they must be done *now*, and that I am *meant* thus to utilize the splendid health I have had, unbroken, for the last year and a half, and the working powers that are fully as great as, if not greater, than I have ever had. I brought with me here the MS., such as it is (very fragmentary and unarranged) for the book about religious difficulties, and I meant, when I came here, to devote myself to that, but I have changed my plan. It seems to me that *that* subject is one that hundreds of living men could do, if they would only try, *much* better than I could, whereas there is no living man who could (or at any rate would take the trouble to) arrange and finish and publish the second part of the 'Logic.' Also, I *have* the Logic book in my head; it will only need three or four months to write out, and I have *not* got the other book in my head, and it might take years to write out. So I have decided to get Part II finished *first*, and I am working at it day and night. I have taken to early rising, and sometimes sit down to my work before seven, and have one and a half hours at it before breakfast. The book will be a great novelty, and will help, I fully believe, to make the study of Logic far *easier* than it now is. And it will, I also believe, be a help to religious thought by giving *clearness* of conception and expression, which may enable many people to face, and conquer, many religious difficulties for themselves. So I do really regard it as work for *God*.[16]

Dodgson's articles in *Mind* and Logic pamphlets of 1894 acted as a kind of hors d'oeuvre to *Symbolic Logic Part II*. *A Logical Paradox* in its finalized version appeared as the celebrated Barbershop Paradox, a hypothetical problem involving three barbers, Allen, Brown and Carr, one of whom must always be in to mind the shop. Allen, who has been ill, cannot go out without Brown, who is clumsy. The customer does not want to be shaved by Brown or Allen, and weighs up the likelihood of Carr's being available. Two incompatible hypotheticals lead to the two apodoses that simultaneously, 'Brown is in', and 'Brown is out'.

The 'lying' dilemma which Dodgson worked out in May 1894 and which apparently formed the basis of *A Theorem in Logic*, printed in June of that year, is extended in the problem of the crocodile and the baby. A crocodile undertakes to restore a baby he has snatched to the mother if she says truly what she will do with it. If not, he will devour it.

> 'You will devour it!' cried the distracted mother. 'Now', said the wily crocodile, 'I *cannot* restore your baby: for, if I do, I shall make you speak *falsely*, and I warned you that, if you spoke *falsely*, I would *devour* it.' 'On

the contrary,' said the yet wilier Mother, 'you cannot *devour* my Baby: for
if you do, you will make me speak *truly*, and you promised me that, if I
spoke *truly*, you would *restore* it!'

Symbolic Logic Part II indicates that Dodgson had broken through the
barriers of traditional argumentation in a number of important areas.
He had anticipated the work done by Leopold Löwenstein between
1915 and 1922 by inventing an automatic validity test for a substantial
part of the logic of terms; he had applied truth tables and matrices more
than a quarter of a century before these came into general use; and he
had devised a 'Method of Trees' to ascertain whether hypotheticals
assumed to be false annexed to hypotheticals assumed to be true would
result in fallacious or ridiculous conclusions. His witty presentation
makes the difficult subject-matter palatable, and he provides eighty
new exercises which are invaluable in the modern classroom situation.
Though Wilson wrote of 'the extraordinary illusions Dodgson is liable
to, from want of study of anything like real logic or even real process of
thinking', Dodgson's methods of checking validity and reaching conclusions are of immense value to the contemporary logician.

The proposed book on 'Great Religious Difficulties' was never completed; but one chapter of it, written in 1895 and circulated privately to
family and friends, was published after his death by his nephew and
biographer, Stuart Dodgson Collingwood, in *The Lewis Carroll Picture
Book*. Entitled 'Eternal Punishment', it dealt with the problem of
whether the concept of eternal punishment meted out by God was
compatible with the belief in the infinite goodness and boundless mercy
of God. The theme was by no means a new one. In 1878 Dr Frederick
William Farrar, Dean of Canterbury and author of *Eric, or Little by
Little*, had published a religious treatise based on his series of five
sermons preached in Westminster Abbey called *Eternal Hope*. This had
immediately sparked off a spirited minor religious controversy in which
many were moved to rush into print. Among the protagonists who
published contributions to the topic were H. R. Bramley, W. J. Phill-
potts, C. F. Childe and John Charles Ryle, the well-known evangelical
Bishop of Liverpool, a Christ Church MA whom Dodgson heard
preach in Oxford. But most celebrated of Dr Farrar's opponents was
Dr Pusey, whose attack was entitled *What is of Faith as to Everlasting
Punishment?*

In *Eternal Hope* Dr Farrar comments on:

1) The Physical torments, the material agonies of eternal punishment.
2) the supposition of its necessarily endless duration for all who incur
   it.
3) the opinion that it is thus incurred by the vast mass of mankind;
   and

4) that it is a doom passed irreversibly at the moment of death on all who die in a state of sin.

Farrar believed that animals were without souls, and that their inevitable fate of sinking into eternal oblivion was infinitely more merciful than the sure knowledge that some of one's fellow human beings would face eternal damnation. He wrote:

> *If the popular doctrine of Hell were true*, I should be ready to resign all hope, not only of a *shortened*, but of *any* immortality, if thereby I could save, not *millions* but *one single human soul* from what fear, and superstition, and ignorance, and inveterate hate, and slavish letter-worship, have dreamed and taught of Hell. I call God to witness, that so far from regretting the possible loss of some billions of aeons of bliss by attaching to the word **αἰώνιος** a sense, in which scores of times it is undeniably found, I would here and now, kneeling on my knees, ask him that I might die as the beasts that perish, and for ever cease to be, rather than that my worst enemy should endure the Hell described by Tertullian . . .

Though Dodgson in *Eternal Punishment* was taking up a common controversial theme, he brought to it something new and original. His treatment was to take a set of propositions which he handled exactly as he would have handled the propositions in *Symbolic Logic*. The propositions he set out were:

I) God is perfectly good.
II) To inflict Eternal Punishment on certain human beings, and in certain circumstances, would be wrong.
III) God is capable of acting thus.

These propositions he examined in depth. The first proposition he found proven by intuition, facts of spiritual history and answered prayer. 'This being whom we call "God" *loves* us, with a love so wonderful, so beautiful, so immeasurable, so wholly undeserved, so unaccountable on any ground save his own perfect goodness, that we can but abase ourselves to the dust before Him,' he wrote. Proposition III follows naturally from proposition II, for if indeed God has declared his intention of inflicting infinite suffering for sins committed in finite time, he will undoubtedly do as he says. The infliction of continuous suffering for continuous sin seems to Dodgson just, whereas the infliction of infinite suffering for finite sins does not. The question then arises whether God has in fact declared his intention of inflicting infinite suffering for finite sin. Given that the authority for God's intention is the Bible, Dodgson now draws up a fresh set of propositions:

I) God has not declared that He will act thus.
II) All that the Bible tells us, as to the relations between God and man, are true.
III) The Bible tells us that God has declared that He will act thus.

The acceptance of the first proposition entails the rejection of the other two. Discussing Biblical Inspiration in relation to II, he writes:

> The theory of *Plenary* Inspiration – which asserts that *every* statement in the Bible is absolutely and infallibly true – has been largely modified in these days, and most Christians are now, I think, content to admit the existence of a *human* element in the Bible, and the possibility of *human* error in such of its statements as do not involve the relations between God and Man. But, as to these statements, there appears to be a general belief that the Bible has been providentially protected from error: in fact, on any other theory, it would be hard to say what value there would be in the Bible or for what purpose it could have been written.

Dodgson is accordingly thrown back on rejecting proposition III, and this he does, first as Farrar did, upon rejection of the strict translation of the word αἰώνιος. Dodgson's argument is developed with absolute precision, but he is forced to base it to some extent on a presumed truth, or axiom, which tends to lessen its value as an exercise in logic. Though he concedes the possibility of human error in the Bible in some instances, it seems a pity that he hinged his argument on this issue on an error of translation rather than on a human element in the basic data in the Bible.

Had Dodgson lived to complete his projected 'Great Religious Difficulties' he might well have included a chapter on physical pain and suffering, for this was a subject to which he devoted a great deal of consideration, particularly during his later years. To some extent his thoughts were channelled in that direction by his correspondence with Mary Brown, whom he had met when she was a little child on the beach, and with whom he continued to correspond even though they never met again. In December 1889 he wrote to her, 'How can I *help* loving one who has gone on loving me all these years without one single meeting to revive that memory of me since that long-ago when she sat on my knee as a little girl?'[17] Mary's letters often dealt with religious problems of her own. She was particularly shattered when in May 1887 her mother suffered a serious accident. Whenever any other human being came to him for religious guidance, Dodgson was prepared to go to infinite trouble to explain God's purposes as he saw them. In April 1890 he wrote:

> It seems to me, that for every one of us, life is really a sort of school, or training time, or trial time, meant *chiefly* for the building up of a character, and of disciplining the spirit, so that by its own choice of good rather than evil, and of God's will rather than self-will, it may rise to a higher and higher stage of Christian growth, and get nearer and nearer to God and more and more like Him, and so more fit for higher forms of existence. Perhaps we are not at all fit, at first, for such an existence as we shall enter after death. I fancy that the mere goodness of an innocent child is not the perfection of man's nature, or what is needed by a

spirit, to be fit to dwell in His visible Presence: it may need a gradual training of the will – perhaps even the knowledge of what *evil* is, in order to make the choice of *good* more real.[18]

Dodgson saw clearly that physical suffering could not always be a punishment for sin, since it sometimes began in sinless infancy. His conception of the purpose of suffering was that it might raise the soul to a yet higher glory and make the pure yet more pure. At the same time he interpreted the blessing of good health as a frequent sign that God expected service for others in some appropriate form. To Mary Brown Dodgson wrote, 'My life is so strangely free from all trial and trouble that I cannot doubt my own happiness is one of the talents entrusted to me to "occupy" with, till the Master shall return, by doing something to make other lives happy.'[19]

At Christmas 1890 Dodgson with much misgiving, particularly in regard to his stammer, resumed preaching. His first sermon was at St Mary's, Guildford, and such was his fear of being unable to go through with it, that he actually called at the house of the incumbent to cancel the arrangement; finding that he was not at home must have seemed like a clear indication that he was meant to preach. From that day forward he preached at Guildford fairly frequently when he was staying at 'The Chestnuts'. At Oxford he began preaching once a term to the College servants at the request of his friend Warner. But after a time he ceased to be asked, and consulted Dean Paget as to the reason. The Dean replied that it was because a decision had been taken to use only those who were accustomed to parochial work.

In December 1896 H. L. Thompson, who had been newly appointed Vicar of St Mary's, Oxford, invited him to preach to the under-graduates. Dodgson was clearly most willing to undertake any work for God to which he was called, but felt he must first acquaint Thompson with the reasons given by the Dean for not calling on him to preach again. Knowing the Dean's friendship towards him, Dodgson saw how difficult it would be for him to tell him that his sermons were not worth hearing, and he therefore urged Thompson to consult the Dean for his reasons, and in the light of them to decide whether or not to confirm his invitation. In due course Thompson renewed his application, and Dodgson preached to the undergraduates twice in 1897.

He had preached his first sermon at Eastbourne on 10 September 1893, and in August 1897 first addressed the junior congregation at the Children's Service at Christ Church. This was so successful that he promised to repeat it at the Children's Service at the Church of St Mary Magdalen in St Leonards. For his address he told the allegorical story of 'Victor and Arnion', which he developed the following week, though it still remained unfinished. In a letter to his sister Louisa dated 1 September

1897 he expressed his happiness at doing distinctly clerical work for God in the shape of sermons, and of 'Victor and Arnion' wrote, 'It grows on my hands. Perhaps I shall print it some day.' He did not live to see this project through, but a later address to the Children's Service was published in St Mary Magdalen Church Magazine (St Leonards) in October 1897.

In the last few months of his life Dodgson devoted a considerable amount of time to a literary project of his cousin, Georgie Wilcox (Mrs Egerton Allen). It was not the first time he had put himself out on behalf of a friend or relative with a worthy literary project. He had entered into correspondence with Macmillan's regarding a book by his Guildford friend, William Follett Synge. The latter had produced a book of verse with the extraordinary title *Bumblebee Bogo's Budget*, published in 1887. Dodgson gave him a great deal of help, and at his death had several copies of the book in his possession. Georgie Wilcox's book was called *The Lost Plum Cake*; Dodgson had noted that it was passed for press in May 1896, but it did not come out until 1898, though it bore the date 1897. Two close friends of Dodgson's were involved in the work: Mrs E. L. Shute, at whose studios he often called and sketched, who provided nine full-page illustrations, and Miss E. Gertrude Thomson, who designed the red and gold cover with an optical illusion, which Dodgson describes:

> The *reader* of this little book has *also* the singular privilege at his command, in connection with the *cover*. . . . Holding the book at the middle point of each side, and turning it about till the light (which should come from *behind* him) causes what looks like little hills on the red cover to glitter, he can then fidget it about – he will soon catch the knack – till the gold ornamentation seems to lift itself a good half-inch off the cover; and he can easily persuade his *eye*, if not his intellect, to believe that, in turning the book about, he is causing the gold to cover now one part of the red and now another.

This little book is written throughout in words containing no more than four letters and he recommends it as a picture-book which children could bring into church, and read during the sermon. 'Let me seize this opportunity of saying one earnest word to the mothers into whose hands this little book may chance to come, who are in the habit of taking their children to church with them,' Dodgson wrote.

> However well and reverently those dear little ones have been taught to behave, there is no doubt that so long a period of enforced quietude is a severe tax on their patience. The hymns, perhaps, tax it least; and what a pathetic beauty there is in the sweet fresh voices of the children, and how earnestly they sing! . . . The lessons, and the prayers, are not wholly beyond them: often they can catch little bits that come within the range of their small minds. But the sermons! It goes to one's heart to see, as I often do, little darlings of five or six years old, forced to sit still through a

weary half-hour, with nothing to do, and not a word of sermon that they can understand. . . . Would it be so *very* irreverent to let your child have a story-book to read during the sermon, to while away that tedious half-hour, and to make church-going a bright and happy memory —

But the book, which went into a second edition in 1927, contained another surprise, pointed out by Denis Crutch:

An interesting copy of this edition was sold at Sotheby's on 13 November 1973 (part of Lot 309). It contains a presentation inscription from the grown-up original of the 'Fred Dale' of the book, which includes the following surprising paragraph: 'Years ago my aunt and god-mother wrote this book for little boys, and her cousin who wrote *Alice in Wonderland* got it printed for her and wrote a preface for the 1st edition and (this is a sort of a secret) he wrote the last chapter.'[20]

This was the last published work which Dodgson wrote. As he moved to the end of his life he viewed the approach of death without fear, and indeed, though he felt a feverish compulsion to work as long as health and strength remained to him, he almost welcomed it. 'I sometimes think what a grand thing it will be to be able to say to oneself, "Death is *over* now; there is not *that* experience to be faced again".'[21]

On 23 December 1897 Dodgson returned to Guildford as usual for the Christmas holidays; but when on 5 January 1898 he received a telegram telling him that his sister Mary's husband had died suddenly, he wrote to her that he had developed a feverish cold of the bronchial type and that because of the risk of ague, Dr Gabb had forbidden him to travel to Southwick to attend the funeral. But with characteristic generosity he sent her a cheque for £50 so that she should not be short of ready money; and to his nephew Stuart Collingwood he sent a long letter of practical advice relating to the funeral.

Though Dodgson's illness had at first seemed trifling, Dr Gabb ordered him to bed when bronchial symptoms developed. His breathing now became hard and laborious, and he had to be propped up with pillows. On 13 January he seemed to have a premonition of the approach of death. 'Take away those pillows,' he said. 'I shall need them no more.'[22] At about 2.30 on the afternoon of 14 January 1898 one of his sisters, who was in the room with him, noticed that the laboured breathing suddenly stopped.

The simple funeral service was conducted at St Mary's Guildford, by Dr Paget, Dean of Christ Church, and the Rector, Canon Grant. A moving account of the occasion was given by Dodgson's old friend, E. Gertrude Thomson:

A grey January day, calm, and without sound, full of the peace of God which passeth all understanding.

A steep, stony, country road, with hedges close on either side, fast quickening with the breath of the premature spring. Between the with-

ered leaves of the dead summer a pure white daisy here and there shone
out like a little star.

A few mourners slowly climbed the hill in silence, while borne before
them on a simple hand-bier was the coffin, half hid in flowers.

Under the old yew, round whose gnarled trunk the green ivy twined,
in the pure white chalk earth his body was laid to rest, while the slow bell
tolled the passing

'Of the sweetest soul
That ever looked with human eyes.'[23]

REFERENCES

1   Green, p. 502.
2   Ibid, p. 457.
3   D.F.C. 27/5/3.
4   Selwyn H. Goodacre, 'The Illnesses of Lewis Carroll', *The Practitioner*,
    August 1972.
5   Morton N. Cohen and Roger Lancelyn Green, 'Lewis Carroll's Loss of
    Consciousness', *Bulletin of the New York Public Library*, 1969.
6   Christ Church Ms. 36/2.
7   D.F.C. 21/6/2.
8   Selwyn H. Goodacre, 'The Illnesses of Lewis Carroll', *The Practitioner*,
    August 1972.
9   Christ Church Ms. 36/2.
10 Florence Becker Lennon, *The Life of Lewis Carroll*, 1972, p. 236.
11 Christ Church Ms. 13.
12 J. O. Johnston, *Life and Letters of Henry Parry Liddon*, 1904, p. 108.
13 'The Mathematical Manuscripts of Lewis Carroll', *The Princeton Library
    Chronicle*, XVI (1954–5).
14 Handbook, p. 183.
15 *Symbolic Logic Part I, Elementary*, 1896.
16 Collingwood, pp. 330–1.
17 D.F.C. 19/4/1.
18 Green, p. 566.
19 Collingwood, p. 325.
20 *The Lewis Carroll Circular*, No. 2, November 1974, ed. Trevor Winkfield,
    p. 70.
21 Collingwood, p. 330.
22 Ibid, pp. 347–8.
23 *The Gentlewoman*, 5th February 1898.

Select Bibliography

For most frequently quoted books, please see *Note about Abbreviations*, page 7.

ABBOT & CAMPBELL (eds), *Letters of Benjamin Jowett*, 1899.
ANON, *Hints for Oxford*, 1823.
BARTLEY, W. W. III, *Lewis Carroll's Symbolic Logic*, New York, 1977.
BENHAM, W. AND DAVIDSON, P. T., *Life of Archibald Campbell Tait*, 1891.
BILL, E. G. W. AND MASON, J. F. A., *Christ Church and Reform 1850 – 1869*, 1970.
BLAKE, KATHLEEN, *Play, Games and Sport: The Literary Works of Lewis Carroll*.
BOND, W. H., 'The Publication of *Alice's Adventures in Wonderland*', *Harvard Library Bulletin*, Autumn 1956.
BOWMAN, ISA, *Lewis Carroll as I Knew Him*, 1972.
BUMP, JEROME (ed.), *The Rectory Magazine*, Austin, Texas, 1976.
COHEN, MORTON N., 'The Electric Pen', *Illustrated London News*, Christmas 1976.
COHEN, MORTON N., 'Letters from Wonderland', *New York Times Book Review*, 15 November 1970.
COHEN, MORTON N., 'So You Are Another Alice', *New York Times Book Review*, 7 November 1971.
COHEN, MORTON N., 'Love and Lewis Carroll', *The Times Saturday Review*, 20 November 1971.
COHEN, MORTON N., 'Alice in Analysis', *Sunday Telegraph Magazine*, 19 March 1978.
COHEN, MORTON N. AND GREEN, ROGER LANCELYN, 'Lewis Carroll's Loss of Consciousness', *Bulletin of the New York Public Library*, 1969.
COLLINGWOOD, STUART DODGSON, *The Lewis Carroll Picture Book*, 1899.
CRUTCH, DENIS, AND SHABERMAN, R. B., *Under the Quizzing Glass*, 1972.
Daresbury Parish Magazine, August 1906.
DE PREZ, EDNA, 'Where the sun came peeping in at morn', *Cheshire Life*, April 1974.
FISHER, JOHN, *The Magic of Lewis Carroll*, 1973.
FURNISS, HARRY, *Confessions of a Caricaturist*, 1902.
FURNISS, HARRY, *Some Victorian Men*, 1924.
FURNISS, HARRY, 'Lewis Carroll', *Strand Magazine*, April 1908.
GARDNER, MARTIN, *The Annotated Alice*.
GARDNER, MARTIN, *The Annotated Snark*.
GATTÉGNO, JEAN, *Lewis Carroll: Fragments of a Looking Glass*, 1978.
GERNSHEIM, HELMUT, *Lewis Carroll: Photographer*, 1949.
GOODACRE, SELWYN H., 'The Illnesses of Lewis Carroll', *The Practitioner*, August 1972.
GOODACRE, SELWYN H., 'Lewis Carroll's Rejection of the 60th Thousand of *Through the Looking-Glass*', *The Book Collector*, Summer 1975.

GREENACRE, PHYLLIS, *Swift & Carroll: a Psychoanalytic Study of Two Lives*, New York 1955.

HARDY, A. E. GATHORNE, *Gathorne Hardy, First Earl of Cranbrook: A Memoir*, 1910.

HARGREAVES, ALICE AND CARYL, 'Alice's Recollections of Carrollian Days – as told to her son, Caryl Hargreaves', *The Cornhill Magazine*, July 1932.

HASSALL, A., *Christ Church, Oxford*, 1911.

HEATH, PETER, *The Philosopher's Alice*, 1974.

HUXLEY, FRANCIS, *The Raven and the Writing Desk*, 1976.

JOHNSTONE, J. O., *Life of Henry Parry Liddon*, 1904.

LENNON, FLORENCE BECKER, *The Life of Lewis Carroll*, 1972.

LEWIS CARROLL SOCIETY, THE, *Jabberwocky: the Journal of the Lewis Carroll Society*, Quarterly, from Autumn 1969.

LEWIS CARROLL SOCIETY, THE, *Mr Dodgson: Nine Lewis Carroll Studies*, 1973.

LEWIS CARROLL SOCIETY, THE, *Three Letters on Anti-Vaccination*, 1976.

LEWIS CARROLL SOCIETY, THE, *A Day of Sea Air*, 1977.

LEWIS CARROLL SOCIETY OF NORTH AMERICA, THE, *Lewis Carroll Observed*, E. Guiliano (ed.), 1976.

LEWIS CARROLL SOCIETY OF NORTH AMERICA, THE, *The Wasp in a Wig*, Martin Gardner (ed.), 1977.

LIDDON, HENRY PARRY, *The Life of Edward Bouverie Pusey*.

MACKENZIE, BEATRICE AND GUY, 'Lewis Carroll Shown in a New Light', *The New York Times Magazine*, 24 May 1930.

MANVELL, ROGER, *Ellen Terry*, 1968.

McDERMOTT, JOHN FRANCIS (ed.), *The Russian Journal and other Selections*, New York, 1935.

MÜLLER, MAX, *My Autobiography*, 1901.

NEWMARK, CHARLES H., *Recollections of Rugby, by an Old Rugbean*, 1848.

NOWELL-SMITH, SIMON, *Letters to MacMillan*, 1967.

PHILLIPS, ROBERT, *Aspect of Alice*, 1971.

PUDNEY, JOHN, *Lewis Carroll and His World*, 1976.

ROWELL, ETHEL, 'To me he was Mr Dodgson', *Harper's Magazine*, February 1943.

RUSKIN, JOHN, *Praeterita*, 1885.

RUSKIN, JOHN, *The Art of England: Lectures given in Oxford*, 1883.

ST JOHN, CHRISTOPHER, *Ellen Terry and George Bernard Shaw: a Correspondence*, 1931.

SUTHERLAND, ROBERT D., *Language and Lewis Carroll*, The Hague, 1970.

TAYLOR, ALEXANDER, *The White Knight: a Study of C. L. Dodgson*, 1952.

TENNYSON, HALLAM LORD, *Alfred Lord Tennyson: A Memoir*, 1899.

TERRY, ELLEN, *The Story of My Life*, New York, 1968.

THOMPSON, H. L., *Memoir of Henry George Liddell*, D.D., 1899.

THOMPSON, H. L., *Christ Church*, 1900.

TRENCH, MARIA, *The Story of Dr Pusey's Life*, by the Author of Charles Lowder, 1900.

TUCKWELL, WILLIAM, *Reminiscences of Oxford*, 1900.

WARD, G. R. M. (translator), *Oxford University Statutes*, 1845.

WATTS, M. F., *George Frederick Watts*, 1912.

WEAVER, WARREN, *Alice in Many Tongues*, Wisconsin, 1964.

WEAVER, WARREN, 'Lewis Carroll, Mathematician', *The Scientific American*, April 1956.

WEAVER, WARREN, 'The Mathematical Manuscripts of Lewis Carroll', *The Princeton Library Chronicle*, XVI (1954–5).

WENHAM, L. P., *The History of Richmond School, Yorkshire*, 1958.

WILCOX, WILLIAM, 'A Letter from Lewis Carroll', *Strand Magazine*, May 1901.

WINKFIELD, TREVOR (ed.), *The Lewis Carroll Circular*, No. 1, May 1973.

WINKFIELD, TREVOR (ed.), *The Lewis Carroll Circular*, No. 2, November 1974.

Index